INTRODUCTION

THIS is the second in a series of volumes devoted to the history of the United States since 1890 to be published by the Ohio State University Press. The series, whose over-all title is MODERN AMERICA, is intended to facilitate publication of scholarly articles in all areas of recent American history. The editors hope that MODERN AMERICA will provide a publication outlet for monographic studies as well as synthetic and interpretative essays.

The present volume is devoted to the reappraisal of the 1920's, a decade Arthur S. Link has called "the exciting new frontier of American historical research." [1] Historians have become increasingly aware that beneath the glitter of the Jazz Age profound and far-reaching changes in American life were taking place. During the last fifteen years, as one of the contributors to this volume has recently pointed out, scholarly interest in the 1920's has mounted.[2] The

---

[1] Arthur S. Link, "What Happened to the Progressive Movement in the 1920's," *American Historical Review*, LXIV (1959), 834.

[2] Burl Noggle, "The Twenties: A New Historiographical Frontier," *Journal of American History*, LIII (1966), 299–314.

essays in this volume have a twofold purpose: to provide a synthesis based upon existing scholarship and also to break new ground by investigating hitherto unexplored problems.

In "1919: Prelude to Normalcy," David Burner shows how the manifold tensions generated by World War I came to an explosive head along a broad front in 1919 and suggests that Harding's election did represent a "return to normalcy." Burl Noggle's "Oil and Politics" reassesses the foremost political scandal of the era in the larger context of government-business relations. Although the image of the decade is one of prosperity, investigation has revealed significant exceptions. Gilbert C. Fite depicts the plight of agriculture in his article on "The Farmers' Dilemma, 1919–1929"; Mark Perlman examines the weakness of organized workers in "Labor in Eclipse"; and David Brody, in "The Rise and Decline of Welfare Capitalism," explores the short-run success of management's efforts to block unionization.

Perhaps the most far-reaching changes of the decade took place in the realm of ideas and attitudes. Three of our contributors study the negative side of the picture: the resistance—bitter, yet often poignant—of the old to the new. Paul A. Carter's "The Fundamentalist Defense of the Faith" traces the fundamentalist reaction to the encroachments of science and secularism. Robert Moats Miller, in "The Ku Klux Klan," takes a penetrating and sobering look at the decade's most notorious example of intolerance. In "Prohibition: The Impact of Political Utopianism," William Gusfield applies insights from sociology to assess the significance of the "noble experiment."

Of more long-range importance than the defense of the old was the triumph of the new. Frederick J. Hoffman's essay analyzes the developments in fiction that were so important in shaping the modern-day image of the 1920's. Gilman Ostrander's "The Revolution in Morals" surveys the breakdown of Victorian mores. John Burnham, in "The

New Psychology: From Narcissism to Social Control,"
shows how the "new psychology" reflected, and in turn
speeded, the transformation underway in American life.
In the concluding essay "Metropolis and Suburb: The
Changing American City," Charles N. Glaab explores the
urban "revolution."

With this volume, David Brody joins the board of editors
for the series, replacing Everett Walters, who has withdrawn because of the pressures of his duties as vice-
president for academic affairs, Boston University. The
editors wish to express their appreciation to Dr. Walters
for his indispensable assistance in launching this project.

The editors also extend their thanks to the contributors,
to the many historians who have expressed interest in
MODERN AMERICA, and to Mr. Weldon A. Kefauver, director
of the Ohio State University Press. Without Mr. Kefauver's
co operation, assistance, and long-suffering patience, this
volume would never have appeared. We particularly wish to
thank Mrs. Catherine M. Bremner for preparing the Index.

The next volume in the series, currently in preparation,
will be devoted to American foreign policy in the twentieth
century. Suggestions for future volumes are welcomed.

JOHN BRAEMAN
ROBERT H. BREMNER
DAVID BRODY

CONTENTS

Change and Continuity
in Twentieth-Century America:
The 1920's

1919: Prelude to Normalcy

DAVID BURNER

AN eminent psychologist predicted that after World War I "personal loves, personal jealousies, and the pursuit of personal gain will not function as they customarily did"; instead, the age would be one of altruism. The editors of the *Nation* also thought that class interests were going to be submerged in favor of the general welfare. Cosmic optimism of this kind represented the idealistic fervor of America's first international war; it was soon to prove itself groundless, dissipating in a postwar period of strikes, high prices, unstable markets, spotty employment, racial unrest, and acrimonious foreign-policy debate. And beneath the particular stresses of the era was a mood of rural-urban suspicion and anger, rekindled by the debate over prohibition but of a kind that has traditionally appeared in American politics.[1]

If the tensions of 1919 gave the lie to war idealism, those tensions were, nonetheless, to a large extent the product of America's involvement in the great conflict. Institutions and customs that once maintained the social equilibrium had been altered or destroyed, in part by the governmental controls of wartime, in part by the emotional and social

[1] James R. Mock and Evangeline Thurber, *Report on Demobilization* (Norman, Okla., 1944), p. 28; *Nation*, CVII (Nov. 2, 1918), 503.

disturbances of war itself. Workers, having become accustomed to a measure of war prosperity and to collective bargaining enforced by the War Labor Board, anxiously sought to preserve their gains as government prepared to withdraw from the economy; but labor faced employers even more resolute in wishing to restore the days of "open shop," and applying in their struggle against collective bargaining the rhetoric of the "American Plan." Farmers cried for various forms of aid from a Congress deaf to their pleas, and as price supports came near to ending, entreated with a cabinet equally unmindful of their plight. In northern cities Negroes attempted to hold on to their wartime jobs as soldiers returned home looking for work. Negroes themselves came back from the trenches, bringing with them an aggressive edge their fathers had never possessed. Following the success of the Russian revolution and its spread to Central Europe, an ambitious attorney-general, aroused by frightened citizens, clashed with liberals of all shades in his ill-defined attempt to suppress revolutionary plots. Debate on the League of Nations separated idealist from realist, and realist from isolationist. Vainly, the progressive worked to resist the course of reaction.

The atmosphere of conflict was thickened by a state of mind for which the war itself had in large part prepared the condition. The war had imposed upon the American people a discipline beyond their normal experience; in turn, their hopes for the postwar era expanded indefinitely, only to be followed by disillusionment and frustration. Our participation in World War I, moreover, was too brief to expend the reserve of fighting spirit manufactured by the Committee on Public Information. That wartime propaganda agency had planned a symphony in creed and emotion that was to reach its crescendo by the middle of 1919. Though the war ended sooner than had been expected, the emotion lingered on, no longer fixed and steadied by the pursuit of victory.

Problems of foreign policy split the progressives into their internationalist and isolationist components. Bull Moosers of Theodore Roosevelt's bellicose stamp deserted their progressivism entirely in their frenzy for war, while the more pacific of President Wilson's followers grew disillusioned as the prospects for reform were everywhere forgotten. No issue could have divided the progressive movement more irreparably than the World War. The conflict itself, moreover, had assaulted the reformers' faith in progress and human virtue. In any case, progressivism was not likely to flourish in the repressive atmosphere of wartime conformism. The principal reform of 1919 was prohibition, which further divided the progressives, this time into their rural-urban camps. The main branches of the reform movement went to seed amid the materialism and reaction that followed the war.

The postwar period, particularly 1919, was a time of much more intense reaction than the 1920's themselves. Progressivism faltered after 1918 because the mood upon which it had succeeded was largely destroyed after the war. During President Wilson's first term the national temper had clearly been progressive; after the war his second term reveled in reaction; the progressive Wilson himself, not Harding, initiated the postwar conservatism. "Can anyone," asked Walter Lippmann late in 1919, "name a single piece of constructive legislation and administration carried through since the armistice?" [2]

Demobilization caught the country by surprise, for no one expected the war to end as quickly as it did. Official

[2] In the opinion of a historian who wrote recently on the period: "From the winter of 1918–1919 to Harding's inauguration in March, 1921, the federal government's policies, both executive and legislative, that affected business, labor, agriculture, and the consumer were thoroughly conservative."—David Shannon, *Between the Wars, 1919–1939* (Boston, 1965), p. 16. For "Recent Opinion on the Decline of the Progressive Movement," see Herbert F. Margulies' article of that title in *Mid-America*, XLV (October, 1965), 250–68. Lippmann wrote in the *New Republic*, XX (Nov. 12, 1919), 315.

planning began a scant month before the Armistice, although some farsighted individuals and groups had earlier recommended action. Prominent among them was the War Industries Board, which repeatedly petitioned the President to appoint competent study groups as European nations had done even before we entered the war. The Board argued for gradual demobilization, vocational education, and the creation of a "buffer industrial army" to be employed in public works. Secretary of the Interior Franklin K. Lane pushed his own plan for the reclamation of arid lands to be settled by veterans; and Assistant Secretary of Labor Louis Post suggested a far broader program of developing the nation's natural resources. But the government failed to take the lead in reconstruction, and private organizations and individuals made more imaginative proposals. Some segments of labor believed that the government should continue to operate the railroads and utilities. William F. Ogburn of the National War Labor Board suggested the enactment of a minimum-wage law. George W. Perkins of Bull Moose fame called for profit-sharing after the war. Matthew Woll, chairman of the AF of L Reconstruction Committee, wanted the government to aid needy industries while stipulating the conditions that were to prevail to restore free speech and to avoid militarism. The National Municipal League recommended federal housing, control of living costs, and generous financing under the United States Employment Office for the placing of veterans in private occupations. A conservative association of business papers, on the other hand, declared that reconstruction would of necessity require the prompt return of the railroads to private ownership, and even that stalwart liberal journal, the *Nation,* concerned over the residual federal powers that the war had called into use, argued for a gradual relaxation of federal controls.[3]

[3] Secretary of War Newton D. Baker wrote to Senator James A. Reed of Missouri that "the collapse of the Central Powers came

Wilson, engaged in the war effort and then in negotiations for the treaty of peace, had little time for such things. Though he briefly contemplated appointing an advisory reconstruction commission under the chairmanship of Bernard Baruch, he distrusted the work of the European commissions. In December, 1918, he told Congress that the government did not know how to control reconstruction. "People would go their own way," he insisted. His only pertinent suggestion—one he repeated to a conference of governors and mayors the following March—was that the government might undertake public works, including the reclamation of unusable land; whatever control there must be, he said, could be exercised through existing agencies. Schemes of reconstruction in Congress also went awry, deadlocked in factionalism, abandoned in the rage for economy, or shunned as socialistic. Partisanship in particular stalled planning: in September and October, 1918, Congress debated whether reconstruction was a presidential responsibility or, as in the era of reunion, a Congressional affair. Legislators feared that the President might dominate Congress, and this fear Wilson had no desire to encourage

more quickly than even the best informed military experts thought possible."—Apr. 3, 1919, Justice Department File 370–163, National Archives. Marc Karson, *American Labor Unions and Politics, 1900–1918* (Boston, 1965), pp. 114–15; Louis Post to Elwood Mead, May 14, 1918, Labor Department File 46–8, National Archives; John C. Sparrow, "History of Personnel Demobilization in the United States Army," U.S. Department of Defense, 1951, pp. 14–15. (Mimeographed.) Ogburn's plan is discussed in *Survey*, XLI (Dec. 14, 1918), 337; Woll's in *Nation*, CVII (Nov. 2, 1918), 505; see also *ibid*. (Nov. 9, 1918), 545, CVIII (Jan. 4, 1919), 5, and (Jan. 18, 1919), 84. Mock and Thurber, *Report on Demobilization*, pp. 36, 54–55, 101–4; John M. Clark, *Demobilization of Wartime Economic Controls* (New York, 1944), *passim;* Dixon Wecter, *When Johnny Comes Marching Home* (Cambridge, Mass., 1944), *passim; Saturday Evening Post*, CXCII (Mar. 1, 1919), 20. See also the articles of E. Jay Howenstine, Jr., "Demobilization After the First World War," *Quarterly Journal of Economics*, LVIII (November, 1943), 91–105; "Lessons of World War I," *Annals of the American Academy of Political and Social Sciences*, CCXXXVIII (April, 1945), 180–87; and "Public Works Program After World War I," *Journal of Political Economy*, LI (December, 1943), 523–37.

—perhaps he was thinking ahead to the day when he would need Congressional support for his peace treaty. By the time the war had ended, no central agency had been established to return the country to peace. Most government regulation was terminated on January 1, 1919; by March almost none remained.[4]

Some decisions had to be made about demobilization. In Britain the government for a time tried moving soldiers with needed industrial skills to the head of the demobilization schedules, but widespread resentment in the camps forced an end to the practice. Secretary of War Newton Baker preferred a somewhat similar program under which soldiers with jobs awaiting them would be the first to be discharged. Yet such a program would work great inequities. For example, those soldiers most recently drafted —and therefore most likely to be holding some claim to their former jobs—would receive priority. Furthermore, such a carefully planned demobilization would require costly investigations into the demand for labor, at a time when Congress was in a mood for economy. It was finally decided to discharge largely by military unit, usually at a point near the soldier's own home. The men were dismissed as rapidly as possible; carrying gas masks and helmets as souvenirs, the greater number reached their homes by the summer of 1919.[5]

The War Department, hitherto totally involved in waging the fight, had been charged with demobilizing the troops. The United States Employment Office, a branch of the Department of Labor, helped soldiers to find jobs; but in March, 1919, the economy-minded Sixty-seventh Congress curtailed its funds. Business interests apparently opposed

[4] Mock and Thurber, *Report on Demobilization*, pp. 38, 108–10.

[5] Churchill, *The Aftermath* (London, 1928), pp. 41–55; for a contemporary guide to British planning, see *Nation*, CVIII (Jan. 25, 1919), 119–21. See also Sparrow, "History of Personnel Demobilization," p. 453

the continuation of the agency. They feared the extension of wartime economic control of any kind; at least a few were ready to capitalize on the cheap labor and means for strikebreaking that unemployment provides. Further, businessmen charged the agency's social workers and reformers with favoritism toward organized labor. The opposition of private employment agencies, which accused the Employment Office of inefficiency, also contributed to its demise, as did the more diffuse antiadministration sentiment of Congress. Despite the housing shortage caused by the migration to the city, the Senate directed the United States Housing Commission to stop all work on government housing projects not 75 per cent completed. And although there was a great need for the kinds of non-military public building that had been suspended by the war, the Senate in January, 1919, defeated a federal works bill that would have provided for veterans, and in the House several bills for the employment of soldiers were unsuccessful. Nor would the Congress extend the lives of governmental agencies that might have given effective help in adjusting to peace. Only the Council of National Defense, a wartime co-ordinating agency, was favored with appropriations, but it was essentially a fact-finding body.[6]

When a conference of governors and mayors met with Wilson early in April, Governor Calvin Coolidge of Massachusetts echoed the widespread complacency: "Ninety per-

[6] On the federal employment agency, see *New York Times*, Jan. 14, 1918, p. 13; *Survey*, XLI (Feb. 18, 1919), 662–63; and *Nation*, CVIII (Feb. 15, 1919), 244–45. In February, 1919, Congressman Pat Harrison was advised by telegraph that "propaganda of private interests against Employment Service has so influenced House Appropriations Committee" that it would soon be discontinued. In June an Indiana businessman advised another congressman that the Service had fomented labor trouble, was inefficient and inimical to states' rights. Labor Department Files 129–14 and 129–14–E, National Archives. As late as December, 1919, Wilson asked Congress for additional help in finding jobs and farm land for ex-servicemen. *Literary Digest*, LXIII (Dec. 13, 1919), 14.

cent of the boys," he said, "were able to take care of themselves." The governor of Indiana, the state that contributed the largest number of volunteers to the army, expressed his constituents' disdain of federal controls. The refrain, let the economy return to natural forces, was repeated endlessly. Reconstruction meant some effort to channel released manpower in a rational way. In fact, demobilization was chaos.[7]

Contributing to the unsettled political conditions of postwar American society was an economic dislocation brought on by the return of peace. But the extent and nature of the dislocation must be identified with some care, for on the surface conditions appeared quite good.

Demobilization of the armed forces itself was soon completed; by the fall of 1919 the service contained only its normal component of men. The demobilization produced some brief hardship early in 1919, but no lasting unemployment problem; nor did the mass revocation of military orders induce an immediate deflation. As Paul Samuelson has pointed out, *"Economically,* the first World War lasted until 1920." The economy was kept active: money was spent on demobilization itself, consumer savings and dismissal pay for veterans were soon in circulation as shelves were restocked and as servicemen returned, business contracts were settled, the military deficit had to be financed, and the Treasury desired to postpone any contraction until after the floating of a last major war loan and further loans to European countries. These monetary policies sparked a revival in automobile production, housebuilding, and numerous related industries that eased the readjustment for the nine million workers formerly engaged in defense work and the four million soldiers returned to

[7] Mock and Thurber, *Report on Demobilization,* pp. 62, 65; *Nation,* CVIII (Mar. 20, 1919), 459.

peacetime life. Industrial production declined a maximum of 10 per cent by the middle of 1919, but in the last six months of the year it reached a new high. Such figures do not record the vast shifting of jobs and resulting hardships that must have occurred in 1919. Yet extensive unemployment would not appear until 1920, when government spending and industrial expansion both halted—partly through the deliberate contraction policy of the administration.[8]

The postwar period was, then, prosperous. Why was the public dissatisfaction so intense? A major reason was a steady rise in the cost of living that angered and perplexed consumers. Despite the wartime controls on prices of certain items, the cost of living almost doubled between 1914 and 1920, and in New York City it rose 28 per cent between 1919 and 1920 alone. The people, according to a correspondent of Mark Sullivan, were "more interested in the price of beefsteak and a pair of shoes" than in Wilson's League of Nations. The administration had proposed that an industrial board in the Commerce Department be allowed to set maximum prices, but George Peek, lacking authority to keep steel prices down, resigned as its head in May, 1919. Not until April of 1920 did the price index begin to fall. Added irritants were the scarcities that persisted after the war as labor unions struck and the economy pursued its uneven course. Viewing the high cost of living as the nation's greatest postwar problem, the Federal Reserve Board acted against the inflation of 1919 and early 1920 by raising the rediscount rate, curtailing credit, and discouraging expansion. A major depression began in

[8] Paul Samuelson and Everett E. Hagen, *After the War* (National Labor Relations Board, Washington, D.C., 1943), p. 21; George H. Soule, *Prosperity Decade* (New York, 1947), pp. 83–84; Elmus R. Wicker, "A Reconsideration of Federal Reserve Policy during the 1920–1921 Depression," *Journal of Economic History*, XXVI (June, 1966), 223–38.

1920, soon enough to contribute to the defeat of the administration in the fall election.[9]

To many Americans, labor appeared responsible in considerable part for the country's economic and social unrest. "Men are either blindly for or blindly against labor," reported the journalist Lincoln Colcord. For in 1919 labor and capital were engaged in a bitter struggle. The war had upset the balance of power established in the prosperous days of the progressive era. As unions grew in size and power, labor's aspirations also expanded. Yet while the war added to the gross income of labor and the government required employers to accept collective bargaining, war also brought its frustrations: the administration discouraged the closed shop and sometimes required short apprenticeships, and inflation ate into wage increases. "It is doubtful," one economist wrote, "if in the long run real wages were appreciably bettered by the war." In addition, labor was restless after months of abnormal exertion in wartime industry. Business also grew stronger in the war, and former competitors learned the blessings of government-sanctioned co-operation. More important, business lost some of the tarnish of the muckraking era, as the strength of American industry contributed its important part to winning the war. But management too was troubled, by high taxes that lasted into 1919 and by the failure of government to award just compensation for some of the voided war contracts. Business was frightened by the apparent growth of radicalism and nervous over the threat of government ownership. Will Hays, the Repub-

[9] For cost-of-living figures, see *New York Times*, May 3, 1920, p. 1; Samuelson and Hagen, *After the War*, pp. 13, 31; and U.S. Department of Labor, *Bulletin of the U.S. Bureau of Labor Statistics*, CCCLVII (May, 1924), 466; John A. Peters to Mark Sullivan, 1920 [?], Sullivan Papers, Hoover Institute on War and Peace; Frederic L. Paxson, *Postwar Years: Normalcy, 1918–1923* (Berkeley, Calif., 1948), p. 45; Houston, *Eight Years with Wilson's Cabinet, 1913–1920*, (New York, 1926), II, 105 ff.

lican national chairman, called the businessmen "supremely loyal" and "entitled to every consideration, including the right to run their own business." "We need a businessman for President," declared the *Saturday Evening Post*. The combatants were all the more tenacious because they clashed in an atmosphere of class consciousness over issues of fundamental importance, including collective bargaining and the open shop. When labor forced the hand of capital in a series of massive strikes, the public was forced to take sides.[10]

Unfortunately for labor, the public was in no mood to champion its cause or to tolerate its strikes. During the war the laboring man's living standard had sometimes risen to middle-class levels, and white-collar workers were disturbed that their wages had risen only 5 to 10 per cent. While their pugnacity offended most of their countrymen, laborers were largely unsuccessful in obtaining their goals. In September, President Wilson asked workers not to strike for higher wages, since strikes would raise even further the high cost of living; and he denounced the Boston police strike as a "crime against civilization." To assuage the hard feelings between capital and labor, he called a National Industrial Conference to meet in October. But the AF of L

[10] Colcord is quoted in *Nation*, CIX (Nov. 15, 1919), 636. A good essay on the inevitability of postwar friction between capital and labor is William F. Ogburn, "Capital and Labor," in Frederick A. Cleveland and Joseph Schafer (eds.), *Democracy in Reconstruction* (New York, 1919), pp. 305–26; see also Isaac Lippincott, *Problems in Reconstruction* (Boston, 1919), p. 229 and *passim*. The economist quoted is Harold U. Faulkner, *American Economic History* (8th ed.; New York, 1960), p. 594. On the breaking of war contracts, see Cleveland and Schafer (eds.), *Democracy in Reconstruction*, and Benedict Crowell and Robert Forrest Wilson, *Demobilization: Our Industrial and Military Demobilization After the Armistice, 1918–1920* (New Haven, Conn., 1921), pp. 126–44. Will Hays is quoted in *Nation*, CIX (Dec. 18, 1919), 733. *Saturday Evening Post*, CXII (Oct. 4, 1919), 28. A typical case of employee discontent over the loss of collective bargaining occurred among telephone workers; see Felix Frankfurter to William B. Wilson, Sept. 2, 1919, Labor Department File 16–603, National Archives.

withdrew on the grounds that representatives of the employers refused—in the face of the steel strike then under way—to affirm the principle of unrestricted collective bargaining that had widely established itself during the war. When the bituminous coal miners went out on strike in November, Attorney-General Palmer obtained two federal court injunctions against the strikers that aroused labor's ire. Following the example of some businessmen, the Attorney-General styled the strikers radicals and their conduct a rehearsal for communist revolution. Wilson estranged the Railway Brotherhoods by refusing to support the revolutionary Plumb plan that would have nationalized the railroads and given the workers a share in their management and profits.[11] Despite the generous arbitration of Secretary of Labor William B. Wilson in the coal strike and the President's efforts on behalf of the steel workers, labor's dissatisfaction with the economic and political status quo increased as rapidly as the public's dissatisfaction with labor. In early 1920 the Esch-Cummins Act came dangerously close to requiring compulsory government arbitration of labor disputes—a thing that in an era of conservative federal administration would hold little promise for the worker—and the antistrike provision of the act also offended labor. Samuel Gompers blamed this act and the

[11] Progressive Republicans especially feared the abuse of public interest on the part of labor unions. George H. Mayer, *The Republican Party, 1854–1964* (New York, 1964), p. 386. Editorial reaction of the country's newspapers to the strikes of 1919 is contained in *Literary Digest*, LXIII (Oct. 25, 1919), 11–14, and (Nov. 22, 1919), 11. On Palmer's use of the injunction, see Franklin K. Lane to Woodrow Wilson, Oct. 19, 1919, Serial VI, File 5085, Wilson Papers, Library of Congress; Gompers to Lee Seamster, Mar. 29, 1920, Gompers Papers, AFL-CIO Building, Washington, D.C.; William B. Wilson to James Duncan, Apr. 22, 1920, William B. Wilson Papers, Pennsylvania Historical Society. For the reaction of the railway brotherhoods to the President's discarding of the Plumb plan, see *New York Times*, Feb. 24, 1920, pp. 1–2. *Nation*, CIX (Sept. 6, 1919), 326–27; *New York Times*, Oct. 23, 1919, p. 1; and *Outlook*, CXXIII (Sept. 3, 1919), 5.

"unrest in the country" on Congress. Sometime in 1920, it would appear, the workers decided that they had lost the industrial war of 1919, and labor militancy receded. By and large, both the activities of unions and the incidence of strikes declined in the 1920's when labor completed its strategic retreat.[12]

Farmers found themselves in their familiar dilemma of squaring the higher cost of living with declining market prices for their crops. Although the 1918 Congressional elections had marked the departure of many farmers from the Democratic party, the Department of Agriculture made little effort to forestall further desertions. For a time the postwar agricultural market prospered as foreign demand sustained the expanded wartime production. But farmers felt uneasy in 1919, knowing that government price supports would end in the spring of 1920. Since we were now a creditor nation and since European borrowing was gradually diminishing under the War Finance Corporation, foreign exports now also declined sharply. And even though farm mortgages had more than doubled since 1914, Secretary of Agriculture David Houston—a southerner viewed with considerable suspicion by western farmers—along with his successor, Edwin T. Meredith, awaited indifferently the end of price supports. To heighten further the agrarian dislike of the Wilson administration, the adoption of the Esch-Cummins law in January, 1920, returning the railroads to private hands was followed by a rate increase of 35 to 40 per cent, and the Federal Reserve Board gave no effective help to agriculture. Unlike the laborer, the farmer did not participate in the complacency of the twenties; agrarian feeling increased in militancy and raised its

[12] David Brody, *Labor in Crisis: The Steel Strike of 1919* (Philadelphia, 1965), pp. 102–11. Gompers is quoted in *American Federationist*, XXVII (July, 1920), 656–57. Labor before and during the Great Depression is the subject of Irving Bernstein's *A History of the American Worker, 1920–1933: The Lean Years* (Boston, 1960).

protest as it looked upon relative health that eventually
came to prevail throughout the economy.[13]

The economic trouble of 1919 was not a depression;
that was to follow from 1920 to 1922. What disturbed
America after the war was an uncertainty about the future,
an uneven distribution of prosperity, and the threat of
depression.

Closely joined to the unsteadiness of the postwar economy
was an injurious psychological mood. Wilson's son-in-law,
William Gibbs McAdoo, observed in 1920 that "there is a
strange poison in the air." [14] There was indeed. The poison
had gathered during the war, and even with the coming
of peace and the elimination of the immediate center of
infection it was working its way throughout the social
body and mind.

The duty of spreading a patriotic war spirit had fallen
to the highly efficient Committee on Public Information.
The unit owed much of its effectiveness to its chairman,
George Creel, a Denver progressive who shrewdly worked
upon chauvinistic feelings already present in American
society and brought to a new intensity a national mood
that blended aggression and sincere idealism, patriotic
dedication and xenophobia. The success of the Creel Committee, as measured by sales of war bonds and subscrip-
tions to Liberty Loans, went beyond anyone's expectations.
Liberals in government failed to foresee, however, that
wartime propaganda and repression, like any strong drug,

[13] United States Department of Labor, *Statistical Abstract, 1920*
(Washington, 1921), p. 464; Arthur S. Link, "The Federal Reserve
Policy and the Agricultural Depression of 1920–21," *Agricultural
History*, XX (July, 1946), 166–75. Secretary of the Treasury Houston
curtailed the Federal Reserve Board's extension of credit to foreign
countries for the purchase of agricultural goods. Crowell and Wilson,
Demobilization, p. 179.

[14] McAdoo to Jouett Shouse, Sept. 17, 1920, McAdoo Papers,
Library of Congress.

might have harmful aftereffects in a time of peace. The psychological gratifications of war were hard to surrender.

In Bolshevism, symbol alike of anarchy and of traitorous retreat from the wartime alliance, the aroused American temper found in postwar days a new object to replace the defeated Hun. Stories of Bolshevik cruelty replaced those of German atrocities, and of course it was rumored that Germans had instigated the Russian upheaval. Indeed, Bolshevism was the enemy in Siberia, where in February, 1919, American troops suffered considerable casualties. And when the international ambitions of the Bolsheviks became publicized, organizations such as the American Vigilantes' International sprang up to combat them, and the newly formed American Legion went on the alert: both organizations were products of the wartime experience. At the same time the Russian Revolution provided a fresh vision for the socialists and communists of America. Though it was unrelated to Bolshevism except in the imaginations of superpatriots, the massive labor agitation of 1919 added to the fear of insurrection from the left.

During the war the Creel Committee had asked citizens to report those who spread pessimistic stories about the war or cried for peace. In response the American Protective League arose. Made up of business and professional men, it acquired a semi-official status during the war as an arm of the Bureau of Investigation. The League publication *The Spyglass* directed its postwar attention to the communist menace. The first of many antisocialist riots instigated by veterans occurred in New York just a few weeks after the war had ended. Soldiers seeking employment in large cities frequently turned violently upon socialist agitators. The formation of the Comintern the following March further heightened the prevalent anxiety. Soon the various representatives of public sentiment were calling on the Justice Department directly to act against

18 CHANGE AND CONTINUITY: THE 1920's

all radicals as well as to keep wartime political prisoners in jail. And at the head of the department was a man with both an aggressive temper and presidential ambitions.

Although Attorney-General Palmer at first displayed a judicious attitude in keeping with his earlier career as a liberal, political opportunism and a lifelong distrust of foreigners and their ways eventually warped his sober judgment. The explosion of a bomb in front of his house spurred him to a fanaticism of one who believed himself persecuted. Red propaganda, he reportedly claimed, gave him "the creeps," and he maintained that the Reds were not going to "get him." But his notorious actions occurred only after alarmist reports from J. Edgar Hoover, newly appointed head of the antiradical division in the Bureau of Investigation, convinced him that the country faced a revolution.[15]

Of course, in 1919 many events caused understandable public anxiety. The Seattle general strike in the winter seemed unlike anything in the native tradition of labor dissent, and the May Day bombs and riots appeared to make clear the radical origins of at least some of the agitation. In reality, the Seattle strike was aimed only at intransigent employers and the May Day riots were as often as not set off by nervous citizens. But when bombs exploded

[15] In April, 1919, Palmer told Governor Cox of Ohio that current charges of pro-Germanism in the Cincinnati schools "consisted chiefly of gossip" and "hearsay." Palmer to Cox, Apr. 30, 1919; see also Palmer to John Lord O'Brien, Apr. 27, 1919; Justice Department Files, National Archives. As late as June, 1919, Palmer argued that more repressive legislation would play into the hands of the radicals. *Nation*, CVIII (June 14, 1919), 927. And even in November he thought some of the Senate bills "too drastic." Palmer to John S. Starkweather, Nov. 17, 1919, and Palmer to Senator Lawrence C. Phipps, Nov. 19, 1919. Justice Department File 100–374, National Archives. On Palmer's subsequent attitude, see Stanley Coben, *A. Mitchell Palmer: Politician* (New York, 1963), pp. 155–56, 185–86, 198–99, 203, 205, 207, 212; and Donald Johnson, *The Challenge to American Freedoms: Word War One and the Rise of the American Civil Liberties Union* (Lexington, Ky., 1963), pp. 120–75.

in eight cities in early June, public apprehension continued to mount with some reason. The Overman Judiciary Subcommittee of the Senate titillated the public with stories of the Bolshevik threat of the "nationalization of women," and the Lusk Committee of the New York State Assembly descended upon the Rand School in New York City. Strikes had reached their greatest frequency in August, 1919; but the most important ones, including those in coal and steel, occurred in the fall. The Boston police strike of September and the Armistice Day massacre at Centralia, Washington, erased whatever uncertainty remained in the public mind about whether the issue was indeed radicalism. That it was a foreign threat was seemingly illustrated by the tenacity of immigrant strikers during the steel strike.

Late in 1919 and after, Palmer, ignoring fundamental canons of human and civil rights, caused the unlawful imprisonment of hundreds of aliens suspected of revolutionary sentiment. Even while opposing immigration restriction, he attempted summarily to deport as many foreign-born radicals as he could. Anthony Caminetti, commissioner of immigration in the Department of Labor, temporarily prevailed on his superiors to condone many deportations. The policy itself was not new, but its massive implementation was. The Red scare intensified the social and political reaction that flourished in 1919; the scare was not unrelated to the strength of nativism in the 1920's, exemplified by the rapid growth of the Ku Klux Klan.[16]

[16] Stanley Coben has contributed a new interpretation of the Red scare. He interprets it as a complicated social-psychological movement in response to a national disequilibrium induced by radicalism, major strikes, federal controls, the high cost of living, and an unsteady economy. Coben finds the term "revivification movement," as it is formulated by one anthropologist, to be applicable to the Red scare; the phrase describes a mass attempt to verify accustomed ways of thinking and to destroy foreign influences. "A Study in Nativism: The American Red Scare of 1919–20," *Political Science Quarterly*, LXXIX (March, 1964), 55 ff.; F. L. Wallace, "Revivification Movements," *American Anthropologist*, LVIII (1956), 264–81.

The "deportations delirium" itself ended abruptly early in the election year of 1920. Palmer's predictions of social unrest failed to materialize, and he encountered the opposition of aroused liberals. Even George Creel, no insignificant spokesman for full-blooded Americanism, worked with the American Civil Liberties Union to free imprisoned radicals. Finally, Palmer met his match in Acting Secretary of Labor Louis Post. The authority to deport radicals lay only with the Secretary of Labor, and Post—convinced by an Industrial Workers of the World brief concerning encroachment on the rights of radicals—repeatedly reversed Justice Department decisions. To remove the obstacle, an angry House Committee started impeachment hearings against Post; but despite his seventy-one years, the Acting Secretary stymied the committee with a storehouse of irrefutable and damning facts about deportation cases. Curious citizens who came to scoff at Post remained to applaud when he reprimanded the committee members for abusing the Bill of Rights.[17]

[17] William Preston, Jr., describes the power struggle as one between J. Edgar Hoover of the Bureau of Investigation backed by Palmer, and Post supported by Secretary of Labor William B. Wilson, whom, incidentally, Frederic C. Howe and others thought to be carried along by the prevalent hysteria late in 1919. Preston, *Aliens and Dissenters*, pp. 224–25; Howe, *The Confessions of a Reformer* (New York, 1925), p. 327; Howe to W. B. Wilson, Oct. 9, 1919, William B. Wilson Papers. According to the *Detroit News*, Apr. 23, 1920, the President, perhaps through fear of angering organized labor, sided with Post against Palmer—a corroboration of Wilson's alleged caution to the Attorney-General not to let the country "see Red." The *New York Times* account of the impeachment hearings appeared on May 9, 1920, p. 12. Post's version of the episode is in his *The Deportations Delirium of Nineteen-Twenty* (Chicago, 1923); the acting cabinet officer acquiesced in the deportations of some 550 radicals, about 20 per cent of the names sent to him by Palmer. Post declared that the American Legion, which honored him by setting up a special Louis F. Post impeachment committee, suffered from "groundless fears" induced by a "psychological condition." Labor Department File 167–255A, National Archives. U.S. Department of Labor, *Annual Report of the Commission on Immigration, 1920* (Washington, 1921), pp. 32–34; *Annual Report . . . , 1921* (Washington, 1922), p. 14. See also Robert K. Murray, *Red Scare: A Study*

While the Red scare was in progress, conditions of another sort were generating irrational angers. As never before, the Negro was coming into major contact, and often major collision, with white society. The war years were a time of mass migration from the rural South to the urban North. Between 1915 and 1920 the Negro population of New York rose 66 per cent to 152,000; in Chicago it increased 148 per cent to 109,000; in Cleveland, 307 per cent to 34,000; and in Detroit, 611 per cent to 40,000. And in Europe, Negroes fired guns, wore honored uniforms, and experienced some measure of social equality; they were prepared—some of them—for militancy. Inevitably, as colored neighborhoods expanded into contiguous residential areas and recently demobilized soldiers competed with Negroes for jobs, passions flared. Barred from a number of unions, Negroes were hired as scabs during the steel strike. Race riots broke out in several cities, including Washington, Chicago, Omaha, and Knoxville; hundreds of lives were lost. Lynchings rose from thirty-six in 1917 and sixty in 1918 to seventy-six in 1919, and then declined sharply in the twenties. And in 1919 the revived Klan began its meteoric rise, gaining some 100,000 members in the South.[18]

---

in *National Hysteria, 1919–1920* (Minneapolis, 1955), pp. 247–49. Concerning Palmer's defense, there is Johnson, *The Challenge to American Freedoms*, pp. 161–62; and U.S. Congress, House Committee on Rules, *A. Mitchell Palmer on Charges Made against Department of Justice by Louis F. Post and Others*, Hearings, 66th Cong., 2d Sess., 1920. Palmer on Post is in Secretary of State Robert Lansing's Private Memoranda, Apr. 14, 1920, Lansing Papers, Library of Congress. For Wilson's own attitude on wartime propaganda, suppression, and related matters, see Harry Scheiber, *The Wilson Administration and Civil Liberties, 1917–1921* (Ithaca, N.Y., 1960), pp. 40–41.

[18] The statistics on Negro population are quoted in Oscar Handlin, *The American People in the Twentieth Century* (Cambridge, Mass., 1954), p. 111; those on lynchings are from Jessie P. Guzman *et al.* (eds.), *The Negro Yearbook, 1952* (New York, 1952), p. 278. Brody, *Labor in Crisis*, pp. 162–63.

In its larger significance, the Post-Palmer skirmish was symptomatic of emerging political disorder within the Democratic party. The administration had lost its power to discipline and stimulate Congress to act on pressing national problems. This near abandonment of party discipline, especially on the part of Wilson, goes far in itself to explain the temper of the nation. Neither were the Republicans able to muster the leadership the times seemed to require.

During the first months of the peace Wilson's schedule made it impossible for him to provide domestic leadership. He spent the month after the Congressional elections of 1918 preparing for the Paris Peace Conference. On December 2 he left for Paris, and, except for a ten-day trip home in the late winter to sign bills and attend to unavoidable domestic duties, his work kept him abroad until July 8, a period of about seven months. On the trip home he met his cabinet, talked to a fairly complacent conference of governors and mayors about unemployment, and had dinner with members of the Senate Foreign Relations Committee; but a ten-day whirlwind of activity could not replace constant presidential concern and leadership.[19]

In the weeks to come the fight over the League of Nations consumed much of Wilson's time, and he continued to give little attention to domestic and party affairs. "There is no real note of leadership coming out of the White House," complained the *Nation* in August. Although weakened by a severe attack of influenza, Wilson began on September 3, 1919, a tour to generate support for his League. On September 25 he had a physical breakdown in Pueblo, Colorado, and shortly afterward suffered a paralyzing

[19] In this period Wilson sent three messages to Congress that touched only peripherally upon political and social reform. Perhaps he could have worked more actively for reform had he returned to America sooner or had his health not given out. For the messages, see *New York Times*, Dec. 2, 1918, pp. 1–2; May 21, 1919, pp. 1–2 (cabled from Paris); and Aug. 9, 1919, pp. 1–2.

cerebral hemorrhage. Since that affliction often leaves some
of the bodily and mental functions unimpaired and a few
of Wilson's visitors during the last year and a half of his
presidency found him apparently hale, their testimony has
occasionally been taken as evidence that his illness did not
seriously damage his capacities. But the opposite was the
case. The stroke prevented him from performing effectively
the complex activity of a President; he was rarely able to
work more than an hour or two a day or to sustain more
than a few minutes of dictation. In the middle of 1920
Doctor Cary T. Grayson, Wilson's physician, spoke of the
President's gradual mental deterioration. Nor is it possible
to separate emotional from intellectual impairment. Had
illness not struck him down, Wilson might have continued
as the strong party leader he had described in his *Congressional Government.* As it was, his party floundered for
lack of direction, all the more so because earlier he had
accustomed it to the vigorous leadership of a prime minister. Few Democratic leaders, "thanks to Mr. Wilson's
domination of his party," observed the *Nation,* "retain any
special capacity for independent thought or constructive
statesmanship.[20]

The President's absence forced an unaccustomed degree
of independence on even the least active cabinet members,
whom he had regarded condescendingly as administrators
rather than as members of an important political body.
Secretary of the Treasury McAdoo, the most competent
executive, had already resigned. Inexperienced though they
were at independent leadership, the more ambitious secretaries jumped at the opportunity to direct government policy. The most flagrant exercise of autonomous power was

[20] *Nation,* CVII (Nov. 9, 1918), 545; CIX (Aug. 2, 1919), 133.
On Wilson's illness, see John Garraty, *Woodrow Wilson* (New York,
1956), p. 182; Arthur Walworth, *Woodrow Wilson* (2 vols.; New York,
1958), I, 400; and the thorough bibliographical note in John Blum,
Joe Tumulty and the Wilson Era (Boston, 1951), p. 312 (see also
pp. 214, 216).

by Attorney-General Palmer, who issued his famous injunction against the United Mine Workers less than two months after Wilson's collapse. Palmer's actions in the Red scare severely divided Wilson's advisers: Joe Tumulty, Robert Lansing, and Albert S. Burleson supported him in opposition to William B. Wilson, Franklin K. Lane, and Josephus Daniels. Secretary of State Lansing acquired Wilson's enmity by calling cabinet meetings without the President's consent. According to Daniels and others, Lansing wanted Vice-President Thomas Marshall to take over the government. Bitterly contentious Postmaster-General Burleson "created everywhere a sense of extreme sensitivity." The new executive leadership frequently took on a conservative character. Fundamental decisions on economic policy lay chiefly with Carter Glass and David F. Houston, successors to McAdoo in the Treasury; and both Houston and Glass wanted the ailing postwar economy to mend itself. Lincoln Colcord of the *Nation* diagnosed the situation in an article entitled "The Administration Adrift":

> So with the President out of commission, it has been Carter Glass and Mr. Burleson, and Mr. Houston, all Bourbon southerners, who have dominated the Administration and formulated its policies during this critical time. . . . There seems little doubt that the leaders of the Bourbon Democracy have utilized the full power and prestige of the Presidency to work their own ends.[21]

Another indication of the President's declining role as leader was his failure to provide a progressive domestic program. Conservationists in particular were discouraged;

[21] Between the end of the war and the election of 1920, six of the nine cabinet officers had to be replaced. Wilson's conception of party government is discussed in Arthur Link, *Wilson: The New Freedom* (Princeton, N.J.: 1956), pp. 145–47. David Houston, among others, recalls the encroachments by the Congress on executive domain after Wilson's illness. *Eight Years with Wilson's Cabinet*, II, 71–90; Houston to Woodrow Wilson, Apr. 15, 1920, Houston Papers, Library

but for a liberal filibuster, a "giveaway" leasing act would
have passed early in 1919. Even such significant legislation
as was passed after 1918—the progressive General Leasing
and Water Power acts of 1920, for instance—had for
the most part been initiated long before the meeting of the
Sixty-sixth Congress, whereas other measures, such as the
Transportation and Merchant Marine acts of 1920, were
steps backward from the radical nationalization of wartime. In referring to the railroad act, the *New Republic*
condemned "the unfortunate legislation of 1920. . . . It
was the product of a mediocre, spineless and leaderless
Congress." A decade later the same journal observed:
"Wilson through the force of his own personality carried
his party into a position of progressivism which was not
native to it and from which it promptly backslid as soon
as his individual authority was removed. By 1920, there
was little evidence left in the party of the spirit which in
1913 was busy inaugurating the Federal Reserve Board
and so many other measures of reform." The last years of
the Wilson administration offered little to Americans of
progressive persuasion, while federal acts of political
repression disgusted liberals.[22]

The *Nation* agreed that "the breakdown in the executive
branch of government is everywhere apparent." But, it
added, "the breakdown is none the less serious" in Congress. Intimidated by the mounting national debt, Congress
felt obliged to practice economy. Even the magazine that
mourned the inactivity of Congress preached that "rigid
economy in government expenditures is imperatively required in the interest of the American people." The *Saturday*

---

of Congress. On Wilson's declining role as party leader, see George
Creel, *The War, the World, and Wilson* (New York, 1920), p. 134.
Richard F. Fenno, Jr., *The President's Cabinet* (New York, 1959),
pp. 58–59. Colcord article is in *Nation*, CIX (Nov. 15, 1919), 635–36.

[22] *New Republic*, XX (Nov. 12, 1919), 315; LVIII (May 8, 1929),
320; J. Leonard Bates, *The Origins of Teapot Dome*, pp. 165, 180,
200 ff.

Evening Post could think of little else. The Senate was less conservative than the House, which spent much of its time in 1919 debating various peacetime sedition bills. But the Senate, beginning in the spring of 1919, was so immersed in the debates over the League of Nations and the Treaty of Versailles that it became, in the view of the *Nation,* "literally impervious to the condition of the country." No important accomplishment can be credited to the Congress in 1919, save for the ratification of constitutional amendments propelled by the thrust of the progressive era, the war, and various pressure groups.[23]

The one issue that might have rallied liberal support was the League of Nations, and yet in fact the League added to disharmony. It was indeed on foreign policy more than on any other issue in the postwar era that the progressive movement fragmented. For a time the League was able to ride the crest of an internationalism expounded by Wilson in his cherished wish to "make the world safe for democracy"; it was promoted to a degree by the same spirit of wartime idealism that also unleashed the more chauvinistic impulses of the day. Evidence of the League's initial strength was ubiquitous. Newspapers supported it overwhelmingly, and even thirty-two state legislatures endorsed some kind of international organization. But the League— still little more than a pleasant notion in most people's minds—was pushed into the background by the immediacy of the domestic program, and a shift in the sentiment of the people was soon to come.[24]

[23] *Nation,* CIX (Dec. 6, 1919), 711; (Dec. 13, 1919), 735, 743; *Saturday Evening Post,* CXC (Dec. 7, 1918), 20; CXCII (May 17, 1919), 28.

[24] William Allen White later wrote of "a height of aspiration" lasting from the Armstice to early 1919. But "perhaps there was no reality to that day," he said, "but only an emotional fiz [*sic*]. . . . " —White to W. D. Guthrie, July 10, 1923, White Papers, Library of Congress.

The President's conduct at Versailles helped to trigger
the reaction against the League. Republicans were the first
to be estranged. Already, in his appeal in 1918 for a Democratic Congress to further his policies, Wilson had invited
a partisan response from the Republican party; and by
failing to take influential Republicans with him to Paris,
or to keep the Senate leaders informed of the treaty-
making progress, he further widened the breach. Wilson's
highhanded indifference to the Republicans—his apparent
assumption, at Versailles and thereafter, that it was the
duty of the Senate Republicans, as it was the duty of the
Democrats, to provide a rubber stamp for a Wilson treaty
—lost him a good deal of the support that he might otherwise have commanded. Of course, if Wilson had triumphed
in peace as he had in war, the Republican cause would
have been less hopeful. But he did not. The Republicans,
by fastening their argument upon Article X of the League
Covenant—a controversial statement guaranteeing the integrity of national boundaries—and by representing the
provision as a binding commitment that would involve
American soldiers in an unending series of wars and police
actions, brought many of their listeners to a new idea of
the League as an instrument not for peace but for
bloody international adventure. And Wilson stiffened the
opposition when he assailed the anti-League senators as
"bungalow-minds" whose heads were "knots tied to keep
their bodies from unravelling." [25]

[25] It is possible, of course, that the President could on no account
have secured Republican co-operation. However tactful he might have
been, a handful of powerful isolationist Republican senators would
have threatened the chairman of the Senate Foreign Relations Committee with a party bolt in 1920. And despite Henry Cabot Lodge's
own milder sentiments, Lodge might have backed the isolationists, if
only to prevent a revolt within his party similar to the Bull Moose
rebellion of recent and searing memory. On May 10, 1919, Colonel
House wrote in his diary that Wilson "has built up a fire there [in
the Republican Congress] which is now beginning to scorch him and

A more surprising effect of Wilson's performance at
Versailles was the desertion of many ardent liberals who
could have been expected to rekindle the idealism of 1917
and 1918. Unprepared for the conflict between ideals and
self-interest, they abandoned the Treaty of Versailles after
becoming convinced that the President had betrayed his
own principles. And by tying the League to the treaty, he
invited greater opposition than he would otherwise have
encountered. For example, the *New Republic* observed in
1920 that the Fourteen Points really belonged to the liberals of the world, not to Wilson, who had negotiated them
so badly. Those liberals who had been suspicious of Wilson
from the first had their fears confirmed; for those who
trusted him, the disillusionment was far more shattering.
The protests of some of Wilson's own advisers increased
the ranks of those who wanted no part of a League tied
to a punitive and "reactionary" peace treaty—one that
perpetuated existing injustices and so could only lead to
another war—and mounting evidence of Allied perfidy in
bringing on the war also disillusioned the liberals. The
Nation imaginatively charged that the international bank-
ing interests, operating through Elihu Root, were pushing
the League. Domestic events confirmed their suspicions that
the President had relinquished his role as a reform leader.
The shambles at Versailles was matched in their eyes by
the repression of the Palmer raids.[26]

The Republicans were hostile, the liberals cool or confused, and old-stock Americans were increasingly alarmed
over foreign entanglements. The Democrats could ill afford
to draw into the League debate still another and steadily

---

it will become worse and worse as his term wanes. It was all so
useless and it has hampered him in the exercise of his public work."
    [26] *New Republic,* XXIV (Sept. 9, 1920), 18; *Nation,* CIX (July 5,
1919), 3.

expanding force in American politics: the organized immigrant, perhaps more intractably hostile to Versailles than
was any native American faction apart from the staunchest
isolationists. Yet in his January plea that the election of
1920 be a "solemn referendum" on the League, Wilson laid
the party open to the animosity of the national minorities.
Political bosses, such as Charles Murphy of New York,
Thomas Taggart of Indiana, and George Brennan of Illinois
pleaded against the idea. They saw that to make the League
a central issue in the campaign would shatter Democratic
foreign blocs in Boston, New York, Chicago, and other large
cities—would hopelessly alienate immigrants or Americans
of immigrant extraction for whom the Treaty of Versailles
represented a slighting, a betrayal, or an oppression of the
old countries. For once the chauvinism of the immigrant
was joined to the chauvinism of the native isolationist.

Long before the presidential campaign of 1920, wartime
idealism flagged in the face of the continuing and fruitless
debates in and out of the Senate, along with Wilson's infuri-
ating proprietary attitude toward the League. A growing
weariness first arose among Republicans, immigrants, and
disillusioned liberals; and gradually, the skepticism perme-
ated the mind of the whole nation. The press, antagonized
by Wilson's censorship policies as well as his poor handling of the news from the Versailles conference, was in
a mood to promote the change in sentiment. It was the
fate of the Democratic party to become a political scapegoat
in the League struggle wherein the issues were unclear and
distorted. One correspondent wrote to Franklin Roosevelt:
"I fear . . . that the Wilson League of Nations is about
the most effective millstone that any party, bent on suicide,
has tied about its neck to date." [27]

[27] Barbara Leahy to Franklin Roosevelt, June 9, 1920, Roosevelt
Papers, Franklin D. Roosevelt Library, Hyde Park, New York.

What kind of public and political tone was to dominate in the 1920's? Would there be a frenzied effort to revive a lost and innocent past? The Red scare had suggested something of this; but by the end of 1920 the American people were firmly on another course. In the decade of the 1920's they would, as usual, pursue the good life. Not that the age of normalcy solved problems; rather, its non-combative posture ignored them and awaited their disappearance. Normalcy was a victory for the middle elements in American life, for the deep-rooted consensus of the American experience that easily outlasted the conflict of the postwar months. The brief span of the reaction supports the view that much of the disturbance of 1919 was superficial rather than serious.

In 1919 people had hurried to resume a way of life that was gone; by the summer of 1920 they had accepted its disappearance and hastened to embrace the new order. When Attorney-General Palmer opened 1920 with his raids on radicals, twenty-two New York clergymen denounced the deportations delirium, a Philadelphia United States District Attorney resigned in protest, and in Minnesota veterans condemned the attacks on free speech. When five Socialists were expelled from the New York Assembly early in 1920, conservatives, including Charles Evans Hughes and Warren Harding, protested their dismissal. May Day came and went without the radical violence predicted by Palmer, and Americans could scoff with the *Nation*: "Who was Queen of the May this year? Why, A. Mitchell Palmer without a doubt." The Congressional sedition laws were forgotten, and new popular fads diverted attention from politics to pleasure, from the League of Nations to the baseball teams of the American League. In contrast to Wilson, who could not forgive Eugene Debs his honest hatred of war, Warren Harding—though for purely political reasons—was to commute the Socialist leader's thirty-

year prison sentence. Soon, Walter Lippmann would write
that there were no parties, no leaders, and no issues. The
1920's had begun in earnest. There were disturbances: a
serious depression lasted from 1920 to 1922, farming never
came out of its economic slump, and the Klan replaced the
Red hunters. But at no time in the decade was American
society to be so confused and distraught as in the single
year 1919.[28]

[28] An editorial appearing in the *Saturday Evening Post* in May,
1920, in some ways heralded the coming of normalcy: newspapers had
exaggerated the recent discontent, the *Post* asserted, whereas in
reality life was pretty ordinary. CXCII (May 15, 1920), 28. The word
"normalcy" was supposedly coined by Warren Harding when he
misread it for "normality" in his inaugural address. In fact, normalcy
had its niche in the English language long before. For two nineteenth-
century usages, see the *Oxford English Dictionary* (Oxford, 1933)
VII, 208. *Nation*, CX (May 8, 1920), 607 The Lippmann essay, "The
Causes of Political Indifference," first appeared in the spring of 1921
and is collected in *Men of Destiny* (New York, 1927), pp. 18–34.

Oil and Politics

BURL NOGGLE

THE Teapot Dome affair, both as scandal and as symbol of shoddy politics in the 1920's, has been long in need of reappraisal. For some forty years, descriptions and evaluations of the great scandal have been monotonously uniform. Historians, Democrats running for office, journalists searching for historical metaphors—all have said much the same thing about Teapot Dome.

College-level textbooks occasionally offer a dispassionate narrative of the essential facts, but more commonly they serve up moral condemnations: "Vulgarity and scandal" in the Harding administration "were the sordid fruits of normalcy." [1] The "tortuous and sordid details of the oil scandals" added up to a "sorry mess." [2] The "loose morality and get-rich-quickism of the Harding era flared forth spectacularly in a series of scandals," with Teapot Dome the "most shocking of all." [3] In his *Only Yesterday* (1931), a book that was the first to treat the 1920's as a historical unit,

[1] John M. Blum, *et al.*, *The National Experience* (New York, 1963), p. 603.

[2] Samuel Eliot Morison and Henry Steele Commager, *The Growth of the American Republic* (5th ed.; 2 vols.; New York, 1963) II, 653.

[3] Thomas A. Bailey, *The American Pageant* (2nd ed.; Boston, 1961), pp. 784–85.

Frederick Lewis Allen entitled his chapter on the Harding
administration "Harding and the Scandals." Allen gave
some ten pages to Teapot Dome, calling it "the aristocrat
among the scandals." [4] Twenty-five years later, Arthur M.
Schlesinger, Jr., wrote that Albert B. Fall (Teapot Dome's
central figure) was "without shame." [5]

In making such judgments, historians are keeping alive a
version of Teapot Dome as old as the affair itself. The Teapot Dome story began to reach the front pages of the nation's newspapers—began, that is, to become a public
"scandal"—about mid-January, 1924. During the next
three months editorial commentary and reports on public
pulse-taking were rampant. In early February the *Freeman* saw Teapot Dome as a valuable object lesson in the
"whole disreputable and thieving business of government
by politics." [6] A *New York Times* editorial of February 3
stressed "the evil" that had been wrought by some of the
Teapot Dome plotters, men who had committed "an incalculable wrong." [7] In late February the *Christian Advocate*
found in Teapot Dome "sickening evidence" of an "ethical
paralysis" in America.[8] By the beginning of March, newspapers throughout the country, were editorializing upon the
scandal. The Rochester (N.Y.) *Post Express* found that the
"political immorality which had forecast the decadence of
nations throughout history is beginning to rear its head in
our own United States." The Charlotte (N.C.) *Observer*
quoted favorably a religious journal's opinion that "the very
indignation that the faithlessness of a few officials has
aroused from sea to sea, is very good evidence that the

[4] Frederick Lewis Allen, *Only Yesterday* (paperback ed; New
York, 1959), pp. 86–112.

[5] Arthur M. Schlesinger, Jr., *The Crisis of the Old Order* (Boston,
1957), p. 52.

[6] "Teapot Dome," *Freeman*, VIII (Feb. 6, 1924), 509–10.

[7] *New York Times*, Feb. 3, 1924, II, 6:1.

[8] *Christian Advocate*, Feb. 21, 1924, p. 20.

public sentiment of the country is on the side of honesty and uprightness." [9]

Such public indignation rose and fell through the next three years. The Teapot Dome story soon lost its early sensationalism, but periodically it returned to the national headlines. Early in 1927, after a jury had acquitted Albert B. Fall and Edward L. Doheny of conspiring to defraud the government, a *New Republic* columnist lamented the jury's failure to accept evidence of "impropriety . . . , duplicity and lying that . . . had shocked the decency of America's honest citizenry." [10] In March, 1928, in response to some current revelations, Republican Senator Arthur Capper of Kansas delivered a broadside that no critic of Teapot Dome has ever surpassed: "The smudge of oil being smeared blankly across the pages of history is repulsive to the . . . entire country. The trail is slimy, odorous, reeking with corruption. [For] ways that are dark and tricks that are vain, for intrigue and plot, for impudent daring, for melodramatic episodes, for duplicity, craft and cunning the conspiracy of Teapot Dome is the equal of any of the major crimes carried out by unscrupulous and infamous freebooters in the Middle Ages. It is more medieval than modern." [11] The *World's Work*, meantime, took in less history for comparison when it judged Teapot Dome to be "a record of deception, lying, fraud, and graft without parallel in the last century of our national politics." [12]

Public response during the 1920's and historical appraisals since then have not, of course, been unanimous. From the very beginning, critics of the scandal had their

[9] "Sinister Shadows behind the Oil Scandal," *Literary Digest*, LXXX (Mar. 1, 1924), 1–9.

[10] J. M. Landis, "The Fall-Doheny Verdict," *New Republic*, LXIX (Jan. 19, 1927), 239–41.

[11] *New York Times*, Mar. 19, 1928, II, 2.

[12] "Money and Nerve in Politics," *Worlds Work*, LVI (May, 1928), 9–10.

own detractors. Senator Thomas J. Walsh of Montana, who
led the Senate investigation into Teapot Dome, sometimes
suffered vicious assaults. One editorialist called him a hyena,
and then defined the animal as "a carnivorous quadruped
. . . long . . . celebrated for the great size of its neck and
jaws, its voice, and its propensity for robbing graves." [13]
In May, 1924, in a summary analysis of the Senate inquiry
to that time, Felix Frankfurter noted that "various powerful forces" were trying to discredit the investigation, that
influential Republicans were beginning to denounce the
Senate committee itself, and that public condemnation was
now being reserved "for the exposers and not for the
exposed." [14]

Many political observers in the 1920's recognized much
of the condemnation of Teapot Dome for what it was—a
grasp for party advantage by Democrats seeking to magnify
a Republican scandal. One journalist in April, 1924, pointed
up a lesson to be learned from the affair—"the way partisan
politics messes up justice." Teapot Dome had given both political parties the chance "to mount their protected soap
boxes in [Congress] and scream their suspicions, rumors,
and slanders to the four winds." After all, he admitted,
congressmen were not only lawmakers; they were also candidates for re-election, "leaders and henchmen of two rival
organizations struggling for advantage." The journalist
Stanley Frost, whose articles on the Teapot Dome affair
were always insightful and sometimes prescient, made the
glum observation in March, 1924, "We Americans might
as well prepare to live from now till election day in an
atmosphere filled with oil and mud and reverberant with
drums. Political Washington has settled down to . . . such

[13] See, for example, *Congressional Record*, 68th Cong., 1st Sess.
(Feb. 8, 1924), 2056, for reprints of editorials.
[14] Felix Frankfurter, "Hands Off the Investigation," *New Republic*, XXXVIII (May 21, 1924), 329–31.

a [presidential] campaign of vituperation as has not been known for more than a generation." [15] And then there was the chairman of the board of Bethlehem Steel, who in March, 1924, complained that hysteria over the oil scandal was hampering business.[16]

Despite these variations, the central evaluation or "image" of Teapot Dome has always been clear: a nefarious and secret deal, sodden with graft and corruption, carried out with conspiratorial intent for purely personal gain. That any other view is even possible may seem naïve or irresponsible or both. Yet other approaches are feasible. The morality—or lack of it—in the Teapot Dome affair may be left to the moralists, who admittedly have plenty of evidence to work with. The historian, although free (and some would say certain) to make such judgments, can find in the history of Teapot Dome many other themes suitable for study. Graft and corruption are not all that the scandal's history contains. Some of the highest drama and some of the most ingenious maneuvering in modern American politics took place during, and because of, the Teapot Dome scandal. Teapot Dome has quite rightly come to epitomize politics in the twenties, and it is the politics rather than simply the immorality that needs to be examined and emphasized.[17]

[15] Frank Crane, "Oil and Dirty Waters," *Current Opinion*, LXXVI (April, 1924), xxxii; Stanley Frost, "Oil, Mud, and Tom-Toms," *Outlook*, CXXXVI (Mar. 12, 1924), 423–25.

[16] *New York Times*, Mar. 11, 1924, p. 1. For a careful study of responses to the Teapot Dome affair by businessmen, see Robert A. Waller, "Business and the Initiation of the Teapot Dome Investigation," *Business History Review*, XXXVI (Autumn, 1962), 334–53.

[17] J. Leonard Bates, "The Teapot Dome Scandal and the Election of 1924," *American Historical Review*, LX (January, 1955), 303–22, was one of the very first studies of Teapot Dome's political history, done by a professional historian concerned more with determining what happened than with merely repeating the usual morality tale. David Stratton also has done some careful essays of this kind: see his "Behind Teapot Dome: Some Personal Insights," *Business History*

The expression "Teapot Dome" is older than the scandal of the same name. Originally, Teapot Dome was the name of a government oil reserve in Wyoming, set aside in 1915 for exclusive use and benefit of the United States Navy. Progressives, conservationists, and scientists in government service had led a concerted drive during the progressive era for a new oil-leasing policy. Believing that the country's domestic oil supply would, without government regulation, become inadequate for the future needs of the economy and of the U.S. Navy, they agitated for conservation and restriction policies. In 1909 President William Howard Taft withdrew from private entry over a million acres of oil-bearing lands in California and Wyoming. In 1912 Taft established within the California area two naval petroleum reserves, Elk Hills (Reserve No. 1). and Buena Vista Hills (Reserve No. 2). In 1915 President Woodrow Wilson added Teapot Dome (Reserve No. 3) in the Wyoming area.[18]

The Teapot Dome reserve lay just south of the town of Midwest, in the northeast quadrant of the state. Overlooking the area is an eroded sandstone formation, one resembling a disfigured human hand but named Teapot Rock. Men in the oil business associated the oil dome with the landmark and called the reserve Teapot Dome. In turn,

Review, XXXI (Winter, 1957), 385–402; and "Splattered with Oil: William G. McAdoo and the Presidential Nomination," *Southwestern Social Science Quarterly*, XLIV (June, 1963), 62–75. On this latter topic, and for still another example of the dispassionate approach, see Lee N. Allen, "The McAdoo Campaign for the Presidential Nomination in 1924," *Journal of Southern History*, XXIX (May, 1963), 211–28. In my *Teapot Dome: Oil and Politics in the 1920's* (Baton Rouge, 1962), I sought to shift attention away from the question of guilt, as such, and to concentrate upon the scandal's effects in party politics.

18 J. Leonard Bates, "The Midwest Decision, 1915," *Pacific Northwest Quarterly*, LI (January, 1960), 26–27 and *The Origins of Teapot Dome: Progressives, Parties, and Petroleum, 1909–1921* (Urbana, Ill., 1963), pp. 14–25; Noggle, *Teapot Dome*, pp. 16–17.

the reserve supplied the name for the great scandal of the Harding administration.

There was much that was fortuitous in the history of Teapot Dome, and especially in the very discovery of the scandal. The Senate investigation that exposed the affair grew in an unforeseen fashion out of a conservation feud, one that had begun well before 1920 but one that quickened after Harding's election in that year. Between 1909, when the California oil lands were withdrawn from private entry, and 1921, when the new Harding administration began to formulate an oil policy, much legislative and bureaucratic wrangling over national oil resources and oil policy had taken place. The basic question had been whether or not the government should lease the reserves to private interests and, if so, under what terms. Businessmen wanted to tap the reserves—and had support from some influential politicians. Conservationists, also with political support, fought to keep them out. The oil-leasing policy of Harding's secretary of the interior, Albert B. Fall, as well as the policies of conservationists who opposed him, was a continuation into the 1920's of this running fight that had begun a decade earlier.[19]

Harding's nomination in 1920 actually pleased Gifford Pinchot and many other old progressives and conservationists concerned with the country's oil supply. They had, of late, built up deep resentment against the Wilson administration. They felt that Wilson himself, his attorney-general A. Mitchell Palmer, and his secretary of the interior Franklin K. Lane had, in their recent policies, turned reactionary. The Wilson administration was not, to them, a friend of the conservation movement. In contrast, they felt that Harding could be persuaded to support a progressive program, in-

[19] Bates, *Origins of Teapot Dome, passim.*

cluding a policy of conservation. Pinchot visited Harding in Marion, Ohio, in mid-summer; afterward, he declared himself pleased with Harding's views.[20]

After his sweeping victory in November, Harding named Albert B. Fall as secretary of the interior. Fall, senator from New Mexico since 1912, was an aggressive and impetuous southwesterner, whose manners and values perfectly matched the stereotype of the folklore frontiersman.[21] As senator, Fall bitterly fought against the conservation program of Wilson's administration. Gifford Pinchot wrote of him: "On the record it would have been possible to pick a worse man for Secretary of the Interior, but not altogether easy." Later, another conservationist wrote: "Fall was condemned as absolutely unfit for such a post by every detail of his record in the Senate. He had been an exploiter and a friend of the exploiters. He had always opposed the conservation movement." [22]

What Fall thought about the naval petroleum reserves was quite clear—they should never have been established.[23] Yet upon moving into the Department of the Interior, Fall did not attempt an immediate change in oil policy. That he was an anticonservationist is clear. That he was an ambitious man of forceful action and independent thinking is also clear. But that he immediately set out to lease or sell

[20] *Ibid.*, pp. 210–12; Noggle, *Teapot Dome*, pp. 5–6. In 1924 charges were to arise that oil company money was improperly at work during the Republican convention. It is clear that oilmen, with their money and their lobbyists, descended upon the convention, but their connection with Harding's nomination and with his subsequent cabinet appointments is not clear at all. His nomination may have been a colossal error in judgment, but the party leaders backed him as a compromise in a deadlocked convention, not because of shady maneuvers by his supporters in the oil business. See Wesley M. Bagby, *The Road to Normalcy* (Baltimore, 1962), pp. 79–100; Noggle, *Teapot Dome*, pp. 3, 141–43.

[21] *Ibid.*, pp. 8–11.

[22] Pinchot to Samuel McCune Lindsay, Mar. 6, 1921, Box 239, Gifford Pinchot Papers, Division of Manuscripts, Library of Congress; John Ise, *The United States Oil Policy* (New Haven, 1926), pp. 365–66.

[23] Bates, *Origins of Teapot Dome*, p. 226.

the petroleum reserves for personal gain, or even from honest conviction, is not clear at all. He did, however, begin a policy that stirred up rumors and that aroused the suspicion of certain conservationists.

Among these latter critics was Harry A. Slattery, an old Pinchot supporter who more than any other single person set in motion the investigation that uncovered the Teapot Dome scandal. In 1920 Slattery was practicing law in Washington.[24] Shortly after Fall took office, Slattery heard a rumor that Fall, through executive order of President Harding, had acquired control of the petroleum reserves. Harding did, in fact, issue such an order, dated May 31, 1921, transferring them from the Navy Department, which had been given control of them only a year earlier. Fall wrote it for him and Secretary of the Navy Edwin Denby approved it. On June 1 the administration announced the transfer, thus confirming Slattery's earlier fear. Albert Fall now controlled the naval oil reserves.[25]

Slattery promptly went to see Senator Robert M. La Follete, Republican of Wisconsin, a veteran conservationist. La Follette encouraged Slattery in the latter's proposal to investigate the transfer. This Slattery did, over a ten-month period. Gradually, he came to the conclusion that Fall was planning a massive program of throwing open the federal domain for sale and exploitation.[26]

[24] From 1909 to 1912 Slattery had been secretary to Gifford Pinchot; between 1912 and 1917 he had served as secretary of the National Conservation Association. Throughout his career he was an investigator, counsel, legislative draftsman, and confidant for conservationists in public and private life. See Noggle, *Teapot Dome*, pp. 4–5.

[25] Slattery to Pinchot, Apr. 25, 1921, Slattery Papers, Duke University Library; Senate Committee on Public Lands and Surveys (68th Cong., 1st Sess.), *Leases upon Naval Oil Reserves* (3 vols.; Washington, 1924), I, 177–78; *New York Times*, June 2, 1921, p. 12.

[26] Statements by Robert M. La Follette, Jr., at a dinner in honor of Slattery, Cosmos Club, Washington, D. C., June 25, 1932, quoted in *Congressional Record*, 72d Cong., 1st Sess. (July 15, 1932), 15457–58; memorandum of Ralph Sucher, Feb. 24, 1932, Slattery Papers; Slattery to Gifford Pinchot, June 21, 1921, and June 23, 1921, *ibid.*

One of Fall's proposals was to transfer the Forest Service from the Department of Agriculture to his own Interior Department. When Slattery reported this plan to Gifford Pinchot, the former Forester reacted instantly. Pinchot had, over the years, developed an intense supicion of the Interior Department and any and all of its secretaries. He fought all attempts to transfer the Forest Service to its jurisdiction. The Service was, he felt, the key agency in the conservation movement that he had helped to establish. Pinchot now joined Slattery and La Follette in what was rapidly becoming an anti-Fall crusade. Between the spring of 1921 and early March, 1922, Pinchot engineered a newspaper campaign against Fall's policies, principally his proposed transfer of the Forest Service and his plans for administrative changes in Alaskan forests.[27]

Near the end of this year-long assault on Fall, Harry Slattery discovered the first evidence of a scandal in oil. Learning that Fall had begun to grant drilling rights in the California reserves to the Pan-American Petroleum and Transport Company of millionaire Edwin L. Doheny, Slattery wrote to La Follette, suggesting that the senator call for a Senate investigation into all oil leases made by Fall. Slattery had little more than hunches at this point— he was suspicious, but evidently his proposal to La Follette was simply a tactical move in the "Fall war," as he called it. He had no clear evidence of any corruption or malfeasance by Fall.[28]

La Follette was at first reluctant to ask for a Senate inquiry. But then Fall, on April 7, 1922, leased the entire Teapot Dome reserve to Harry Sinclair's Mammoth Oil

[27] Noggle, *Teapot Dome*, pp. 20 ff.

[28] Slattery to La Follette, Mar. 15, 1922; La Follette to Slattery, Mar. 20, 1922; Slattery to H. H. Chapman, Apr. 19, 1922; and Slattery to Philip Wells, Mar. 20, 1922, Slattery Papers.

Company. Two weeks later, Edward L. Doheny received further drilling rights in the California oil reserves. In fact, as the Senate inquiry would later reveal, Fall leased to him the entire Elk Hills reserve. La Follette, responding to these actions and to more and more rumors and protests that Slattery and other correspondents were communicating to him, asked the Senate to investigate Fall's oil-leasing policy. On April 29, 1922, the Senate voted approval of his proposal. Initiative now passed to the investigators, the Senate committee on Public Lands and Surveys.[29]

La Follette had chosen his committee of inquiry with care. The logical choice, the Naval Affairs Committee, was weighted with administration supporters. The Public Lands Committee contained Reed Smoot (Utah), Irvine Lenroot (Wisconsin), and other Republican stalwarts; but it also included Republican insurgents George W. Norris (Nebraska), Edwin E. Ladd (North Dakota), and Peter Norbeck (South Dakota), as well as strong-willed Democrats Thomas J. Walsh (Montana) and John B. Kendrick (Wyoming). This latter group was not likely to pigeonhole La Follette's resolution or neglect its task out of partisan calculation. Nevertheless, hearings did not begin until eighteen months after the Senate had approved the investigation. Perhaps Smoot and other stalwarts did work for a delay beyond the 1922 Congressional election, but the hesitancy and the deliberation of Thomas J. Walsh was perhaps even more significant.[30]

La Follette had urged Walsh to "take the leadership in investigating." Walsh, already burdened with numerous committee assignments, was reluctant. Then in June, 1922, in compliance with the Senate resolution, Fall sent to the

29 Noggle, *Teapot Dome*, pp. 34–42.
30 *Ibid.*, pp. 43–46.

committee a truckload of documents. During the next six-
teen months—from June, 1922, to October, 1923—Walsh
made what he called "a critical analysis of the lease." He
studied past legislation relevant to the leasing, and he sent
letters to "all journals which had exhibited any special
interest in the subject," asking for the sources of their
published statements. Slattery and Pinchot, and to a degree
even La Follette, had been quick to suspect corruption.
Walsh was aroused more slowly. Not until early 1923 did
he display any real misgivings over Fall's conduct. Finally,
on October 22, 1923, when the hearings began, Walsh took
informal command of a committee containing a Republican
majority and a Republican chairman.[31]

Between April, 1922, when the Senate agreed to investigate Fall's policies, and October, 1923, when the hearings
began, Fall had resigned, Harding had died, and Calvin
Coolidge had moved into the White House. Fall had resented Pinchot's campaign against him and had bitterly
struck back at what he called "vicious propaganda" and
"Pinchotism." [32] But Fall did not resign merely because of
Pinchot's opposition; nor did the pending Senate investigation alone drive him from the cabinet. As early as
February, 1922—two months before La Follette's request
for an investigation—there were rumors of Fall's resignation. Loss of influence in New Mexico politics, where he
had long been a power, and disappointment over his relative
unimportance in the cabinet had supposedly turned Fall's

[31] Belle C. and Fola La Follette, *Robert M. La Follette* (2 vols.;
New York, 1953), II, 1051–52; Thomas J. Walsh, "The True History
of Teapot Dome," *Forum*, LXXII (July, 1924), 1–12; J. Leonard
Bates, "Senator Walsh of Montana, 1918–1924: A Liberal Under
Pressure," (Ph.D. dissertation, University of North Carolina, 1952),
309–10; Harry A. Slattery, "From Roosevelt to Roosevelt," MS in
Slattery Papers; *Leases upon Naval Oil Reserves* (1924), pp. 24–68.

[32] *New York Times*, Mar. 7, 1922, p. 2, quoting a letter from Fall
to "Chairman of one of the principal committees of the House." The
latter was N. J. Sinnott, chairman of the Committee on Public Lands.
See Fall to Sinnott, Mar. 3, 1922, Box 7, Albert B. Fall Papers, University of New Mexico.

thoughts toward resigning.[33] Several New Mexico newspapers expressed regret when Fall did resign early in 1923.
Harry Slattery was jubilant and believed that " the threat
of the coming . . . investigation drove Fall out of the
Cabinet." [34] Whatever motivated Fall when he resigned, his
public character was untarnished. Nine months later, he
would be wholly discredited.

The Walsh committee, beginning work on October 22,
1923, uncovered little of significance during its first two
months of activity.but then late in November and early in
December, witnesses testifying before the committee revealed that Fall, early in 1923, had suddenly begun making
costly improvements on his New Mexico ranch—at about
the same time he had leased Teapot Dome. Late in December, Fall, informing the committee of his financial status,
declared that he had borrowed $100,000 in cash from Ed-
ward B. McLean, publisher of the Washington *Post*. But
McLean, when questioned about the loan, denied making it.
Now under intense pressure from Walsh, Fall admitted to
a lie, saying he had found "other sources." [35]

With this development, a dull and unrewarding Senate
inquiry suddenly became the Teapot Dome scandal. Fall's
confession was the first of several dramatic revelations. One

[33] For an early analysis of Fall's possible resignation, see the
Santa Fe *New Mexican*, Feb. 19, 1922, which reported that "eastern
papers" for some time had been carrying the rumor. Meantime, the
New York Times, Mar. 12, 1922, VII: 1, carried a special story on
Fall's differences with Harding and the cabinet. For stories on Fall
as a state boss and for some account of his waning influence in the
state after becoming secretary, see the Santa Fe *New Mexican* for
Aug 24 and Sept. 15, 16, 20, 26, and 27, 1920; Aug. 2 and 19, and
Sept. 3, 1921; and Aug. 22 and 23, 1922. See also George Curry,
George Curry, 1861–1947, An Autobiography, ed. H. B. Hening (Albu-
querque, 1958), pp. 292–93; and Fall to Herbert B. Holt, July 22, 1922,
and Fall to C. E. Mitchell, July 31, 1922, Fall Papers.

[34] Rio Grande *Republic*, Jan. 4, 1923; Rio Grande *Farmer*, Mar.
22, 1923; Slattery, "From Roosevelt to Roosevelt," pp. 90–91.

[35] *Leases upon Reserves* (1924), pp. 1430 ff., and pp. 1649 ff.;
New York Times, Dec. 28, 1923, p. 2, and Jan. 12, 1924, p. 2; Walsh,
"True History of Teapot Dome," and Walsh to Fall, Jan. 11, 1924,
Fall Papers.

that quickly followed it was Edward L. Doheny's calm statement to the Wash committee that he had been the "other source" of Fall's $100,000—and that his son, Edward, Jr., had carried it to Fall's office, in cash, "in a little black bag." Doheny emphasized his friendship for Fall as motive for the loan, the two men having been prospectors together in Mexico and the Southwest years earlier.[36]

In itself Fall's lie was perhaps the most fateful statement he ever uttered, and was one he deeply regretted the remainder of his life. That he had, in truth, received a loan from Doheny, the oilman to whom he had leased the Elk Hills reserve—this was, if anything, even more incriminating. Then, immediately after Doheny revealed himself as Fall's creditor, the Walsh committee learned that in 1923, just after Fall's resignation, Sinclair had sent Fall "$25,000 or 30,000 in bonds." [37]

During the next three months—January through March, 1924—the Teapot Dome hearings were a national sensation. Charges and countercharges, insinuations of guilt and corruption in high offices, and maneuverings for political advantage seemed to possess Washington. Democrats jubilantly made the most of this Republican scandal. That 1924 was a presidential election year merely added zest (and sometimes desperation) to the uproar. In January the Democratic national committee began publicizing "the rape" of Teapot Dome.[38] President Coolidge directed Attorney-General Daugherty to send a competent staff member to all hearings before the Walsh committee and to take any action necessary to protect the interests of the federal government.[39] Daugherty himself, as well as Secretary of the

[36] *Leases upon Reserves* (1924), pp. 1771 ff.

[37] *Ibid.*, pp. 1713–17.

[38] Marion Banister, *The Lands Ye Possess* (Washington, 1924).

[39] Coolidge to Daugherty, Jan. 24, 1924, Justice Department, General Records, Records of Naval Oil Reserve Investigations, 1924–29, Box 107, National Archives.

Navy Denby, came under heavy criticism and finally both men resigned—Denby in February, Daugherty in March.[40]

From January into spring charges persisted that Coolidge, as well as Secretary of Commerce Hoover and Secretary of State Hughes, had sat in certain cabinet meetings where Fall's leases were discussed and approved.[41] In early February William Gibbs McAdoo's bright chances for the Democratic presidential nomination suddenly turned dim when Doheny testified that he had once employed McAdoo as legal counsel.[42]

As such revelations and rumors piled up, public excitement arose in proportion, and in Congress partisan debate swelled. The Santa Fe *New Mexican* noted: "The oil lease probe is spreading. The deeper you get into it the more bottomless it appears." [43] Albert Fall allayed none of this discussion when, in February, he appeared before the Walsh committee and refused to testify on the grounds that his answers might tend to incriminate him.[44] Later in the month, Coolidge appointed special government counsel with unlimited authority to handle prosecution of the oil leases.[45]

[40] The attacks on Denby and Daugherty, and the pressure on Coolidge to fire them, can be followed in *New York Times*, Jan. 30, 1924, pp. 1, 2; Feb. 7, 1924, p. 4; Feb. 22, 1924, pp. 1, 4, and Feb. 28, 1924, pp. 1, 3; and Mar. 29, 1924, p. 1; *Cong. Rec.*, 68th Cong., 1st Sess. (Feb. 11, 1924), 2055–68, 2245; *ibid.* (Feb. 29, 1924), 3299 ff.; Denby to Coolidge, Feb. 17, 1924, Box 98, Coolidge Papers, Division of Manuscripts, Library of Congress; F. P. Corrick to C. Bascom Slemp, Mar. 3, 1924, Box 48, *ibid.*; Slemp to Corrick, Mar. 19, 1924, *ibid.*; Slemp (?) to Daugherty, Mar. 27, 1924, unsigned copy in Box 98, *ibid.*; Daugherty to Coolidge, Mar. 28, 1924, and Coolidge to Daugherty, Mar. 28, 1924, Box 98, *ibid.*

[41] Noggle, *Teapot Dome*, pp. 82–84.

[42] *Ibid.*, pp. 99–105; 110–14; Lee N. Allen, "The McAdoo Campaign for the Presidential Nomination in 1924," pp. 220–22; David H. Stratton, "Splattered with Oil," pp. 62–75; and David B. Burner, "The Democratic Party in the Election of 1924," *Mid-America*, XLVI (April, 1964), 92 ff.

[43] Santa Fe *New Mexico*, Feb. 14, 1924.

[44] *Leases upon Reserves* (1924), 1961–63.

[45] *Cong. Rec.*, 68th Cong., 1st Sess. (Feb. 16, 1924), 2547–65, and 2637 ff.

But Democrats continued to attack Coolidge for inaction
and complacency, and even charged him with guilt by association with Fall, a man now thoroughly discredited.[46]

Then the scandal began to abate. Through March the
excitement did not lessen; but as April gave way to May,
no new revelations arose to feed the scandal. The elaborate
newspaper reports, the detailed magazine articles and analyses, the extravagant accusations from editors and from
Congress—all diminished or disappeared. Attendance at the
hearings shrank away, until finally not a single spectator
showed up. On May 14, 1924, the committee adjourned.[47]

The scandal was far from ended. In the 1924 presidential
campaign the Democrats played Teapot Dome for all it was
worth.[48] Between 1924 and 1929, court trials in California
and Wyoming restored the naval reserves to the government
and produced new evidence of still more money passing
into the hands of Albert Fall, as well as into the coffers
of the Republican national committee.[49] In January, 1928,
the Walsh committee began another—though briefer—inquiry, an attempt to dissect the workings of the Continental
Trading Company, Ltd.

In 1924 government agents working for Coolidge's special
counsel, Owen Roberts and Atlee Pomerene, discovered the
existence of this corporation. In November, 1921, a group
of oil men, Harry Sinclair among them, had held an organization meeting in New York City; later, they received
incorporation in Canada. Several of the organizers were
officers in major oil companies, a condition they promptly

---

[46] Noggle, *Teapot Dome*, pp. 114, 118, 123–36, and 149–51.

[47] *Leases upon Reserves* (1924), 3586.

[48] Bates, "The Teapot Dome Scandal and the Election of 1924,"
and Noggle, *Teapot Dome*, chap. viii.

[49] *Ibid.*, pp. 144–46, 179–86, 200–201, 211. Francis X. Busch,
Enemies of the State (New York, 1954), contains a 79-page summary
of these trials. For a legalist's analysis of the cases, see Charles G.
Hagland, "The Naval Reserve Leases," *Georgetown Law Journal*, XX
(March, 1932), 293–328.

exploited to their own profit and their companies' loss. As members of the Continental Trading Company, they contracted to buy 33,333,333 barrels of crude oil at $1.50 a barrel from a company controlled by Colonel A. E. Humphreys, himself one of the Continental organizers. On the same day they sold this contract to two oil companies, one headed by Harry Sinclair, the other by James E. O'Neil, each of whom was also a Continental organizer. Sinclair and O'Neil, as heads of their respective companies, agreed to buy the oil at an increase of 25 cents a barrel. They took delivery of the oil directly from Humphreys, but paid for it through Continental. Between January 1, 1922, and May 26, 1923, over 8,700,000 barrels of oil had exchanged hands under this agreement and the Continental organizers had netted a profit of more than $2,000,000, which they invested in Liberty bonds. Roberts and Pomerene managed to learn that Fall received at least $233,000 worth of these bonds. This left $2,770,000 worth of bonds unaccounted for.[50]

In the fall of 1927 Paul Y. Anderson, a reporter for the St. Louis *Post-Dispatch,* began a search for the missing bonds. Unable to gain information or co-operation from the Treasury Department or the Department of Justice, he persuaded Senator George W. Norris to ask for a Senate investigation. On January 9, 1928, the Senate agreed, and once more the Public Lands Committee—Walsh in charge—brought Albert Fall under scrutiny and Teapot Dome into the midst of national politics.[51]

The committee soon determined that Harry Sinclair had delivered the $233,000 worth of Liberty bonds to Fall and

[50] Noggle, *Teapot Dome,* pp. 180–83. See also Carl Taeusch, *Policy and Ethics in Business* (New York and London, 1931), pp. 197–221, for a discussion of the Continental Trading Company.

[51] James W. Markham, *Bovard of the Post-Dispatch* (Baton Rouge, 1954), pp. 100 ff.; George Norris to O. K. Bovard, Jan. 9, 1929, and Norris to Bovard, Jan. 25, 1929, Tray 7, Box 7, Norris Papers, Division of Manuscripts, Library of Congress; *Cong. Rec.,* 70th Cong., 1st Sess. (Jan. 9, 1928), 934–, 1185.

had later loaned him $36,000 more. Thus, from Sinclair, Fall had received a total of $304,000. Doheny's $100,000 loan (plus another $5,000 that Doheny mentioned) meant that Fall had received at least $409,000 from the two men to whom he had leased the Teapot Dome and Elk Hills reserves. Further testimony revealed that some of the Continental profits had gone to the Republican national committee.[52]

These revelations produced a new wave of political charges, denials, and strategic moves. But the Continental inquiry never reached the fevered intensity of the 1924 investigation. In the 1928 presidential campaign Democrats tried to exploit the scandal. Senator Thomas J. Walsh, Teapot Dome's great prosecutor, campaigned for the Democratic nomination, but Al Smith easily defeated him in the early primaries.[53] As they had done in 1924, Republicans studiously ignored Teapot Dome. The scandal had little perceptible effect on the election's outcome.[54]

On July 20, 1931, having been tried and sentenced for bribery, Albert Fall entered prison in Santa Fe, New Mexico. Doheny and Sinclair, also tried, went free. Senator Norris had once suggested that it was impossible to convict a hundred million dollars in the United States. The businessman-as-hero image of the 1920's may have saved mil-

[52] Senate Committee on Public Lands and Surveys (70th Cong., 1st Sess.), *Leases upon Naval Oil Reserves* (Washington, 1928), 3–68, 357–416, 459–481, 549–54, and 575 ff.

[53] Noggle, *Teapot Dome*, pp. 201–3; Paul A. Carter, "The Other Catholic Candidate: The 1928 Presidential Bid of Thomas J. Walsh," *Pacific Northwest Quarterly*, LV (January, 1964), 1–8.

[54] I have briefly considered this question in *Teapot Dome*, pp. 200–209; two recent and broader studies of the election are Ruth C. Silva, *Rum, Religion, and Votes: 1928 Re-examined* (University Park, Pa., 1962); and Paul A. Carter, "The Campaign of 1928 Re-Examined: A Study in Political Folklore," *Wisconsin Magazine of History*, XLVI (Summer, 1963), 263–72.

lionaires Sinclair and Doheny from conviction, even though the United States Supreme Court had nullified their leases.[55]

Albert Fall's conviction ended the legal history of Teapot Dome. Already, the 1928 campaign had demonstrated the ineffectiveness of the scandal as a political weapon, and court action in the 1920's altered the policy that Fall had sought to establish. The Teapot Dome scandal ended with the decade that produced it. Thereafter, it survived as history, as morality tale, and as political folklore.

For the political historian of the twenties, Teapot Dome offers some insight into political behavior and political values of the decade. This great scandal, cutting deep in many directions, seems to confirm conventional images of life in the 1920's: an inept Harding and his cronies, gross favors for American business, and widespread immorality and irresponsibility, all in contrast to the progressive era that preceded the decade and the New Deal that followed it. This view, of course, is not entirely wrong, but it is too simple. Something more needs to be said. Within the past decade or so, historians have begun to question the old view that America in the 1920's was merely a dreary period of reaction sandwiched between two eras of reform. Arthur S. Link, in 1959, was one of the first historians to call attention to this new approach that scholars were attempting. Link agreed that the prewar progressive movement "unquestionably declined" in the twenties, but he denied that it was dead. We must, he wrote, "recognize that the progressive movement was certainly not defunct

[55] Noggle, *Teapot Dome*, pp 200–201, 184–85, 211. Sinclair served a few months in jail in 1929 for contempt of the Senate and for criminal contempt of court. Doheny, at least technically, may have properly been found innocent. Under the U.S. criminal code, the offer of a bribe was a separate and distinct offense from the acceptance of one. In each case, the intent of the transaction, as it existed in the mind of the defendant, determined or refuted the guilt. I have

in the 1920's; that on the contrary at least important parts of it were very much alive." [56]

The Teapot Dome affair illustrates this very well. The scandal has been—and should be—used to point up some reactionary and irresponsible traits of politics in the twenties. But it can also be used to reveal the endurance of progressivism.[57] To begin at the very beginning, men who had been progressives before the war initiated the Senate inquiry that uncovered the scandal. Carrying into the 1920's the same aspirations and behavior they had manifested earlier, Harry Slattery, Gifford Pinchot, and Robert M. La Follette went after Albert Fall in 1921-22 as they had gone after Richard A. Ballinger in 1909–10, and for much the same reason.[58]

These conservationists had helped to create the prewar conservation movement; in the twenties, they never once slackened their interest in sustaining that program.[59] During the decade conservation may not have enjoyed the positive support that Theodore Roosevelt had once given

---

discussed this matter very briefly in *Teapot Dome*, p. 211. See also an article, *New York Times*, March 30, 1930, III: 7, edited by Current Events Committee of American Association of Legal Authors; and Charles Hagland, "The Naval Reserve Leases," p. 327.

[56] Arthur S. Link, "What Happened to the Progressive Movement in the 1920's?" *American Historical Review*, LXIV (July, 1959).

[57] It is difficult to establish a working definition of progressivism, but as used here the term refers to the nation-wide movement for reform that took place in the United States before World War I, a reform movement recognized by its participants and since then studied by historians. My particular use of the term and my evidence for its "survival" in the twenties will, I trust, become clearer in the remainder of this essay.

[58] On the Ballinger-Pinchot affair, see Elmo R. Richardson, *The Politics of Conservation* (Berkeley and Los Angeles, 1962), 51 ff. On parallels between this affair and the Teapot Dome inquiry, see Noggle, *Teapot Dome*, pp. 21–22.

[59] M. Nelson McGeary, *Gifford Pinchot: Forester-Politician* (Princeton, N. J., 1960), shows fully Pinchot's career as conservationist; on Slattery, see Noggle, *Teapot Dome*; La Follette's support for conservation is shown in La Follette, *Robert M. La Follette.*

it and that Franklin D. Roosevelt would later provide. But neither did the conservationists fade away (or promote a return to nineteenth-century style land-grabbing, depletion, and exploitation). The twenties may have been a return to McKinleyism in some ways, but not in conservation.[60]

Pinchot and Slattery may well have prevented Albert Fall from gaining control of the Alaskan forests. They obviously were responsible—Slattery especially—for turning La Follette's attention to Fall's oil policy and to an investigation of his leases. That investigation was a windfall for conservationists. Evidently, in 1921–22, Pinchot and his supporters had only a general suspicion of Fall and wanted only to drive him from office—to repeat the maneuver they had used against Richard A. Ballinger, an earlier secretary of the interior who had opposed them. This they did.[61] Then, after the Senate investigation uncovered scandal and Teapot Dome became a sensational political issue, President Coolidge and, later, President Hoover took actions that benefited the conservation program, actions that the conservationists had not foreseen but ones that they now welcomed. In December, 1924, Coolidge established a Federal Oil Conservation Board, instructing it to determine the best methods for conserving the government's oil supply. Secretary of the Interior Hubert Work claimed in 1925 that creation of a new conservation board in the Geological Survey was "for the purpose of placing every possible safeguard around the leasing of the Nation's estate." In March, 1927, Coolidge revoked Harding's executive order

[60] Donald C. Swain, *Federal Conservation Policy, 1921–1933,* clearly demonstrates the achievements in conservation during the 1920's.

[61] In explanation of his resignation, it is debatable as to which influenced Fall the most—the attacks on his policy by his opponents in conservation, or his disappointments over failure to become a dominant figure in the Harding cabinet, even while he was losing power he had once held in New Mexico. See Noggle, *Teapot Dome,* 52–55.

that had transferred the oil reserves to the Interior Department.[62] Hoover, eight days after taking office, announced a new oil conservation policy: "complete conservation of government oil in this administration." Two days later, on March 15, 1929, he announced that the Interior Department would review some 20,000 existing oil leases in order to determine whether the holders were complying with the law.[63]

It is difficult to determine how much of this presidential action was designed to offset the damage Teapot Dome had caused the Republican party. Both Coolidge and Hoover may have been more concerned about the oil market than about political scandal. In establishing the FOCB, Coolidge was trying to control production and raise prices for the oil industry, which was suffering from overproduction. Certainly, Hoover in 1929 was trying to decrease production; and his actions were entirely in keeping with the neo-mercantilism that he had worked for during the 1920's even before the Teapot Dome scandal had erupted.[64] The policies of both Presidents reflected their concern for the oil industry, but there is no doubt that each man was also

[62] Secretary of Interior, *Annual Report* (Washington, 1924), 8 and 31; *Federal Oil Conservation Board Hearings, February 10 and 11, 1925* (Washington, 1925), viii-ix; Hubert Work, *The Department of the Interior: A Review for 1925* (Washington, 1925); *New York Times*, July 2, 1925, p. 2.

[63] *New York Times*, Mar. 13, 1929, p. 1; and Mar. 16, 1929, p. 7. See also Ray L. Wilbur, *Two Years of the Department of the Interior, 1929–31* (Washington, 1931), p. 1; and Herbert C. Hoover, *Memoirs of Herbert Hoover* (New York, 1952), II, 237 ff.

[64] Swain, *Federal Conservation Policy, 1921–1933*, pp. 62–66, discusses the oil conservation policies of Coolidge and Hoover, though not with reference to Teapot Dome. Joseph Brandes, *Herbert Hoover and Economic Diplomacy* (Pittsburgh, 1962), shows Hoover's attempts, while secretary of commerce, to develop a partnership between government and business "along lines consonant with the national welfare." See also William Appleman Williams, *The Contours of American History* (Cleveland and New York, 1961), pp. 425 ff.

trying to offset the political effects of the oil scandal. In such ironic fashion, a scandal in oil helped to further the oil conservation movement in the 1920's.

Not only did progressives launch the Teapot Dome investigation and thereby motivate a conservation program, but they also—most of them nominally Republicans—carried on a running verbal attack against the scandal throughout the mid-1920's. Besides La Follette, the three most conspicuous senatorial critics of the scandal were Thomas J. Walsh, George W. Norris, and Republican Senator William E. Borah of Idaho. La Follette's resolution in April of 1922 launched the inquiry. Later in 1922, La Follette chaired a Senate subcommittee that investigated the high prices of gasoline and other petroleum products. He turned over to Walsh much of what this committee discovered, including evidence that increased suspicions of Fall's policies. During his 1924 bid for the presidency on the Progressive party ticket, La Follette and his running mate Burton K. Wheeler made much use of Teapot Dome.[65]

Walsh and Norris worked largely through the Public Lands Committee, using it as a forum for attacking the Coolidge administration and the scandal. Walsh's role as prosecutor of Teapot Dome is a familiar story, but his crucial importance needs emphasizing. During the first weeks of hearings in the fall of 1923, Walsh alone carried the burden of inquiry. Reed Smoot and Irvine Lenroot, two Old Guard members of the committee, were totally negative. Peter Norbeck, one of several maverick Republicans on the committee, observed in February, 1924, that "most of the Republican members and some of the Democratic members . . . were not very anxious to stir up that Teapot Dome

[65] U.S. Senate, *High Cost of Gasoline and Other Petroleum Products*, 67th Cong., 2d Sess. and 4 Sess. (4 vols.; Washington, 1923) ; Noggle, *Teapot Dome*, pp. 49–50, and 168.

business. Senator Walsh had to fight his way through all along." [66]

George Norris was a notable exception to this judgment. Several months after the hearings had begun, Walsh wrote to Norris: "Until you came I never had . . . one word of encouragement or even sympathy from the majority side, at best I guessed that Ladd and Norbeck were not unfriendly." [67] Throughout the investigation in 1924 and 1928, in private correspondence and in the Senate, Norris was a consistent critic of the scandal and of its Republican principals. As early as January, 1924, before all of the damaging details of the scandal had been revealed, Norris suggested that Fall's leasing contracts were due to "deep, disgraceful fraud and corruption." In March Norris wrote to a Nebraska constituent that "a good many prominent Republicans" were "continually [throwing] water on this investigation. They have in many cases and in many ways tried to prevent the full disclosures of the truth." Such critics Norris deplored; and in particular he was "not at all satisfied with Coolidge . . . a partisan more than anything else." [68]

It was Norris who, in 1928, reopened the Senate inquiry that, led by Walsh, explored the workings of the Continental Trading Company.[69] Again, it was Norris who, in the 1928 presidential campaign, found the Republican platform "a sad disappointment to every progressive citizen," for it was, among other things, silent "on the disgraceful . . . disclosures of the naval oil leases." The same men who controlled the Republican convention, said Norris, had "fought every

[66] Norbeck to Harry King, Feb. 2, 1924, cited in Gilbert C. Fite, *Peter Norbeck: Prairie Statesman* (Columbia, Mo., 1948), p. 113.
[67] Walsh to Norris, Feb. 18, 1924, Box 7, Tray 7, Norris Papers.
[68] *Cong. Rec.*, 68th Cong., 1st Sess. (Jan. 30, 1924), 1669–70; Norris to Rev. B. F. Eberhart, March 8, 1924, Box 1, Tray 2, Norris Papers.
[69] Noggle, *Teapot Dome*, pp. 186 ff.

. . . step to uncover any of these disgraceful and treasonable frauds." [70] Near the end of the 1928 campaign, Norris issued a plea for all "Progressives" to support Democrat Al Smith. "When I think of the oil scandals and the debauchery and the crime . . . in high places," said Norris, "I think of [the past] seven years with a sense of humiliation and shame, and I feel like condemning myself when I remember that . . . I did my mite toward putting the Harding Administration in power." As for Hoover, Norris found the same men backing him who had defended Fall; and Hoover himself, during the Senate committee's "weary grind toward the facts," had remained "as silent as a sphinx" while knowing of the crimes.[71]

If Norris was the leading Republican progressive among the Teapot Dome critics, Walsh, meantime, was the tireless and relentless Democratic prosecutor. He grilled reluctant witnesses, he endured verbal attacks from Republican newspapers and even from fellow members of the Public Lands Committee, he uncovered vital information, and he published articles on the affair and delivered to the Senate judicious summaries of the committee's findings.[72]

Borah was, next to La Follette and Norris, the most acrid Republican critic of Teapot Dome. Early in 1924, Borah demanded that Attorney-General Daugherty resign because of his presumed connivance in the Harding scandals, as well as his negligence in turning up evidence for the Senate committee's use. At this time Borah believed that

[70] Norris statement to press, June 16, 1928, copy in Tray 1, Box 5, Norris Papers.

[71] *New York Times*, Oct. 28, 1928, p. 28.

[72] See Noggle, *Teapot Dome, passim*, for a study of Walsh's role in the inquiry. For Walsh's analysis of the committee's work in 1924, see his "What the Oil Inquiry Developed," *Outlook*, May 21, 1924, pp. 96–98; also his "The True History of Teapot Dome." More elaborate is the (Walsh) majority report of the Committee on Public Lands and Surveys, *Cong. Rec.*, 68th Cong., 1st Sess. (June 6, 1924), 10938–10949.

the best tactic for the Republican party was to "clean out." [73] In March, 1928, in keeping with this tactic, Borah made a dramatic gesture to cleanse his party. After the Public Lands Committee in 1928 had determined that Harry Sinclair had contributed some of his Continental Oil Company profits to the Republican national committee, Borah repudiated the contribution. On March 5 he appealed to national chairman William M. Butler to purge the party of the "stigma" of "oil money" by returning to Sinclair all donations he had made. The party could not "in honor and decency" keep the money, since the whole Continental transaction "had in view an ulterior and sinister purpose." Borah believed that "plenty of Republicans" would contribute "from one dollar up to any reasonable sum to clear their party of this humiliating stigma." [74]

Republicans reacted to Borah's plan at once. William Allen White wrote to him: "You are on the right line. . . . The louder you talk the better it will be for the party. We can't go into the campaign of 1928 with the blight upon us of tainted money." [75] Not enough Republicans agreed with Borah's plan, however, to contribute the necessary amount to Sinclair. Borah did receive hundreds of letters and as many small contributions. By March 30, he had collected only $6,184. In mid-April Borah began returning the money to those who had contributed. [76]

Teapot Dome, then, became a scandal because progressives sought it out, found it, probed it, and exploited it.

[73] C. O. Johnson, *Borah of Idaho* (New York, 1936), pp. 288–89; *New York Times*, Feb. 19, 1924, pp. 1–2; Borah to Mrs. Olive Stott Gabriel, Mar. 7, 1924, cited in J. Leonard Bates, "The Teapot Dome Scandal and the Election of 1924."

[74] Borah to Butler, Mar. 5, 1928, Box 763, William E. Borah Papers, Division of Manuscripts, Library of Congress. See also *New York Times* Mar. 12 and 13, 1928, p. 1.

[75] White to Borah, Mar. 13, 1928, Borah Papers.

[76] For a list of the contributors, the amounts they gave, and other records kept by Borah — including his bank deposit book — see "Sinclair Fund," Borah Papers.

At least two interpretations of their actions and attitudes are possible. To an extent, La Follette and his fellow Republican insurgents undoubtedly took a stand against Teapot Dome because it was a political liability to their party. In this respect they were neither more nor less progressive than any other Republican—Coolidge himself moved shrewdly and subtly to offset the scandal's effect.[77] But they also appear to have spoken and acted against Teapot Dome because it was a scandal involving an old bête noire of progressivism, "big business," including in this case two oil millionaires, Doheny and Sinclair, neither of whom had ever shown much sense of public responsibility. La Follette, Norris, Borah, Pinchot, and other Republican progressives opposed Teapot Dome partly because of the big businessmen they could assault and the natural resources they could protect—two traditional elements of progressivism. They also, as hard-headed politicians, hoped to cleanse their party. But this, too, reveals a residue of progressivism in the 1920's, since to cleanse meant to uncover what progressives had long assumed to be the unfortunate "reality" of politics—the vested interest, the bribe, the dishonest politician, the immoral businessman.[78] While this progressive activity hardly adds up to a major reform program, it does, especially in view of the amount of money and oil involved, deserve emphasis as a progressive achievement in the 1920's.

In at least one instance, instead of calling forth progressivism, Teapot Dome undermined it by seriously damaging William Gibbs McAdoo's chances for the Democratic presidential nomination in 1924. As early as the summer of 1923, McAdoo was a serious contender for the Democratic prize. By early 1924, he appeared to be the leading contender. When the Democratic national commit-

---

[77] Noggle, *Teapot Dome*, pp. 80–151, *passim*.
[78] Hofstadter, *Age of Reform*, p. 200.

tee met in Washington on January 15, newspaperman
Frank Kent reported great optimism among McAdoo supporters. A poll of the committee showed that more than 60
of a total of 106 were for McAdoo. Atmosphere in the
Washington hotel lobbies, wrote Kent, "was a McAdoo
atmosphere and the McAdoo control of the committee was
conceded." Reports and private correspondence from many
sections of the country, meantime, revealed considerable
support for McAdoo.[79] But then on February 1, 1924,
Edward L. Doheny testified before the Public Lands Committee that he had once employed McAdoo as legal counsel
for his Pan-American Petroleum Company. Doheny's testimony had been deliberately provoked by Senator Lenroot,
acting upon instructions from Senator James A. Reed of
Missouri. Reed was himself campaigning for the Democratic
nomination and knew that Doheny's testimony would
embarrass McAdoo.[80]

Doheny did more than embarrass McAdoo. He effectively
demolished his bid for the nomination. By pure association
McAdoo was linked to scandal, and at once his political
support began to crumble.[81] McAdoo himself refused to
give up, but some of his major supporters—including
Bernard Baruch, who had been helping to finance his campaign—now began turning to other candidates.[82] McAdoo
still entered the convention with about three hundred delegates pledged to him. If Teapot Dome had injured him,
other issues gave him support. Rural, Protestant, and prohibitionist elements in the party from the South and the
West remained loyal to him, partly as a means of opposing

[79] Noggle, *Teapot Dome*, pp. 60–61, 99; Allen, "The McAdoo
Campaign," pp. 212–20; Stratton, "Splattered with Oil."
[80] Noggle, *Teapot Dome*, p. 100; Allen, "The McAdoo Campaign,"
p. 220; Stratton, "Splattered with Oil."
[81] Noggle, *Teapot Dome*, pp. 101–3; Allen, "The McAdoo Campaign," pp. 221–22; Stratton, "Splattered with Oil."
[82] Noggle, *Teapot Dome*, pp. 104–5, 136–41.

Al Smith, who was strong among urban, Catholic, and repeal-minded delegates from the Northeast.[83]

The Democratic convention of 1924 was a suicidal brawl, as Smith and McAdoo forces held fast for over one hundred ballots, with neither able to gain the necessary two-thirds majority. On the 103rd ballot, after some complex maneuverings by and for several lesser candidates, and after McAdoo released his own delegates, the convention nominated John W. Davis of West Virginia.[84] Teapot Dome alone had not spoiled McAdoo's chances. The deadlock between Smith and McAdoo reflected a fundamental division in the Democratic party, which in turn mirrored a significant fact of American life in the 1920's—the conflict between rural, Anglo-Protestant America and a newly rising urban and secular society. Yet had McAdoo never been tainted with Teapot Dome, he just may have attained the margin of votes he needed to defeat Smith and to gain the nomination.

McAdoo was not a clear-cut progressive, although he called himself one and sought to appeal to farmers, to organized labor, and to other groups traditionally associated with progressivism.[85] He never once censured the Klan, which openly supported him. One of McAdoo's strategists once suggested, "there is no sense in denouncing the Klan and entering upon the impossible task of competing with Smith for the Catholic vote, for that is just what it amount[s] to." [86] Frank Freidel has perhaps characterized McAdoo best in calling him a "mildly progressive Democrat." [87] By any standard, however, he was more of a

[83] Burner, "The Democratic Party in 1924," pp. 95 ff.

[84] *Ibid.;* and Noggle, *Teapot Dome,* pp. 163 ff.

[85] Allen, "The McAdoo Campaign."

[86] Diary of Breckenridge Long, July 15, 1924, Breckenridge Long Papers, Division of Manuscript, Library of Congress.

[87] Frank Freidel, *Franklin D. Roosevelt: The Ordeal* (Boston, 1954), p. 166.

progressive than was John W. Davis[88]—though like Davis,
McAdoo likely would have been drubbed by Coolidge in
the 1924 election.[89]

The effect of Teapot Dome upon McAdoo's candidacy
points up the paradox that the scandal's history so often
displayed. In 1924 this Republican scandal was a far
greater disadvantage to McAdoo, Democrat, than it was
to Calvin Coolidge, Republican. Coolidge, in fact, exploited

[88] It may be argued that Teapot Dome, by weakening McAdoo,
strengthened Smith; that Smith's strength in 1924 helped to gain
him nomination in 1928; and that even though he lost badly to Hoover,
Smith brought a host of new voters into the Democratic party in 1928,
voters who would support the New Deal—which was, to some extent,
in the progressive tradition. Also, Smith in 1924 was probably more
of a progressive than was McAdoo, though here use of the word
"progressive" is most ambiguous: Smith represented a new urban and
"liberal" element that, entering politics in the 1920's, came to power
in the New Deal; McAdoo, on the other hand, was more of a carry-
over from the Wilson administration of a prewar variety of progressivism. See Howard Zinn's discussion, in *LaGuardia in Congress*
(Ithaca, 1958), pp. 260–73, of the twenties as a transition from
prewar progressivism to New Deal liberalism; also William E.
Leuchtenburg, *The Perils of Prosperity, 1914–32* (Chicago, 1958),
137–39. Samuel Lubell, *The Future of American Politics* (New York,
1952), discusses the shift taking place in metropolitan areas away
from the Republican and into the Democratic party in the 1920's, a
shift that Smith's own background encouraged, and one that might
not have occurred as readily in 1928 if McAdoo had been the
Democratic candidate.

By such indirect fashion, then, Teapot Dome may have contributed
after all to progressivism in the 1924 campaign. But this is a most
indeterminate matter, and the reasoning process here calls for so
many assumptions and deals with so many variables that it can
only be offered as speculation. For example, although Smith may have
been more of a progressive than McAdoo—or at least more representative of a newer variety—he was, by any standard, almost as
"conservative" as Hoover in the 1928 campaign; and both Zinn and
Leuchtenburg consider LaGuardia a better example than was Smith
of the "new progressivism" arising in the twenties.

[89] On the election, see Burner, "The Democratic Party in the
Election of 1924," pp. 109–13; Bates, "The Teapot Dome Scandal and
the Election of 1924," *passim;* and Noggle, *Teapot Dome*, chap. viii.
Two useful contemporary analyses are Hugh L. Keenlyside, "The
American Political Revolution of 1924," *Current History*, XXI
(March, 1952), 833–40; and Arthur Macmahon, "The United States:
Domestic Politics," *Political Science Quarterly*, Supplement (March-
December, 1925).

the scandal to political advantage. As vice-president, from March, 1921 to August, 1923, Coolidge had little if any connection with the Teapot Dome affair. But as successor to Harding, he inherited responsibility for that unfortunate man's administration—including the actions of his cabinet. Coolidge had been president less than six months when the scandal erupted. At first, Coolidge said and did virtually nothing to offset or to counter the damage that the scandal did to his party. But then, slowly, Coolidge began to take action to cope with the liability. He did so shrewdly and effectively. Once he had accepted the enormity of the scandal and had realized the need for action, he moved with deliberation, maintaining a delicate balance between too little concern and too much. He eased Harry Daugherty out of the cabinet, replacing him with respectable Harlan Fiske Stone. He appointed special counsel, who soon began carrying cases to court and winning decisions; and his secretary of the navy, Curtis D. Wilbur, inaugurated an oil conservation program that contrasted markedly with Albert Fall's. While acting in such ways beneficial to his party, Coolidge at the same time conveyed the impression that the scandal was not nearly so dastardly as his Democratic critics pretended.[90]

Teapot Dome was not a major issue for Coolidge to overcome in the 1924 election; however, in so far as voters were disturbed over the corruption theme, Coolidge was probably attractive to them. He had reformed his cabinet, had appointed prosecutors, and had begun an oil conservation program. In addition, Coolidge himself had a certain appeal. As Walter Lippmann suggested soon after the election, Americans liked Calvin Coolidge. In a time of luxury and pleasure, they installed in the White House "a frugal little man who in his personal life is the very antithesis

[90] For discussion of Coolidge's activities, see Noggle, *Teapot Dome*, pp. 80–176, *passim*.

of the flambouyant ideal that everybody is frantically
pursuing. . . . At a time when Puritanism as a way of
life is at its lowest ebb among the people, the people are
delighted with a Puritan as their national symbol." [91]

Coolidge won in 1924 not merely because he overcame
the Teapot Dome issue. But since the Democrats, in the
face of the Harding scandals, failed to win, many commentators then and later concluded that the American
voter was apathetic over corruption in government[92]—
which may be one reason why so many historians have
moralized over Teapot Dome more than they have described
or analyzed it. Yet as this essay has attempted to show,
Teapot Dome is not simply a morality tale. It is above all a
political story, one that is often complex, often ambiguous,
often paradoxical. The Senate investigation might never
have been made had the conservationists not been alarmed
over Albert Fall's appointment and his early policies. The
inquiry, once begun, developed as it did because of the work
of several key figures, most of them politicians, and men
who were for the most part progressives. The oil conservation policies of Coolidge and Hoover developed, to an extent
at least, as a response to the scandal. Especially in 1924,
but also in 1928, scandal motivated some dramatic political

[91] Walter Lippmann, *Men of Destiny* (New York, 1927), pp. 15–16.
Writing in 1930, Gamaliel Bradford explained Coolidge's success in
much the same way: " . . . The average American saw in Coolidge
just the virtues that were supposed to constitute the American ideal
and supposed to have made America. Coolidge incarnated thrift, self-
denial, plain and simple living, straightforward, hard-headed honesty.
The average American had heard that his fathers had these virtues
and had made a great nation by means of them. He saw with a sigh
that he had not much taste for them himself, and that his children
had much less than he; but there was all the more reason why he
should turn to a President who embodied them completely."—"The
Genius of the Average: Calvin Coolidge," *Atlantic Monthly*, CXLV
(January, 1930), 11.

[92] Bates, "The Teapot Dome Scandal and the Election of 1924,"
effectively challenges the conventional view that Americans were
merely "apathetic" toward scandal in 1924.

maneuverings, as Democrats tried to exploit the affair and Republicans to minimize it. It was probably more than coincidence that both Senate investigations came during a presidential election year. Yet Teapot Dome did not handicap Coolidge in 1924, nor Hoover in 1928. Coolidge effectively overcame the scandal in 1924; the two powerful issues of liquor and religion buried it in 1928. Thereafter, Teapot Dome survived in politics mostly as a byword and, at that, one imprecise in meaning and dubious in effectiveness.

For the politician, Teapot Dome has lost whatever partisan usefulness it once had. For the political historian, serious contemplation of the affair has only begun.[93]

[93] As the references in this essay indicate, several books and articles on the scandal have appeared within the past decade. These studies have by no means exhausted the subject. David H. Stratton is at work on a biography of Fall, and J. Leonard Bates is completing a study of Walsh. Biographical studies of other principals in the story are needed, as are studies of other "Harding scandals"—for example, an appraisal of Harry Daugherty's conduct as attorney-general would be relevant. The complex legal history of Teapot Dome (the trials and court decisions) needs analysis. In the realm of social and intellectual history, the scandal and the public response to it may reveal something about attitudes toward business and toward government officials in the twenties. In addition, the scandal and the Senate inquiry need to be studied in relation to other periods and other problems—for instance, a study of the investigative functions of Congress, with the Teapot Dome inquiry being compared to other investigations. Eventually in studies of Teapot Dome, the principle of diminishing returns may set in; but that time appears to be far off.

The Farmers' Dilemma, 1919-1929

GILBERT C. FITE

DURING the 1920's American farmers experienced difficult and frustrating times. Most other major segments of the economy enjoyed unprecedented prosperity, but agriculture suffered from high costs of operation, heavy debt burdens, and relatively low prices. Annual per capita income of people living on farms averaged only $273 in 1929; the average for all persons was about $750. Looking back at the postwar decade, one Oklahoma farmer wrote: "We have been in bad shape here ever since the war. . . . Everybody in this part of the country has been in the same boat for years, a sinking one." [1]

In contrast to this discouraging picture, American farmers had enjoyed unusually good times between 1900 and 1920. The period before World War I has been labeled the "golden era" of American agriculture, and the war itself enhanced the growing prosperity. Farmers found themselves in better circumstances because the rate of agricultural expansion slowed down after 1900 and the demand by a growing urban population for farm products increased. This brought supply and demand into a better balance than

[1] L. D. Jones to Senator Elmer Thomas, Dec. 12, 1931, Thomas Papers, University of Oklahoma Library.

had existed in much of the late nineteenth century, or later in the 1920's. Since there were no large surpluses, farm commodity prices advanced sharply. For example, in 1900 wheat brought 62 cents a bushel, but by 1916 it sold for $1.43 and went higher after the United States entered World War I. Cotton prices rose from about nine cents a pound to seventeen cents in the same period. The growing value of farm products prompted the Country Life Commission to write in 1909 that "there has never been a time when the American farmer was as well off as he is today." [2]

Increased farm prices did not in themselves assure agricultural prosperity. The welfare of farmers depends basically upon the relationship between the prices of their commodities and the prices of non-farm goods that they must purchase. It is the exchange value between farm and non-farm products that is of vital concern to agricultural producers. In this respect farmers were fortunate in the early years of the twentieth century because farm prices rose faster than industrial prices. For instance, the value of ten leading agricultural crops rose 72 per cent between 1900 and 1909, while the prices of a selected list of non-farm commodities increased only 12 per cent. The price relationship was considered so fair to farmers in the years from 1909 to 1914 that farm prices were later considered to have been at "parity" with other prices in that period.

Farmers also benefited from rising land prices. The value of land and buildings increased from an average of $19.81 per acre in 1900 to $39.60 in 1910, and shot upward to $69.38 by 1920. In some states the advance was phenomenal. The price of South Dakota farm land, for instance, rose

[2] *Report of the Country Life Commission*, 60th Cong., 2d Sess., Sen. Doc. 705, p. 21. *Agricultural Statistics, 1962* (Washington, 1963), pp. 1–2; and *Yearbook of Agriculture, 1909* (Washington, 1910), pp. 9–33.

more than 300 per cent between 1900 and 1910. In short, farmers made money by just holding land.[3] Thus the combination of rising commodity prices and increasing land values meant better times for farmers in the years before World War I. The tremendous demands for food and fiber during the war further contributed to agricultural prosperity. Net income of farm operators exceeded $8 billion in both 1917 and 1918, and reached nearly $9 billion in 1919. This was more than double the figure for 1916. The South had its first $2 billion cotton crop in 1919 when average farm prices rose to thirty-eight cents a pound. As a result of this newly found prosperity, farmers expanded their operations, improved their facilities, and enjoyed a better standard of living.

In 1920, however, farm conditions changed radically. Agricultural prices began to weaken in the summer, and within six to twelve months farmers were engulfed in a serious postwar depression. For example, in June, 1920, the farm price of wheat averaged $2.58 a bushel, but by December 1 it had dropped to $1.43. A year later the price had declined to less than $1 a bushel. Cotton that brought thirty-seven cents a pound in July, 1920, commanded only fourteen cents in December when much of the crop was going to market. Hog and cattle prices did not drop seriously until November and December, but by June, 1921, prices were from 40 to 50 per cent below what they had been a year earlier. Secretary of Agriculture Henry C. Wallace declared that in 1921 most agricultural products sold "at bankruptcy prices." Wallace explained that price drops came "as a stunning surprise to a majority of farmers." Though they had expected some postwar decline, he

[3] U.S. Bureau of the Census, *Agriculture,* 1950, General Report, II (Washington, 1952), pp. 48–53.

said, they had not anticipated anything "so severe as what actually happened." [4] Because of these sharp price declines, net income to farm operators in 1920 was more than $1 billion below the figure for 1919. By 1921, however, net farm income was down more than 50 per cent from the year before, totaling only $3.3 billion, the lowest since before 1910. Land values also tumbled, wiping out billions in capital investment. [5]

But statistics fail to tell the story of human tragedy on the farm. The experience of a Missouri cattle-feeder was typical of thousands of livestock farmers who were ruined by falling prices. In October, 1919, U. A. Towns bought 200 head of stocker steers at what he thought was a low price. After wintering and pasturing them during the following summer, he put them in the feed lot in September, 1920. When he marketed the first 100 head, in February, 1921, they brought $2,000 less than they had cost, not to mention his grain and labor. Moreover, there was no chance of getting anywhere near the original outlay for the other 100 head. Towns told Secretary Wallace that he had to borrow money to pay his taxes and interest, and in addition, he was forced to negotiate a second mortgage on his farm. [6] If owners were hard hit, conditions were even worse for tenants. One farmer wrote to Secretary Wallace that his neighbor, a hard-working renter who farmed 320 acres, had turned everything over to his landlord on December 1, 1921, "save one team which they hitched to an old wagon, put in their household goods, got in the wagon themselves, and drove away to get work at day labor and make a new start in life." [7] A Georgia share-

[4] *Yearbook of Agriculture, 1921* (Washington, 1922), p. 11; *ibid.*, 1922 (Washington, 1923), p. 2.

[5] *Yearbook of Agriculture, 1921*, pp. 529, 612, 693, and 724; and *Agricultural Statistics, 1962*, p. 510.

[6] Towns to Wallace, Jan. 2, 1922, Bureau of Agricultural Economics files, USDA, National Archives.

[7] Quoted in *Yearbook of Agriculture, 1922*, p. 8.

cropper who had a wife and "8 head of children" said that he was unable to feed or clothe his "naked and barefooted" family, and that they would be better off in an orphan's home.[8]

The postwar price declines placed farmers in an especially difficult economic position because costs of operation remained high. Production expenses for the 1920 crop were the highest on record and continued heavy in subsequent years. Prices of equipment and machinery, labor, taxes, interest, transportation, and other costs were excessively high in relation to the very low prices brought by most farm products. For example, by 1921–22 taxes paid on farm real estate averaged 226 per cent above that of 1913–14,[9] and beginning in August, 1920, railroad rates advanced from 25 to 40 per cent, just in time to raise the cost of marketing much of the current farm crop.[10] Moreover, during the war many farmers had gone heavily into debt to buy land and to expand their operations. Between 1910 and 1920 farm mortgage debt had risen from $3.2 billion to $8.5 billion, and the yearly interest charges had increased from $203 million to $574 million. Non–real estate agricultural loans totaled an additional $3.5 billion by 1920, and interest rates were often as high as 10 per cent for this type of credit.[11]

Rapidly declining agricultural prices and continued high operating expenses placed farmers in an oppressive cost-price squeeze by 1921. Farmers in the postwar period were in exactly the opposite position from that in the prewar years. Considering the farm price index in 1913

[8] Idua Sapp to Secretary Wallace, Dec. 13, 1921, Secretary's Correspondence, USDA, National Archives.

[9] *Yearbook of Agriculture, 1922*, p. 1002.

[10] James H. Shideler, *Farm Crisis, 1919–1923* (Berkeley and Los Angeles, 1957), pp. 58 ff. Shideler's book is the best and most comprehensive account of farm problems and the suggestions made to solve them in the early 1920's.

[11] *Historical Statistics of the United States from Colonial Times to 1957* (Washington, 1960), pp. 286–87.

as equaling 100, by 1921 corn had dropped to 59, wheat
to 78 and cotton to 48. The purchasing power of several
basic farm products in 1921 was only 67 per cent of what
it had been in 1913.[12] The practical effect of this unfavorable price relationship can be better understood by looking
at specific illustrations. A suit of clothes, for instance, that
cost a North Dakota farmer the equivalent of 21 bushels
of wheat in 1913 required 31 bushels in 1923. It took 63
more bushels of wheat to purchase a wagon in 1923 than
it did a decade earlier. To be sure, other segments of the
economy were also in trouble by 1921; but the agricultural
situation was different in that, as one economist emphasized, farm "prices fell *first*, fell *fastest*, and fell *farthest*."
This explains why farmers were in a singularly unfavorable
economic position.[13]

Farmers initially blamed most of their difficulties on
poor credit facilities, high interest rates, heavy transportation charges, rigged markets, inadequate tariffs, and a
drop in foreign trade. When the Joint Commission of
Agricultural Inquiry studied the farm situation in 1921, it
concentrated on credit, transportation, and marketing and
distribution.[14] These questions did affect the welfare of
farmers, and certain reforms would have been helpful to
hard-pressed producers. However, the "farm problem," as
it came to be known, went much deeper and was more
complicated than these discussions and proposals implied.
Agriculture was an industry out of balance. That is, production exceeded demand at prices profitable to farmers.

[12] George F. Warren and F. A. Pearson, *The Agricultural Situation* (New York, 1924), p. 67; See also the figures published in the
Congressional Record, 67th Cong., 1st Sess. (June 21, 1921), p. 2792.

[13] Clarence A. Wiley, *Agriculture and the Business Cycle Since
1920* (Madison, Wis., 1930), p. 14.

[14] Report of the Joint Commission of Agricultural Inquiry, *The
Agricultural Crisis and Its Causes*. H. Rep. 408, 67th Cong., 1st
Sess. (1921).

In economic terms this meant that there was more land, labor, and capital devoted to farm production than was needed to meet both domestic markets and export trade. The main problem was one of surpluses.

Supply and demand had gradually moved toward a somewhat better balance before World War I. However, the tremendous need for food and fiber of the United States and its allies during the war years encouraged heavy production, especially of wheat and pork. Farmers harvested 73.7 million acres of wheat in 1919 compared to only 52 million acres in 1913, and wheat acreage continued large during the 1920's. Gross production of crops rose about 15 per cent between 1913 and 1920. There were also about twelve million more hogs on farms in 1919 than five years earlier. During the half dozen years before 1920, farmers geared their production to abnormal demands and failed to consider the drastically changed conditions that would come with peace. World War I disrupted a long-run adjustment needed in the agricultural sector of the economy to bring supply and demand into better balance.

Unfortunately for the welfare of agriculture, American farmers expanded their productive capacity at the very time other major agricultural countries were also enlarging their output. This meant that after World War I American farm surpluses had to compete in world markets with the products of Canada, Australia, Argentina, Brazil, and other countries. Although United States farm products were able to compete quite successfully for their share of the foreign export trade, the prices of raw materials and primary food products were low in world markets after the war due to heavy production and lack of purchasing power in the war-torn countries of Europe. The worst aspect of the problem was that the domestic price of wheat, cotton, tobacco, and other staple crops was largely determined by the surplus that had to be sold abroad. In other words, the low foreign price set the domestic price of crops like wheat and cotton, which depended heavily upon export sales. And no amount of tariff protection could effectively raise prices as long as farmers produced large surpluses. The main problem then was how to deal with excess agricultural capacity and overproduction in order to keep burdensome surpluses from depressing the domestic price level.

Much of the increased productivity on American farms resulted from increasing efficiency in the use of resources. Encouraged by the United States Department of Agriculture and acting on their own experiences, farmers introduced new crops, bought labor-saving machinery, applied more fertilizer, and adopted better management practices. The most important change was the rapid expansion in the use of tractors. Between 1920 and 1929 the number of tractors on farms increased from 246,083 to 852,989. These and other changes improved the efficiency on many American farms. While crop acreage and livestock numbers remained about the same between 1919 and 1929, farm output jumped 20 per cent. At the same time population rose only 16 per cent.[15] Increased efficiency undoubtedly helped individual farmers, but the over-all effect was to depress prices and penalize the whole agricultural industry. This was a paradoxical situation whereby the welfare of individual farmers often conflicted with the condition of agriculture as a whole.

The agricultural dilemma was also complicated by other factors. Because of the large number of farms (more than six million in 1920), uncertain weather, insects, disease, and other influences, farmers were unable to control their production even if they knew in advance about how much of a commodity the market would take at profitable prices. Since they could not regulate total production, they could

[15] *Yearbook of Agriculture, 1934,* p. 25.

not influence the price of their commodities. On the other hand, industry regulated its production. A farm machine manufacturer did not produce the maximum number of reapers but only made as many as he could sell at a profitable price. A good example of the difference between the position of agriculture and industry can be seen in the period between 1929 and 1933. As demand weakened following the stock market crash, farm machine and motor vehicle production was cut some 80 per cent, while prices were reduced from only 6 to 16 per cent. But even though agricultural prices declined about 63 per cent in those four years, production dropped a mere 6 per cent. Since a farmer's income is determined by quantity times price, low prices may actually encourage him to produce more in order to get enough money to pay operating and living expenses. When he does this, he adds to the problems of all farmers.

Farmers were at a further disadvantage in dealing with other economic groups. As individual producers, they could not bargain effectively over either the price they paid for non-farm goods or the price they received for their commodities. Part of the difficulty was that farmers dealt with representatives of large and powerful corporations. Three large tobacco companies bought nearly half the tobacco in the 1920's, thirteen flour mills purchased more than 50 per cent of the wheat, and three meat packers bought more than one-fourth of the cattle and hogs marketed. At the same time a half-dozen farm machine manufacturers produced most of the agricultural machinery, and many of the other things that farmers bought were produced by big corporations. As a matter of fact, both the price of what the farmer bought and what he sold was set by others. When he took wheat to the elevator, he received the established price or did not sell his grain. When he bought a plow, he paid the asking price or returned home without the machine. The individual farmer was simply in no position to influence the price of commodities he sold or purchased. This was one of the main reasons that agriculture suffered from inequality or disparity of income. Farmers were penalized for being old-style competitive operators in an economy dominated by large corporations that administered their prices.[16]

Moreover, the supply and demand situation in agriculture was unlike that of many other industries. The demand for several basic farm commodities was inelastic; lower prices did not bring a proportionate increase in consumer purchases. In the case of bread and potatoes, for example, people will pay higher prices if the supply is scarce, but they will not buy much more even at considerably lower prices. In other words, if the price of potatoes drops from $1.00 to 50 cents a bushel, consumers will not buy twice as many bushels. Moreover, gradual dietary changes reduced the demand for certain basic products like wheat and potatoes in the 1920's. The annual per capita consumption of potatoes averaged about four pounds less during the 1920's than in 1919. This was a drop of some eight million bushels, or between 2 and 3 per cent of total production. Per capita wheat consumption declined from an average of 217 pounds in 1909 to 180 pounds in 1925.[17] The declining rate of population growth in the postwar decade also affected the demand for farm products. On the other hand, the widespread shift from horse to tractor power freed millions of acres of land for food production that had previously been needed for horse feed.

Farmers were also confronted by rigid and fixed expenses that were a severe burden. The cost of interest and taxes alone rose from 6 to 8 per cent of total cash farm income

[16] Carl T. Schmidt, *American Farmers in the World Crisis* (New York, 1941), pp. 45–97. Schmidt has an outstanding discussion of the basic problems facing farmers.

[17] *Agricultural Statistics, 1962*, p. 62.

before World War I to 8 to 14 per cent in the 1920's.[18] Since farmers had no control over the price of their products, they could not pass these fixed costs on to consumers in the form of higher prices as was customarily done by businessmen. Altogether, farmers were in a most unfavorable position.

By 1921 it was widely recognized that agriculture was in deep trouble, but not many people, farmers or others, really grasped the fundamental problems confronting the agricultural industry. Few saw the problem in terms of an excess of resources devoted to farming. Furthermore, the "conventional wisdom" held that it was dangerous to reduce the agricultural sector of the economy. This did not mean that farmers should not try to adjust their operations to market requirements. Indeed, it made sense to cut the output of crops in surplus and diversify production to meet changing demands. But farm spokesmen were suspicious of any program that might hurry the decline of agriculture's relative position in the economy. Most Americans seemed to believe that farming had special character-building virtues for both individuals and the nation as a whole, and that agriculture was the very basis of a prosperous economy. Secretary of Agriculture Wallace wrote that forcing people to the cities in abnormal numbers was not good for either the farm communities or the nation. Reflecting his agricultural fundamentalism, Wallace argued that industry, commerce, and labor could not prosper very long if agriculture were depressed. The "unchallenged" truth was, Wallace wrote, "national prosperity must rest on a sound and prosperous agriculture." [19]

The drastic fall in farm prices in 1920 brought frantic demands that the federal government do something to help farmers. Secretary of Agriculture David F. Houston wrote

[18] Schmidt, *American Farmers in the World Crisis*, p. 81.
[19] *Yearbook of Agriculture, 1923*, pp. 10–13.

that "the agitation for relief became hysterical," [20] and
his successor Henry C. Wallace said that "visionary schemes
of all kinds are presented." [21] Most farm spokesmen flatly
rejected the idea that farmers could and should be expected
to weather the severe deflation on their own resources. A
wide variety of proposals designed to assist farmers was
advanced, including plans to enlarge agricultural exports
and schemes for outright government price-fixing of major
crops. Several bills were introduced in 1920 and 1921 to
establish fixed prices for farm commodities by government
fiat. It is not surprising, however, that these measures
failed. Besides being opposed by Democratic and Republican leaders, they ran counter to the growing popular
demand in 1920 and 1921 to take the government out of
business. Speaking in 1921 against the proposal of Senator
George W. Norris to have the government purchase surplus
farm products and sell them abroad on credit, Senator
Henry Cabot Lodge remarked: "It puts the United States
into active business. I think at this time the more we take
the United States out of business and the less we put it
in the better." [22]

Although the Harding administration opposed placing the
government in the business of handling farm products or
setting their price, it was not unsympathetic to the farmers'
plight. Since, however, administrative and Congressional
leaders did not understand the basic economic handicaps
under which farmers operated in the economy, the proposals for relief tended to treat the symptoms rather
than the underlying problems. Most farm relief proposals
advanced in 1921 and 1922 called for more generous credit,

[20] David F. Houston, *Eight Years with Wilson's Cabinet* (2 vols.;
New York, 1926), II, 109.

[21] *Yearbook of Agriculture, 1921*, p. 15.

[22] *Congressional Record*, 67th Cong., 1st Sess. (July 19, 1921),
p. 4039.

higher tariff duties, regulation of the grain exchanges and packers, and improved co-operative marketing.

Under growing insistence from agricultural leaders and farm constituents, Congress passed a series of so-called farm relief bills during the Harding administration. Much of the political pressure was exerted by the farm bloc. This was a bipartisan group first organized in the Senate in May, 1921, under the leadership of Senator William S. Kenyon of Iowa, and subsequently in the House by Iowa Congressman L. J. Dickinson. In May, 1921, Congress passed the Emergency Tariff Act, which raised duties on many farm commodities, including cotton. This legislation could not, and did not, raise prices of farm products of which there was an exportable surplus, but the principle of protecting the home market had a wide appeal to misinformed farmers and their leaders. The three major farm organizations, the Grange, Farm Bureau, and Farmers Union, all favored this law.[23] In July and August Congress amended the Farm Loan Act to furnish more capital for the Federal Land Banks. It was hoped this would indirectly help farmers with their credit problems. Moreover, the War Finance Corporation, which had been revived late in 1920, was permitted to expand its lending power by $1 billion in a law passed in August, 1921. The Packers and Stockyards Act was passed at about the same time. The result of years of agitation, this law authorized the secretary of agriculture to extend some supervision and control over packers and stockyards, who, farmers believed, had been exploiting producers.

In 1922 Congress passed the Grain Futures Act to regulate dealing in futures, and the Capper-Volstead Co-operative Marketing Act, which specifically exempted

[23] James R. Connor, "National Farm Organizations and the United States Tariff Policy in the 1920's," *Agricultural History*, XXXII (January, 1958), 32–43.

farm marketing associations from the antitrust laws. The
Intermediate Credits Act was approved early in 1923. It
set up twelve Intermediate Credits Banks to make loans
to banks and other financial institutions that handled farm
credit. This law reflected the general belief among farm
groups that credit contraction had been a major cause in
the price declines of 1920 and 1921.[24]

The agricultural question probably received more Congressional attention than any other single issue during the
Harding administration. Many farm bills were passed,
Congressional debate was extensive and sometimes heated,
and the whole nation became aware that there was a "farm
problem." But farmers received more sympathy and attention than real help. None of the legislation passed between
1921 and 1923 got to the heart of farmers' basic difficulties
of surpluses and price disparities. Congress, as well as
most farm leaders, advanced the old nostrums of credit,
co-operative marketing, and regulation of dealers in agricultural products. The only proposal to deal directly with
the surplus problem was Senator George W. Norris' bill
that would have established a government-financed export
corporation to buy up farm surpluses and sell them abroad
on credit. But this departed too far from the accepted economics of Harding and the conservative Republicans, and
went down to defeat in August, 1921.

Although Secretary Wallace believed that legislation
might be of some assistance to farmers, he recognized that
these laws were only doctoring symptoms. Referring to
credit legislation, Wallace wrote: "Better prices for the
crops the farmers have to sell and lower prices for the
things they have to buy are far more needed than an
opportunity to go further in debt." [25] But Wallace had no
pat answers for the plight of farmers. Like others, he was

[24] Shideler, *Farm Crisis*, chap. vi.
[25] *Yearbook of Agriculture, 1921*, p. 15.

searching and struggling for something that would bring genuine relief to a sick industry. He recognized the need for more study of agricultural economics and wrote in 1921 that "had we in the past given as much attention to the economics of agriculture as we have to stimulating production, it is not too much to say that at least some of the troubles which now beset us might have been anticipated and avoided." [26] In July, 1922, Wallace organized the Bureau of Agricultural Economics in the Department of Agriculture with Henry C. Taylor as chief. The Bureau employed a group of outstanding economists to study all aspects of agriculture, but during its early years the BAE considered itself a "fact-finding, information-giving and service-rendering institution" rather than an agency to develop policy.[27]

Secretary Wallace urged farmers to adjust their production to market conditions and believed that the United States Department of Agriculture had a responsibility to inform farmers of probable demand. The Secretary favored voluntary reduction of acreage among cotton growers in 1921, and wrote to his son, Henry A., who was editing *Wallace's Farmer* back in Des Moines, that "we should cut down production to our own needs, or a little more." [28] Indeed, there was considerable support for cutting wheat, cotton, and corn acreage in 1921 and 1922 as a means of bringing supply and demand into better balance. The Wallaces, Harry N. Owen, editor of *Farm, Stock and Home* in St. Paul, economists, a few congressmen, publishers, and some business leaders supported this move. The editor of the Washington *Post* wrote on May 14, 1924, that "the remedy is plain: let American wheat growers quit trying

[26] *Ibid.*, p. 16.
[27] Henry C. and Anne Dewees Taylor, *The Story of Agricultural Economics in the United States 1840–1932* (Ames, Iowa, 1952), p. 644.
[28] Henry C. Wallace to Henry A. Wallace, Sept. 18, 1922, Secretary's File, USDA, National Archives.

to compete with cheap foreign wheat and cut their production down to home needs." [29] Farmers did not generally favor this kind of advice, and by 1924 total crop acreage was only about one million acres less than the high years of 1918 and 1919. Wheat acreage was down, but that of cotton and corn was up.[30]

Meanwhile, Congress set up a Joint Commission of Agricultural Inquiry in 1921 to study the farm situation. The Commission described many of the problems plaguing farmers, but its recommendations were confined mainly to orderly marketing. Secretary Wallace then called a National Agricultural Conference that met in January, 1922. Although numerous proposals for helping farmers were discussed, the Conference's principal contribution was to publicize ideas, clarify the problems, and emphasize the difficulties in solving the farm dilemma.[31] Although by 1922 and 1923 farm problems had been thoroughly explored and some agricultural legislation had been passed, the basic question of the disparity between farm and non-farm prices still remained. The continued seriousness of this problem finally brought a new approach to solving agriculture's difficulties.

It was George N. Peek and Hugh S. Johnson, officials of the Moline Plow Company, who proposed a practical plan to achieve equality for agriculture. During 1920 and 1921, as farm leaders and government officials sought an answer to farm ills, Peek and Johnson watched their sales of agricultural implements decline. Viewing this situation, Peek exclaimed that "you can't sell a plow to a busted

[29] Quoted in Gilbert C. Fite, *George N. Peek and the Fight for Farm Parity* (Norman, Okla., 1954), p. 133. Representative G. M. Young of North Dakota declared that if farmers were to get cost of production plus a reasonable profit, they must have "intelligent crop control." *Congressional Record*, 67th Cong., 2d Sess. (Jan. 12, 1922), pp. 1142–43.

[30] *Yearbook of Agriculture*, 1925, p. 102.

[31] *Report of the National Agricultural Conference, 1922*, 67th Cong., 2d Sess., House Doc. 195, p. 195.

customer," and set out to analyze the problem and come up with a solution. Like others who had studied the matter, Peek and Johnson saw that surplus production depressed the price of staple crops to the world level and that a tariff had no effect in raising the price of commodities of which there was an exportable surplus. As it was, farmers bought in a protected market where industry benefited from tariffs while they sold their products at world prices. This situation, they believed, was largely responsible for the disparity in prices between farm and industrial commodities. Peek and Johnson, and those who came to support their plan, did not attack the tariff system. They were economic nationalists who believed that tariffs were largely responsible for America's higher standards of living. "America could make no greater blunder at this crisis than to abandon protection," Peek wrote; but he and Johnson argued that agriculture must be brought under the umbrella of the tariff system so that "it will do for agriculture what it does for industry." To achieve this goal, it was necessary to remove or segregate the surplus portion of a crop that depressed the prices to about the world level. Once the price-depressing surpluses were eliminated from the home market, farm prices would then rise behind a tariff wall. There were two ways of dealing with the surplus problem: cut production to only what the domestic market would absorb, or dump the excess abroad. Peek favored the latter approach, and advocated segregating the surpluses and selling them in foreign markets at world prices and then maintaining tariff-protected domestic prices at home.

Effective tariff protection for farmers, Peek declared, would give their products a "fair exchange value" with non-farm goods and place agriculture on an economic equality with industry. Peek's objective was to raise the price of farm commodities to the point where they would have the same purchasing power as they had in the favorable period from 1909 to 1914. Here was the idea of parity prices for farmers. This concept went back at least to the 1890's, but Peek and Johnson were the first to advocate incorporating the principle in national farm legislation.[32] They suggested that Congress set up a government corporation that would buy agricultural surpluses and sell them abroad for whatever they would bring. Any losses on this operation were to be paid by the farmers through an equalization fee or tax on each unit of a commodity sold.[33] In other words, though a government corporation would administer the program, it would be self-supporting.

Peek's approach to the farm problem was important in at least three major respects. It broke new ground in policy matters by stating, first, that parity prices were a practical legislative goal and, second, that the means to achieve this objective was through an agency of the federal government. Moreover, it broke the restrictive bonds on farm thinking that held that government aid should be confined to education, credit, co-operative marketing, or regulation of business.

During 1922 and 1923 Peek actively promoted his plan of "equality for agriculture" among farm leaders, economists, businessmen, and government officials. He presented it before a committee of the National Agricultural Conference in January, 1922, and this group resolved that Congress and the President "should take such steps as will immediately re-establish a fair exchange value for all farm products with that of other commodities." However, no action followed this committee resolution. Peek was especially anxious to get Secretary Wallace's support. Though

[32] Fite, *George N. Peek and the Fight for Farm Parity*, chap. iii. See also Robert L. Tontz, "Origin of the Base Period Concept of Parity," *Agricultural History*, XXXII (January, 1958), 1–13; James H. Shideler, "Development of the Parity Price Formula," *ibid.*, XXVII (July, 1953).

[33] George N. Peek and Hugh S. Johnson, *Equality for Agriculture* (1st ed.; Moline, Ill., 1922).

Wallace was friendly to the idea, he did not commit himself. Some economists in the Department were openly critical of the ratio-price scheme, although Henry C. Taylor, chief of the Bureau of Agricultural Economics, was sympathetic.

Despite the lack of encouragement, Peek did not give up. He wrote letters, talked with farm leaders, especially in the Farm Bureau, and continued to seek support in the United States Department of Agriculture. During 1922 he sent out hundreds of copies of a pamphlet, *Equality for Agriculture,* that outlined his views. IIis main problem was to reach the Congressional and administrative power structure. This was not easy, but the continued farm depression, especially in the wheat belt, helped Peek win political support for his plan. Farmers in the northwest were constantly bombarding their congressmen, the President, the Secretary of Agriculture, and farm organization leaders with demands for price-lifting legislation. As Peek's proposals became known, policy-makers began to hear from the grass roots. Moreover, neither the farm organizations nor the administration was offering anything that might meet the farm demand for higher prices. Late in 1923 Senator Thomas J. Walsh of Montana wrote that "the farmers of my state . . . are giving their endorsement to the so called Johnson-Peek plan for an agricultural export corporation." Another Montanan wrote that it was "spreading like wildfire" among farmers and small businessmen. Thus the Peek plan was conspicuous in its appeal for support. Of course, there were frequent demands for outright government price-fixing of farm products, but no one really believed that Congress would enact legislation to implement this idea.[34]

By late 1923 the Peek proposal had gained a surprising amount of backing at the grass roots and was beginning

[34] Walsh to George W. Norris, Dec. 27, 1923; A. H. Stafford to Walsh, Dec. 20, 1923, Walsh Papers, Library of Congress.

to win important support in Washington. In the Department of Agriculture, economists and Secretary Wallace were wrestling with the problem of just how far the federal government should go in trying to help farmers. On September 22, 1923, Taylor sent Wallace a memorandum in which he discussed various approaches to the farm problem, and concluded: "The question is, shall we adhere to the policy of providing information on a basis of individual and collective action and await the very gradual recovery of agriculture through growth and readjustments of population; or, shall we undertake to bring about a more immediate solution of the problem by direct governmental action which will re-establish pre-war price relations at an early date." [35] Taylor did not answer his own question, but in November Secretary Wallace gave his guarded endorsement to the Peek principles. In a report to the President on the wheat situation, he wrote that the "most careful consideration" should be given to setting up an agricultural export corporation to handle surplus crops. It would be the duty of the corporation, he said, "to restore, so far as possible, the pre-war ratio between wheat, and other farm products of which we export a surplus." [36]

With strong support in the wheat belt, from northwestern congressmen and senators, and from some agricultural leaders, and now approval by Secretary Wallace, the next step was to draw up a measure for Congressional consideration. By November, 1923, Charles J. Brand, a consulting specialist in the Department of Agriculture, was busy writing a bill. After some modifications it was introduced in January, 1924, by Senator Charles L. McNary of Oregon and Representative Gilbert N. Haugen of Iowa. The McNary-Haugen

[35] Taylor and Taylor, *The Story of Agricultural Economics*, p. 594.

[36] *Yearbook of Agriculture, 1923*, p. 150. For a discussion of the role of the secretaries of agriculture in the 1920's see Gladys L. Baker *et al.*, *Century of Service; The First 100 Years of the United States Department of Agriculture* (Washington, 1963).

bill called for establishing an agricultural export corporation capitalized at $200 million with power to buy enough surplus agricultural commodities to bring the domestic price up to the "ratio price." The ratio price was that figure which gave a commodity the same purchasing power that it had in the period from 1905 to 1914, a time when the exchange value of farm products was considered favorable. By taking the all-commodity index and comparing it to the price of wheat in 1923, for instance, wheat should have been bringing $1.53 a bushel to have the same buying power or exchange value that it had in the prewar years. Actually, wheat was selling for only 92 cents a bushel.

It is easiest to illustrate how it was thought the plan would work by considering wheat. Under the McNary-Haugen bill, the export corporation would buy enough wheat to maintain the ratio price in the domestic market and then it would sell the surplus abroad at world prices. The loss on foreign sales was to be recouped by placing a small tax on the farmer for each bushel he sold. For example, if the United States produced 800 million bushels of wheat and consumed 600 million bushels domestically, there would be 200 million bushels to sell abroad. The difference between the ratio price and the world price in 1923 was about 61 cents a bushel, which would mean a loss to the export corporation of $122 million dollars on the 200 million bushels disposed of in foreign markets. In order to pay this, a tax or equalization fee on each of the 800 million bushels sold would have to be about fifteen cents. But since the farmer received the full ratio price of $1.53 for his wheat, he would still have $1.38 a bushel instead of 92 cents, even after paying the 15-cent tax.

Thus the heart of the plan was to get near-parity prices for basic farm crops by segregating and disposing abroad of the price-depressing surpluses. To protect higher domestic prices, a flexible tariff provision was added to keep out imports. The bill covered only eight so-called basic crops: wheat, flour, corn, cotton, wool, cattle, sheep, and swine. Cotton was later dropped. It was believed that if the major crops were helped, most of agriculture's problems would be solved. The McNary-Haugen bill was primarily a marketing device that, as Henry A. Wallace later explained, would give farmers "the centralizing power of the Federal Government so they could dump enough of their surplus abroad to raise prices in the domestic market." [37]

After about four months of hearings, debate, and discussion, the first McNary-Haugen bill was killed in the House of Representatives by a vote of 223 to 155, and Congress adjourned without passing any major legislation. Opposition to the measure was intense. President Calvin Coolidge was among the leading opponents. He believed that farmers could work out their own problems or at least get some help by expanding their own marketing co-operatives. The President's position had been made clear in his first annual message. He said that "no complicated scheme of relief, no plan for government fixing of prices, no resort to the public treasury will be of any permanent value in establishing agriculture." [38] Lined up behind Coolidge were businessmen, especially those in the grain trade, metropolitan editors, most southern Democrats, professional economists, and many farm journals. Critics charged that the bill was unworkable and economically unsound. The main objection, however, was that it would put the government in the business of handling farm products; and that was considered un-American.

[37] Henry A. Wallace, *New Frontiers* (New York, 1934), p. 148. For a discussion of the first McNary-Haugen bill see Fite, *George N. Peek and the Fight for Farm Parity*, pp. 59–63. Peek discussed his idea of how the plan would work in "The McNary-Haugen Plan for Relief," *Current History*, XXIX (November, 1928).

[38] *Congressional Record*, 68th Cong., 1st Sess. (Dec. 6, 1923), p. 100.

Though the opposition to surplus-control and price-lifting legislation was organized and nation-wide, supporters were disorganized and represented mainly sectional interests. Most of the favorable votes came from the wheat states and the western part of the corn belt. Southerners were not interested in the proposal because at that time cotton was selling considerably above the ratio price. Miscellaneous support from Secretary Wallace, an occasional business leader like Bernard Baruch (Peek's old boss on the War Industries Board), a scattering of individual farm leaders, and a few local bankers and businessmen did not represent enough political power to enact this type of legislation.

It became clear in the fight over the first McNary-Haugen bill that the farm dilemma was political as well as economic. The broad diversity of agricultural interests made it extremely difficult to present anything approaching a united front in Congress. Wheat-growers, livestock-raisers, dairymen, cotton and tobacco farmers, and vegetable-raisers had relatively little in common. Also, there were conflicts of interest within particular crop and livestock regions. Cattle-feeders, for instance, did not want higher grain prices. The same kind of farm program was not suitable for all farmers.

Furthermore, agricultural power in Congress was slowly but surely weakening in the face of a rapidly rising urban population. For the first time the census of 1920 revealed that more Americans lived in cities than on farms or in small towns. Although no reapportionment was made on the basis of the 1920 census, in 1930 Minnesota, Iowa, Kansas, Nebraska, and the Dakotas lost representation. Thus the problem before Peek and supporters of the McNary-Haugen bill was twofold. They had to develop a program that would attract as many farmers and farm leaders as possible, and then organize rural political power to push the legislation through Congress. It was obvious

in the summer of 1924 that if the McNary-Haugenites
were to obtain any major farm relief they must have organization, leadership, and money. During the next two years
Peek and his associates developed the most powerful
agricultural lobby in the nation's history.

On July 11, 1924, about one hundred and fifty farm
leaders met in St. Paul to consider the next move in the
fight for farm relief. Among those present were Peek;
Henry A. Wallace; Frank W. Murphy, a Minnesota farmer
and lawyer; Charles E. Hearst of the Iowa Farm Bureau;
William Hirth, leader of the Missouri Farmers Association;
C. H. Hyde, vice-president of the Farmers Union; and
George C. Jewett, head of American Wheat Growers Associated. The American Council of Agriculture was organized
out of this meeting to "secure the enactment . . . of legislation embodying the principles of the McNary-Haugen bill
and thus secure for American agriculture equality with
industry and labor." [39] The American Council of Agriculture was a non-partisan group designed to provide central
direction and united leadership in the battle for McNary-
Haugenism. Peek was elected president. He moved to Washington in January, 1925, and set out to marshal the farm
relief forces into an effective pressure group. At this
juncture southern farm leaders were conspicuous by their
absence.

Meanwhile, farm relief advocates had to face the discouraging reality of Coolidge's re-election. To make matters
even worse, Secretary Wallace, a loyal friend of surplus-
control legislation, died on October 25, 1924, and was replaced a few months later by William M. Jardine, president
of Kansas State College. Like Coolidge, Jardine believed
that farmers could best solve their problems through

[39] "Report and Record, Agricultural Conference, July 11 and 12,
1924." Mimeographed copy, Peek Papers, Western Historical Manuscripts Collection, University of Missouri.

co-operative marketing and voluntary adjustments in production. Furthermore, increased prices in 1924 took some
of the urgency out of demands for price-raising legislation.
Wheat rose nearly 40 cents a bushel, and, although cotton
prices were lower, a larger crop gave farmers about the
same returns that they had received in 1923 when cotton
reached 31 cents a pound. In 1925 total farm income went
up about 7 per cent, and the parity index figure for all farm
crops, according to the Secretary, increased to 87 by the
end of the year.[40]

In an effort to improve farm marketing and to divert
attention from surplus-control legislation, Coolidge gave
his active support to co-operative marketing in 1925. In
January a National Agricultural Conference called by the
President recommended co-operative marketing as the best
relief for farmers, along with more credit, lower freight
rates, and higher tariffs on some agricultural products.[41]
When Coolidge addressed the annual meeting of the American Farm Bureau Federation the following December, he
again emphasized his devotion to co-operative marketing
and closed by saying that the "future of agriculture looks
to be exceedingly secure." Agriculture was indeed secure,
quipped humorist Will Rogers, "by at least two mortgages." [42] To the McNary-Haugen supporters, co-operative
marketing was nothing but a sop thrown to farmers to quiet
their demands for effective price-lifting legislation.

By 1925 the farm issue was joined. Coolidge, with the
strong support of Secretary of Commerce Herbert Hoover,
Jardine, and conservatives in Congress, believed that the
role of government should not be extended beyond advising
farmers on marketing and production, and perhaps liberal-
izing farm credit and tinkering with tariffs. The adminis-

[40] *Yearbook of Agriculture, 1924*, pp. 2–3, 17–18; *ibid.*, 1925, p. 2.
[41] 68th Cong., 2d Sess., Sen. Doc. 190 (Jan. 28, 1925).
[42] Washington *Post*, Dec. 20, 1925.

tration flatly rejected both the need for, and wisdom of, federal handling of farm commodities.

On the other hand, the McNary-Haugenites insisted that agriculture was still suffering from basic disadvantages that only surplus-control legislation could solve. They especially objected to the suggestions that farmers should cut production. When Hoover told the President's Agricultural Conference that "the fundamental need is balancing of agricultural production to our home demand," critics interpreted this to mean that farmers must give up their foreign markets while industrialists pushed their own overseas exports. "Non-export for the farmer and aggressive export for the manufacturer," Mark Sullivan wrote, would definitely subordinate farming to other industries.[43] Peek and his backers saw this as a sinister move by the industrial interests to benefit themselves without any regard to the position of farmers. They tried to play on the deep agrarian sympathies of Americans: "Shall we industrialize America at the expense of agriculture . . . ?" The implication was clear. Unless something like the McNary-Haugen bill was passed, American farmers would drift into peasantry.[44]

In May, 1925, the farm lobby was strengthened by formation of the Grain Belt Federation of Farm Organizations. This organization became popularly known as the Corn Belt Committee and was headed by William Hirth. At the same time Peek was busy widening the support for surplus-control legislation among businessmen and farm organizations. In December, 1925, Sam H. Thompson, a supporter of the McNary-Haugen bill, was elected president of the American Farm Bureau Federation. This was a sign of growing insistence by farmers for price-raising measures. Peek won the backing of Frank O. Lowden,

[43] Mark Sullivan, "The Waning Influence of the Farmer," *World's Work*, LI (April, 1926), 657–61.

[44] For a discussion of this entire question see Fite, *George N. Peek and the Fight for Farm Parity*, chap. viii.

former governor of Illinois and popular in farm circles. The most important support, however, originated with the Iowa Bankers Association. The Hawkeye bankers took the lead in calling an "all agricultural area" marketing conference in Des Moines in January, 1926, attended by representatives from eleven states. The conference endorsed the idea of creating a farm export corporation and authorized Governor John Hammill of Iowa to appoint two men from each state to carry on the farm relief fight. A subcommittee of this executive committee of twenty-two worked closely with Peek, who set up offices in Washington and Chicago to promote farm relief legislation.

By 1926 Peek and a few close associates were coordinating the activities of the American Council of Agriculture, the Corn Belt Committee, and the executive committee of twenty-two. Never before had farmers enjoyed such strong representation in Washington. Farm lobbying had at last come into its own. Although the Farmers Union and the Farm Bureau had their own offices in Washington, they worked closely with the special pressure groups directed by Peek. Only the Grange remained aloof from the central farm relief efforts. The Grange supported the export-debenture plan, a scheme to raise prices on exportable surpluses by paying an export bounty. In February, 1926, Chester C. Davis was brought into the farm relief campaign as a paid worker after serving as commissioner of agriculture in Montana. In order to finance the farm lobby, Peek and his associates tapped the agricultural organizations, wealthy friends, and contributed much out of their own pockets. For example, Bernard Baruch initially gave $5,000, and later, Mark Woods of Nebraska contributed a similar amount. Several of the farm organizations gave fairly substantial sums, but often money was short and Peek had to pay office expenses himself.[45] Nonethe-

45 *Ibid.*, pp. 148–58.

less, constant pressure was applied on Congress to pass a McNary-Haugen bill.

Throughout 1925 and 1926 the McNary-Haugenites not only increased their political power but significantly modified their legislation. By giving co-operatives a larger role in price-support operations, they hoped to win support from some of the large co-operatives and to reduce opposition from the Coolidge administration. The McNary-Haugen bill of 1926 provided for a federal farm board with power to help remove surpluses of basic crops—cotton, corn, wheat, butter, cattle, or swine—if favored by the co-operatives. The board could arrange with co-operatives, processors, or others who handled farm products to sell the surpluses abroad or hold them in storage for higher prices. A revolving fund of $375 million was to be provided by Congress to handle surplus operations, but the ultimate cost of dumping crops abroad was to be met by the farmers themselves through the equalization fee. Peek's original ratio-price plan was abandoned, and prices were to be raised to the world price plus the tariff.

Under this bill, the co-operatives would play a much larger role. The federal farm board was not to engage in price-lifting activities unless they were first approved by the co-operatives, and it was anticipated that the co-operatives would also have an important part in the actual handling and disposing of surpluses. Yet the essential principles for which farm groups had been fighting were maintained. Though it appeared that the McNary-Haugenites had made some significant compromises with those who had opposed their first bill, a measure incorporating these revisions was defeated in May, 1926, by a House vote of 212 to 167.[46]

[46] Murray R. Benedict, *Farm Policies of the United States, 1790–1950* (New York, 1953), p. 225. See Chapter X in Benedict for his account of the campaign to achieve surplus-control legislation.

So far, the strength behind McNary-Haugenism had rested in the corn and wheat states. The need was for a western-southern coalition in Congress—a marriage of corn, wheat, and cotton. Some southerners began to warm up to the McNary-Haugen plan in 1925 when cotton prices fell nearly 10 cents a pound, but most southern farm leaders were still primarily interested in co-operative marketing. Peek was a political realist. In seeking southern support early in 1926, he told the directors of the American Cotton Growers Exchange "to write their own ticket." Peek said he was willing to modify the McNary-Haugen bill to meet southern wishes in return for "their cooperation in helping us get what we want." [47]

The cotton people did not want a two-price, export-dumping plan like that favored by the wheat men. They simply favored some central agency that could keep periodic surpluses from depressing prices. They generally favored using the co-operatives to bring about more orderly marketing, assisted perhaps by some kind of federal farm board.

Although the McNary-Haugenites gained some southern support during 1926, it was the dramatic drop in cotton prices to as low as 10 cents a pound in the fall of 1926 that brought the South into a full-fledged partnership in the fight for farm relief. Moreover, the McNary-Haugen bill introduced in January, 1927, was a compromise measure that included southern demands. This bill provided for setting up a federal farm board that would work through the co-operatives to dispose of surpluses of basic crops, including cotton, tobacco, wheat, rice, corn, and hogs. To finance orderly marketing through the holding of crops, or

[47] Peek to Frank O. Lowden, Mar. 24, 1926, Chester C. Davis Papers, Western Historical Manuscripts Collection, University of Missouri; Fite, *George N. Peek and the Fight for Farm Parity*, chap. x.

to pay losses on export-dumping, a fee or tax was to be levied on each unit of the commodity sold. This was to be collected, however, as the board decided in the "transportation, processing, or sale" of a product. Until these fees could be collected, Congress would provide $250 million. Perhaps the most important change in this bill was the elimination of any special price objective other than to prevent surpluses from "unduly depressing" agricultural prices.

Amidst charges of "vicious lobbying," the grain and cotton forces finally won a signal victory by passing the McNary-Haugen bill in February, 1927. But the flush of success soon turned to gloom when President Coolidge killed the measure with a lengthy veto. Relying on advice from Hoover and Jardine, as well as his own deeply held beliefs, Coolidge said that the bill was unsound, unconstitutional, and violated "the philosophy of our government" and "the spirit of our institutions." Coolidge also objected to the equalization fee as a "vicious form of taxation," and argued that increased prices would encourage production and intensify the surplus problem. Economic arguments were subordinated in his message to a defense of laissez faire.[48]

Although not greatly surprised, leaders in the farm fight were bitterly disappointed. During 1927 they regrouped their forces, modified the bill in hopes of meeting some of Coolidge's objections, and repassed the measure in May, 1928. In his second veto message the President still insisted that the bill was unconstitutional and "was repugnant as ever to the spirit of our institutions, both political and commercial." The campaign was over; the war was lost. And no one recognized this better than the McNary-Haugenites. The conservative little Yankee from Vermont

[48] Fite, *George N. Peek and the Fight for Farm Parity*, p. 179.

had been able to thwart legislation that probably had more western and southern farm support than free silver or any other issue ever considered by Congress up to that time.

Blocked by White House action, farm leaders now sought to get a friend of agriculture nominated by the Republicans at the convention in June, 1928. When Hoover obtained the nomination, Peek, Chester Davis, and others looked to the Democrats. Democratic standard-bearer Alfred E. Smith could not, however, attract much farm support outside of the traditional Democratic South. He knew practically nothing about agriculture, and, besides, he alienated many midwestern and southern farmers because he was a Catholic and favored the repeal of Prohibition. Hoover, consequently, not only carried the traditional Republican Midwest but won several southern states as well.[49]

Hoover's election created a feeling of resignation among the old McNary-Haugen crowd. He had probably been the strongest and most effective opponent of surplus-control legislation during the Harding and Coolidge administrations. Like Coolidge, Jardine, and other conservatives, Hoover believed that the best way to help farmers was to strengthen the co-operative marketing organizations. He agreed that the federal government could properly assist in achieving this objective through advice and loans to the commodity associations.[50]

With McNary-Haugenism hopelessly defeated, Hoover was free to proceed with his brand of relief. During the presidential campaign he had promised that, if elected, he

[49] Gilbert C. Fite, "The Agricultural Issue in the Presidential Campaign of 1928," *Mississippi Valley Historical Review*, XXXVII (March, 1951).

[50] Benedict, *Farm Policies of the United States, 1790–1950*, chap. xi; and Theodore Saloutos and John D. Hicks, *Agricultural Discontent in the Middle West, 1900–1939* (Madison, Wis., 1951), chap. xiv. Saloutos and Hicks also have excellent chapters on other aspects of farm policy in the 1920's.

would call a special session of Congress to deal with farm problems. In June, 1929, Congress passed the Agricultural Marketing Act. The new law called for placing "agriculture on a basis of equality with other industries," an objective that the McNary-Haugen campaign had popularized. This was the voice of Jacob, but the hand of Esau! Agricultural equality was to be achieved through orderly marketing and strengthening the farm co-operatives. Congress appropriated $500 million that could be loaned to co-operatives to construct facilities, to merchandise commodities, to hold products off the market, and for other purposes. In case of unusually large and price-depressing surpluses, the law permitted formulation of stabilization corporations that could purchase excess crops in order to maintain satisfactory prices. If the stabilization corporations suffered operating losses, these were to be paid out of the $500 million appropriation. A Federal Farm Board was provided to administer the new farm relief law.[51]

Passage of the Agricultural Marketing Act climaxed Peek's efforts of nearly five years. Up to 1924 Peek and his supporters had pushed the rather radical idea that a corporation of the federal government should guarantee ratio, or near parity, prices for basic farm commodities used in domestic consumption by purchasing price-destroying surpluses and dumping them abroad. Beginning in 1925, however, emphasis shifted to orderly marketing through farm co-operatives. The changed approach aimed to reduce Coolidge's opposition and at the same time gain political support from the large commodity groups. By 1928 the

[51] Benedict, *Farm Policies of the United States*, chap. xi; Saloutos and Hicks, *Agricultural Discontent in the Middle West*, chap xiv. The Agricultural Marketing Act soon failed, partly because it was not designed for depression conditions and partly because it made no provision to control large and continuing surpluses. By 1931 the Federal Farm Board had lost some $345 million in a hopeless attempt to stabilize farm prices. It then abandoned efforts to maintain higher prices, and the law remained a dead letter on the statute books during the rest of the Hoover administration.

positions of the McNary-Haugenites and the co-operatives
had been compromised to the point where only two principal
differences separated the Agricultural Marketing Act and
the last McNary-Haugen bill. First, the Hoover measure
provided government funds for supporting prices rather
than taxing each unit of a commodity through an equalization fee. Second, there was no provision for export-dumping
in the Hoover plan. Farm relief leaders had moved toward
a policy aimed primarily at improved marketing facilities
by enlarging and strengthening the farmers' own co-
operatives. What started out in 1922 and 1923 as a sharp
break from the past in agricultural policy ended up in the
same conservative groove that characterized most of the
American economy in the 1920's.

The main reason that the farm movement of the 1920's
continued in a conservative vein was because its leading
spokesmen were fundamentally conservative. The views of
George Peck and Calvin Coolidge on political economy were
closer than either would admit. They both believed that
government had a role to play in economic development
and prosperity. The main difference was not that Peek
favored government help for farmers and Coolidge did not;
it was that Peek wanted to assist farmers and Coolidge
favored extending government help to industry. Peek in
1924 quietly voted for John W. Davis, who was as conservative as Coolidge. There is no indication that Peek even
thought of voting for La Follette. Another sign of conservatism in the farm movement is that much of the
argument in favor of doing something for agriculture was
based on the belief that prosperous, land-owning farmers
were the main bulwark against radicalism and socialism.
In other words, a little government help to raise agricultural prices and to provide a better life on the farm was a
means of preserving traditional American institutions.[52]

[52] Fite, *George N. Peek and the Fight for Farm Parity*, pp. 124–25.

Despite its basically conservative nature, the drive for farm relief during the 1920's was highly important. The McNary-Haugen campaign pointed up as never before the unfavorable position of agriculture in the nation's economy. It emphasized, too, that greater efficiency was not the sole answer, especially when more production simply resulted in additional surpluses. Farmers were also educated, although not with complete success, to the importance of co-operation and organization as a means of improving their economic position. It became clear that somehow farmers, at least those who produced a particular crop, must get together so they could act in unison. Otherwise, they could exert no influence over the prices of their products. There were differences of opinion as to whether farmers could achieve this goal through their own co-operatives or by using the centralizing power of government, but unity was essential if farmers were to have any influence over the price of their commodities.

Furthermore, the question of surpluses held the center of attention and stimulated consideration of production control by restricting acreage. Most of the McNary-Haugenites did not favor any plans that would force or strongly encourage acreage reduction. Yet a discussion of surpluses could not help but raise the question of reduced acreage as one means to deal with overproduction. Almost unwittingly, the McNary-Haugenites helped to publicize the idea of getting higher agricultural prices by cutting acreage.

Perhaps the most significant thing about the farm relief campaign in the 1920's was the emphasis upon the parity-price concept. This became a symbol in the farm mind, and parity prices actually became the goal of the Agricultural Adjustment Act of 1933. Moreover, the idea became widely accepted that the federal government had a responsibility to help farmers achieve this price goal. Thus farm policy-makers did not achieve significant concrete results in the

1920's, but they did prepare the way for an extensive agricultural program after the election of Franklin D. Roosevelt. Their main objective, parity prices, and the means to achieve this goal, the federal government, were incorporated in New Deal legislation.

Thus it was in the field of ideas, not in the solutions offered, that the McNary-Haugenites were most important. The McNary-Haugen bills probably would not have achieved what the farm groups hoped for. If that type of surplus-control legislation would have worked at all, it would have been only on a temporary basis. The McNary-Haugen bills contained at least two serious weaknesses. Foreign reaction to American dumpings would surely have resulted in other nations putting up barriers against American farm produce. Second, higher prices would undoubtedly have stimulated production and added to the already burdensome surpluses. Farm spokesmen in the 1920's did not seem to realize that the continuing mechanical, chemical, and biological revolution in agriculture would create much larger surpluses in the future. This meant that adjustment and control measures would have to be much more drastic than they contemplated.

Meanwhile, farmers struggled to improve conditions through their own efforts. They increased their efficiency, enlarged their operations, and jealously guarded expenditures. Thousands quit farming altogether. Between 1920 and 1930 the number of farms declined by 159,695, and the average size rose from 148 to 157 acres. Prices for some farm commodities had become quite favorable by 1928, but the crushing burden of debt left over from the World War I period, heavy local taxes, and high costs of production caused trouble for even the larger and more efficient operators. By 1930 some 42.4 per cent of the farmers were tenants, compared with 37 per cent in 1919. A great deal about the economic and political situation of farmers can be seen in the following letter of a cotton-grower who lived near Mangum, Oklahoma. Writing to President Hoover in the fall of 1930, he said that he had mortgaged his cotton crop, six mules, and three cows in order to borrow $600 to meet expenses. He wrote:

> Cotton is selling now at six cents per pound and I can't pay out to save my life at the price. I voted for Coolidge expecting relief, he promised it. He said we would have to help ourselves, we made too much. You promised farm relief, but our products have gone lower than they have been since before the World War. . . . I am past fifty years old, and have voted for every Republican President in my time and the last few years have made me a pauper. But guess I will fall in the Republican ranks. But this year will wind me up as to farming. . . .[53]

At the end of the 1920's, agriculture still faced an economic and political dilemma. Farmers simply did not have the unity of interests, the organization, or political power to achieve their economic objectives. Moreover, they were handicapped in the struggle for a fair share of the national income by the individualistic nature of their industry. It was not until the entire nation sank into depression, and practically all parts of the economy turned to the federal government for help, that farmers got the assistance they believed was rightfully theirs. George N. Peek was a John the Baptist crying in the wilderness throughout the 1920's; Franklin D. Roosevelt was the Messiah.

[53] Garfield Todd to Herbert Hoover, Oct. 10, 1930, Secretary's File, USDA, National Archives.

Labor in Eclipse

MARK PERLMAN

I. THE QUESTION

UNIONS symbolize many things. They are protective organizations designed to stabilize employment and working
conditions. They are business organizations designed to
improve the economic, social, and possibly the political
fortunes of their members, their leaders, and various groups
in general society. They are reform organizations working
with an eye to specific or even general social problems.
They are even simple cluster organizations that serve personal and social purposes such as education, insurance, and
lobbying. And not infrequently, they are social-movement
organizations grasping for an ethos; and if they are able
to define it, they give such expression to that ethos as is
meaningful to their function, their members' aspirations,
and to the time.

It is common to note the decline of American unionism
in the 1920's. At the beginning they were (relatively)
large; at the end they were small. At the beginning they
expressed confidence (if not exactly assurance) ; at the
end, they were cautious. At the beginning they had many
plans and dreams; at the end they concentrated simply on
survival. Perhaps the topical word is frustration. By the

end of the 1920's they seemed barely able to hang on to their members, let alone raise the banner and march into battle.

But stress and adversity do have a very few advantageous products. As one catastrophe piles on another, the natural or rational thing for a unionist to do is to seek what he needs through some means other than unionism. By the same token, those who must deal with labor will develop other ways to organize and control their employees. If, at the end, there is something that adversity has not completely destroyed, the very hardiness of that something demands respect and investigation. Thus, this essay has, as one of its purposes, the indirect goal of identifying the hardy element of American unionism that survived the period of trial.

"The use of history," Emerson claimed, "is to give value to the present hour and its duty." Dean Inge put the point even more directly when he commented that "our chief interest in the past is as a guide to the future." For these reasons particularly, the opportunity to look at "labor in the eclipse" (by which was certainly meant "unionism in the eclipse" in the 1920's) is a chance to see the significance of the changes in the light afforded by today's events.

This essay is organized about several points. First, we look at the decline of unionism from 1920 to 1930 in quantitative terms. Second, we ask what caused the decline, not so much because we are interested in identifying the crucial individuals or the critical moments, but because we want to know what factors were operative. Third, we ask what unionism had come to mean to its members by the end of the period, or, was there an emergent ideology that seemed to stand out more and more as the other faces of unionism shriveled and were cast aside.

Finally, we consider the eclipse experience in the face of our own knowledge of what came later and what seem now to be the problems. What did the experience reveal about the American worker, the American employer, and their thoughts about each other? What did it tell us about the economics of unionism, about the role of economic growth, and even about its attitude toward itself?

II. The Decline

MEASUREMENT OF THE DECLINE

The vintage year of trade union membership was 1920, when there were 5,047,800 members. This number was almost twice as large as the membership figure of 1913 (2,716,300), and the ratio was even better than the 1915 figure (2,582,600). Membership had swelled because of war-time prosperity and because the federal government had encouraged unionism in war industries. It had grown because the 1916 Adamson Act, giving the railway unions legislatively directed concessions, suggested to many workers that unions could accomplish meaningful achievements.

The prosperity had continued throughout 1919, and the glow of success continued to suffuse the unions. Yet there were sophisticated observers who saw blight setting in. And they were right. They suggested that the easy wartime wage gains, the rapid upgrading of personnel, the generous resolution of grievance disputes, all characteristic of the war and postwar periods, were not likely to continue. They also believed that the antiunion crusades of many individual employers and such employer organizations as the National Metal Trades Association were likely to be resumed with a vigor that would astound the forgetful union rank-and-file.

Even when the informed observers mentioned that unionism's gains had been geographically concentrated in the larger cities, at railroad division centers and in the Northeast and Midwest, that the citadels of antiunionism had not been cracked, the analysis fell on deaf ears.

Professor Leo Wolman has done much of the authoritative work regarding the size of union membership. His
figures show that by the end of the period (1930) membership had fallen to 3.4 million; by 1933 it was to fall to
3.0 million. Table 1 gives Wolman's figures. Examination
of it suggests that the great lossses were between 1920

TABLE 1

REPORTED UNION MEMBERSHIP

YEAR	TOTAL WOLMAN*	IAM				
		ABSOLUTE		ANNUAL CHANGE		% Deviation of Wolman's Figures from Perlman's
		Wolman† (000)	Perlman‡ (000)	Wolman	Perlman	
1913	2,716.0	71.0	74.0	....	....	— 4.2%
1918	3,467.0	143.6	229.5	....	....	—37.8
1919	4,125.2	254.6	331.4	77.3%	14.4%	—23.2
1920	5,047.8	330.8	282.5	29.9	—14.8	+11.7
1921	4,781.3	273.6	206.9	—17.3	—26.8	+13.2
1922	4,027.4	180.9	148.3	—33.9	—28.3	+12.2
1923	3,622.0	76.4	104.7	—57.8	—30.4	—27.0
1924	3,536.1	71.7	79.6	— 6.2	—25.9	— 9.9
1925	3,519.4	71.4	72.0	— 0.4	— 9.5	— 0.8
1926	3,502.4	71.4	71.6	0	— 0.9	— 0.3
1927	3,546.5	72.3	71.0	+ 1.3	— 0.9	+ 1.0
1928	3,479.3	74.5	69.0	+ 3.0	— 2.8	+ 8.0
1929	3,442.6	77.0	71.6	+ 3.4	+ 3.8	+ 7.5
1930	3,392.8	78.0	69.4	+ 1.3	— 3.1	+12.4
1931	3,358.1	77.6	63.6	— 0.5	— 8.4	+22.0
1932	3,144.3	70.7	58.9	— 8.9	— 7.4	+20.0
1933	2,973.0	75.0	61.1	+ 6.1	+ 3.7	+22.7

* Wolman, *Ebb and Flow in Trade Unionism*, p. 16
† *Ibid*, p. 177
‡ Perlman, *The Machinists: A New Study in American Trade Unionism*, p. 206.

and 1924. Thereafter, there were either fairly small gains
or relatively small losses.

Wolman's figures are estimates made by a reasonably
skeptical mind, and although they suffer from some almost
obvious shortcomings, they are still the best we have available at this time. He got them from the AF of L or the
railway unions organizations, and the figures represented
the number that each union used as a basis for its representation claim (and tax) in the roof organization. Here
we run into the first difficulty. Unions paid a representation
tax to the AF of L (if they were affiliated). The amounts
they chose to pay were governed by several considerations,
only one of which was their actual membership. The other
factors included the state of the affiliate's treasury and
whether and how much the affiliate wanted to influence
AF of L policy.

Another problem of measuring union size is more thorny.
Union policies regarding definition of membership have
always varied widely. Some hold that an individual can be
counted for internal representation purposes by his local
only if he is currently dues-paying (usually delinquency of
three to six months is permitted in order to allow for the
inexperience of local treasurers); others are quite lax about
internal representation matters and base their estimates of
membership really on the size of per capita payments to
the national (international) organization that the local
makes. The impact of these differences in union policies
and practices makes estimates of the relative sizes of
different unions subject to irregular distortions.

Dr. Wolman's figures for 1920–21 represent a possible
overstatement of true membership numbers. That is, did
union leaders' confidence in their ability to hold onto their
wartime gains lead them to report inflated figures either
because they believed that the losses were temporary or

because they feared that employers would become more aggressive if convinced that unions were losing worker appeal?

A comparison of Dr. Wolman's figures for the International Association of Machinists and the figures that developed from my own research in the IAM's general secretary-treasurer's office records is interesting in this connection. Wolman's figures in Table 1 for 1920 exceed my own by almost 50,000 members (11.7 per cent). In 1923 his figures were 27 per cent too low. But as will also be gleaned from column 7 of Table 1, the relationships are not consistent in amount or even in direction. Annual changes in membership, columns 5 and 6 of Table 1, also illustrate how neither the quantities nor their signs (plus or minus) illustrate stability between Wolman's figures (those given to the AF of L) and my own (coming from the IAM's confidential files). Any survey of the IAM history of the period will suffice to explain how the pressures mentioned above influenced its payments to the AF of L (which Wolman relied upon). The decade was one of general retrenchment, although after 1926 (when a civil war within the IAM was resolved), there was a small regular increase through 1930. After 1930 the Great Depression served to cut union membership, even though the IAM (for one) permitted unemployed members to maintain their affiliation at the monthly cost of only ten cents.

IMPLICATIONS OF THE NUMERICAL DECLINE ON AF OF L POLICY

Not all sectors of American industry were identically affected by the loss in membership. Dr. Wolman's figures in Tables 2 and 3 show some interesting points.

Among the occupations only one, mail carriers, showed an increase in percentages of workers organized. Most showed substantial declines; the declines were relatively

small only in a very few. It is quite clear that the mail
carriers were not affected by the private-employer animus
against unionism.

TABLE 2

PERCENTAGE OF EMPLOYEES ORGANIZED
BY SELECTED OCCUPATION*
(HAVING OVER 100,000 EMPLOYEES)

OCCUPATION	1920		1930	
	Number (000)	Percentage Organized	Number (000)	Percentage Organized
Bakers, bakery workers.....	127	21.2	181	10.8
Barbers	183	23.3	261	19.0
Blacksmiths, forgemen, and hammermen	295	17.6	148	3.0
Brick & Stone masons......	139	50.0	170	49.4
Carpenters and joiners.....	892	40.5	934	32.3
Compositors, linotypers, etc..	140	46.4	184	39.6
Electrical workers	190[1]	6.1†	605	22.8
Locomotive engineers and firemen	201	....‡	168	96.4
Machinists, millwrights, and toolmakers	934	33.9	774	8.9
Mail carriers	(91)	(24.8)	121	75.3
Molders, founders, and casters	124	43.4	105	19.1
Painters, decorators, and paperhangers	344	29.1	557	18.7
Plumbers & gas and steam fitters	214	33.5	244	17.5
Stationary engineers	242	12.4	256	12.5
Stationary firemen	144	19.9	159	5.1
Schoolteachers	752	0.8	1,044	0.5
Teamsters & chauffeurs.....	926	11.9	1,273	7.7
Waiters and cooks..........	....	....	959	4.5

* Sources: 1920 data from Leo Wolman, *Growth of American Trade Unions 1880–1923* (New York: National Bureau of Economic Research, 1924), pp. 156–57; 1930 data from Leo Wolman, *Ebb and Flow*, pp. 222–23.
† Pertains only to telephone operators
‡ Data rejected as unreliable (i.e., well over 100 per cent unionized).

Table 3 tells much the same story. Generally, the percentage of workers in unions fell. The sole exception was among street railwaymen. Again, their activity has to be explained as a special phenomenon, namely, situations where the employer was occasionally a public authority or

TABLE 3

PRINCIPAL DIVISIONS OF INDUSTRY, PERCENTAGE OF
TRADE UNION ORGANIZATION AMONG EMPLOYEES

DIVISION OF INDUSTRY	1910	1920	1930
Mining, quarrying, crude petroleum and gas production, total	27.8%	39.6%	22.4%
Coal mining	36.8	50.9	33.0
Other mining	14.9	13.9	3.3
Quarrying	7.8	5.8	4.4
Crude petroleum and gas production..	....	24.4	1.0
Manufacturing and mechanical industries including construction, total..........	11.4	22.2	12.2
Transportation and communication			
Transportation, total	19.5	39.6	22.1
Motor and wagon transportation....	4.5	11.7	6.2
Steam railroads	27.6	53.2	38.6
Street railways	23.6	50.0	57.6
Water transportation	33.2	80.9	30.4
Communication, total	9.0	19.9	7.7
Service industries, total	2.0	4.9	3.2
Clerical service	1.7	8.6	5.4
Commercial service	0.8	1.0	0.3
Professional service	3.1	4.6	3.6
Domestic and personal service, recreation and amusement	2.2	4.2	3.0

Source: Lee Wolman, *Ebb and Flow*, p. 118.

a private corporation fearful of violence and the possibility of franchise cancellation.

Usually, the skilled were the bulk of union membership, but it is clear also that the bulk of skilled workers was generally (but not always) non-unionized.

Nor were all American unions affected in the same way by the general downswing. If we rely on Wolman's figures (and in the absence of any others, we must), the pattern

TABLE 4

RELATIVE IMPORTANCE IN ORGANIZED LABOR
OF PRINCIPAL GROUPS OF UNIONS BY
REPORTED SIZE OF MEMBERSHIP

	1910	1920	1929	1933
Mining, quarrying, and oil	12.8%	8.7%	7.9%	11.9%
Building and construction	21.4	17.6	26.7	19.6
Transportation and communication..	22.5	24.9	25.9	20.5
Clothing	4.6	7.4	6.3	11.3
Paper, printing, and bookbinding....	4.2	3.2	4.7	5.1
Metals, machinery, and shipbuilding..	9.2	17.0	6.1	6.1
Textiles	1.0	3.0	1.0	0.5
Food, liquor, and tobacco	5.7	3.6	1.9	1.9
Public Service	2.7	3.2	7.2	10.0
Total percentage identified	84.1	88.6	87.7	86.9

Source: Wolman, *Ebb and Flow*, pp. 87, 88, and 91.

is quite interesting and can be concluded from Table 4, which purports to show the strength of the various voices in the ranks of organized labor. What stands out is the relative growth of the building-trades unions' role and the relative stability of the transportation and communication industry (where increases in union membership on the rail-

roads were offset by growth of such non-union sectors as
the telephone- and automobile-connected operations).

On the whole, the AF of L was dominated by the building-
trades unions. Internecine conflict between them may occasionally have immobilized policy-making, but usually theirs
was the biggest voice. That voice was given its timbre both
by the relative size of its respective membership and by the
seniority rights its representatives enjoyed in the AF of L
executive council. The railway unions were not then (nor
are they now) AF of L affiliates. The largest metal-trades
union was the IAM, but until 1926, when its international
president (William A. Johnston, a "radical") was replaced,
the IAM had virtually no positive impact on AF of L policy.
The mineworkers union, led by the redoubtable John L.
Lewis, was isolated both because Lewis was unpopular and
because of organizational weakness. Basic steel and the
auto industries were unorganized, and consequently, they
had no voice in the AF of L council. The typographical
union was strong in the newspaper sector; yet its membership was not large. The lithographers were even relatively
more unionized but even smaller in absolute numbers.

What I have suggested, then, is that American unions
really had only three possible stable points of focus; the
railway operating brotherhoods (outside of the AF of L),
some parts of the printing industry, and the building trades.
The operating brotherhoods had difficulties with several
managements, but by 1926 had managed to get the managements to develop a program of governmental intervention
that assured unions basic continuity; they usually represented the vast majority of the eligible workers, although
certain large railroads were exceptions. The building trades
unions (which I identify as the citadel of the AF of L), on
the other hand, generally had to depend upon co-operation
of the many small contractors in the industry who could,
if they were willing, pass on the costs of wage benefits
(changes in the factor market) to their customers. Since

factor markets (where the agents of production were hired) and the product markets (where the products were sold) were both local, it was not hard to maintain union stability unless the local contractors were vehemently antiunion. Many of them were, it should quickly be added. But where a desire to work with the building-trades unions existed, the employers, whose earnings were often tied to a fraction of labor cost, profited and did not substitute machinery for labor. Yet in spite of this unique factor/product relationship, Wolman found that between 60 and 68 per cent of all carpenters were *not* union members during the period 1920–30. Seventy to almost 80 per cent of electrical workers were *not* union members. Other similar figures could be cited for the plumbers, painters, plasterers, and so forth. So the decibel level of the building-trades unions' voice in the AF of L councils was tempered by a general knowledge that they were not really in control of their own sub-industries.

THE PATTERN OF DECLINE

At the end of World War I union leaders were aware that their greatest strides had been made in industries where the sympathetic attitude of the Wilson administration had been economically most easily expressed. They had few illusions that the antiunionism of the pre-Wilson period on the part of many employers had really been changed during the war. Moreover, they were also aware that the swelled ranks of their organizations contained many workers who believed that unionism and union membership provided benefits without sacrifices.

Their decision was to try first to convert by talking what had been the antiunion citadels into a more agreeable attitude. The Wilson administration staged two postwar labor-management conferences. Both were unsuccessful, or as one writer summarized the record, were dominated by

Mr. Gompers' eloquence and Judge Gary's (U.S. Steel Corporation) silence.

Labor unions also tried to combine their resources to force recognition by U.S. Steel, a (if not *the*) bastion of the open shop. The "Great Steel Strike" of 1919 lacked many virtues as such operations go; principal among them was victory. And from that time on, it was apparent to any discerning mind that the prewar antiunion sentiment was once again going to be the rule (cf. Table 5).

In some of the areas where unionism had gained strength during the war, it became weak afterward simply because the sub-industries vanished; munitions manufacture is an excellent example. Yet many munitions firms turned to manufacture other things and did not vanish. Here the record shows frequently the impetuousness of the members, unaccustomed to the real sacrifices that maintaining a union requires, and the inability of the officers to restrain the demands *and remain in office*. The men demanded wage increases to compensate for the loss of overtime and forced the leadership to condone strikes when negotiations failed. The strikes also failed. They were expensive, exhausted the unions' pecuniary reserves, and left the employers angry, the members disillusioned and frustrated, and the leadership, if anything, discredited. Such was the story in the International Association of Machinists; it can be repeated if one looks in the records of many other unions. What needs to be added, of course, is that management in these firms lost whatever enthusiasm or patience it had for unions and pursued open-shop policies.

The AF of L leadership was only too well aware that the union movement lacked the money resources to win by fighting the employers. So, it proposed conciliation once again. At the 1923 Portland, Oregon, meeting of the AF of L executive council, the famous Portland Manifesto was issued. Its offer was for labor to eschew governmental intervention and thereby to reject even the barest trace of

TABLE 5

PRINCIPAL DEFEATS OF AMERICAN LABOR UNIONS, 1920–30

Year	Industry	Union	Issue	Remarks
1919	Steel	AF of L interunion group	Recognition	Union kept out of industry
1920 ff.	Coal	Mineworkers	Wage cuts, grievances, and recognition	Union generally pushed out of industry.
1921 ff.	Building trades in New York and Chicago	Building trades	Wages	Racketeering became an issue, and unions lost public confidence.
1921	Maritime	International Seamen's Union	Against wage cuts and three-watch system	Union pushed out of industry.
1921–22	Meatpacking	Meat Cutters and Butcher Workmen	Against wage cut	Union pushed out of industry.
1922	Railroad	Shopcraft Unions	Wage cuts and refusal of representatives to arbitrate	Unions generally defeated; rise of B&O plan.
1927	Textiles	Textile workers	Recognition and wages	Union largely kept out of industry.

socialism. The corpus of socialism had been rejected years before. The key phrase in the message was "The continuing clamor for extension of state regulatory powers under the guise of reform and deliverance from evil can but lead into greater confusion and more hopeless entanglements." Labor, so the Manifesto promised, would work directly with management, and a new era of peaceful industrial relations was promised. If the Manifesto represented the outstretched hand of organized labor, business did not rush to grab it. In fact, business ignored it.

Business even ignored the orders of the governmental board administering labor conditions in the one industry where the law seemed to require an appreciable willingness to abandon unilateral decision-making, i.e., the railroads. The shop-crafts unions were not happy with what the governmental officials ordered, and they were even more astounded when the railroads refused to comply. The courts upheld the railroads' right to intransigence, and the 1922 strike began. It ended in union defeat. Disaster was averted only because a very few of the railroads' managements were basically not antiunion; President Willard of the Baltimore and Ohio worked out with the shop crafts a compromise productivity program that several unions accepted as a means of salvaging something, if only continued recognition.

SOME LIMITED SUCCESSES

Some unions, particularly those in the garment industry, went more willingly up the road of joint responsibility for productivity improvements and cost control. Meyer Pearlstein, an officer of the International Ladies' Garment Workers' Union in the Cleveland market, was one who showed how unions could work sympathetically with employers in the face of the latter's problems. Few employers, however, offered the reverse.

One exception to that last generalization was the railroads, not to the shop-crafts unions but principally to the operating brotherhoods. The Transportation Act of 1920 had proved a failure; the railways dishonored it when it had served their immediate purpose to do so, and it brought them no peace when they needed it. Because of the work of a Chicago attorney, Donald Richberg, the two sides (union and management) did work out their differences and presented jointly a plan to Congress to reform the handling of labor disputes on the railroads and the allied transportation intermediaries. Congress passed the plan in 1926; it was strengthened by amendment in 1934 and continues to be the predominant legislation in the field. It looked most satisfactory in its first two decades of operation; since then, its results have seemed less and less attractive.

Unionism, as I have suggested, was on the defensive virtually everywhere. The railroads seemed to be the one exception, and they were only partially so.

III. THE DECLINE AS EXPLAINED

There is an understandable temptation to explain decline as a result of poor decisions, bad timing, or villainy of key individuals. Although it may be true that any or all of these factors may play a significant role at a critical moment in history, yielding to the temptation to explain everything by resort to one or more of these three factors seems to me to be erroneous. The decline of American union growth during the 1920's can be partly explained by these

factors, but there were other factors as well. In this section
I want both to suggest some of them and to consider how
they affected the others, mentioned earlier.

CAUSES ASSOCIATED WITH GENERAL ECONOMIC GROWTH

Different rates of growth of specific industries.—A principal problem of American union leaders was that the
industries in which they were relatively strong tended to
grow more slowly than those where they were relatively
weak. Thus growth worked against the interests of
unionism.

Another way to consider the same point is to note that
there were three major shifts in the characteristics and
composition of the labor force during the period. The
biggest, the shift from the farm to urban employment, will
be discussed later, but it worked against the interests of
unions. Second, the proportion of the labor force occupied
as manufacturing operatives or as white-collar and service
workers (types for which unionism had had previously
little or no appeal) grew significantly. And third, women
played an increasingly important role in the labor force,
and they, too, had rarely been enthusiastic in large numbers
about unionism.

Some older industries were replaced (harness-making by
auto repair shops or concert gardens by radios). Others
were destroyed by law (brewing and saloon-keeping). And
some were weakened simply by the force of new inventions:
local transit companies gave way to private automobiles.

On the whole, as I have suggested, industrial growth was
greatest in the areas where unionism was weak, and somewhat less in the areas where unionism was relatively strong.

Technology.—We have already suggested that new industries came into being and hurt established industries.

Behind this change was often a radical shift in technology that induced a demand for a completely new kind of labor. It was this change on the production line, a shift away from traditional to assembly-line production, rather than the AF of L's "inability to absorb industrial workers" that caused the problem. It is a frequently repeated error to claim that the AF of L consisted only of craft unions. In the first place, there were actually several industrial unions of the AF of L even before 1895; in the second place, very few of the predominantly craft unions were really completely craft-organized or even craft-dominated. And finally, craft unions had since 1895 rarely withstood the opportunity to take on production workers, if the latter could be incorporated without pain or expense. An example of this was the Machinists' absorption under its aegis of the production workers in "its plants."

Nonetheless, the AF of L's problem was aggravated during the 1920's when there was a general shift in American industry from the traditional methods of production to mass production or assembly-line organization. The product market, as Adam Smith might have observed, had grown, thus permitting (even encouraging) work specialization, with each employee performing a small number of carefully defined tasks. A vast output of product at a low unit cost resulted. What also resulted was each worker realizing that he was no longer a "wheel" (much less a "big wheel"); what he had become was a "cog". Whether this change actually destroys the self-esteem of a new worker is a topic open to debate. It seems that it did do much to destroy the self-perception of craftsmen accustomed to the previous patterns of production. The unions' traditional strength had been among craftsmen, and this shift had significance for American unions in a variety of ways; among these was the stepped-up recruitment of new types of workers, generally women or migrants from rural areas. These new types saw in the factory an opportunity to get good wages providing she or he did as he was told. These women workers and "green hands" competed quite successfully with older craftsmen, since, working with machinery and intense management supervision, they could produce products that sold widely for less than the craftsman-produced products. The traditional workers, whether they were truly craftsmen or only thought they were, had often offered to bring the women and green hands into their unions in order to police the job-opportunity area, but the latter were not to be fooled; they well understood that the unions' interest in them might result in improved rates of pay only in the short run. In the long run there would undoubtedly result fewer jobs for them. Union leaders seemed completely unable to break through to these new types of workers. Indeed, they were largely unable to do so until the mid-thirties when the combination of a harrowing depression experience plus federal government aid sufficed to do much that was necessary.

Different rates of regional growth.—What is true of industries is similarly true of regions. Textiles, as an industry, did not fare badly during the 1920's; but New England textiles did. Thus, in so far as the New England mills were the unionized sector of the industry, the textile union fared miserably. The Textile Worker's Union tried to organize the growing southern textile industry, but failed to do so. It failed because of the hostility of the southern employers, who often used the local police forces as veritable extensions of their own plant guards. Employer groups in one region after another, forced by competition even when they were not led by evangelical antiunionists, came to embrace the open-shop movement, often known as "The American Plan," the "Anti-boycott League," or simply the "Open Shop Movement." And as the change occurred, regions as well as industries became known for their antiunionism. Southern Ohio, Detroit, Los Angeles, the South, the Mountain States, all were bastions of this antiunionism; inasmuch as many were also economically expanding areas, the impact on the American union scene of their attitude was large and, over time, expanding. Even in large cities where unionism had strong roots, trouble mounted; public investigations showing racketeering in New York City and Chicago undermined public, and certainly worker, confidence in the building trades unions, to cite but one example.

The point here is not subtle, but nonetheless it is often missed. If the less-unionized areas where the antipathy toward unionism was strong grew much faster than the areas more favorable to unionism, then unionism after a time became *on the average* (throughout the nation, defined as comprising both areas) relatively weaker in terms of its total or over-all strength than it had been "in the beginning." It was just this kind of differential regional growth that did occur in the 1920's. Consequently, economic growth as such worked against union success during the decade.

CAUSES ASSOCIATED WITH EMPLOYER ATTITUDES

It is apparent that employers, on the whole, thought that they could operate their plants without unions. But it would be an error to conclude that employers had learned nothing from unions. Quite the contrary, many of them realized that unions played a positive and significant role in industrial government. However, these employers believed that there was a preferable substitute for a union playing this role, and they set about creating the substitute.

Unions, they reasoned, improved pay, reduced hours, provided grievance procedures, and offered an opportunity for potential leaders to identify themselves. They, as em-

ployers, would do these things, and even outdo the unions.
Pay increases would be generous rather than niggardly.
Hours would be voluntarily reduced. Personnel administrators would be hired both to prevent grievance situations
from developing (by not hiring proven trouble-makers)
and to smooth other obvious inequities where shop committees (without any outside "agitators"—like union representatives) suggested they existed. Finally, promotion
would be given to almost anyone; no more was the bright
worker to be passed over while a not-so-bright relative of
an executive was promoted.

The emphasis was on the appearance of consideration for
workers' feelings. Employers emphasized the necessity of
creating "an atmosphere of appreciation" for their employees. Promotions came easily, and in many instances
there was marked improvement in the communication of
workers' dissatisfactions. The personnel administration
movement emphasized the advantages of the carrot over
the stick, and many workers agreed to accept the pecuniary
and other enrichments at the expenses of loyalty to what
appeared to them to be an unneeded protective device, the
union. Employers agreed to pay high pay rates and to give
lavish benefits; it was useless for unions to point out that
the workers so rewarded only enjoyed a portion (and often
a small portion) of the outcome of increased productivity.

These employer policies are usually identified under the
rubric of "welfare capitalism." But they include the scientific management movement inspired by Frederick Winslow
Taylor and improved upon by H. L. Gantt and Frank and
Lillian Gilbreth. There is also the personnel management
movement, one phase of which was developed by Clarence
Hicks at the Colorado Fuel and Iron Company and later
at Standard Oil of New Jersey, and another phase coming
out of the work of Edward Filene in Boston. What these
plans had in common was a conviction that the functions

that unions performed could be better done by employers, and if they were done by employers, the employer was justified in all senses in keeping unions and unionists off of his property.

All of this, of course, is not to suggest that many employers really had to be convinced that they could perform union functions better than unions could. Many were initially just basically antiunion. Many of the things they offered were given simply and obviously with the intention of weaning workers' affections away from unions. Very often, the employer was not particularly subtle: unionized workers were immediately discharged, and non-unionized workers were made welcome. Any worker who advocated unions was considered a traitor to the firm and was not only discharged but frequently blacklisted in the industry.

One other point on this topic should be added. Rapid technological change, of which there was much, involves not only new machinery and new methods of assembly but also new methods of supervision. During the 1920's American industry, as will be mentioned again later, turned on a large scale to variant forms of Taylorism or "scientific management." One of the original tenets of scientific management was to deal with workers on an individual basis. But that alone was not enough to stop unionism. What scientific management usually preached, and what was even more injurious to the cause of unionism, was the insistence that management stood responsible for determination of worker methods; the individual workers were not to be consulted on how to do the job—they were to be told. Of course, over time some of the rougher edges of scientific management were smoothed off. But during the 1920's the technological change associated with mass production and scientific management worked to the detriment of unionism for no other reason than that the unionism available was a product of an earlier kind of industrial organization.

CAUSES ASSOCIATED WITH GOVERNMENT POLICY

There can be no question but what Wilson's New Freedom incorporated enough of the *élan vital* of the old Socialist-Populist reforms that socialism itself never recovered from the impact. In addition, the patriotic frenzy associated with World War I was channeled from anti-Kaiserism to anti-Bolshevik activity. In so far as the Lenin revolution kindled an interest on the part of American workers, the xenophobic charge of subversive radicalism had to be faced. The raids staged by Attorney-General A. Mitchell Palmer were not discriminating in their targets. Hard as union leaders tried to disassociate their organizations from those that Palmer and others categorized as subversive, the efforts rarely succeeded.

One can also point to other activities. Frequently, state governors used the National Guard to break strikes. Even the attorney-general of the United States under President Harding, Harry Daugherty, gratuitously injected the federal government into the ill-fated shop-crafts strike in 1922. His reasons for doing so can only be explained by his desire to help employers in their avowed battle for the open shop and even for the abolition of unions.

Later it became apparent that unions did need the positive support of governments. In so far as this is true, the lack of any positive prounion position on the part of national, state, or local governments (to say nothing of an antiunion position) explains well the relative loss of union influence during the period.

Another very important reason why unions declined relates to the difficulty union leaders had in reaching prospective members. There were legal factors that must be cited. The "yellow-dog contract" was upheld by the United States Supreme Court in a famous case involving

President John Mitchell of the United Mine Workers and the Hitchman Coal and Coke Company. That case stood as a precedent and increased the already great difficulty that unions invariably had when, in order to talk to "the men," private property had to be crossed.

A recent study has also suggested that there was a systematic attempt on the part of former President Taft to put conservative (even reactionary) lawyers on the bench while he was Chief Justice of the United States Supreme Court in the early 1920's. These men, if the charge is true, had a predilection for issuing injunctive orders against union organizers or leaders. The courts, never particularly sympathetic to unions, became markedly unsympathetic during the 1920's.

CAUSES ASSOCIATED WITH THE EFFECTIVENESS OF UNION OPERATIONS

The Economics of Decline.—Decision-making in unions is a topic all too frequently overlooked by students of labor history. There are many facets of it that should be analyzed: (1) Who makes the decisions? (2) What are the economic, political, social, ideological, and personality factors influencing the decision-maker? (3) What is the role of timing as apart from the substantive characteristics of the decision? (4) Who opposes the decision and why?

Generally, the rule is that in an atmosphere of optimism and expansion it is relatively hard to make a blunder, and that in an atmosphere of pessimism and contraction one can only choose the least bad (there being no really happy) outcome.

Unions are basically political organizations, where the popularity of the leader counts more, particularly in the short run, than his economic insights or moral excellence.

However, it is necessary for us to consider the basic economics of union policies as they developed in the 1920's. Essentially, union leaders have the traditional business concern, namely, how to balance expenditure with income over some type of time period—usually longer than a year and usually shorter than the typical seven to eight years of a business cycle. Union revenue comes mainly from dues and assessments. Unions spend for personnel to conduct union business (usually termed business agents or union representatives, but also lawyers, pickets, and members on strike). There are massive economies in scale vis-à-vis many of these personnel. One representative can handle a great many contracts, but only superficially as to details. If the union employs a large number of representatives in any specified area or industry, each can specialize on a few aspects of the union-employer or union-member relationships. Specialization here, as in Adam Smith's pin factory, creates true productive efficiency.

During the massive decline in membership during the 1920's, unions, on the whole, suffered diseconomies. As their memberships diminished, their revenues fell. As the revenues fell, they could afford fewer agents and, even then, often had to settle for less well-qualified individuals. The cost of organizing (in terms of gross and particularly net gains) became heavier and heavier. The economic burden of union business became larger for each member, i.e., a larger share of the cost of union representation had to be collected from each member. Bad as that might have been during the mid-1920's, when most businesses flourished, by the end of the period the revenue situation was desperate. What naturally had to result was the curtailment of services and a reduction in the amounts that unions could pay to each of its employees.

I believe that my own studies of the Machinists' experience yield relatively typical conclusions. The program least resistant to outside pressures was the business agent system. The organizing and the strike programs during the period involved served the majority of members' interests only indirectly, and were therefore cut back radically. The IAM had to make all labor rates (possibly, but not probably, labor costs) more uniform in an area and an industry because such a change would work to the advantage of the strongly unionized segments of the industries in which IAM members worked. To accomplish this result, employers had to be approached and potential members convinced. Whenever possible, strikes were avoided; but the IAM still occasionally had to authorize walkouts for organizing purposes.

As the depression deepened, per capita allocations fell,

TABLE 6

IAM GRAND LODGE EXPENDITURES ON
SELECTED SERVICE PROGRAMS

YEAR	PER CAPITA EXPENDITURES		
	Organizing	Business Agents	Strike Allocations
1921	$1.26	$0.68	4.33
1922	1.14	.82	4.19
1923	1.22	1.31	.80
1924	1.04	1.25	.59
1925	1.46	1.29	.37
1926	1.55	1.35	.27
1927	1.62	1.38	.19
1928	1.39	1.41	.86
1929	1.79	1.31	.44
1930	1.58	1.35	.13
1931	1.45	1.42	.18
1932	1.05	1.30	.11
1933	.76	1.01	.02

Source: M. Perlman, *The Machinists: A New Study in American Trade Unionism* pp. 220, 223.

and per capita resources fell even more. More and more members maintained a nominal tie to the union by buying "unemployment stamps," which was from the standpoint of the national organization a poor substitute for the usual per capita tax. In such an economic setting the union machinery worked inefficiently or not at all. The conclusion to be drawn is that the efficiency of union activity is worst in depression. It is often not very good during a period of decline, either. Inasmuch as American unions were depressed throughout much of the 1920's, their record is, in terms of how well they performed their usual functions, less than excellent.

Communication problems.—But the size-of-operation factor was not the only one. There were also some very significant social factors. The enactment of Prohibition closed the saloons, where previously a union organizer could contact a large number of men over a relatively short period of time. Before the close-down, if an organizer agreed to stand sponsor for a round of drinks, he usually could expect a reasonably friendly hearing, even if no outright decisions to join were made on the spot. The closing of the saloons, without any logical successor, made it much harder for union organizers to operate. Bad as that situation was, it was made more difficult by the wide sale of automobiles, such as Ford's Model T. Workers not only did not remain in the saloons where they could be contacted, but they didn't congregate at parks or picnic grounds as was the usual pattern for a summer's Sunday prior to the World War I. Instead, many workers packed picnic baskets, the children, and the wife and toured the countryside. Union organizers had a difficult job tracking them down, and when they found them at home, the organizer had frequently to contend with the on-the-spot expression of the wife's fears.

CAUSES PECULIAR TO LABOR LEADERSHIP

Other factors that must be included in this consideration of the causes of decline include several important points regarding union organizations themselves. The old leadership was unwilling to retire and be replaced by younger men. Retirement was not a common feature of life after World War I. Though it was true that the span of life had increased, people were generally not aware of the implications of this with regard to business, government, universities, or even unions. The traditional leadership became less energetic as the men themselves passed sixty-five years of age, to say nothing of the biblical allotment for life.

Yet in many unions there were vigorous struggles for leadership. These struggles occasionally resulted in the installation of younger officers. But invariably, these installations followed a bitter political fight, and did not end it. John L. Lewis retained control of his union (even though charges of fraud flew), but an entire sector of it became disaffected. In the case of the Machinist's Union, the traditional leader, J. J. O'Connell, was defeated by William A. Johnston in 1911. Johnston never managed to consolidate his victory and finally was himself forced out in 1925. His successor, A. O. Wharton, pursued a very cautious policy intended to consolidate the organization. Whereas Johnston had advocated large-scale organizing, Wharton advocated other policies intended to solidify support of the leadership within the organization at the expense of growth in numbers.

Many of the old-time Socialists, who had been active in unions, lost their zeal for unions as an aid to socialism primarily because union leadership disavowed socialism in order to escape the xenophobic charges mentioned earlier. Many of these socialist-radicals became bitter critics of unions and both believed and preached that the union leaders were traitors to the working class generally and to their own members specifically. In some instances it seems quite true that local union leaders were "bought out" by employers and that the local leaders sacrificed the economic interests of their members for bribes, either pecuniary or psychological. Moreover, the dangers of racketeering, always present where power can be concentrated, gripped several important unions in metropolitan areas.

CAUSES ASSOCIATED WITH INDIFFERENCE OR
HOSTILITY OF POTENTIAL MEMBERS

There is no reason to believe that all workers are predisposed in favor of union membership. The abstract or general reasons why some like it have been analyzed in one of my early books, *Labor Union Theories in America.* Professor Selig Perlman has synthesized in his *A Theory of the Labor Movement* what he calls the typical (or "Tom, Dick, and Harry") unionist mentality. Professor Frank Tannenbaum, to cite someone else with another view, also has some insights on the topic of the conservatism of unionists.

But the important point is that unionism does not appeal to a lot of individual workers. Some view it as a blanket smothering the fires of their personal career ambitions. They have faith in their own ability to deal man-to-man with their employers or their immediate representatives, the supervisors. Some feel that the unions' omnipresent shibboleths, "seniority" and that what is good for the group averages out for the good of the individual, may only be correct in theory; and these people do not care about seniority (they are young) or the group (they are industrial transients or casuals). For these individuals unionism *per se* is not good; and if the employer offers them a good personnel policy, they are more than just satisfied.

Other workers are anticapitalist. They look to real proletarian revolution or to widespread political reform. Unionism might appeal to them; American-type unionism generally did not. In the 1920's specifically, they rejected the capitalism-accepting, wage- or job-conscious-oriented unionism of the AF of L. Most of these embraced IWW-ism or the various organizations that the communists (including myriad splinter groups) spawned, baptized, buried, and resurrected. A few were Social Democrats who did not want to "bore from within" (the tactics of the Communists), but preferred to support the method of legal enactment. Hence they put their energies into lobbying for "security by legislation" rather than working for "security by collective agreement."

But if adversity has its problems, it also presents some opportunities. Lack of resources precludes opportunities to make big (or even many small) decisions; but the time not so spent can be diverted to some thinking. The 1920's was such a period. In the next section, we are concerned with the evaluation of the philosophy or theory of American unionism which emerged quite clearly during the decade 1922–32.

IV. The Eclipse As It Affected Refinement of Labor Union Theory

WHAT HAPPENED TO SOCIALISM

At the turn of the century and for about a decade thereafter there seemed to be developing a stable variety (as well as several unstable competitors to it) of socialism within the rather amorphous "labor movement," and even within its much better defined unit, the trade union movement. Max Hayes, representative of the Printers' Union, in one AF of L convention after another challenged Gompers' antisocialist leadership. Hayes's strength was never enough to topple Gompers or even to threaten his antisocialism. But it was enough to give hope that in the near future there lay the possibility of socialist success.

Hayes's socialism (and he was typical of those who influenced the unions most) was not intellectually rigorous. It merely emphasized the brotherhood of man (modified to exclude lesser breeds like the colored, orientals, and perhaps East Europeans) and stressed the necessity of industrial unionism.

The election of 1912 not only presented a breach in the ranks of the Republicans, it also presented a renovated Democratic party. Woodrow Wilson's platform included a great many social reform planks. When Wilson was elected, he believed (as did a majority of the Congress) that a mandate for reform had been given. The New Freedom (as his program was called) absorbed many of the ideas that the Socialists had espoused. Thus at the same time Wilson was adopting many of their objectives, he was giving erstwhile Socialists a reason to vote for one of the established parties. Many Socialists seized the opportunity; the obvious result was a decimation of the socialist ranks. Public interest in socialist reforms as such became weaker. And because of the pacifist sentiment found among many socialist leaders, America's growing participation in the Allies' military efforts intensified public antipathy toward them. It often spilled over to cover socialism, as well. And the unions, like most institutions in a democratic society, tended to absorb the prevailing sentiment (whenever possible). The shift served to confirm and even exacerbate the unions' support of Gompers' antisocialism.

But within the union movement there was also after World War I a change in attitude toward the brotherhood-

of-man concept as it applied to unionism. The great increases in unions' ranks during World War I occurred in
war industries (building, shipbuilding, munitions, and textiles) and on the railroads. The attempts to make these
increases permanent generally failed in the former group.
A bitter lesson was learned. Though there were advantages
to large numbers (emphasizing the brotherhood of man) in
a given union, the disadvantages often outweighed the
advantages. The sense of individual identity got lost, and
many of the new members were at best halfhearted in
their enthusiasm for unionism.

Moreover, the conditions that brought about the increase
in unionism—principally, prosperity—actually served as a
substitute for unionism in many industries. If an individual
was badly treated by his employer, he could get another
job easily; employers knew this was so and consequently
tended to be more considerate in their treatment of their
employees. If an employer refused a pay raise, another
employer, short of labor, usually agreed to the demand
unless the demands were beyond the pale. Employers knew
this to be true also, and consequently were relatively generous in granting pay raises. It is perhaps wise to add that
pay raises were often granted in a variety of ways; overtime was increased, rates were hiked, and upgrading of
positions (promotion) was easy. In any event, the sense
of solidarity of workers and the belief that unions should
be the sword of the working class did not come to be a
popular doctrine, and many of the worst social conditions
that might have been expected to drive workers to unionism
were alleviated by the impact of labor shortage. It was
a case where reform was accomplished by the action of
the market rather than by pressure group activity.

Yet there were those who felt these should have been
popular doctrines. The history of the left-wing labor movement during the 1920's is an interesting one. However, it
attracted little mass support, and if it has a colorful history,

much of the color is in the literature (principally in ballads) it produced.

THE BENEFIT/COST THEORY

There is another theory of unionism, quite "economics"-oriented. This theory, made somewhat popular by Sidney and Beatrice Webb in England and by Professor George E. Barnett in this country, suggests that unionism is an institution that workers embrace when it serves to achieve easily the ends they want. In so far as unions lead to pay raises, job security, and status, workers will embrace them. It is quite apparent that at the beginning of the 1920's, many workers thought that unions could bring them the things they wanted. They supported unions' programs in the steel industry, in the metal trades, in the transportation field, and elsewhere. However, it soon became apparent that unionism was far from successful in these areas. Better deals could be made if one dealt directly with a welfare-oriented employer (i.e., an employer believing in the American Plan). Thus it was logical for workers to reconsider the old question regarding the usefulness of union membership. Professor Barnett, for one, came to conclude that political enactment was a preferred means for providing economic and job security. In his well-known presidential address to the American Economics Association in 1932, "American Trade Unionism and Social Insurance," he rang the death knell of unionism.

THE "WISCONSIN" OR "COMMONS-PERLMAN" THEORY

A third theory of unionism argued that unions alone could provide the necessary job security that workers needed. It was this theory that was most thoroughly developed during the 1920's. If it was synthesized by an academician (as indeed it was), his synthesis was grasped eagerly by many of the leaders of American union organizations. When Miss Florence Thorne brought out Samuel Gompers' autobiography (she was certainly the editor, and probably the ghost writer), she used this theoretical formulation to explain Gompers' objectives. This theory, best known as the Wisconsin, or Commons-Perlman, theory, explains the development of unionism as an attempt by job-conscious workers to stabilize their "ownership" of work opportunity. The theory was developed in Professor Selig Perlman's *A Theory of the Labor Movement*. Miss Thorne incorporated the theme in her work.

What this brand of unionism suggested was that unionists were a special kind of people. They were essentially pessimistic about opportunity, but were willing to accept the mores of a capitalist society, provided that society would modify its concept of ownership to include not only land but jobs too, and then argued that unions had to exist to guarantee rights to jobs.

It would be an error to suggest that this "Wisconsin" theory of unionism was universally accepted. It would also be an error to suggest that all unions' activities could be explained by it. However, the years of disaster between 1920 and 1933 did serve to produce more evidence of the kind upon which Professor Perlman had based his analysis. Later, as conditions changed, other ideas of unionism appeared. The economic-benefit theory was certainly apparent during the New Deal renaissance of unionism. Yet the period of eclipse, namely, the 1920's, did produce something durable, if only a theoretical formulation.

Professor Robert F. Hoxie had earlier described American unions in his book *Trade Unionism in the United States* as principally "business-oriented." His notion of a business union was a union dominated by a passion for business-like efficiency. His use of the term was meant to suggest that American workers had become imbued with the businessman's mentality, which he thought particularistic rather than ideological. Unlike the Barnett kind of formulation, Hoxie's stressed the place of ideology. Thus, although in his view the typical American union was benefit/cost analysis-minded, this aspect or concern was subordinate to a more pervasive consideration: "What was its attitude toward general social reform?" General social reform, he concluded, did not "pay off," and for that reason American unions tended to eschew all opportunities to improve the lot of the public generally and of the working class in particular. There were those who claimed that the job-conscious theory of unionism was simply a rendering of the business-unionism that they believed Hoxie described. Such a conclusion was not warranted. The union theory that emerged attempted to explain not only why unions had to exist (according to the Hoxie formulation, if "no-union" paid off better than any union, then no-union would be used) but it also tried to explain the reason for the essential conservation of labor organizations—namely, the dependence upon the concept of property.

V. A RETROSPECTIVE VIEW

SUMMARY

At the outset we considered some of the many things unions can do. In brief, they serve as protective organizations, business organizations, reform organizations, simple cluster organizations with specific purposes, and the working face of a social movement. In two of the substantive

sections of this paper we have considered the record and
some of the reasons for it. Let us now very briefly ask
what, if anything, provided the services that unions sought
to furnish.

Protective aspects.—Though it is said frequently that in
the 1920's employees had to depend upon the employers'
favor, which is implicitly no protection at all, there were
then (as now) two elements that kept some (even many)
employers from being capricious and overbearing. The first
was custom; for if an employer is overly greedy or immoral,
his reputation suffers, and a poor reputation can in time
hurt him. The second was the market; for if an employer
drove away employees by his inconsiderateness, he had to
replace them with others who required training, and training cost him money. Thus, in principle, there were checks
on the employer. In the face of the record, however, these
checks were ineffective. So there was no substitute for the
relative job protection unions offered. In other countries
arbitration was used: it didn't usually work well, but it was
something. Here there was all but nothing. By the end of
the 1920's the idea of giving unionism a try (i.e., preventing
employers from throttling it) was gaining popularity.

Business aspects.—What raised wages and handled such
grievances as were processed was some employers' willingness to see that it was the ratio of value added to labor
cost that was important rather than simple hourly or
weekly rates of pay. America became an even higher wage
economy than it had been because the scientific-management
people and those influenced by the personnel administration
movement had relatively open minds regarding wages and
career opportunities. Although the economic position of
many workers did not suffer consequently, not as much can
be said for their political and social rights. Companies

dictated what products they had to buy (each major auto manufacturer's employees learned by violence what would happen if they bought a competitor's products). Companies dictated what friends they could not have (union sympathizers, for example). As for the efficiency of the system, morality and market allocation do work; but they work neither quickly nor thoroughly. However, if one considers how inefficient unions became (as suggested in the discussion), the difference between the abstract forces of conscience and cost (on the one hand) and external union representation (on the other) were not great. Neither worked well, and by the end of the period, it was clear that unions possibly might work economically, but only if given an opportunity to grow. Not all employers agreed, as was to be expected, but the trend was in the direction of trying unionism—if only to forestall more radical possibilities.

Reform organizations.—Although there have always been many socialist and other reform unions, they have not prospered in American soil, fertilized as it has been by federalism and only slightly irrigated by the traditional astringent interpretations of common-law precedence over liberal Constitutional construction. American unions operated best when the reforms they proffered were grafted on to the native vines of increased real wages and property rights, including the right to a job unless objective (rather than subjective) factors interfered. The good economic life was preached before all else. Utopian reform, such as it was, came via the political area—i.e., the New Freedom and the New Deal; and later, the Fair Deal, the New Frontier; and now, the Great Society. Unions have in the past (and even more recently of the last decade) offered themselves as pilots for the nation in its sailing forward (we always seem to claim to be progressing in that direction); but success has not been great, and general reform, as such, has been left to the political parties or interested minority groups. The unions' role in national politics has varied. In 1924 (as in 1964) unions "could" support only one candidate. But always the problem remains—are the gains possible in the face of victory worth the losses probable in the face of defeat. Throughout the 1920's the general weakness of the federal government in matters of economic policy tipped (or perhaps should have tipped) the balance in favor of non-participation in political contests. Such a conclusion was similarly warranted if state government was similarly weak in economic policy matters. The reverse conclusion may now be the case because of the expansion of state and federal policy-making activities. But even where governments are active economic-policy formulators, just how unions will line up is not always clear. Yet if unions have not been leaders, neither have they been the stalwart opposition. What union leadership has had to learn is how to steer a middle course—one that neither embraces unnecessary or too soon membership dividing reforms nor destroys the union's reputation for imaginative equity (where injustices previously existed).

Cluster aspects.—The lessons of unions performing non-job-connected functions for the members was not an easy one to master. Unions provided insurance benefits, ran banks, and tried to supplement their members educational opportunities. Each of these activities had program and business aspects. How popular the programs were, of course, depended in good part on the abilities of the leaders and the cultural and personal interests of the members. The business side, however, was influenced not only by these considerations but also by some purely objective elements. Insurance programs have a technical side involving an understanding of "area of risk," "nature of risk," abandonment or protection of "individual equity," and so forth. If unions learned anything in the 1920's, they learned that although these programs could be popular with the membership and although they could provide an otherwise unmet service, technical (even professional) competence was needed. If it was to be had, some control had to be taken from the normal leadership and given to specialists. In the 1920's this transfer was on a few occasions successful; witness the early attempts at union medical clinics and homes for superannuated members. In some instance, the attempts were signal failures; the IAM, to cite one union, failed in its effort to run job-creating firms, an actuarially sound insurance program, a bank, and even a buyers' co-operative.

Social movement aspects.—If the period of the 1920's showed anything clearly, it showed that there was no effective substitute for unionism as the voice of workers protecting their job- and wage-gains. Although it is true that many workers did not like the terms in which these gains were protected, it was clearly apparent that the solution lay in revising the unions' policies rather than in developing an alternative institution. The need for brevity does not permit elaboration of this point, but it can be found in much of the labor literature on scientific management, personnel administration, and in the partial "successor" to both, the "human relations" approach.

THE KEY PROBLEMS AT THE END OF THE PERIOD

Obviously the most important problem that faced American labor at the end of the 1920's and at the beginning of the New Deal was how to increase the size of its ranks. How could unions organize—should they be industrially oriented, should they be large, should they have national or local control, should they be job-conscious or economic reform–conscious? Disagreement about these factors led ultimately to the formation of the Committee for Industrial Organization.

A problem of almost equal importance was how to overcome employer hostility. In an effort to overcome it, unions came to accept the role of continual governmental intervention in labor disputes—even in purely jurisdictional matters. This idea was first proposed by Democratic Senator Robert Wagner of New York and later was administered, with both pro- and antiunion consequences, by the National Labor Relations Board. The extent to which unions and the labor movement should endorse one political instrument, the national Democratic party, was a natural result of unions relying on governmental intervention. In 1936 John L. Lewis, perhaps the most dynamic labor leader of the inter–World War period, abandoned his traditional membership in the Republican party to campaign not only for President Franklin D. Roosevelt but for the candidates whom Roosevelt had endorsed. Lewis' later disillusionment was swift and complete. But the question of unionism's political alliances remained afterwards.

There was also the problem of replacing old leadership. In many cases by this time, the old-timers were dead. A new generation appeared and replaced some of the stalwarts by then in the pantheon of unionism. Not all the new leaders were permanent, but many established great reputations and records. Tied up with, but by no means tied to, this problem of leadership was the evil of racketeering elements in many union organizations. It is not hard to cite an impressive list of unions that had fallen prey to greedy individuals who used the control of the labor market that unions could exercise for their own selfish ends.

Finally, there was the problem of accumulation of revenue. The unions ended the period with small treasuries, little hope for financial improvement in a situation, and levels of operation far below anything approaching optimal effectiveness. Left to their own pecuniary resources, it was probable that most unions could not achieve very rapid improvement in their situations. This is one of the reasons that explains the turning to governmental assistance.

SIGNIFICANCE OF THE 1920's FOR THE 1960's

There are several ways in which the 1920's throw light on the present labor movement. The recent variety of rates of growth and of technological change in the various sectors of American industry and the shift from unionized to non-unionized areas and industries in the country have great similarities to the situation in the 1920's. If the personnel management program of the Standard Oil Company was used then as a model for antiunionism, the unwillingness of the personnel of the International Business Machines Corporation to join unions today has some points of similarity. In the one case, of course, the management was patently antiunion; in the present case the management cannot be patently anything; but the fact is that the workers now have not elected to use unionism as the preferred method for representation of their interests.

Whereas earlier industry grew most rapidly in open-shop localities like Detroit, Cincinnati, or Los Angeles, today the most rapidly developing industrial areas are the Southeast and the "desert states" of Arizona and New Mexico. If the areas that grow fastest economically are antiunion, the portent for union growth is perforce discouraging.

If high real wages plus regular increases without union pressure made workers happy in the 1920's, the same formula seems to work today. Whereas once production operatives, greenhands and/or women workers, seemed hostile to unions and no formula for organizing them seemed to work, so today many white-collar workers remain hostile—or, at best, indifferent—toward unionism.

Once again, unions have the problem of maintaining adequate revenue. The costs of representation have climbed increasingly as dependence upon economists and lawyers, rather than lay bargainers, has increased. The membership of one union after another has shown a reluctance to increase union revenue; and where they have agreed to do so, the agreement has often been accompanied by marked dissatisfaction with the personnel who demanded it.

Again, we have problems of allegedly jaded leadership. In the past few years several key union leaders have lost control of their organizations. But the problem of leadership is not simply a question of its jaded quality. Federal and state legislation has worked to make unions "more democratic." Leaders are no longer able to restrain impetuous rank-and-file dissidents. If it was purportedly the intent of those who framed the legislation to make unions democratic, frequently that end was achieved at the cost of union stability.

It is on the philosophical, ideological, or theoretical level where unionism today best parallels unionism in the 1920's. Critics of the AF of L in the 1920's derided the philosophy that the leading AF of L unions embraced, namely, job-consciousness. Today, among the most active and successful unions are those that appear most to lack the reform idealism, so dear to the hearts of those who study the labor movement. The teamsters, the operating engineers, and even the dying railroad brotherhoods, all are principally concerned with their own parochial interests—principally, the protection of job rights. There are those who decry this emphasis and urge the labor movement to stand for something more. Nonetheless, a reading of the history of the

1920's suggests that it is this very parochialism that is the
hard core of the labor movement. At least, it is arguable
that that aspect has not changed.

SELECTED BIBLIOGRAPHY

BARNETT, GEORGE ERNEST, "American Trade Unionism and Social
    Insurance," *American Economic Review*, XXIII (1933), 1–15.
GALENSON, WALTER. *The CIO Challenge to the AFL: A History of the
    American Labor Movement*. Cambridge, Mass., 1960.
GOMPERS, SAMUEL. *Seventy Years of Life and Labor*. New York, 1925.
GREGORY, CHARLES O. *Labor and the Law*. New York, 1961.
HARRINGTON, MICHAEL, "The Retail Clerks," in *Studies of Compara-
    tive Union Governments for the Center for the Study of Democratic
    Institutions*, ed. WALTER GALENSON. New York, 1962.
HOLLAND, THOMAS, "The Labor Management Conferences." 1950.
    Privately circulated.
HOROWITZ, MORRIS A., "The Structure and Government of the Car-
    penters," in *Studies of Comparative Union Governments for the
    Center for the Study of Democratic Institutions*, ed. WALTER
    GALENSON. New York, 1962.
HOXIE, ROBERT F. *Trade Unionism in the United States*. New York,
    1917.
KAUFMAN, JACOB J. *Collective Bargaining in the Railroad Industry*.
    New York, 1954.
KRAMER, LEO, "Labor's Paradox: The American Federation of State,
    County, and Municipal Workers, AFL-CIO," in *Studies of Com-
    parative Union Governments for the Center for the Study of Demo-
    cratic Institutions*, ed. WALTER GALENSON. New York, 1962.
LECHT, LEONARD A. *Experience under Railway Labor Legislation*.
    New York, 1955.
MASON, ALPHEUS THOMAS. *William Howard Taft: Chief Justice*.
    New York, 1965.
PERLMAN, MARK, "Democracy in the International Association of
    Machinists," in *Studies of Comparative Union Governments for the
    Center for the Study of Democratic Institutions*, ed. WALTER
    GALENSON. New York, 1962.
———. *Judges in Industry: A Study of Labour Arbitration in Aus-
    tralia*. Carleton, Victoria, Australia, 1954.
———. *Labor Union Theories in America: Background and Develop-
    ment*. Evanston, Ill., 1958.
———. *The Machinists: A New Study in American Trade Unionism*.
    Cambridge, Mass., 1961.

PERLMAN, SELIG. *A Theory of the Labor Movement*. New York, 1949 printing.

———, and TAFT, PHILIP. *Labor Movements*. (*History of Labor Movements in the United States, 1862–1932*, Vol. IV.) New York, 1935.

RAYBACK, JOSEPH G. *A History of American Labor*. New York, 1959.

ROMER, SAM, "The International Brotherhood of Teamsters: Its Governmental Structure," in *Studies of Comparative Union Governments for the Center for the Study of Democratic Institutions*, ed. WALTER GALENSON. New York, 1962.

ROTHBAUM, MELVIN, "The Government of the Oil, Chemical, and Atomic Workers' Union," in *Studies of Comparative Union Governments for the Center for the Study of Democratic Institutions*, ed. WALTER GALENSON. New York, 1962.

SAYLES, LEONARD R., and STRAUSS, GEORGE. *The Local Union: Its Place in the Industrial Plant*. New York, 1953.

SEIDMAN, JOEL, "The Brotherhood of Railroad Trainmen: The Internal Political Life of a National Union," in *Studies of Comparative Union Governments for the Center for the Study of Democratic Institutions*, ed. WALTER GALENSON. New York, 1962.

STIEBER, JACK, "Governing the UAW," in *Studies of Comparative Union Governments for the Center for the Study of Democratic Institutions*, ed. WALTER GALENSON. New York, 1962.

TAFT, PHILIP. *The A.F. of L. from the Death of Gompers to the Merger*. New York, 1959.

———. *Organized Labor in American History*. New York, 1964.

———. *The Structure and Government of Labor Unions*. Cambridge, Mass., 1954.

TANNEBAUM, FRANK A., *A Philosophy of Labor*. New York, 1951.

ULMAN, LLOYD, "The Government of the Steel Workers' Union," in *Studies of Comparative Union Governments for the Center for the Study of Democratic Institutions*, ed. WALTER GALENSON. New York, 1962.

WITTE, EDWIN E. *The Government in Labor Disputes*. New York, 1932.

WOLMAN, LEO. *Ebb and Flow in Trade Unionism*. New York, 1936.

The Rise and Decline of Welfare Capitalism

DAVID BRODY

"OUR job primarily is to make steel," the veteran head of
Bethlehem Steel, Charles M. Schwab, told the American
Society of Mechanical Engineers in December, 1927, "but
it is being made under a system which must be justified.
If . . . this system does not enable men to live on an
increasingly higher plane, if it does not allow them to ful-
fill their desires and satisfy their reasonable wants, then
it is natural that the system itself should fail." Schwab's
qualification expressed the key idea of the welfare capitalism of the 1920's. "There has been a change—an enormous
change—and within the last ten years," a director of the
U.S. Chamber of Commerce said in 1929. "We are acquiring
a new industrial philosophy . . . that the fundamentals of
decent and right conduct laid down by Jesus of Nazareth
constitute the soundest, most sensible, and workable economic system possible to devise." Callousness toward labor
was receding into an unlamented past, enlightened businessmen assured themselves. "I have gone through some rather
dark chapters in American industry," recollected Schwab
(whose brilliant business career went back to the bloody
Homestead strike of 1892), "and it is a great joy to me

to realize that humanity rules American industrial life today." [1]

The new outlook promised to transform the country's labor relations. Many businessmen foresaw a future of "concord and plenty," noted the economist Herbert Feis. "The concord is based chiefly on the expectation of cooperation between workers and management. This cooperation is to show itself in a recognition of the worker's needs and desires. . . . The plenty is to be expected by improving industrial technic, by lessening waste, by the gains of common effort marked by goodwill." Concord and plenty seemed within easy reach in 1928. "Much of American industry," said Feis, "is convinced that it has worked out simple means and policies for insuring steady and peaceful advancement of industrial life." [2]

That confidence proved remarkably ill-founded. Within a few years of the stock market crash in 1929, welfare capitalism collapsed in a burst of unexampled industrial strife. From the bitter 1930's there issued a system of labor relations that rested on collective bargaining, not the benevolence of management. In failure, welfare capitalism has been too casually dismissed. Flawed as it was, it seriously attempted to minimize the human problems raised by industrialization. And it was a more vital phenomenon than it has seemed from the modern perspective.

Welfare capitalism had its roots in the emergence of big business in the early years of the twentieth century. Even before, of course, employers had interested themselves in the welfare of their workmen. Pullman had built his model town near Chicago; Proctor and Gamble had started its profit-sharing plan in 1886; others had provided pensions

[1] *Law and Labor*, X (January, 1928), 19; *Nation's Business*, XVII (April, 1929), 89, XVIII (February, 1930), 198.

[2] Herbert Feis, *Labor Relations* (New York, 1928), p. 2.

and encouraged mutual benefit societies. During the indus-trializing era, however, benevolence had been limited by frantic expansion and ruthless competition. As these moder-ated, leeway opened for a departure from the hard labor policy ruled by the cost books and the labor supply. The larger scale of business enterprise increased the resources available to progressive employers. Above all, the consolida-tion movement demanded more enlightened treatment of labor. Less imperative as progressivism subsided, that rationale remained binding in the 1920's.

Consolidationists such as J. P. Morgan intended to restore order to industries "demoralized" by cutthroat competition. Their strategy was, first, to combine warring firms into a giant concern and, second, through its dominance impose "fair" competition on the industry. Business should strive for "cooperation" and "stability," not ruinous warfare. This course would be profitable; it would also be right. Weighty ethics justified fair competition. "From the standpoint of morality," Elbert H. Gary said, the steel industry had been "a shame and a disgrace" before the formation of U.S. Steel. Spreading beyond its original advocates, the doctrine of co-operation dominated American business in the 1920's. "Even the most skeptical devotees of the old dog-eat-dog theory of business competition," said a Chamber of Com-merce officer in 1929, "are being gradually persuaded from the sheer, cold pressure of the facts that . . . war doesn't pay in this complicated world of ours." Owen D. Young of General Electric added: "The Golden Rule supplies all that a man of business needs." [3]

This mode of thinking inevitably influenced labor policy. Morgan's partner George W. Perkins told the National Civic Federation in 1909 that if capital and consumers bene-fited from co-operation, so must the laborer. Ethical stan-

[3] David Brody, *Steelworkers in America* (Cambridge, Mass., 1960), p. 149; *Nation's Business*, XVII (April, 1929), 90, 162.

dards applied to labor relations no less than to business relations, and would foster the same harmony of interests. "Ruinous competition, the crushing of small companies by monopolistic rivals . . . continual strikes—there is no avoiding the punishment such plagues entail," pronounced a business spokesman in 1929. "Take strikes, for example. . . . Ten years ago it was considered part of the game to cut wages without compunction. . . . Today wage-cutting is the last thing any employer wants to resort to. He knows, from experience, that it is wrong and that it makes trouble." Modern business acted on the "sincere belief that the interests of the employer and employee are mutual and at bottom identical." [4]

These precepts depended on new industrial leadership for implementation. As business grew large and complex, control passed into the hands of lawyers and financial men, and they felt the broader obligation of their high places in the great corporations. General Electric's Owen Young, himself a lawyer, argued that "the new idea in management . . . sprang largely from the fact that lawyers were advanced to high managerial posts. . . . If there is one thing that a lawyer is taught, it is knowledge of trusteeship and the sacredness of that position. Very soon we saw rising a notion that managers were no longer attorneys for stockholders; they were becoming trustees of an institution." [5] And labor was among the beneficiaries of that trusteeship.

Public opinion served as a spur to action. Big-business leaders anxiously cultivated national favor. That alone, Elbert Gary and George Perkins had argued during the progressive era, might protect the vulnerable industrial

[4] Robert Ozanne, "A Century of Labor-Management Relations" (in press), chap. vi, p. 4; *Nation's Business*, XVII (April, 1929), 90.

[5] *Nation's Business*, XVII (April, 1929), 164; also, *Fortune*, II (February, 1931), 110 ff.; (March 1931), 94.

giants from antitrust action. The legal dangers lifted, if they did not disappear, in the 1920's. But the sensitivity to public opinion remained, sustained as it was by the conviction of business leaders that theirs was an occupation clothed with the public interest. Earlier, muckraking attacks and government investigations had prodded major reforms in industry. U.S. Steel had finally abolished the seven-day week in 1911 after the crusading first vice-president, W. B. Dickson, had threatened to resign and take the fight outside the corporation.[6] Public relations became less stormy, but not less important, in the 1920's. Businessmen remained sensitive to the country's rising expectations for the treatment of labor. What wants do employees "have a right to see satisfied as far as conditions permit?" asked Charles Schwab in 1927. He listed, among other things, steady employment, a voice in the regulation of their working conditions, opportunity to save and to own stock, and some guarantee of security in old age.[7] This was the measure of national sentiment in the 1920's, so far as business was able to read it.

Initially, welfare work lacked any functional relationship to industrial operations. Businessmen did assert in a vague sort of way that they earned a profitable return on the investment in welfare work, especially in the creation of loyalty and contentment. But the moving impulse came from other than ordinary business considerations. Welfare, said Elbert Gary, was "a simple duty that industry owes to labor"; it was an obligation of the "big, broad employers of labor."[8] In the 1920's that paternal reasoning was joined by a second, more hardheaded argument: employee well-being would increase efficiency.

[6] W. B. Dickson to Sidney Hillman, Jan. 27, 1940, Sidney Hillman Papers, Amalgamated Clothing Workers of America.

[7] *Law and Labor*, X (January, 1928), 14.

[8] Brody, *Steelworkers in America*, p. 117.

When Gerard Swope became president of General Electric in 1922, he spread the new gospel in a series of informal talks to plant officials. Their job, he told Schenectady foremen, was threefold: "production, costs, and relations with men. Usually . . . we think of the first two only . . . The last thing our foremen will remember is the relations with the men who work for him [sic] and that, as a matter of fact, is the most important consideration that bears on the results that any executive is to achieve." The workers were not mere adjuncts to the machinery. "And there isn't anything men expect more than fair treatment; they must be dealt with not only fairly and justly, but with sympathy." Swope pressed home his conclusion: "You are constantly being hounded to increase your output. One of the ways of getting it is to have your men cooperate with you." [9]

The intellectual sources for this line of business thinking derived from the scientific-management movement of Frederick W. Taylor and the emerging science of industrial psychology. Many businessmen, too, had seen for themselves during the war how patriotic fervor had stimulated production. Far from being a fixed item, the workers' performance seemed a prime point for improving industrial operations. The war also drew attention to the neglected problem of labor turnover. For the first time, many employers realized the high costs of replacing experienced men. In the 1920's a low turnover rate became an index of the effectiveness of a company's labor program. The handling of labor assumed major importance for American industrialists. Successful management, Charles Schwab told an engineering audience, "is going to depend more and more upon the management of men than upon the organization of machines and other problems of practical engineering." The future engineer would find little challenge in the technical

[9] Quoted, Gerard Swope MSS., Oral History Collection, Columbia University.

problems. "Industry's most important task in this day of large-scale production is management of men on a human basis." [10]

The industrial-relations movement attempted to place labor policy on a rational, organized basis. It created a professional group of managers (led by such men as Clarence J. Hicks and Arthur H. Young) and experts (such as Industrial Relations Counselors, Inc.) backed by college courses, research and publications, and professional organizations. It centralized labor administration in industrial-relations departments and defined an area of decision-making in the business enterprise comparable to sales, production, and finance. It rationalized the recruitment and handling of labor—above all, by stripping the foremen of the power to hire and fire. The National Industrial Conference Board emphasized "that the individual employee represents a definite investment, and that sound business principles require that the investment be capably handled in order that it may yield a fair return." Advanced businessmen saw personnel administration "not as frill or as a vehicle for the fulfillment of philanthropic impulses, but as a natural and business-like method of dealing with the . . . work force to secure results." [11]

Yet the new approach also buttressed the welfare philosophy of big business. For labor's well-being contributed to industrial-relations objectives. Modern economic life created insecurities among employees, acknowledged E. K. Hall of the American Telephone and Telegraph Company. "We must find ways and means to help our workers get their worries out of their minds so they can get on the job 'rarin to go'." Freed from anxiety over accident and illness, old age and unemployment, men would work with a better

[10] *Law and Labor*, X (January, 1928), 19.
[11] National Industrial Conference Board, *Industrial Relations* (New York, 1931), p. 104.

will. Many employers placed great faith in stock ownership. "A sense of proprietorship affords a powerful incentive to arouse interest in the performance of work," pronounced Charles Schwab.[12] And the contributing firm would reap further dividends in the form of low turnover, high quality recruits, and labor peace. Welfare found a business justification in the approach of personnel management and, since responsibility for such activities fell to industrial-relations departments, also an administrative home.

The welfare plans proliferating in the 1920's were designed to meet the major hazards of modern industrial life. One group of schemes encouraged men to acquire property. Some companies operated savings plans, often with the incentive of high interest rates or special bonuses. Many firms adopted home-ownership plans that provided employees with various kinds of technical assistance and financial aid. Stock-purchasing plans exerted special appeal in the prosperous 1920's. Most schemes offered special inducements for employees to purchase and hold company stock. By 1927, 800,000 employees had invested over a billion dollars in 315 companies. Other programs protected workmen and their families from losses resulting from accident, illness, old age, and death. Group insurance valued at $7.5 billion covered close to six million workers in 1928. More than 350 companies gave pensions in 1929. Besides granting these basic protections, companies improved plant conditions and safety, provided medical services and visiting nurses, underwrote sports and classes, distributed land for gardening, and assisted workmen in all manner of personal problems. The costs mounted high for major firms: U.S. Steel's expenditures averaged over ten million dollars a year in the 1920's. Such generosity, Judge Gary assured the stockholders in 1923, was justifiable "because it is the

[12] *Law and Labor*, X (January, 1928), 15; XI (March, 1929), 53.

way men ought to be treated, and secondly because it pays to treat men in that way." [13]

Both considerations supported employee representation, the most celebrated labor experiment of the decade. The idea had found a small group of advocates before World War I, above all, in John D. Rockefeller, Jr. Overcoming a personal aversion to public speaking, the younger Rockefeller lectured across the country about the plan introduced at his Colorado Fuel and Iron Company in the aftermath of a bloody miners' strike in 1913-14. World War I provided a more forceful influence. Urgently desiring labor peace, many employers became willing to experiment. Simultaneously, the government itself adopted a variant of the idea; in over 125 cases, the War Labor Board ordered companies to instal shop committees. Although many smaller firms discarded the arrangement immediately after the Armistice, other employers were won over by employee representation, and a number of large companies—among them, Youngstown Sheet and Tube, International Harvester, Goodyear Tire and Rubber, Yale and Towne Manufacturing—voluntarily introduced the plan in 1918–19. Following the postwar labor crisis, 317 companies joined the movement by which workmen elected fellow workers to speak for them before management.[14]

More than any other item in the program of welfare capitalism, employee representation was couched in idealistic terms. When a strike broke out at the Consolidated Coal Company in Pennsylvania in 1922, the younger Rockefeller, a major stockholder, publicly denounced the operators for denying "their employees all voice and share in determining their working conditions and any adequate

[13] United States Steel Corporation, *Stockholders' Meeting, April 16, 1923*, p. 9.

[14] National Industrial Conference Board, *Collective Bargaining Through Employee Representation* (New York, 1933), pp. 12–13.

machinery for the uncovering and adjustment of grievances. The day has passed when such a position can justly be maintained . . . in a country like ours. . . . Employees in every industrial unit [have] a fundamental right, namely, the right to representation in the determination of those matters which affect their own interests." Rockefeller's letter, widely praised, reflected the thinking of enlightened employers. "Industrial democracy" had become a national byword during World War I. "It would be strange if the people of the United States came out of the War [for democracy in government] without any concessions to the growing demand for more democracy in industry," a steel trade journal had remarked.[15] Bitterly divided on other matters, the President's Industrial Conference of October, 1919, was practically unanimous on the proposition that workingmen had a right to representation with employers. Employee representation continued to exert a powerful idealistic appeal throughout the 1920's.

The practical benefits received equal emphasis. The National Industrial Conference Board reported that executives found plant morale significantly improved by employee representation.

> It facilitates quick adaptation to special or changing conditions, when passive opposition would bring about the failure of plans. It engenders greater interest in the job, which leads to the offering of suggestions as to short cuts and improvements that in the aggregate may mean considerable savings for the company. The works council provides a meeting place, where management and working force can consider calmly, on the basis of accurate information rather than rumor, their respective positions and problems. . . . Beyond the settlement of grievances and, better, their prevention, is the broader and more constructive accomplishment

[15] Raymond B. Fosdick, *John D. Rockefeller, Jr.* (New York, 1956), p. 179; Brody, *Steelworkers in America*, pp. 225–26.

of employee representation in welding together management and working force into a single, cohesive productive unit.

Charles Schwab observed that Bethlehem's plan stimulated "constructive cooperation along the lines of increased efficiency, elimination of waste, and improved methods and quality and quantity of products. Along with this development has come a growth in morale and in sympathy and understanding between employees and officials." They had "an unobstructed channel through which their unity of interest may be promoted." [16]

Employee representation seemed the capstone of welfare capitalism. Its other activities advanced the material well-being and personal security of workingmen. Employee representation catered to their minds. "The men must be dealt with as thinking men," Gerard Swope lectured to General Electric foremen. Through the representation plans, workers could air their grievances and ideas, and in turn receive an understanding of the policies of their employer. Employee representation, concluded a labor expert, rested on "the citizenship theory of labor relations." [17]

Employers of the 1920's explained their labor policies as an expression of right conduct and as an effort to raise industrial efficiency. But welfare capitalism meant more than that. It sustained a power system that granted management full authority over the terms of employment. Contemporary labor programs, remarked the economist Sumner H. Slichter in 1929, "are one of the most ambitious social experiments of the age, because they aim, among other things, to counteract the effect of modern technique

[16] National Industrial Conference Board, *Collective Bargaining*, pp. 39–40; *Law and Labor*, X (January, 1928), 16.

[17] Swope MSS., Columbia Oral History Collection; Irving Bernstein, *The Lean Years* (Boston, 1960), p. 170.

upon the mind of the worker, to prevent him from becoming class conscious and from organizing trade unions." This aim, more than considerations of humanity or efficiency, measured the ultimate value of welfare capitalism to most of its advocates.[18]

When labor trouble threatened U.S. Steel in 1919, Judge Gary told the subsidiary presidents that "there is nothing we can do better than to be sure we are liberal in the protection of our workmen and their families. . . . Make the Steel Corporation a good place for them to work and live." Fair and generous treatment would leave "no just ground for criticism on the part of those who are connected with the movement of unrest." Some benefits—housing, pensions, profit-sharing—gave men a specific stake in their jobs. But the entire welfare effort presumably made workers loyal and contented. Union leaders objected to such programs, a steel trade journal observed, "because they realized that it was resulting in non-union men becoming more closely attached to the companies by which they were employed." Personnel methods reduced the resentments common to industrial employment, guaranteeing equitable, orderly treatment to all and opportunity for training and advancement to the talented few. "To the best men," remarked Sumner Slichter, "promotion thus becomes a more certain and often an easier way of gaining higher wages than is trade union action." [19]

Employee representation hit most directly at the union threat. In 1918 and 1919 many plans had been inaugurated to ward off an imminent danger of unionization. Immediately after the Armistice, Arthur H. Young warned the

[18] Sumner Slichter, "The Current Labor Policies of American Industries," *Quarterly Journal of Economics*, XXXXII (May, 1929) 432.

[19] United States Steel Corporation, *Meeting of Subsidiary Presidents, January 21, 1919*, pp. 21, 24, 33; *Iron Age*, June 3, 1920, p

head of International Harvester that labor agitation was sure to intensify and grow more radical. He urged the quick adoption of his employee representation plan, not only to safeguard the company's open shop, but to serve as an example for American industry generally.[20] In other cases where labor organization had established itself—for instance, the plants of the major meat packers and the shop crafts of the railroads—employee representation replaced the unions as they were driven out. Clearly, the plans were intended to substitute for trade unions, both as a justification to the public and an answer to employee needs.

The difference was, however, fundamental. The American Federation of Labor, said an industry spokesman in 1922, "requires a continuing state of war and the constant preaching of enmity and antagonism." The representation plans, on the other hand, "aimed at the settlement of disputes on a basis of fairness and justice rather than by argument of superior force." Labor and management had mutual, not antagonistic, interests; and employee representation would harmonize those interests. Differing in structure and even in emphasis, the plans agreed on one point: they did not diminish the power of employers. "Management must lead and must accept the responsibility for carrying on industry," said C. B. Seger of the U.S. Rubber Company in discussing employee representation. "Intelligent leadership, however, presupposes that leaders will keep those whom they lead informed and it presupposes also that they will be responsive to those led." Charles Schwab was privately blunt about Bethlehem's widely praised plan: "I will not permit myself to be in a position

---

1608; Slichter, "The Current Labor Policies of American Industries," p. 433.

[20] Ozanne, "A Century of Labor-Management Relations," chap. vii, p. 7.

of having labor dictate to management." [21] Assuredly, labor did not under the company unionism of the 1920's.

At the time, welfare capitalism seemed a sure guarantee of the existing power system of American industry. In 1929 a business spokesman announced that "the end of the strike era is in sight, and that the next five years will see an unparalleled gain in relationships of mutual understanding and good will between employee and employer." [22] The prediction could not have been more mistaken. Those five years marked the start of the industrial upheaval that would end in a powerful union movement and collective bargaining in American industry. Welfare capitalism would leave a permanent legacy of benefits to workingmen and of methods of personnel administration. But the welfare approach did not prevent American labor from turning against its employers and demanding a share of power in the industrial system. And that was the essential test of the labor relations of the 1920's.

Why did welfare capitalism fail? Historians have inclined to see an inherent weakness. Irving Bernstein, for instance, concludes: "The central purpose of welfare capitalism— avoidance of trade unionism—could be achieved only temporarily because paternalism failed to come to grips with the main issue: a system of shop government placed in a climate of political democracy and universal suffrage." [23] Bernstein's thought is congenial to the modern view that deplores the arbitrary control of one man by another and that favors the division of private power among different voluntary groups. It is comforting to think that welfare

[21] *Iron Age*, February 2, 1922, p. 356; S. A. Lewisohn and P. T. Moon (eds.), "Constructive Experiments in Industrial Cooperation," *Proceedings of the Academy of Political Science*, IX (January, 1922), 545–46; A. Pound and S. T. Moore (eds.), *They Told Barron* (New York, 1930).

[22] *Nation's Business*, XVII (April, 1929), 90.

[23] Bernstein, *The Lean Years*, p. 187.

capitalism never was a success, never persuaded the American workingman that he was best off as a ward of his employer, and never could have survived once wage earners received a free choice protected from employer retaliation.

Welfare capitalism certainly fell short of the glowing claims of the speechmakers. It was, for one thing, a minority phenomenon, limited to the large prosperous firms. The methods of personnel management, widely introduced on a piecemeal basis, frequently lacked the essential administrative base. One survey found industrial-relations departments in 6.5 per cent of companies employing under 500 men, in approximately 30 per cent of companies employing between 500 and 2,000 men, and in 50 per cent of those over 2,000. The National Industrial Conference Board reported that some welfare activities were quite general by the end of the decade: over 90 per cent of surveyed companies operated safety programs; 70 per cent, group insurance; 60 per cent, mutual aid associations. But only one out of five provided formal pension plans, stock-purchase opportunities, savings and loan facilities. There was similarly a gap between promise and fulfilment on the matter of wages. As the decade passed, employers gave increasing public support to the "doctrine of high wages" (which "not only promote the happiness and welfare of the men, and secure their cooperation . . . but also create purchasing power"). Yet even its strongest advocates failed to translate the idea into action: wages rose insignificantly during the 1920's.[24] Nor was there much improvement in hours. The most notable improvement occurred when the steel industry ended the twelve-hour day in 1923. The reform actually was forced on Judge Gary and his colleagues by the pres-

[24] National Industrial Conference Board, *Effect of Depression on Industrial Relations Programs* (New York, 1934), pp. 4–10; National Industrial Conference Board, *Industrial Relations*, p. 54; American Iron and Steel Institute, *Yearbook* (1929), p. 33.

sure of public criticism and ultimately the intervention of President Harding himself. On the whole, welfare capitalists lacked sympathy for shorter hours, and the work week did not shrink appreciably during the 1920's.

Nor was there reason to assume the perfect operation of the labor policies of the New Era. Employee representation was a case in point. At the end of the decade the plan covered a million and a half men, over 80 per cent of them in some forty companies with work forces of over 5,000. So the resources and professional help available to such large corporations gave a maximum chance for the success of employee representation. Yet rarely, if ever, did a meaningful relationship result. Herbert Feis sat in on one meeting of the Employees Conference Committee at the Ivorydale plant of Proctor and Gamble. No important matters were discussed; no enthusiasm was displayed on either side. "The men are not reaching forward through the plan," concluded Feis; "the management has ceased to attempt any great achievement through it." [25] At International Harvester and Colorado Fuel and Iron, promising plans likewise disappointed their creators.[26] Significantly, all three had suffered from an identical betrayal during the severe recession of 1921: wage cuts made either arbitrarily or with the barest pretense of consultation. Other plans, begun hastily and with obvious ulterior purposes, had even less likelihood of achieving any real vitality.

The shortcomings of welfare capitalism, both of commission and execution, surely stemmed principally from the monopoly of power in employer hands. To that extent, modern historians correctly assessed welfare capitalism. Yet its failings did not mean an inability to ward off trade

25 Feis, *Labor Relations*, pp. 60, 71.

26 B. Selekman and M. Van Kleeck, *Employes' Representation in Coal Mines* (New York, 1924), pp. 247 ff.; Ozanne, "A Century of Labor-Management Relations," chap. vii.

unionism. Organized labor failed to recover the million and a half members lost during the severe postwar recession, not to speak of making further gains. "Our trade union movement is going through most extraordinary experiences," John Frey of the AF of L wrote in bafflement in 1929. "After business began to revive in 1923, it was found that the former method of organizing did not bring the same results as in previous years. . . . New methods in organizing are required to meet the new conditions in industry which confronts [sic] us." [27] The newest, for which no improved technique would answer, was the evident satisfaction of the American workingman with the status quo.

Professor Sumner H. Slichter, a most sensible observer, considered organized labor's weakness as less the result of welfare benefits and industrial-relations techniques than of prevailing employment conditions. The 1920's was a time of steady work in a weak labor market, stable wages, and declining living costs, hence, modestly rising real earnings.[28] Those facts rendered less important the flaws of welfare capitalism, but not the concept itself. For welfare capitalism exceeded the sum of its formal activities. It was also an idea: that management accepted an obligation for the well-being of labor. For that, employers claimed credit in the 1920's, and they had some reason for so doing. The labor surplus and slipping living costs actually permitted wage-cutting, had employers so inclined. Charles Schwab told the American Iron and Steel Institute in May, 1929, that the industry's prosperity must be shared with labor: "We cannot give consideration to the responsibilities that repose upon us in the steel industry without being impressed with a real sense of trusteeship . . . for hundreds of thou-

[27] John Frey to F. Kummer, June 28, 1929, Frey Papers, Library of Congress.
[28] Slichter, "The Current Labor Policies of American Industries," pp. 428, 430.

sands of families. We seek to prosper ourselves but above
all we seek the welfare, progress and happiness of our
people. (Applause)" That meant, he said, good wages and
steady employment.[29]

By every measure and every account, American workers
wanted nothing more. "The desire for steady employment
and higher earnings became more dominant in the minds
of the workers than the feeling for industrial freedom and
independence," admitted the labor expert Lewis Lorwin.
In their study of "Middletown," the Lynds found that
employed workingmen were content to enjoy their Fords
and radios, indifferent to the concentration of power in
their employers. Management made the same assessment.
Ralph Easley of the National Civic Federation confidentially
polled railroad officials in 1929, seven years after the bitter
shopmen's strike: did they detect any revival of interest in
trade unionism? Almost invariably (one railroader feared
communist influence on his immigrant workmen) the
answer came back a confident "no." "In our shops since
the strike of 1922, the shop employees have been very
quiet," wrote the head of the Chicago and Alton Railroad.
"The employee is much happier than under the old [union]
regime. . . . He is a peaceful worker and a peaceful citizen
and he wants to be let alone in that state." The statistics
confirmed the absence of discontent. Industrial disputes in
1929 involved less than a sixth the number of men in 1916,
and a seventeenth the number in the peak year of 1919.
The turnover rate had fallen sharply, according to one 1927
survey running at 40 per cent of the prewar rate.

To Sumner Slichter in 1929, paternalism unhappily
seemed permanent; he could only suggest that it might
better issue from the government than from private industry. The Frenchman André Siegfried arrived at a similar

[29] American Iron and Steel Institute, *Yearbook* (1929), pp. 33,
36–37.

conclusion: "The American workman, when he realizes that society assures him a comfortable income, is ready to accept the existing organization of industry." [30] But industry actually could not assure that income. Therein lay the fatal weakness—really akin to the sin of pride—of welfare capitalism. Employers confidently undertook responsibility for labor's well-being. That obligation, in the end, they could not fulfil.

"Why work so hard for Mr. Hoover?" General Electric's Owen Young chided a political friend in September, 1928. "Not that he does not deserve it from his supporters, but perhaps he does not need it. . . . Worse things can happen to a country than to have a liberal party in power once in a while. . . . In any event, nothing very serious is going to happen to this country however the election turns out." [31] Few employers of labor had any greater premonition of economic disaster. Fewer still made any provision to meet it.

A month after the stock market crash in October, 1929, President Hoover called into conference Myron Taylor, Owen Young, Walter Teagle, Alfred P. Sloan, Pierre du Pont, and others of the nation's chief industrialists. Confiding his fear that a general depression would follow the Wall Street crisis, the President asked for a pledge against wage-cutting. The magnates readily assented. Actually, they needed no White House prodding. Wage maintenance had become part of the doctrine of "stability" that governed the oligopolistic industries. On October 25, in the midst of the crash, Schwab had lectured the Iron and Steel Institute

[30] Bernstein, *The Lean Years*, p. 81; William G. Baird to Ralph Easley, Nov. 9, 1929, National Civic Federation Papers, New York Public Library; National Industrial Conference Board, *Industrial Relations*, p. 14; Slichter, "The Current Labor Policies of American Industries," pp. 429, 435.

[31] Owen D. Young to Marie M. Meloney, Sept. 22, 1928, Meloney Papers, Columbia University Library.

on the importance of maintaining prices. Noting that the industry's prosperity was unimpaired, Schwab joked about "the smile of uncertainty upon the faces of a few who thought last week they were very rich and not quite so rich this week (laughter)." But, he insisted, steel had a "stabilized price structure" based on manufacturing cost plus a fair rate of return on the investment. The big steel firms would not permit "slight but inevitable fluctuations" to "disturb the healthy balance that has been established." That necessarily held for wages as well. "If you are going to sell your goods and eliminate your profit and expect to get it out of the men in the mills you are greatly mistaken," U.S. Steel's J. A. Farrell sternly admonished those who proposed wage cuts six months after the crash. "Wages are not coming down in the steel industry. . . . We all know that just as soon as they go down, if they should, Mr. Customer gets it." [32] Wage maintenance offered manifold benefits—humanitarian, psychological, and economic (everyone was saying that consumption was the key to prosperity). But the policy depended on industry determination to hold the price line.

Employment lacked that amenability to managerial control. As demand fell, production had to fall and diminish the amount of available work. The depression hit the automobile and textile industries first, and then spread with increasing force to other sectors of the economy. In past depressions American industry had simply laid off excess men, and so did most smaller firms now. But the proponents of welfare capitalism undertook instead to spread the work. The rubber companies of Akron went on a six-hour day, and many companies shifted to eight hours at this time. The other approach was to rotate men. Using this method,

[32] Herbert Hoover, *Memoirs. The Great Depression, 1929–1941* (New York, 1952), pp. 43–44; American Iron and Steel Institute, *Yearbook* (1929), pp. 294–97, 302, (1930), p. 42.

U.S. Steel maintained on its payroll 94 per cent of its regular work force in January, 1931, while it was operating below half of capacity. The roll of participating companies included probably every important exponent of welfare capitalism, and then enlisted others as work-spreading gained the support of the National Association of Manufacturers, the Chamber of Commerce, and the Hoover administration, and even spawned an organized Share-The-Work movement. By 1933, according to a Commerce Department survey, work-sharing existed among four-fifths of the country's firms and created one-fourth of all part-time jobs.[33]

Share-the-work naturally evoked the criticism that it merely made "the poor keep the poor." (Only the rarest of employers—the Kellogg Company, for instance—raised wages to compensate for the shorter hours.) Candid employers admitted some validity to the charge. But did critics offer them a better alternative? Nor did the plan let business off so easily. A Bethlehem Steel executive listed the ways by which the company supplemented work-sharing— extending credit, making work, advancing pensions, providing garden plots and seed. And rotation of men had operational drawbacks. "If low cost production and profits were the only aim of industry in these days," said a business spokesman citing a typical case, "it would probably be wiser for the employer . . . to keep 400 on at full time and let the least efficient 200 join the ranks of the wholly unemployed." That ruthless practice of past depressions "has given way to the belief that the human relationship must be considered." Paul W. Litchfield of Goodyear Tire and Rubber believed "the six hour day in most cases economically unsound . . . but as the rubber industry in Akron employs the bulk of workers engaged in industry, we are

[33] Bernstein, *The Lean Years,* p. 479.

permitting social conditions to govern, and are trying to keep as many men at work as possible." Work-sharing in steel seemed to Charles Schwab an "unexampled achievement of management." "Our men have stuck by us through thick and thin, and we are going to stick by them." [34]

To some extent, that responsibility covered even the growing jobless numbers. In October, 1930, Schwab urged steel men to care "in part at least for those people who have no jobs at all. . . . We should . . . take such measures as may be necessary to carry everybody connected with the steel industry safely through this depression." And Myron Taylor added inspirationally:

> . . . We shall have to dig deep into our purses to assist those in want . . . and who must be cared for. They shall be cared for! And we of this great industry will do generously our part in this great service to humanity! . . . Let it be said of the steel industry that none of its men is called upon to ask help of the public. (Applause)

When the journalist William Hard visited Braddock, Pennsylvania, the following winter, he found U.S. Steel's Edgar Thomson Works dispensing groceries to 753 jobless employees, and other local plants were doing likewise. "Unemployment is a responsibility of industry very largely," asserted a trade journal, "and industry should take the leadership in practical plans for relief." Some companies established loan funds (General Electric, Goodyear, International Harvester, Standard Oil of New Jersey) or direct relief (Westinghouse) for unemployed men. Some attempted to select workmen for layoffs on a basis of need and number of dependents. Finally, a few firms (Standard Oil

[34] *Nation's Business*, XIX (February, 1931), 132, XX (October, 1932), 32; Bernstein, *The Lean Years*, p. 478; American Iron and Steel Institute, *Yearbook* (1931), p. 32; *Steel*, Dec. 12, 1932, p. 13.

of New Jersey, American Rolling Mill, Hills Brothers) acknowledged a kind of property interest of long-term employees in their jobs and made money settlements to those who were permanently let go.[35]

Meanwhile, management thinking turned to reform. Even in the 1920's, unemployment had drawn attention, partly because the problem existed in the midst of prosperity and partly because welfare capitalism emphasized the working-man's security. Concrete results were negligible—only a bare thirteen companies started formal programs—but the main lines of private action did emerge. One avenue was an annual guarantee of work. In 1923 Proctor and Gamble began its famous plan of promising the employees of its soap-making plants 48 weeks of full-time work a year. Essentially, this approach challenged management to stabilize operations and devise labor practices that would regularize employment. Lacking Proctor and Gamble's unusually stable market, few employers dared make guarantees, but General Electric, Bethlehem Steel, and other firms did begin to improve job stability. Once the depression struck, the practices that had been developed were utilized generally in the work-sharing programs—for example, shifting men from department to department, cutting hiring to a minimum, building up inventories, and doing maintenance work in slack seasons. The other approach was to create an insurance reserve, either by the employer alone or on a matching basis with employees, that would provide unemployment benefits of limited duration. General Electric and fourteen Rochester firms, led by Eastman Kodak, introduced insurance plans during the first two depression years. The U.S. Chamber of Commerce thought

[35] American Iron and Steel Institute, *Yearbook* (1930), pp. 252, 545; *Nation's Business*, XIX (February, 1931), 128, 129, XX (November, 1932), 55; *Electrical World*, Nov. 7, 1931, p. 815; William Hard, "Ingots and Doles," *Survey*, Feb. 1, 1932, pp. 453–58.

these confirmed the expectation "that long-range provisions for unemployment are becoming a settled policy of American industry." [36]

Before the National Electrical Manufacturers Association on September 16, 1931, Gerard Swope of General Electric outlined the most ambitious private program to emerge from the crisis. His plan incorporated the two basic concepts of employment stabilization and insurance reserves (as well as provisions for workmen's compensation, life insurance, and pensions), but placed them in an unprecedentedly broad context. Swope argued that the individual firm could not cope effectively with unemployment. Stabilization required industry regulation through trade associations, which in turn would come under some form of federal supervision. Unemployment insurance had to be on a national basis so that coverage continued when a man moved from job to job. The Swope plan evoked tremendous interest, partly because of its controversial features. Whatever the dangers (especially regarding the proto-NRA aspects) he found in the proposals, the enlightened businessman could not question that Swope was right in his urgent concern over unemployment. "That this condition has ever been present in such periods detracts nothing from its wrongness. That industry must . . . first ameliorate and untimately eliminate it, must be the reaction of every one who gives thought to what is taking place." [37]

[36] *Nation's Business,* XVIII (August, 1930), 11, XIX (April, 1931), 104. The General Electric plan is printed in *Law and Labor,* XII (August, 1930), 180–83. On the Proctor and Gamble plan, see Feis, *Labor Relations,* chap. x; H. Corey, "Solving the Unemployment Riddle," *Nation's Business,* XIX (April, 1931), 17–20.

[37] The Swope plan is printed in *Law and Labor,* XII (October, 1931), 217–22. See also Swope MSS., Columbia Oral History Collection; David Loth, *Swope of G. E.* (New York, 1958), chap. xiv; J. G. Frederick (ed.), *The Swope Plan: Details, Criticisms, Analysis* (New York, 1931).

Had the economy revived at about the time of Swope's speech, welfare capitalism would have emerged unscathed, indeed, enhanced. "This depression has shown us the extent to which business has become conscious of and accepted its social responsibility," wrote a Chamber of Commerce editorialist. "The employer has learned that labor is something more than a commodity to be bought in the cheapest market." Schwab expected that "the far-sighted and sound handling of our workers' interests . . . will stand out in bold relief as the major accomplishment of American management today." By maintaining wages and spreading employment, business was "keeping our economic organization in orderly condition and guarantee[d] the purchasing power of the public as soon as better conditions resume." But conditions did not improve. They worsened, and worsened further, and bumped down finally to an unimagined bottom of economic stagnation. In 1932 auto production dropped to 20 per cent of capacity, steel to an incredible 15 per cent. After that terrible year, Schwab considered it "a tribute to the sagacity and flexibility" of the steel industry's leaders "that most of our companies are still intact, despite huge losses." [38] But, in the meanwhile, welfare capitalism fell into an irredeemable shambles.

The economic collapse cut short any progress toward private unemployment insurance. Few companies followed the lead of General Electric and the Rochester firms. To supplement General Electric's relief and insurance efforts, Gerard Swope persuaded his board of directors to approve a guarantee of minimum earnings of half of normal for six months beginning November, 1931. "Conditions became steadily worse," Swope recalled years later, "and I was very thankful when the six months guarantee period ended.

[38] *Nation's Business*, XX (February, 1932), 14–15; American Iron and Steel Institute, *Yearbook* (1933), p. 28.

. . . This was too ambitious a plan for any one company to undertake." Nor did he have greater success with his grand plan for industry-wide action. He continued to urge it, but, as he himself admitted, "not with very much effect." While industry remained inactive, sentiment was building up for public unemployment insurance; it gained the support of Governor Roosevelt of New York, was intensively studied by the Ohio Commission on Unemployment Insurance, and even passed into law in Wisconsin. The threat renewed employer support for private insurance in the early months of 1933. Admitting past error, Schwab asserted that the steel industry would build up reserves "to help meet any future depression." If laws were passed, they "should be so drawn as not to affect or impair voluntary activity by forward-looking industries. Otherwise, years of progress and voluntary action would be endangered." [39] As a seasoned businessman, Schwab should have known better than to try to trade on exhausted credit.

The immediate antidepression measures likewise were failing. The wage line could not be held. In steel, prices moved downward despite pleas from industry leaders. The fact was that money was still to be made by a few tightly run, ruthlessly competitive firms like E. T. Weir's National Steel Corporation. And wage rates crept downward as part of the hard game. "I think it is a pretty cheap sort of business when . . . men . . . are working three days a week, and then cut that three days a week another 10 percent," exploded James Farrell of U.S. Steel before the Steel Institute in May, 1931. "Now that . . . is not the idea of the old line companies." But they were soon obliged to follow. When U.S. Steel announced a 10 per cent cut effec-

[39] Swope MSS, Columbia Oral History Collection; American Iron and Steel Institute, *Yearbook* (1933), p. 36. On the position of the U.S. Chamber of Commerce, see *Nation's Business*, XXI (January, 1933), 70, XXI (June, 1933), 18. Swope himself came down on the side of public insurance.

tive October 1, 1931, wage maintenance died in steel and in industry generally. A few weeks later, Ford abandoned the seven-dollar day (which he had dramatically proclaimed after Hoover's request for wage stability in November, 1929) and by November, 1932, had the minimum down to four dollars. Average hourly earning for production workers in manufacturing fell from 51.5 cents in 1931 to 44.2 cents in 1933. The collapse of wage maintenance revealed the vulnerability of even the largest companies. "None of us can escape the inexorable law of the balance sheet," Schwab admitted after the first reduction in steel. And after a second in the spring of 1932: "We cannot escape the dictates of present conditions." [40]

Corporate helplessness had far worse consequences on employment. Work sharing became hardly more than a cruel joke as production dried up. In the winter of 1931, Goodyear employees were working eighteen hours a week. Bethlehem Steel acknowledged in December, 1931, that under its rotation plan men "are now getting [less] than is necessary to sustain life." How much worse, then, was their plight ten months later when the company's operations had fallen nearly 90 per cent while its regular work force remained only 15 per cent below normal. Meanwhile, the jobless rolls lengthened alarmingly, especially in the heavy industries. General Motors had employed an average of 233,286 people in 1929, 116,152 in 1932; Ford, 101,069 in 1929, 56,277 in 1932. In some desolated industrial towns the employed worker became a rarity; the steel center of Donora, Pennsylvania, had 277 persons at work out of a population of 13,900 in March, 1932. Total jobless estimates crept upward from eight million in July, 1931, to a sickening fifteen million in March, 1933—one out of three in the

[40] "National Steel: A Phenomenon," *Fortune*, IV (June, 1932), 90 ff; American Iron and Steel Institute, *Yearbook* (1931), pp. 41, 342, (1932), 33–34; A. Nevins and F. E. Hill, *Ford: Expansion and Challenge, 1915–33* (New York, 1957), p. 588.

labor force. Long before that, the industrial giants had ceased to talk about caring for their own, or even assuming that the relief task could be handled with local resources. In June, 1932, leading Chicagoans pleaded for federal relief for their city: the list included the heads of Armour, Wilson, Cudahy, International Harvester, Inland Steel, Bendix, and U.S. Gypsum.[41]

The situation was actually worse than it seemed in Chicago and New York corporation offices. Industrial workers were not only losing hope in the promise of welfare capitalism; many were turning actively and fiercely against their employers. They did so despite the patently good intentions of management, for depression had the peculiar effect of spoiling even honest acts of benevolence. The fact was not obvious at a distance; close up, it could be perceived here and there.

In May, 1931, 2,000 workers spontaneously walked out of a rubber-goods plant in Mishawaka, Indiana, not far from South Bend. The strike bewildered the management. The plant boasted a long history of good labor relations, first as an independent firm, and now under the control of U.S. Rubber, a leading practitioner of welfare capitalism. When hard times hit the plant in 1930, the company did its best to protect the workers through work sharing. "As a matter of fact," wrote Cyrus S. Ching, the able labor relations chief of U.S. Rubber, "I believe that in our efforts to take care of the situation, the management may have gone further than what might have been considered good business." Making a significant concession to end the strike, the open-shop company agreed to discuss grievances with an employees' committee elected by secret ballot. "We have the extreme desire for the good will of the employees," a

[41] *Nation's Business,* XX (November, 1932), 55; Bernstein, *The Lean Years,* pp. 317, 467; Nevins and Hill, *Ford: Expansion and Challenge,* pp. 587, 588; *Law and Labor,* XIV (January, 1932), 6.

company representative assured the committee in September. At that very time a federal conciliator found the workers dangerously angry. Three of "the best type men" warned him that they would kill the superintendent if they went out again. Notwithstanding its best efforts, the company found itself sitting on a powder keg.

The depression had demanded a series of hard decisions. "With a greatly reduced amount of business, and with a reduction in the price of goods, the need of economies has been felt more . . . than ever before," explained the superintendent. To meet the competition, he embarked on a drastic program, introducing new equipment and methods, cutting wages an average 10 per cent after a survey of day and piece rates, hiring an industrial engineer to start time-and-motion studies, and, finally, replacing straight piece work with a task-and-bonus system that figured earnings on an hourly basis plus a bonus for all production over the standard fixed by time-and-motion methods. The new pay plan set off the rebellion in May. The strikers charged that the standards were impossibly high, that many operatives had to start an hour or two early to make an efficiency rating that would keep them on the payroll, and that earnings fell from a third to a half for much more work. Company explanations and assurances did not lessen the hatred for "the heartless and inhuman task and bonus system."

The management faced a bitter predicament. The same depression conditions that called forth humane efforts demanded tough business decisions. What was worse, the benevolent acts themselves compounded the trouble. Had they cut the ranks ruthlessly so as to give the remaining employees full-time work, the Mishawaka managers felt that the task-and-bonus system would have operated better and raised no opposition. Other well-meant measures likewise backfired. The company had agreed to shift some men

to female jobs to keep them employed, and soon came under
attack for paying them starvation wages.

> If we had laid those fellows off at the time we didn't have any of
> their kind of shoes . . . and built up production on Savoys with
> women, we would have saved ourselves a lot of grief. . . . And
> we didn't have the work for them, we could have laid them off
> legitimately.

When the managers reacted accordingly, they merely
worsened matters. The second period of labor trouble in
September, 1931, occurred because of the layoff of fifty
men. The employees' committee requested further work
spreading and, when the company refused on the ground
that it wanted to assure enough work for the remaining
workers over the winter, accused the management of discriminating against union men. In May, 1932, the firm had
to cut wages another 15 per cent, but provided that the
reduction would operate only in those weeks when the
men had four days' work, doubtless hoping thereby to
guarantee a living wage. The men, however, believed it
was a trick. Certain that the company would schedule
just enough work to effectuate the reduction, they went on
strike again. So the bitterness deepened despite company
pleas that "we haven't been selfish. We have perfectly
clean hands." [42]

This was the terrible irony: just as everything redounded
to management's credit in the 1920's, so now to its discredit
in the depression. The Mishawaka experience was excep-
tional only because it resulted in overt trouble (possibly

[42] Correspondence, memoranda, and minutes of company meetings
with employees' committee, 1931–32, Mishawaka plant, United States
Rubber Company, Federal Mediation and Conciliation Service Files,
Record Group 174, National Archives.

because of the presence of both union and communist sentiment). But everywhere resentment was silently building up. When it burst out under the aegis of the New Deal, the air would be filled with charges of inhuman speed-up, of ruthless rate-cutting, of rampant favoritism in the disposition of work. These grievances sharpened the edge of bitterness over the basic complaint of unemployment.

On January 18, 1933, Goodyear's Paul W. Litchfield confided to a friend "that we are drifting like a rudderless ship into waters that become more and more dangerous. There appears to be an increasing spirit of dejection and disillusionment wherever one goes. . . . The problem of unemployment is underlying all other ills." Litchfield's despair was partly over the intense suffering during the terrible third winter of depression. (The most poignant expression of that sympathy was an earlier outburst by Daniel Willard of the Baltimore and Ohio Railroad that, if he were a jobless worker with a family, he would steal before he would starve.) But it sprang also from a sense of helplessness in the face of economic collapse. Welfare capitalism rested ultimately on confidence in the strength of the big employers. They guaranteed the well-being of their workmen, and in turn received loyalty and good will. But the guarantee had not been honored. In August, 1932, Myron Taylor observed that U.S. Steel was "at the mercy of business just like any other corporation." [43] It was a fatal admission for welfare capitalism.

Careful observers read the signs of the future. In June, 1929, a shrewd labor official, John Frey, had felt defeated

[43] P. W. Litchfield to Ralph Easley, Jan. 18, 1933, National Civic Federation Papers; *Fortune*, XIII (June, 1936), 113. The formal welfare activities tended to be cut back to only a surprisingly small extent; the stock purchase plans, naturally enough, were the chief victims of the depression. National Industrial Conference Board, *Effect of Depression on Industrial Relations Programs, passim.*

by "the development of cunningly devised schemes for making trade unionism difficult to maintain." Two years of depression changed Frey's mind about union prospects.

> So many workmen here have been lulled to sleep by the company union, the welfare plans, the social organizations fostered by the employer . . . that they had come to look upon the employer as their protector, and had believed vigorous trade union organization unnecessary for their welfare. When we get out of this depression . . . I look forward to a period of organizing much more extensive than any we have ever had except during the period of the war. . . .
> The fact is that the existing banking and industrial system has failed to justify the faith people have placed in them. The capitalist system as represented by these institutions have [sic] broken down for the time being.[44]

But Frey, no more than anyone else, estimated the force with which labor would shortly turn on American industry.

Welfare capitalism could not sustain the management-dominated system of labor relations. The failure was not inherent in its functioning in the 1920's, but sprang rather from an extraordinary turn in the business cycle. American industrial relations might well have continued on its paternalistic course but for the Great Depression.

[44] John Frey to F. Kummer, June 28, 1929, July 28, Oct. 29, 1931, Frey Papers.

The Fundamentalist Defense of the Faith

PAUL A. CARTER

THE shambling defense attorney, hooking a thumb under one of his red galluses, with his other hand held out for inspection a lump of rock laden with fossil shells. When he claimed, in defiance of Bible chronology, that the relic was ten million years old, the large, balding, wide-mouthed man on the witness stand retorted: "It is better to trust in the Rock of Ages than to know the ages of the rocks"; and an excited member of the audience shouted, "Amen!" But the year was not 1925, and this scene was not played in Dayton, Tennessee, during the trial of *Tennessee* v. *John Thomas Scopes*. It took place thirty years later when a land-grant college troupe put on the play *Inherit the Wind,* with its re-creation of the celebrated "monkey trial," in their home state; and that "Amen!", however disconcertingly it might have rung in the ear of an eastern intellectual liberal, was also "audience involvement" to a degree that the theater aims at but does not always attain.[1]

[1] I have this incident from a member of the show's cast. A slightly different account, making it "the road company" of the Broadway play to which this happened, is in Richard Hofstadter, *Anti-Intellectualism in American Life* (New York, 1963), p. 129.

Equally spontaneous was a line uttered on a fine spring day in 1962 by one of a group of university students who were gathered at the river, not for baptisms and prayers, but for that most modish of New Frontier recreations, water-skiing. Strengthened by a Lutheran confirmation class text-book, with its assurance that God had "created the many species of plants and animals," which were "not the result of a natural development from a single form, as claimed by the evolutionary theory," [2] one shapely coed pointed a painted toenail at some green algae at the water's edge and declared, "I'm glad I don't have to believe we're descended from *that*."

These incidents suggest that historians of Fundamentalism, myself included, have erred in describing that movement as a spent or dying force.[3] But Thomas C. Oden, a seminary professor who taught in a region of the United States where "the fastest-growing religious communities" were "not the defensive 'status quo' churches of culture-Protestantism (Presbyterian, Methodist, Disciples, and others) but such aggressive fundamentalist groups as the Churches of Christ, Pentecostals and Jehovah's Witnesses," reminded us once again in 1962 that "world views already discarded by the intelligentsia have a way of perpetuating themselves far beyond their expected life span." Biblical Fundamentalism "maintains remarkable grass-roots strength among the organization men and the industrialized mass society of the 20th century," Oden wrote, and "it would be a sad illusion for liberal Protestantism"—and for

[2] Jacob Tanner, *The Junior Confirmation Book* (Minneapolis, 1943; tenth printing, 1953), p. 6.

[3] Church historians have been more observant than many of their secular colleagues on this point: cf., e.g., Sydney E. Ahlstrom, "Continental Influences on American Christian Thought Since World War I," *Church History*, XXVII (1958), 257.

the secular academic intellectual, he should have added—
"to imagine seriously that fundamentalism is dead." [4]

Perhaps the continuing power of the movement appears
most vividly when one looks away from the conventional
old-line Protestant denominations and observes, in almost
any American city today, the proliferation of Assemblies
of God, "holiness" churches, gospel missions, Bible taber-
nacles, Soul-Saving Stations, and *iglesias pentecostales,* all
often housed in the store-front churches characteristic of
Harrington's poverty-stricken "other America," but also
(and increasingly) erecting churches that are of substantial
architecture, or purchasing older houses of worship that
were originally built for "mainstream" congregations. And
in the "mainstream" itself there has been the phenomenon
of Mr. Billy Graham, hobnobbing with Presidents and ex-
changing pleasantries before the camera with Jack Benny
and Jack Paar.

It is hard to imagine Billy Sunday playing quite so urbane
a role, and it is therefore sometimes suggested that the
latter-day evangelist ought to be distinguished from his
predecessors by some such term as "neo-fundamentalism."
But Billy Graham attended three fundamentalist colleges,
taking his major in anthropology from professors who
taught him that the theory of evolution was false; and one
has but to observe the man in action, with the Book as
his only stage prop and with his almost liturgical reitera-
tion, "The Bible teaches us . . . ," to be reminded that the
prefix "neo-" qualifies the word "fundamentalism" a good
deal less than it does the word "orthodoxy." [5]

[4] Thomas C. Oden, "Fundamentalism's Weak Christology," *Christian Century,* LXXIX (1962), 1350 f.

[5] William G. McLoughlin, *Modern Revivalism: Charles Grandison
Finney to Billy Graham* (New York, 1959), p. 477, uses the word
"neofundamentalism" to describe the movement after World War II;

Moreover, the intent faces picked out of the crowd in the telecast of a Graham "crusade" are as likely to be those of people from Cleveland or Boston as they are to be those of people from "down South" or "out West". The Southern Baptist Convention, in which Graham was ordained, has long since broken out of the South to plant flourishing new congregations as far afield from the classic "Bible belt" as Hawaii, Alaska, and Maine. In the sixties it surpassed the combined northern and southern membership of the Methodist church and became the largest Protestant denomination in the United States,[6] still numbering many a Fundamentalist, young and old, in its ranks, some of them in positions of denominational power.[7] As for Fundamentalism "out West," the Lutheran Church—Missouri Synod, among major Lutheran bodies in America the one in which resistance to the theory of evolution has been most stoutly maintained,[8] in our own times has not only remained an important social and political force in many midwestern and High Plains states but also, like the Southern Baptists, has new parishes thriving everywhere, including such unlikely places as southern New England and suburbia.

but in further discussion he shifts to categories of "ultra" and "moderate" fundamentalism, terms that would have been equally applicable to the fundamentalism of the twenties. On Billy Graham's own use of the word "fundamentalist" *vide ibid.*, p. 501.

[6] The Methodist church, 10,234,986; the Southern Baptist Convention, 10,395,940. *Time*, May 8, 1964, p. 74. But Claire Cox, writer on religion for United Press-International in New York, reminds us, in *The New-Time Religion* (Englewood Cliffs, N.J., 1961), p. 23, that "electronic brains can tell man in a moment how many days it will take him to get to the moon, but when it comes to determining how many persons are affiliated with religious organizations, statisticians might just as well be counting on their fingers."

[7] For an example of the exercise of this power as recently as 1962, see the editorial, "A Desecration of Liberty," *Christian Century,* LXXIX (1962), 1375 f.

[8] For evidence of this continuing resistance, see *Lutheran Witness Reporter*, official organ of the Lutheran Church—Missouri Synod, I (May 9, 1965), pp. 2, 3, and *passim.*

Nor has this continuing conservatism been limited to clergymen. Anticlerical liberalism (in America, as elsewhere) perennially imagines a democratic and common-sensical people who would rid themselves quickly of religious bigotry and backwardness were it not for the machinations of reactionary priestcraft; there is more than a touch of this in Stanley Kramer's filmed version of *Inherit the Wind*, for example. But a Methodist pastor, writing in 1957 of "the cleavage between the beliefs of the average church-goer and his minister," insisted that it was the *clergy* of his generation, educated by the seminaries "far beyond the understanding and religious position of the laity," whose personal religious convictions were often "far more liberal and unorthodox than they would dare to admit in public" [9] —a judgment which, if valid, would suggest that Fundamentalism at mid-century may be even more pervasive than the mere persistence of preaching that relies for its proof upon the biblical text would indicate.

Surprise, and sometimes alarm, at the vitality of "that old-time religion"—and particularly at its adoption by the young—have characterized intellectuals' encounters with Fundamentalism from the beginning. One pilgrim to the South in the summer of 1964, from New York's Union Theological Seminary, told with obvious concern of having met "persons who had renounced the training they had once received [as Episcopalians, no less!] . . . in favor of a biblical and ethical fundamentalism strong enough to chill the heart of anyone who dreamed that an advance had been made beyond the Scopes Trial." [10]

The Scopes trial in its day had similarly come in some quarters as a rude awakening. "We thought that forty years ago in America religion had become adjusted to the

[9] James B. Moore, "Why Young Ministers Are Leaving the Church," *Harper's Magazine*, CCXV (July, 1957), 66.
[10] Letter to the editor, *Christian Century*, LXXXI (1964), 1338.

evolutionary theory," the president of Brown University
wrote in 1923, "as it was adjusted in the sixteenth century
to the far more startling Copernican theory"; instead, he
noted by way of current example, "in one college a new
professor happened in his first lecture casually to use the
terrifying word 'Evolution.' Whereupon the whole class
hissed him." [11] In 1927 Granville Hicks interviewed Hilyer
Straton, son of one of the leading fundamentalist pulpit
performers of the day, and was taken aback to learn that
along one sector of the battle line no "Revolt of Youth"
was taking place: "Half my crowd Sunday evenings are
under twenty-five," the youthful minister declared. "Do
you think the modern generation is bound for the dogs?"
Hicks asked him. Young Straton smiled—and well he might,
as an enthusiastic student minister with a busy Philadelphia
parish turning out for two preaching services every Sunday—and replied, "That's where Father and I disagree." [12]

In the first article of a series on "The War in the
Churches," published in 1923, Rollin Lynde Hartt painted a
portrait of the liberal intellectuals, many of them "dwellers
in apartments looking out across the Gothic quadrangle[s]
of famous theological seminaries," who vibrated between
"underestimating the enemy's strength" (or his intelligence) on the one hand, and, on the other, giving way to
panic, and perhaps to compensatory overestimates of
Fundamentalism's strength, when they experienced the
movement in its raw and vigorous reality; or discovered,
as Glenn Frank did in the thick of the fight, that orthodox
leaders seemed to have a "much better sense of generalship
than liberals. . . . The Fundamentalists have succeeded in

[11] William H. P. Faunce, "Freedom in School and Church,"
World's Work, XLV (1923), 509.

[12] Granville Hicks, "The Son of a Fundamentalist Prophet,"
Christian Register, CVI (1927), 197. "Father" in this case was
John Roach Straton, of whom more anon.

giving the liberal and intelligent leaders of the church the appearance of renegades." Hartt thought it significant that Fundamentalist and Modernist each accused the other of being heavily subsidized—an explanation that permitted both sides to escape the logical dilemma of how a view regarded as unpopular should seem to be so widely accepted.

Much of the liberal polemic of the twenties contained the ambivalent notion that Fundamentalism was both dying in ill repute and at the same time dangerously threatening to prevail.[13] Harry Elmer Barnes, for example—a liberal by the canons of the twenties—asserted in the Preface to *The Twilight of Christianity* that Fundamentalism had "burned its bridges behind it" and that it was "only a matter of time until it must decay and disintegrate." Two hundred pages later, however, he was not so sure: "The situation is likely to get worse, as the figures indicate that the sects harboring the Fundamentalists are those which are growing most rapidly." In like manner Kirsopp Lake, professor in the Harvard Divinity School, conceding Fundamentalism's "energy, determination, organization, and . . . clearly intelligible position," predicted that in the long run the "Modernist" view of religion would no doubt prevail, but it might be a very long run indeed: "If any one of the . . . parties wins completely and speedily, it is likely to be the Fundamentalists." And in *Religion in Human Affairs,* a book intended as a text for university courses in sociology, Clifford Kirkpatrick prophesied: "Doubtless each successive generation will contain a smaller and smaller proportion of aggressive Fundamentalists"; but he then recalled how the scientific-minded nineteenth century had somehow produced

---

[13] Rollin Lynde Hartt, "The War in the Churches," *World's Work,* XLVI (1923), 473; "Fighting for Infallibility," *ibid.,* XLVII (1923–24), 52. Glenn Frank's statement, from *Century Magazine,* CVI (1923), 637 ff., was reprinted in Eldred C. Vanderlaan (ed.), *Fundamentalism versus Modernism* (New York, 1925), pp. 92 f.

Joseph Smith[14] and Mary Baker Eddy, and wondered, "Who can tell what religious leaders, prophets and messiahs will arise to lead men back to the old ways of thought" in the twentieth or twenty-first?[15]

Stewart Cole, the first historian of Fundamentalism, concluded his study with the observation that the recent controversy in the church had "changed few minds." Probably there remained in 1931 "as many conservative believers as there were two decades ago." Cole criticized the liberals of his day for having "resorted to the logical rather than the psychological method" in evaluating the faith of their orthodox brethren. They had weighed fundamentalist doctrines in the balance of science and scholarship and found them "contrary to genuinely modern beliefs," Cole concluded; and then they had committed the intellectual's characteristic blunder of assuming that if only other men's thought processes were informed and enlightened, general agreement would result. But to bring Protestant churchgoers "abreast of the problems and ideals that characterize the age," Cole predicted, would be "an exceedingly heavy educational task" for the next generation of church leaders —a task which, judging from the continuing strength of Fundamentalism into the fifties and sixties, those leaders failed to accomplish.[16] Indeed, the problem for the historian

[14] No account of Fundamentalism's impact on twentieth-century America would be complete without some mention of Mormonism, which has long outgrown its purely regional significance, but remains thoroughly literalist in outlook — indeed, to the Fundamentalists' literally inspired scriptures it adds several others of its own. My own high-school class's baccalaureate sermon was preached by a Latter Day Saints stake president who went out of his way to confute Darwin, dramatically reading from Genesis 1 and closing the pulpit Bible with a thump.

[15] Harry Elmer Barnes, *The Twilight of Christianity* (New York, 1929), pp. vi, 219; Kirsopp Lake, *The Religion of Yesterday and To-morrow* (Boston, 1925), pp. 159 ff.; Clifford Kirkpatrick, *Religion in Human Affairs* ("Wiley Social Science Series"; New York, 1929), pp. 399, 481.

[16] Stewart G. Cole, *The History of Fundamentalism* (New York, 1931), pp. 325, 328 f., 337.

of the twenties is not so much one of accounting for the
later decline of Fundamentalism, as Cole, Norman Furniss,
and Ray Ginger have assumed,[17] as it is one of discerning
elements in the movement that account for its continuing
vitality.

The showdown between Fundamentalism and Modernism
was long in the making.[18] Sixty-six years had elapsed
between the publication of Darwin's *Origin of Species* and
its constitutional testing (so to speak) in the Scopes trial.
But as early as 1873, Charles Hodge, the formidable
Princeton theologian, had rhetorically asked, "What is
Darwinism?" and answered himself, "It is Atheism." [19] On
the other side of the fence, Phillips Brooks had written
from Boston in 1887 that he was "more and more sure
that the dogmatic theology in which I was brought up"—
well before the Civil War, since Brooks was born in 1835
and ordained deacon in 1859—"was wrong." A biographer
of Phillips Brooks added a footnote detailing the issues
over which his subject had diverged from that dogmatic
theology, and these turn out to have included "its literal
theory of inspiration and its conception of Scripture as a
whole; its indifference to intellectual culture; its insistence
upon the necessity of acknowledging a theory of the Atonement"; and its tendency to limit church fellowship to the

[17] *Ibid.*, pp. 309 ff.; Norman F. Furniss, *The Fundamentalist
Controversy, 1918–1931* (New Haven, Conn., 1954), p. 181, and the
same author's essay in H. H. Quint *et al.* (eds.), *Main Problems in
American History* (Homewood, Ill., 1964), II, 200; Ray Ginger, *Six
Days or Forever? Tennessee v. John Thomas Scopes* (Boston, 1958;
paper, New York, 1960), p. 182. Cf. the Afterword at the end of
this essay.

[18] Robert T. Handy argues convincingly that the controversy had
been coming to a boil ever since the original settlement of North
America. "Fundamentalism and Modernism in Perspective," *Religion
in Life*, XXIV (1955), 381 ff.

[19] Quoted in Frank Hugh Foster, *The Modern Movement in
American Theology* (New York, 1939), p. 47. Foster was a partici-
pant in most of the controversies he describes.

"elect"—all adding up to a dissent from a point of view that unmistakably foreshadowed modern Fundamentalism.[20]

The heresy trials that shook the Protestant churches, and particularly their theological seminaries, in the eighties and nineties are also a part of this story; and it must be noted of those earlier controversies that by and large the Modernists had won them. Going further than mere Modernism in his attacks on orthodoxy had been the itinerant freethinker Robert G. Ingersoll, as archetypal a figure of the Gilded Age as the shoe salesman-turned evangelist, Dwight L. Moody; and while the multitudes at Moody's public meetings were singing Ira Sankey's gospel hymns, a host of critics, more systematic if less eloquent than Ingersoll, had quietly been thinking out a world view that left little if any place for "that old-time religion." In short, the world in which the famous "five points" of Fundamentalism[21] were put forth in 1895 was a world that subjected all such concepts to devastating attack—sometimes in sorrow, sometimes in anger, sometimes even by inadvertence, but always unremitting and inescapable.

There is a sense in which it can be said that without Modernism—and the anticlerical scientism that went beyond it—there could have been no Fundamentalism, in precisely the sense that without the New Deal–New Frontier —and the anticapitalist philosophies that went beyond them —there could have been no Goldwater Republicanism. Fundamentalism is not *simply* "the old-time religion"; the

[20] A. V. G. Allen, *Life and Letters of Phillips Brooks* (New York, 1901), III, 252.

[21] The version of the "five points" adopted as a "deliverance" (resolution) by the northern Presbyterian General Assembly of 1910 lists the following: the infallibility of the Bible, the virgin birth of Christ, the substitutionary atonement, Christ's bodily resurrection, and the factuality of miracles. Full text reprinted in E. C. Vanderlaan (ed.), *Fundamentalism versus Modernism*, p. 21. Earlier versions than the one of 1910 made the second coming of Christ one of the Five Points. (Although it lies just beyond the scope of the present essay, a study of the relationship between Fundamentalism per se and apocalyptic millennialism would add much to our understanding of religion and society in America.)

mere affirmation of an inherited tradition is not at all the same thing as the affirmation of that tradition (or a more or less reasonable facsimile) after it has gone through a period of public eclipse by a rival faith. One can thus speak of Fundamentalism as "new" in the twentieth century, despite the relative antiquity of orthodox Protestantism, in the same way one can speak of a "new" American right in the time of the Cold War, despite the relative antiquity of orthodox laissez faire economics.

It would be easy to push this parallel one step further, and simply identify Fundamentalism as the religious version of radical rightism. The continuing vitality of the one could then be seen as a function of the recurrent upsurges of the other, and we could settle back into the familiar groove of an economic or psychosocial interpretation of history. To put the matter into fundamentalist language, "Ye shall know them by their fruits" (Matt. 7:16), and by that test there is clear evidence for the identification; to make the point, one has only to compare William Bell Riley in 1926, labeling "those professors in our modern universities who . . . in their devotion to the Darwinian theory dare to dethrone God" as "the outstanding leaders today" of "Sovietism" [22], with Helen Wood Birnie in 1960, lecturing on the presumed atheist and materialist views of American college and high-school teachers as "Communism's Secret Weapon" and testifying that she had withdrawn her two boys from "the godless public schools" lest they be taught the theory of evolution.[23] The line of evolutionary descent from Riley (and Gerald Winrod and Billy Sunday) to Mrs. Birnie (and Billy James Hargis and Harvey Springer) is

[22] W. B. Riley, *Inspiration or Evolution* (Cincinnati, 1926), p. 102, quoted in Furniss, *Fundamentalist Controversy*, p. 18.

[23] Notes taken by the author at one of "Sister" Birnie's public meetings. For further documentation of this modern right-wing Fundamentalist's evangelistic effectiveness in some far Northwest communities, see Gretchen Billings, "A Political Profile," *People's Voice* (Helena, Mont.), XXI (Feb. 12, 1960), 2, and *ibid.*, XXI (Mar. 17, 1961), 4.

all too clear.[24] There have even been survivors from the one generation of right-wingers to the others: witness the career of Gerald L. K. Smith, who was twenty-seven years old at the time of the Scopes trial and was still going strong in the presidential election campaign of 1964, in which "for the first time in my mature life," this extremist declared, "a major political party has nominated a candidate for President worthy of respect." [25]

But descent and overlap do not quite add up to identity. Some latter-day Fundamentalists have bitterly resented being equated with the far political right; thus John W. Bradbury, editor of the *Watchman-Examiner,* a paper that in the fifties, as in the twenties, was a bastion of biblical evangelicalism, complained in 1952 of "religious vigilantes" who "cannot be classified . . . with the original Fundamentalists. They may appropriate the name, but they know not the spirit of the movement." [26] In any case, it would be a historiographic error to extrapolate backward from the "apparently cordial marriage" between the radical right and fundamentalist religion[27] in the more recent years and assume therefore that all that it is necessary to say about the meaning of Fundamentalism in the twenties has been said.

The most systematic defense of the basic fundamentalist tenets may be found in twelve paperback volumes of essays

[24] On Winrod, see P. A. Carter, *The Decline and Revival of the Social Gospel* (Ithaca, N. Y., 1956), p. 54; on Sunday, William G. McLaughlin, *Billy Sunday Was His Real Name* (Chicago, 1955), *passim;* on Hargis, Willie Morris, "Houston's Super-patriots," *Harper's Magazine,* CCXXIII (October, 1961), 48 ff.; on Springer, Ralph Lord Roy, *Apostles of Discord* (Boston, 1953), especially p. 199.

[25] Quoted in Gladwin Hill, "Gerald L. K. Smith Still in Business," *New York Times,* Oct. 11, 1964, p. 75.

[26] Quoted in Roy, *Apostles of Discord,* p. 226.

[27] It has been suggested that the ultranationalism of this union may ultimately be destructive for the marriage: "One wonders whether people like Billy James Hargis and Fred Schwarz will not compromise fundamentalism so seriously that in large regions of the country it will no longer be recognizable as religion."—Elwyn A. Smith, "Rightism: Revivalism Revived," *Christian Century,* LXXIX (1962), 1387.

published and distributed between 1909 and 1914 under the over-all title *The Fundamentalists: A Testimony to the Truth*. At that time, such spokesmen for Protestant social concern as Shailer Mathews and Washington Gladden, Walter Rauschenbusch and Josiah Strong, most of them Modernists in their theology, were enjoying a considerable vogue. What did the framers of *The Fundamentals* think of the Social Gospel? The answer is difficult since nearly all of the several dozens of essays in *The Fundamentals* were characterized less by "right-" or "left-wing" views than by the absence of political discussion altogether. Their apolitical quality contrasts sharply with the neo-Fundamentalism of recent years.[28] In this comparative ignoring by the earlier fundamentalist writers of the burning public questions of their day—the welfare of the workers, the control of the trusts, the purity of food,[29] and elections—it is tempting to find a kind of conservatism by default. This, however, would be an argument *ex silentio*, and any such argument runs certain risks. In the discourse of *all* preachers, be they fundamentalist or modernist, social liberal or social reactionary—or none of these—there is necessarily much that is of a purely devotional, doctrinal, or pastoral nature. The reader from outside the faith under consideration, for whom most of the material may have no meaning, is prone to skim it and dig down for the occasional nugget of sociopolitical comment, assuming that this is the heart of the

[28] Louis Gasper, *The Fundamentalist Movement* (The Hague, [1963]), documents the more overtly political quality of the present-day "neo-" Fundamentalism as compared with the earlier period. See also Richard Hofstadter, "Fundamentalism and Status Politics on the Right," *Columbia University Forum*, VIII (Fall, 1965), 18–24.

[29] An interesting exception to early Fundamentalism's indifference to secular social questions is Alfred W. McCann, who worked in a testing laboratory under Harvey Wiley and subsequently became what might be called a pure-food vigilante; it was said that he had "initiated two hundred and six successful prosecutions of food adulterators and . . . never lost a case."—Alfred W. McCann, *The Science of Eating* (New York, 1918), p. vi: cf. pp. 162, 386 ff. McCann later wrote one of the more imposing of the anti-evolution tracts, cited *infra*. The psychology of all this would be fascinating to explore, but would take us far afield from our present subject.

matter; indeed, the assembling of many such nuggets may
well have inclined historians to view the liberal Social Gospel ministry before 1914 as having been even more activist
than in fact it was.

But we do not have to proceed entirely by inference. The
comparative neglect in *The Fundamentals* of political and
economic issues does not go quite to the point of total silence.
Unfortunately for our present purpose, the little that we
do find of this sort of thing in *The Fundamentals* is somewhat inconclusive, even contradictory[30]—until we reach the
last article in the closing volume of the series. In this final
item, *The Fundamentals* suddenly got to the point: the
article was entitled "The Church and Socialism." The
author, Charles Erdman, was the son of William J. Erdman,
one of the founders of the Moody Bible Institute in Chicago,
and himself a professor at Princeton Theological Seminary,
one of the most important American intellectual fountain-
heads of Fundamentalism, and a member of the editorial
committee having general supervision over publication of
The Fundamentals. Here at the end, the reader might surmise, the "two Christian laymen," Lyman and Milton
Stewart, who had patiently and anonymously supported the
venture with their California oil earnings, could at last
have expected their due. But if a Christian defense of free
enterprise was what the Stewart brothers expected for
their money, so to speak, that was not what they got. There
were those in the church, Erdman admitted, "quite comfortable under what they regard as orthodox preaching,
even though they know their wealth has come from the
watering of stocks and from wrecking railroads, and from

---

[30] Cf., e.g., Charles Gallaudet Trumbull, "The Sunday School's
True Evangelism," in A. C. Dixon *et al.*, (eds.), *The Fundamentals: A
Testimony to the Truth* (Chicago, n.d. [1909–14]), XII, 61, as against
Robert E. Speer, "Foreign Missions or World-Wide Evangelism,"
ibid., 70. Also cf. Arthur T. Pierson, "Our Lord's Teachings about
Money," *ibid.*, X, chap. v, and similar brief comments by the same
writer in Vol. I, 70 ff. and Vol. IX, 67.

grinding the faces of the poor." But, he bluntly declared, "The supposed orthodoxy of such preaching is probably defective in its statements of the social teachings of the Gospels. One might be a social bandit and buccaneer and yet believe in the virgin birth and resurrection of Christ; yet one cannot be a Christian unless he believes . . . [that] to live for Christ means to live for Him in every sphere and relationship of life, whether employer or employee, capitalist or laborer, stock-holder or wage-earner." As for socialism —a term that until comparatively recently had "suggested a dream of fanatics"—Erdman continued, it now embodied "the creed and hope of intelligent millions" as a "serious protest . . . against the defects of the present economic system, against special privilege and entrenched injustice, against prevalent poverty, and hunger, and despair."

A "New American Rightist" of our own day would find such a critique of socialism outrageously disappointing, if not downright subversive; and in such a context it would seem as logical to equate this early mode of fundamentalist thinking with radical social protest as to equate it with the reactionary right. As logical—and as meaningless, for in deepest essence this was not what the fundamentalist controversy was about. "Christianity is a religion; Socialism an economic theory, or a political proposal," Erdman argued. It followed that "a man may be an ardent Socialist and a sincere Christian, or he may be a true Christian and a determined opponent of Socialism." [31] The major social thrust of Fundamentalism, in its earliest years at least, was neither liberal nor conservative in the political sense.

[31] It should be noted that this fundamentalist statement on socialism constituted more of an "opening to the Left" than could have been found in American Catholicism of the period; cf., e.g., William Cardinal O'Connell, "Pastoral Letter on the Laborer's Rights," Nov. 23, 1912, reprinted in John A. Ryan and Joseph Husslein (eds.), *The Church and Labor* (New York, 1920), p. 183: "There is not, and cannot be a Catholic Socialist. . . . The principles of Socialism are utterly opposed to the principles of Christianity."

Rather, it foreshadowed a position like that which was to
emerge in the thirties among churchmen decidedly not
fundamentalist in their outlook: "Let the Church be the
Church"; "The Church is committed to no one social order.
. . . It is opposed to the wrongs and injustice of every
system." [32]

Fundamentalism was not predestined from its inception
to play a rightist role in America. Dogmatic as the authors
of *The Fundamentals* were, they were not so graceless but
that one of them could warn against "the temptation to feel
as if we belonged to a superior order of Christians"; and,
in sharp contrast to the anxieties and angers of the radical
right of a later day, the tone of these essays is in general
quite as much marked by love for God and man as it is by
hate for the devil and Modernists. It is a spirit best summed
up in the reply of a prominent evangelist to a well-bred
young lady who balked at going out as a missionary to the
"dirty Chinese": "I do not think the question whether or
not you love the Chinese is the one to be considered; it
seems to me that the real question is whether or not you
love the Lord." [33]

One does not need to be a religious believer to be moved,
for example, by the testimony of Philip Mauro, a wealthy
and successful, but unhappy, Manhattan attorney who
learned his religion "from a company of exceedingly plain,
humble people, of little education, to whom I regarded
myself as immeasurably superior," and whose meetings
"from the ordinary standpoint would have been pronounced
decidedly dull." [34] The pages of *The Fundamentals* are filled

[32] Charles R. Erdman, "The Church and Socialism," *The Fundamentals*, XII, 112, 108, 109, 111, 113.

[33] R. A. Torrey, "The Personality and Deity of the Holy Spirit,"
ibid., I, 56; Henry W. Frost, "What Missionary Motives Should
Prevail," *ibid.*, XII, 93.

[34] Philip Mauro, "A Personal Testimony," *ibid.*, IV, 109. This
tribute is all the more remarkable coming as it did from a man who
in purely secular matters remained probably the most elitist of all
the contributors to *The Fundamentals*. Cf. Mauro, "Modern Philosophy," *ibid.*, II, 97, 99 ff.

with this kind of discourse, both as testimony and as advice; and on occasion, as when Reuben Torrey, the dean of the Los Angeles Bible Institute, echoed a slogan associated also with the essentially liberal John R. Mott ("the evangelization of the world in the present generation"), the purposes of Fundamentalism and of the Social Gospel could fuse.[35] Not even the blustering nationalism of World War I, which found vehement religious voice in Billy Sunday's notorious "damn-the-Germans" crusade in New York City in the spring of 1917, would entirely shoulder aside this humane and universalist side of Fundamentalism.[36] James M. Gray, dean of Moody Bible Institute in Chicago, where most of the editorial work on *The Fundamentals* had been done, wrote in July, 1917, of a German pastor whom he had planned to bring to Moody when the war intervened:

> He is doing his best today to minister to the German soldiers, and to promote the interest of his fatherland I doubt not, and I expect to do the same for my country. But I love that man still and he loves me; and when this cruel war is over, one of the earliest exchanges of brotherly love I have in mind is to bring him here. . . . [In the meantime] the German Christian is serving Christ in obeying his government and the American Christian is doing the same, and *Christ is able to keep them both and to make them stand.* Nor is either of them required to pray for victory [but rather] for the will of God to be done.[37]

Such utterances in wartime were, of course, exceedingly rare from men of any faith except the foundering one of socialism; and in the red haze of generalized intolerance

[35] John T. Stone, "Pastoral and Personal Evangelism," *ibid.*, XII, 30; R. A. Torrey, "The Place of Prayer in Evangelism," *ibid.*, 106.

[36] Accounts of this crusade may be found in McLoughlin, *Billy Sunday*, pp. xvii–xxix, and Bernard Weisberger, *They Gathered at the River* (Boston and Toronto, 1958), pp. 255 ff.

[37] James M. Gray, "What the Bible Teaches about War," (Chicago, [1917]), p. 15 (italics in the original). First published in *Christian Workers' Magazine*, July, 1917.

that hung so ominously over the postwar years, they became if anything even more rare—which suggests that Fundamentalism may have been not so much one of the causes of that wartime and postwar intolerance, as has so often been assumed, as it was one of its victims.

If the war unleashed hate, it also unleashed disillusionment. Fully to have accepted 100 per cent Americanism as a fighting faith would have involved subscribing to the American ideology of ongoing and inevitable progress, and progress, as J. B. Bury was about to point out, [38] had been searching more than a century for a rationale and had finally found one in Darwinian evolution. One way out of the resulting dilemma for Fundamentalists [39] was to find in the war itself a convincing demonstration that the progressives—and, by implication, Darwin as well—had been wrong.

Many non-Fundamentalists also felt this particular disillusionment. George W. Richards, who would one day write on the topic *Beyond Fundamentalism and Modernism,* wrote in 1923 that the war years had reminded men of "the proximity of savagery to culture. . . . It matters little whether man wears skins or broadcloth, so long as the heart is unchanged." But it was the Fundamentalist who was prepared to follow the logic of this most uninhibitedly to its conclusion: "Darwinism had saturated the war-lords with all the catchwords essential to the prosecution of their designs," Alfred W. McCann asserted, "and the people . . . were prepared to follow to the end, little dreaming of the

[38] J. B. Bury, *The Idea of Progress* (London, 1920; first American edition, New York, 1932), chap. xix.

[39] This dilemma was sensed even by so unreflective a Fundamentalist as Billy Sunday: "If by evolution you mean progress, I go with you. But if by evolution you mean that I came from a monkey, good-night!"—McLoughlin, *Modern Revivalism,* p. 411, quoting the Boston *Herald,* Nov. 14, 1916.

carnage, starvation and disease toward which their 'progressive' evolution was now thundering its flight." [40]

The reference to "the war-lords" suggests the World War I propaganda stereotype of the "Hun," although McCann noted that his German villains (Ernst Haeckel was a favorite) had their French and British counterparts. But other Fundamentalists had felt a challenge from Germany long before American national interest became involved. They quite correctly saw their position undermined not only by the theory of evolution but also by modern critical study of the Bible, an impressive amount of which had been done in German universities. Their warfare against German historical scholarship easily broadened into a more general attack on *Kultur*. The Nietzschean superman, or the propagandist's caricature of him, was a bogeyman for Fundamentalists long before he became one for George Creel and Woodrow Wilson.

"It is notorious to what length the German fancy can go in the direction of the subjective and the conjectural," wrote a contributor to the first volume of *The Fundamentals*. German biblical criticism, the same essayist observed (with some truth!), "deals with the writers and readers of the ancient Orient as if they were modern German professors." This same note of quasi-philosophical objection to the Teutonic penchant for "hypothesis-weaving and speculation" runs through other pages of *The Fundamentals*. One contributor, for example, wittily satirized the skeptical extremism of certain German biblical scholars by applying their kind of reductionist logic to a contemporary figure, to "prove" that Theodore Roosevelt had, like Jesus of Naza-

[40] George W. Richards, *Christian Ways of Salvation* (New York, 1923), p. 261; Alfred W. McCann, *God—or Gorilla?* (New York, 1922), pp. 328 f.

reth never really existed![41] The Peerless Leader of the
anti-evolution forces might not have been at home in a
discussion at quite so sophisticated a level, but he had heard
of Nietzsche; and at the Scopes trial Bryan conjoined the
Nietzschean superman's transvaluation of values to Darwinism, and hurled back at Clarence Darrow the latter's
plea for extenuation in another celebrated trial, made on
the ground "that the teachings of Nietzsche made [Nathan]
Leopold a murderer."[42]

At both the metaphysical and the moral level, Fundamentalists continued to see Germany as the fountainhead of
what they were opposing. When Hitler came to power, some
American Fundamentalists would view the Nazi government as the logical outcome of half a century of godless
German Modernism and declare in effect, "We told you
so."[43]

At the same time, however, the Fundamentalists were
more open-minded in their attitude toward Germany than
contemporary right-wingers are regarding the communist
"menace." Thus, J. Gresham Machen, himself a former
graduate student at Marburg and Göttingen and by all odds
intellectually the ablest of major spokesmen for Fundamentalism, urged a protégé who was contemplating a year of
study abroad in the mid-twenties to spend all of his time
in Germany: "At most of the universities you will be living
in a highly stimulating intellectual atmosphere that will be
entirely foreign to Christianity," he wrote; "not altogether
an easy experience" for an orthodox young man, but one

[41] Dyson Hague, "The History of the Higher Criticism," *The
Fundamentals*, I, 90 ff.; John L. Nuelsen, "The Person and Work of
Jesus Christ," *ibid.*, VI, 103 ff.

[42] Sheldon N. Grebstein (ed.), *Monkey Trial: The State of
Tennessee vs. John Thomas Scopes* (Boston, 1960), p. 129, citing the
original trial transcript, p. 454.

[43] Frederick K. Wentz, "American Protestant Journals and the
Nazi Religious Assault," *Church History*, XXIII (1954), 328 ff.

that would give him "the satisfaction of having come into firsthand contact with those forces which underlie all the doctrinal indifferentism in Great Britain and this country." [44] It would be a rare bird indeed among right-wingers since World War II who would urge a student to spend a year in Moscow or Peking, or Havana, to become acquainted at first hand with the other side!

But even more incongruous than Machen (whom Walter Lippmann called "a scholar and a gentleman") as a progenitor for the radical right of our day was the arch-Fundamentalist of all, William Jennings Bryan. In the apostolic succession of the Democratic party from Andrew Jackson to Franklin D. Roosevelt, Bryan has often been an embarrassment to the academic liberal, and never more so than in the anti-evolution campaign. Indeed, he has been judged by a double standard, so that we are inclined, for example, to remember that he went to Dayton in 1925 to prosecute a schoolteacher and to forget that he went to the Presbyterian General Assembly in 1920 to prosecute his own denomination's war profiteers.[45] But the Great Commoner saw his public career as one self-consistent whole; he felt that his crusades against the scientists and the Higher Critics, like his crusades against the hard-money men and the militarists, were on behalf of popular democracy. Well along in the pages of *In His Image*, his own special-creationist tract, Bryan reaffirmed his lifelong credo: "I fear the plutocracy of wealth; I respect the aris-

---

[44] Quoted in Ned B. Stonehouse, *J. Gresham Machen: A Biographical Memoir* (Grand Rapids, Mich., 1954), p. 241. Stonehouse had access to the Machen family papers.

[45] Willard H. Smith, "William Jennings Bryan and the Social Gospel," a paper read before the Mississippi Valley Historical Association, Cleveland, 1964, p. 12. I am indebted to Professor Smith, who was kind enough to allow me to read this paper in manuscript. It has since been published in *Journal of American History*, LIII (June, 1966), 41–60.

tocracy of learning; but I thank God for the democracy of the heart." [46]

But that, in the opinion of more than a few of his contemporary critics, was precisely what was the matter with Bryan: not that he attacked the principle of "one man, one vote," but that he defended it. The anti-evolution campaign was seen by some of them as a characteristically bad example of popular, one man–one vote democracy in action. Thus the antics of William Bell Riley debating the theory of evolution against all comers but packing the meetings with loyal Fundamentalists, so that his defense of the Bible would be voted to have "won," and of John Roach Straton reacting to the American Museum of Natural History's exhibit on the Age of Man with what amounted to a demand for "equal time" for an exhibit of "The Bible Story of Creation" [47] only served to confirm H. L. Mencken's opinion that "the mob has made its superstitions official." Five years after the Scopes trial, Mencken wrote in praise of the civilized rule of enlightened skeptics during the eighteenth century, and lamented the subsequent "spread of the democratic pestilence"—the results of which in the United States, "where democracy has been carried further than anywhere else," included "such obscenities as Comstockery, Prohibition, and the laws against the teaching of evolution." [48]

[46] William Jennings Bryan, *In His Image* (New York and Chicago, 1922), p. 262. Facing the title page of this work was an advertisement for Bryan's other books, one of which the publisher represented as "the cream of Mr. Bryan's public utterances on Prohibition, Money, Imperialism, Trusts, Labor, Income Tax, Peace, Religion, Pan-Americanism, etc.," strongly implying that at least one sales-conscious copywriter of the twenties saw Bryan's pre- and postwar audiences as essentially one and the same. Cf. also the "Social Gospel" statements in *ibid.*, pp. 146 ff., 205, and the whole of Chapter VI.

[47] On this tactic of Riley's, see Bruce Tarrant, "Minnesota: Modern or Mediaeval?", *Independent*, CXVIII (1927), 28, and Stewart Cole, *The History of Fundamentalism*, pp. 272, 302, 314. On Straton's proposed exhibit, see John Roach Straton, "Fancies of the Evolutionists," *Forum*, LXXV (1926), 250.

[48] H. L. Mencken, *Treatise on the Gods* (New York, 1930), p. 296.

The dilemma posed here was one not for Fundamentalists and their opponents only but for respresentative government itself. "Can the public school, at this stage of the world's history, be dedicated to a literal interpretation of Genesis . . . ? Can the religious frame of mind which this assumes be imposed by law upon educators and pupils?" No, said the liberal Catholic journalist Michael Williams, covering the Scopes trial for *Commonweal*. Yes, said Benedict Elder, editor of the Catholic diocesan newspaper in Louisville: "If its citizens believe that the Bible is true, the state has no right to employ instructors . . . to teach . . . that the Bible is not true." State schools had to be controlled by the state "and not by any professional group —however learned," Elder went on; "After all, the common judgment of the plain people is not to be scorned." [49] Such also was Bryan's conviction when at one point in the Scopes trial he cried, "Your Honor, it isn't proper to bring experts in here to try to defeat the purpose of the people." [50]

At this point in discussions of Fundamentalism by liberals and Modernists, it was (and is) customary to shift from categories of left and right to categories of intellect and ignorance. Thus Clarence Darrow replied to Bryan that the logic of his argument amounted to saying, "It is a crime to know more than I know." [51] And it is further customary to equate these in turn with urban and rural life: one man's vote is the full equivalent of another's provided that both men are equidistant from the centers of modern thought and culture. Walter Lippmann, for example, readily embraced a rural-vs.-urban interpretation of Fundamentalism as the most practical way of arguing it down without falling into the illiberal assumption that the people ought to be governed by their betters:

[49] *Commonweal*, II (1925), 242, 246.
[50] Grebstein, *Monkey Trial*, pp. 125, 79, citing pp. 436, 207, of the trial transcript.
[51] *Ibid.*

> The deep and abiding traditions of religion belong to the country-side. . . . The omnipotence of God means something to men who submit daily to the cycles of the weather and the mysterious power of nature. But the city man puts his faith in furnaces to keep out the cold, is proudly aware of what bad sewage his ancestors endured, and of how ignorantly they believed that God, who made Adam at 9 A.M. on October 23 in the year 4004 B.C., was concerned with the behavior of Adam's children.[52]

One of the most persistent and persuasive of the interpretations of Fundamentalism has set it in a wider context of rural-urban conflict in America, akin to the crusades against Demon Rum and Al Smith, and perhaps also to the pre-nomination struggles of 1964 between Barry Goldwater and those personalities within the Republican party whom the Senator was wont to term the "fat cats back East." John Washington Butler, author of the Tennessee anti-evolution law, was moved to run for the legislature and introduce his bill in large part because a girl from his home town had gone away to college and had come back believing in evolution and not believing in God; this episode has often been cited as a demonstration of the role in the evolution controversy of "cultural lag"—a concept, popular in the 1920's, which is still too frequently employed by historians.[53]

Such an interpretation of Fundamentalism, like the politico-ideological one, must be applied with caution. To be sure, a certain willful ignorance does pervade much fundamentalist discourse; and, to be sure, the record of the Scopes trial—that symbolic heart of the entire controversy —fairly crackles with resentment at the way Chicago, personified in Clarence Darrow, and New York, personified in

[52] Walter Lippmann, *A Preface to Morals* (New York, 1929), pp. 62 ff.

[53] Cf., e.g., Furniss, *Fundamentalist Controversy*, p. 3; Ginger, *Six Days or Forever?*, p. 8; Hofstadter, *Anti-intellectualism*, p. 126.

Dudley Field Malone, were interfering in the private affairs of Dayton, Tennessee. But every tale of a country boy or girl being ruined, intellectually or otherwise, by the liberal ways of a metropolitan university,[54] could be matched by testimony to the contrary, such as that of Harry Emerson Fosdick, next to Darrow the prime target of fundamentalist wrath in the twenties. Discovering the theory of evolution toward the end of his freshman year in college in 1897, young Fosdick had announced to his family "as impressively as I could manage it: 'I have made up my mind that I believe in evolution,'" only to have the wind taken out of his undergraduate sails by his father's reply: "Well, I believed that before you were born." [55]

A Methodist minister who came out of a hamlet that was culturally even more remote from modern America than Dayton to earn a B.A. degree in 1922 and a theological degree in 1925, the year Darrow took on Bryan, later recalled no tension or conflict between a rural upbringing and an exposure to modern science in college. The theory of evolution, this liberal clergyman wrote before 1940, "did not disturb my thinking at all, for it was the most natural explanation of the world of Nature I had known." [56] Thus one country-dweller, as Lippmann suggests, might sense in the powers of nature beyond his own control a transcendant power behind them, which would drive him into fundamentalist religion; but evidently another country-dweller could

[54] E.g., the letter in *Bible Champion*, XXXV (1929), 5, from a college student who had learned "a little about biology and chemistry and physics . . . a little more about history and comparative religion," but enough of all these to decide that "Jehovah is not for me." The editor commented: "What are we doing to save students in these faith-wrecking institutions?"

[55] Harry Emerson Fosdick, *The Living of These Days: An Autobiography* (New York, 1956), p. 49. A slightly different version of this episode is told in Fosdick, *Adventurous Religion* (New York, 1926), p. 107.

[56] "Broken Spires," MS autobiography in the possession of the Rev. Manfred A. Carter of Hampden, Maine, p. 58.

have found in his own firsthand acquaintance with the living things of field and forest a world of experience for which the theory of evolution gave him a fully satisfying explanation. "The study of evolution seemed perfectly natural," the same minister wrote after his retirement in 1962. "The fundamentalism of the [home-town] church must have passed me by. I never did have to get rid of it." [57]

When one uncovers the intellectual roots of the fundamentalist controversy in the warfare of science and theology in the nineteenth century, the cultural-lag hypothesis, with urban high-brows all ranged on one side and rural low-brows all on the other, becomes even harder to sustain as a universal proposition. For on this assumption what is one to make of John Wesley Powell, growing up in a village and educated in one-room schoolhouses and a library-laboratory housed in a private dwelling, then roaming the river banks of an Illinois barely a generation away from the frontier, and in the process insensibly making a first-rate geologist of himself? [58] Free inquiry has never been wholly confined to the intellectual and cultural centers of the nation. In our age of dependence upon large university libraries and astronomically expensive laboratories, we are prone to forget the number of Americans over the years in both town and country who have contrived to educate themselves catch-as-catch-can. And just as there have always been instances of intellect at work in the American countryside (think of Edwards ministering to the Stockbridge Indians while writing *Freedom of the Will*), so there have been important revivalist and biblical-literalist manifestations in town. Fundamentalism in the 1920's claimed many a strategic city pulpit, from Boston's venerable Park Street Church to

[57] Revised draft of *ibid.*, 1963; pages not numbered.
[58] William Culp Darrah, *Powell of the Colorado* (Princeton, N.J., 1951), pp. 11–14, 23–33, 36–46.

W. B. Riley's home base in Minneapolis. The *New Republic* commented on this paradox in an obituary on the "Fundamentalist Pope" of Manhattan, John Roach Straton: "In spirit, he was a Baptist of the old school, attached to the letter of the Old Testament; in technique, he was a New Yorker of the twentieth century." A man who "planned a skyscraper church as a shrine for doctrines in which he believed as literally as did the tent-dwelling patriarchs to whom they were first proclaimed in Palestine" and preached the old-time religion over that most modern of gadgets, the radio, Straton "was typical of a persistent contrast in our national life." [59]

A further difficulty for a purely rural-urban interpretation of the fundamentalist controversy is its international dimension. When Bryan took off his coat in the blazing July heat of Tennessee and "revealed the fact that he was not wearing galluses but a belt, an article of apparel affected only by advanced dressers and advanced thinkers," the drama would seem to have been about as far from the spirit of old Europe as it was possible to get; but of the three million copies of *The Fundamentals* that had been distributed by 1914, approximately one-third had gone outside the United States, half to the British Isles and the balance to the European continent and the rest of the planet.[60] Even if we assume that most of these overseas recipients were British or American Protestant mission workers, no generalizations about the American self-made

[59] *New Republic*, LX (1929), 335.

[60] W. O. McGeehan, covering the Scopes trial for the New York *Tribune*, July 10, 1925, reprinted in the *Sunday Herald Tribune*, Apr. 17, 1955, with a photo of Darrow and Bryan both in shirtsleeves; publishers' statement, *The Fundamentals*, XII (Chicago, n.d. [but published after the outbreak of World War I, from internal evidence]), 4. It is not clear from this statement whether three million volumes or three million sets (of twelve volumes each) was meant as the claimed figure; probably the former.

man, the American rural mind, or American hostility to
scholarship entirely suffice to cover the subject.[61]

Does Fundamentalism, then, come down to unadorned
anti-intellectualism, regardless of race,[62] political creed,
nationality, or regional origin? Once again, *The Fundamentals* are a major interpretive obstacle. These articles
are, most of them, sober. Only one or two of them are really
ranting in tone,[63] and the level of the argument on the
whole is only a hair more illogical than academic discourse
in general—which indeed much of it is; a high proportion
of the authors were professors of theology, many of them
in respectable institutions, and a low proportion of them
could have been classed merely as vulgar evangelists. And
even if we dismissed these essays as irrelevant for understanding the Fundamentalism of the twenties, there would
still remain the enigma of J. Gresham Machen, who was
not only a man of impeccable scholarship himself but one
who turned the sword's point around in the twenties and
accused the liberals of low-browism. "We are opposed with

[61] Articles were contributed to *The Fundamentals* by a professor
in Glasgow; a pastor in Kilmarnock, Scotland, and another residing
at Ballineen, County Cork, Ireland; the bishop of Durham; the
minister of Westminster Chapel and the vicar of St. Paul's, in
London; the former principal of Knox College, Toronto; a canon
of the Church of England in Montreal, and another in London,
Ontario; and a professor emeritus in Stuttgart. Incidentally, even
Bryan was not above quoting British and French writers for their
snob value in supporting his views: cf. *In His Image*, pp. 124 ff.

[62] The subject of Negro Fundamentalism needs exploration. When
E. Franklin Frazier said that "the Negro church and Negro religion
have cast a shadow over the entire intellectual life of Negroes," I
am sure that he had more than segregation alone in mind. Frazier,
The Negro Church in America (New York, 1963), p. 86.

[63] The only essays that really "rant" (in the sense of "to scold
vehemently," Webster, 2nd ed.) are those dealing with (1) the more
outré of the Fundamentalists' sectarian rivals, e.g., Mormonism,
Spiritualism, Jehovah's Witnesses, and (2) the Roman Catholic
church. Cf. T. W. Medhurst, "Is Romanism Christianity?", *The
Fundamentals*, XI, chap. vi, and J. M. Foster, "Rome, the Antagonist of the Nation," *ibid.*, chap. vii. The relationship, and antipathies,
between Protestant Fundamentalism and Catholic rightism in this
country need further study.

all our might," Machen vowed in 1924, "to the passionate anti-intellectualism of the Modernist Church." The entire first chapter of his book *What Is Faith?* (1925) was a polemic against "the intellectual decadence of the day," not only in the church but in secular education with its "absurd pedagogic theories which . . . depreciate . . . the labor of learning facts." [64]

But how could a plea for high standards of intellectual enterprise be reconciled with a categorical rejection of the findings of modern science? The Fundamentalist who did not retreat into *credo quia absurdem*—an answer that a Machen would have rejected as contemptuously as a Mencken [65]—was forced into the assumption that some day, somehow, the whole evolutionary edifice must topple for lack of sufficient evidence and that science itself would conclude that Darwin had been wrong. In the twenties this did not seem as forlorn a hope as it sounds today. Alfred McCann in *God—or Gorilla?*, arguing that scientists' attempts to reconstruct man's subhuman ancestors from fossil remnants were at best hopes and at worst forgeries, went with a debater's unerring instinct in his first chapter to the "Piltdown Man," which of course *was* eventually proved a fabrication. We should bear in mind, too, that the provenance of *Pithecanthropus*, the Trinil or "Java ape-man," was not finally established until 1939,[66] and that "Rhodesia Man" had a hole in its skull that for years was believed to have been made by a bullet! This was later

---

[64] J. Gresham Machen, "Does Fundamentalism Obstruct Social Progress?", *Survey*, LII (1924), 426; Machen, *What is Faith?* (New York, 1925), p. 15.

[65] Machen's *Weltanschauung* is admirably summed up by Lefferts A. Loetscher in "Machen, John Gresham," *Dictionary of American Biography*, XXII, Supp. Two (New York, 1958), pp. 411 f.

[66] Indeed, Trinil Man's discoverer died in 1940 insisting that his find had been no "missing link" but only a large gibbon. Herbert Wendt, *In Search of Adam*, trans. James Cleugh (Boston, 1956; originally published in Germany as *Ich Suchte Adam*), p. 299.

shown to have been the bite of a primeval hyena, but in the meantime it afforded people like McCann much fun at the evolutionists' expense.[67]

As for Darwin's theory of the origin of species by natural selection, it had fallen on evil days. "Discussions of evolution came to an end," the British geneticist William Bateson told the American Association for the Advancement of Science in 1921, "primarily because it was obvious that no progress was being made. . . . Variations of many kinds, often considerable, we daily witness, but no origin of species." Noting Bateson's indiscreet remark that "when such confessions are made the enemies of science see their chance," and ignoring his insistence that "what has been learned [about evolution] constitutes progress upon which we shall never have to go back," Fundamentalists wrote sermons and editorials and whole books whose thesis was that the evolutionists were dogmatizing to cover up their own ignorance. From this point of view, the classic warfare between science and theology anticlimactically came down to a case of my faith versus yours.[68] "It was . . . remarkable," one contributor to *The Fundamentals* had written, "that men of trained intellect should have so promptly accepted at face value [Darwin's] two principal works, in which the expression, 'we may well suppose,' occurs over eight hundred times." [69]

The defender of evolution was put in an awkward position by this kind of attack. If he denied that any such tenta-

[67] Alfred W. McCann, *God—or Gorilla?*, chap. i, "Making the Piltdown Man"; cf. Wendt, *In Search of Adam*, pp. 410 ff. On Rhodesia Man, *ibid.*, pp. 422 ff.

[68] William Bateson, "Evolutionary Faith and Modern Doubts," *Science*, LV (New Series), 56 f., 61. Note the selective quotation from this address in Louis T. More, *The Dogma of Evolution* (Princeton, N.J., 1925), p. 28; and cf. Frank E. Allen, "Dr. Clark Arouses a Furor among Evolutionists," *Bible Champion*, XXXV (1929), 309 ff.

[69] "Evolutionism in the Pulpit," "by an occupant of the pew," *The Fundamentals*, VIII, 27.

tiveness or doubts existed among the experts, a William Bateson—professionally aware that the mechanism of natural selection seemed to have proved unsatisfactory as an explanation of evolution and that the mechanism of genetic mutation was as yet very imperfectly understood—quite properly could be quoted in rebuttal.[70] If he affirmed that supposition, inference, hypothesis is the way science operates, a McCann was ready with the Baconian observation that "science deals with facts known to be facts, and not with opinions supported by conjecture, speculation, assumptions, or theoretical connecting links." [71]

If there is a cultural lag in operation here, it is one not between science and superstition but between nineteenth-century science and twentieth-century science. In the words of A. Hunter Dupree, "The quest for 'hard things' in science seemed a reasonable enterprise in the nineteenth century; it is madness in the twentieth." When Fundamentalists and evolutionists tried to reduce the issues between them to "hard things," the contending parties sounded startlingly alike.[72] For men battling over what they took to be "hard things," the kinds of armistice terms proposed by Modernism—that science deals with "facts" and religion with

[70] Modernists who were trying to have it both ways, preserving both science and some semblance of orthodoxy, often injured their own case by adopting neither the Darwinian theory of natural selection nor the Mendel-deVries theory of mutation but the then current vogue of neo-Lamarckianism, since that hypothesis seemed to "have the inestimable advantage of opposing the materialistic or mechanical theory of life."—More, *The Dogma of Evolution*, p. 211. Ironically, the Soviet Union was in the process of adopting the Michurin-Lysenko version of Lamarckianism for exactly the opposite reason.

[71] McCann, *God—or Gorilla?*, p. 263.

[72] A. Hunter Dupree, "Words or Things in the History of Science," a paper read before the American Historical Association, Washington, D.C., Dec. 30, 1964. Cf. Oden, "Fundamentalism's Weak Christology," p. 1350, in which nineteenth-century historicism, like nineteenth-century scientism, is shown to be a common assumption in disputes between Fundamentalists and liberals.

"values," or that evolution deals with the "how" of man's origin and the Bible with the "why"—were rejected on both sides as illogical compromises or dishonest evasions.[73] American Catholicism probably came the closest to a workable *via media* that anyone achieved in the 1920's on the evolution question,[74] but it was the editor of the *Catholic World* who challenged "anybody to convey to a class the arguments for the evolution of man without revealing, I will not say his own scientific conclusions, but his own theology." [75] In the sixties we have become acquainted with the concept of a social "mainstream," but in the twenties the liberals and conservatives, religiously if not politically, were more inclined to insist that one climb out upon the stream's right or left bank.[76]

[73] For attacks on a middle-ground position from the fundamentalist side, see Francis L. Patton, *Fundamental Christianity* (New York, 1926), pp. 202, 204; Machen, *What is Faith?*, p. 241, and from the liberal-humanist side, Barnes, *Twilight of Christianity*, p. 425, and Lippmann, *A Preface to Morals*, pp. 40 ff. The dilemma of a compromise position is expressed by a man who tried to maintain one in E. Y. Mullins, *Christianity at the Cross Roads* (New York, 1924), p. 123.

[74] For representative Catholic expression on the Bible-versus-Darwin problem, see Arthur Ryland, "The Inspiration of Scripture," *American Catholic Quarterly Review*, XLVIII (1923), 121 f., and T. Lawrason Riggs, "Fundamentalism and the Faith," *Commonweal*, II (1925), p. 345. On the age of man, however, Catholics were not totally immune to the appeal of fossil-debunking in the manner of Protestant Fundamentalists; cf. Cornelius Merrins, "On the Age of Man," *American Catholic Quarterly Review*, XLVIII (1923), 176 ff. And note Mencken's comments on how Roman Catholicism had escaped the logical difficulties of Protestantism "by keeping the Bible in its place," in *Treatise on the Gods*, pp. 338 ff.

[75] *Catholic World*, CXXI (1925), 544. Cf. the valiant efforts of instructors in recent American history to be even-handed in their treatment of Democratic U.S. Presidents and their Republican oppositions—an emotional-pedagogical problem almost exactly comparable to the one under discussion here.

[76] That this tendency of the debate to polarize into opposites was felt in Judaism as well during the twenties may be inferred from Abba Hillel Silver, *Religion in a Changing World* (New York, 1931), pp. 1 f. A comparison between Judaism and Protestantism in America specifically upon the point of the reception and response

It is interesting that although the word "fundamentalism" is still used to describe a recognizable entity (e.g., the sermons of Billy Graham), the word "modernism" has all but dropped out of the American Protestant vocabulary. And in retrospect many of the modernist compromises do sound curiously empty. Thus Edward Scribner Ames, for forty years pastor of University Church (Disciples of Christ), Chicago, wrote of Christianity as being on the verge of a new "great epoch," which he described variously as "the religion of the spirit, as social Christianity, and as the religion of democracy." But by "spirit," he seemingly meant nothing more transcendental than the glow of goodfellowship, as in the term "school spirit"; in fact, he made the parallel explicit: "Our college is our Virgin Mother, to whom we address songs and sentiments of genuine affection." [77] Fundamentalists were quick to deride the shallowness of this kind of Christianity—"You could take the 'C' out of Y.M.C.A. and nobody would ever notice the difference" [78] —and to warn of its total inadequacy for the great crises in life: "For mere popular lectures it is still serviceable; but . . . when despair at the loss of all one has loved

---

to Darwin in the light of biblical criticism would, I think, be most enlightening. Literal insistence on the factuality of Genesis 1–3 has been a common problem in both religious traditions—and is more prevalent to this day in Orthodox Judaism, as in orthodox Protestantism, than one sometimes supposes.

[77] Edward Scribner Ames, *The New Orthodoxy* (Chicago, 1918), pp. 10, 50.

[78] Hilyer Hawthorne Straton, quoted in Hicks, "The Son of a Fundamentalist Prophet," p. 197. That there was some substance to this charge was tacitly conceded in 1930 by the general secretary of the Y's sister organization, who spoke of the growth of "a sense of unreality in the expression of religion," and of "the quiet dropping away in so many Associations of those things that we formerly spoke of as our religious activities."—Anna V. Rice, "The Association As a Religious Movement in the World Today," Eleventh National Convention of the Young Women's Christian Associations of the United States of America, *Proceedings* (New York, 1930), p. 138.

takes possession of the mind . . . when one is on a sick-bed and death approaches . . . just at this time when its help is most needed, this modern religion utterly fails." Or as Lippmann put it, "A man cannot cheat about faith." [79]

All of which suggests that the Fundamentalists may after all have been doing just what they thought they were doing: not merely defending a political ideology, however much some of them talked of the American way of life—for the Jehovah's Witnesses, equally literal in their interpretation of Scripture, were refusing to salute the flag; not only defending an economic system, however much oil money was poured into the dissemination of *The Fundamentals*— for other oil money built Riverside Church, and housed Dr. Fosdick therein; not simply defending the countryside against the city—for the "old-time religion" early discovered, and has perpetuated, an evangelistic style of city-based revivals; not even essentially defending ignorance against intellect—for the claims of intellect in the ivory tower were scarcely lived up to in the encounter in the courtroom that merely pitted authority against authority, "the Bible teaches" against "science says"; but also, and chiefly, defending what the Fundamentalists honestly believed was all that gave meaning to human life, "the faith once delivered to the saints."

Although for many people living through the twenties science had in the words of Joseph Wood Krutch "not only won from us a confidence in her methods, but also made it well-nigh impossible for us to believe in any others," this does not detract from the high seriousness of the fundamentalist defense of faith. Krutch himself—one of the apostles of the gospel of science—acknowledged that the findings of science had indeed robbed human life of its

[79] F. Bettex, "The Bible and Modern Criticism," *The Fundamentals*, IV, 87; Lippmann, *A Preface to Morals*, p. 49.

intrinsic value: "We have grown used . . . to a Godless universe, but we are not yet accustomed to one which is loveless as well, and only when we have so become shall we realize what atheism really means." [80] The terrible darkness of this passage, I have found, still has power to kindle in student readers its author's despair; and from it one can understand why some clung to Fundamentalism in the twenties: God help them, they could do no other.

AFTERWORD

Since this is a frankly revisionist essay, it should be stated that, as even a cursory comparison between this essay and Chapter IV of my *The Decline and Revival of the Social Gospel* (Ithaca, N.Y., 1956) will demonstrate, the historian's views that have been most thoroughly revised are my own. I am indebted to the following for their chastening comments in reviews of my earlier work, particularly as regards its treatment of Fundamentalism: C. Howard Hopkins, in *Religion in Life,* XXI (1957), 303; Sydney E. Ahlstrom, in *Review of Religion,* XXVI (1957), esp. p. 209; and Sidney E. Mead, in *Church History,* XXVI (1957), 397 ff. I have also learned from reviewers with whom I remain in essential disagreement, e.g., Irving E. Howard in *Christian Economics* (Nov. 27, 1956), p. 4, and from those like Daisuke Kitagawa, *Ecumenical Review,* (April, 1957), who agreed with my judgments but restated them in briefer form that led me to doubt their soundness. Although it appeared too late for me to use in this essay, Ernest R.

[80] Joseph Wood Krutch, *The Modern Temper* (New York, 1929); paper, 1956), pp. 154, 78. Mr. Krutch, as is well known, found his way out of those dark woods; but his way has been a highly idiosyncratic and personal one. Perhaps anyone's must be.

Sandeen's paper on the origins of Fundamentalism, which
he read at the American Historical Association meeting at
San Francisco in December, 1965, has opened a fresh and
original line of investigation into the roots of the movement,
particularly in its more formal theological aspects.[81]

[81] Sandeen agrees with my judgment that the movement cannot be
reduced to economic, regional, political, or psychosocial categories:
"Fundamentalism originated in the northeastern part of this continent
in metropolitan areas and cannot be explained as a part of the populist movement, agrarian protest or the Southern mentality." But he
differs from my estimate of the movement as a defense, under fire, of
an existing orthodoxy: "It was . . . marked by some special doctrinal
innovations," which Sandeen sees as having had their origin no earlier
than the nineteenth century. Ernest R. Sandeen, "Towards a Historical Interpretation of the Origins of Fundamentalism," *Church History*, XXXVI (1967), 66–83.

The Ku Klux Klan

ROBERT MOATS MILLER

THE Ku Klux Klan of the 1920's is a study in anxiety rather than in abnormality. The citizens of the Invisible Empire were deeply anxious men, but they were not, save for the psychotic few, moral monsters; and to dismiss these five million hooded Americans as peculiarly depraved is to blink away the banality of evil. The Klan illuminates the need of mediocre men to flee to the mysticism of the primitive collectivity, and serves, therefore, to remind us that Americans are implicated in the totalitarian temper of the modern world. To discern more than a casual relationship between the Klan and twentieth-century collectivism, however, is not to say that the Klan is a study in un-Americanism. These True Believers of the twenties were not converts to an alien ideology; rather, they confessed to a creed shared, in whole or in part, by many Americans in every generation. The Klan illuminates the persistency of dark strains in American history, strains that have been eased but never entirely erased by faithfulness to the countervailing ideals of decency and fair play. Why, however, should these strains become acutely manifest in a decade fondly deemed the apogee of "normalcy"? Admitting that all men in the

modern world bear the burden of anxiety, acknowledging
the racism, nativism, and irrationalism flawing the American past, it remains our task to comprehend what there was
in the social and psychic air of the early 1920's making
many Americans so terribly anxious as to compel them to
seek release in a secret, hooded order which, if spawned in
Europe, would have carried the designation "fascist."

Any attempt to resolve this paradox must begin with the
understanding that the Klan was a many-splintered thing
or, less invidiously, a many-splendored thing. The Knights
were troubled souls, but that which tried their souls varied
from region to region and, indeed, from Knight to Knight.
It was as though an outraged citizenry participated in a
gigantic police line-up to identify the enemies of society,
with each "good" American fingering a different suspect:
uppity Negro, conspiratorial Catholic, avaricious Jew, dirty
Mexican, wily Oriental, bloody-handed Bolshevik, scabrous
bootlegger, fancy "lady," oily gambler, fuzzy internationalist, grafting politico, Sabbath desecrator, wife-beater, home-
breaker, atheistic evolutionist, feckless-faithed Modernist,
scoffing professor, arrogant intellectual, subversive socialist, slick urbanite, simpering pacifist, corrupt labor organizer. Of necessity, the line of suspects was endless because
the evils threatening America appeared legion: miscegena-
tion, mongrelization, Romanism, socialism, urbanism, skepticism, secularism, paganism, modernism, radicalism, internationalism, materialism, Freudianism, relativism, surreal-
ism, alcoholism, sexualism.

These myriad dangers appeared more clear and present
in some regions and to some citizens than others; consequently, it is imprecise to speak of *the* Klan of the 1920's.
Rather, there existed many local Klans operating as virtually autonomous units, and each unit ranked the dangers
in some order of priority, just as each Knight was motivated
(whether consciously or not) by his life experiences.

Fragmented and amorphous, the Klan was yet a fellowship of belief, knitted together by a shared anxiety about
tomorrow and a shared longing for the return of yesterday.
Perhaps, after all, there was only one great enemy: *change!*
Made bewildered and fearful by the swift and surging forces
reshaping "their" country, unwilling or unable to understand this strange, new century, men banded together to
offer resistance. Essentially, then, the Klan was a counterrevolutionary movement. Its core appeal was to those
Americans who, through considerations of rational self-
interest or unconscious emotional needs, dreamed that the
clock might be stopped; and who, as they donned their white
dream robes, knew a momentary identification with a fanci-
ful older and purer community.

The older and purer community of the Klansman's dream
was, of course, a white man's community. "I believe in the
Klan. I don't believe the thing to do at this moment is to go
out and shoot a nigger in the street. But when the time
comes—when it comes—we'll take them down by the busload, by the trainload, that's what we'll do. By the busload.
By the carload! . . . We don't hate Negroes. We love 'em,
in their place—like shinin' shoes, bell-hoppin', street-
sweepin', pickin' cotton, diggin' ditches, eatin' possum,
servin' time, totin' buckshot, river-floatin', etc." Thus spoke
the voice of the Klan in 1965, as articulated by a Jackson-
ville, Florida, barber. "Our main and fundamental objective
is the MAINTENANCE OF THE SUPREMACY OF THE
WHITE RACE in this Republic." Thus spoke the voice
of the Klan in 1867, as articulated by the delegates to
the organizational meeting of the Reconstruction Klan in
Nashville.

Because the Negro was the central target of both the
Reconstruction and mid-twentieth-century Klans, because
both saw the untrammeled Negro as the nation's greatest
menace, the temptation is to interpolate and conclude that

the same Negrophobia dominated the Klan of the twenties. Perceptive historians have not succumbed to this temptation, realizing that the Klan that flowered after World War I reflected the coalescence of many different fears and loyalities. Indeed, students of the Klan in the Southwest, Far West, and Midwest deem the black man an inconsequential factor in the growth of the white-robed order. We may concur that the movements of the 1860's, 1920's, and 1960's, although sharing a common name and ritual, were substantively different. We may even concur that in great areas of the country where the Klan was powerful the Negro population was insignificant, and that, in fact, it is probable that had not a single Negro lived in the United States, a Klan-type order would have emerged, such was the pervasive anxiety of the post-Versailles years.

Yet having escaped the errors of simplism and "present-ism," perhaps in this very sophistication the principle of Ockham's Razor has been forgotten: complex and refined explanations of observed phenomena must not obscure the simple and evident. Just as there is no more demonic theme in American history, so there is none more persistent than that America was a white man's country. White supremacy was an article of faith with almost all modern Europeans and their descendents in the northern New World. Until almost today it was a faith seemingly supported by much scientific and scholarly evidence. Kluxers of every generation have feared the Negro—and consequently have hated him. And Kluxers in every generation have enjoyed the covert endorsement of large numbers of citizens too timid or too hypocritical to enlist under the banner of the fiery cross. The Klan of the 1920's was first, if not foremost, a movement to keep the black man in his place—if necessary, by digging his grave. Its founder, Colonel William Joseph Simmons, was an Alabaman who with a band of Georgians on Thanksgiving night, 1915, ascended Stone Mountain near Atlanta to call "from its slumber of half a century" that Invisible Empire that once had saved the prostrate south from mongrelization. "The present Klan," testified Simmons, "is a memorial to the original organization. In a sense it is the reincarnation among the sons of the spirit of the fathers." As gallant southerners had galloped with torch and mask to the defense of their society imperiled by conquering Yankee and former bondsmen, so their sons would band to resist with equal success the present pretensions of "darkies" who, said Simmons, were "getting pretty uppity." Childhood cloudy fantasies of redeeming Klansmen were given sharper focus on the screen of the darkened Atlanta theater as the good Colonel saw repeated performances (on scrounged passes) of that tarnished epic, *The Birth of a Nation,* a film that wrote "history with lightning," to use Woodrow Wilson's words of mindless approbation; and in both fantasy and film Simmons identified the redemption of his beloved South with the preservation of the existing caste system. It is, therefore, not surprising that all prospective Knights vowed to "faithfully strive for the eternal maintenance of white supremacy." Nor is it a matter of astonishment that when Simmons was maneuvered from control, his successor, Hiram Wesley Evans, reaffirmed the ancient dogma that "God Almighty never intended social equality for Negro and white man," and who, with a coterie of Dallas disciples, implemented the Almighty's wishes by branding with acid the initials KKK across the forehead of a Negro bellhop. As the Klan was reborn in Georgia by southerners determined to rekindle with fiery cross the resistance spirit of their fathers, so it was in Dixie in 1920, 1921, and 1922 that the movement first gained strength. To be sure, presently the Klan penetrated other sections and exploited other anxieties, but its southern "style" and essential Negrophobia was never totally lost. And the 1960's have reminded us of the historic fact that white men in the North when put to the test are scarcely color-blind.

The period immediately following World War I was a time of testing for the white man and a time of terror for the Negro. Even as the guns on the Western Front quieted, racial violence in America exploded. Service overseas gave Negro soldiers a taste of equality and a sense of pride. The migration of thousands to northern cities engendered a feeling of independence. And the millions who remained in the South hoped that President Wilson intended to include American Negroes among the beneficiaries of his new world of democracy. By 1920 their hopes had been shattered and their pretensions corrected. America was to remain, as it always had been, a white man's country. This was the hard lesson learned of a thousand floggings, a hundred lynchings, and a score of race riots in the months following the Armistice—a lesson administered over the land from Washington to Omaha and from Chicago to Longview, Texas. Further, it was an instruction to be repeated throughout the 1920's for the benefit of forgetful Negroes by the revived Ku Klux Klan.

If many Americans were made fearful by the rising tide of color, it is possible that an even greater number trembled over the menace of Rome. In truth, the shadow of the Pope seemed darker than that of the Negro, and anti-Catholicism was the key to the Klan's growth in the Far West and Midwest and, though not initially, perhaps in the South as well. Although Colonel Simmons dreamed of resurrecting the Reconstruction Klan, he in fact reawakened two other resistance movements, the Know-Nothings of the 1840's and 1850's and the American Protective Association of the 1880's and 1890's. In these movements there raged the fever of anti-Catholicism, the oldest and stubbornest variety of

the disease called "nativism," a disease far too common in
the United States to be diagnosed a foreign or un-American
strain. If the conquest of America by Rome seemed a
frightening possibility to nineteenth-century Protestants, to
their twentieth-century sons it was an imminent probability
and, in the great northern cities, an actuality. In the twenty-
five-year period preceding the incident atop Stone Mountain,
the Catholic church gained in membership 114.1 per cent,
and in 1920, the year of the Klan's great surge, Catholics
comprised 36 per cent of the American religious population.
The power, the prestige, the "arrogance" of Catholicism was
everywhere evident in American life; and when Alfred
Emanuel Smith made his first bid for the presidency in
1924, the last, worst fear of Protestants was at hand: the
"Dago of the Tiber" (to borrow a Klansman's characterization of the pope) would now take up residence on the
Potomac.

It is impossible to understand the enormity of the peril
and consequently the enormous appeal of the Klan unless
we comprehend the historic identification between Protestantism and Americanism. Since the first settlements, Protestants had prided themselves on being the senior partners
in the American enterprise, and in the nineteenth century
the American nation and the Protestant denominations had
marched to greatness together. This was entirely appropriate, for there was no discernible tension between the
evangelical churches and society, between piety and patriotism. The Protestant way of faith and the American way of
life were one. What was good for the churches was good for
the country. To be sure, this resulted in a "culture-Protestantism" wherein the churches paid a tragic price for their
comfortable relationship with American culture; rarely was
it found necessary to cry, "Let the Church be the Church!"
The churches were not merely domesticated, they were

virtually emasculated, and like the eunuchs of old, served
as ornaments without seriously disturbing their master's
establishment.

Thus, the prideful cry of the Ohio Klan leader was repeatedly uttered: "We want the country ruled by the sort of
people who settled it. This is *our* country and we alone are
responsible for its future." Protestants viewed the growing
power of Catholicism as not only a threat to their religion
but also to their beloved nation. Indeed, since Protestantism
and Americanism were inseparable, it was impossible to
assault the one without wounding the other. Therefore, the
Klan attracted patriots as well as bigots, appealing to
nationalist loyalties as well as to religious prejudices. Even
irenic-spirited Protestants saw (or thought they saw) in
the authoritarian structure of the Catholic church objective
reasons for opposing its spread in a democratic society. As
in wartime true citizens willingly lay down their lives in
defense of their free institutions, so patriots in peacetime
should freely spend of themselves in the fight against internal subversion. It is instructive that the "Klan verse" of
the New Testament is Romans 12:1: "I beseech you therefore, brethren, by the mercies of God, that ye present your
bodies a living sacrifice, holy, acceptable unto God, which
is your reasonable service." Perhaps we can now understand why the Klan tapped anti-Catholic hostilities even in
areas, such as rural Indiana, where the Catholic population
numbered less than 2 per cent. Social conflict between
Protestants and Catholics over such matters as schools,
local politics, prohibition, and censorship heightened tension
in many communities; but even where abrasive contact was
absent, patriotic Protestants yet feared for the future of
"their" nation.

The very name *Roman* Catholic church was suggestive of
sinister foreign influence, underscoring the essential Americanism of the Protestant denominations. The very militancy

of Catholicism transmuted Protestant tolerance from a virtue to a weakness. And the very authoritarianism of the Church of Rome sharpened the revelation of Protestantism's fragmentation, rendering efforts to quench the conflagration of Catholicism sweeping the land as feeble and ill-directed as the spray from a leaky hose. The Klan carried the hope of Protestant unity and the promise of Protestant militancy. At long last God-fearing men could know, as they assembled around the blazing hillside cross, identification with a mighty supradenominational movement. Like all crusaders, these Klansmen without conscious hypocrisy could cry, "For God and country," and in their righteousness have no sense of shame as they battled the enemies of their faith and nation. "I've attended a lot of church gatherings and conventions," remarked an Exalted Cyclops after the Klan's 1924 national convention, "but I never attended one where the revival spirit was as pronounced as it was at the Klan Klonvocation."

The operative words are "revival spirit," for though anxiety over Catholicism's growth and ambitions was widespread, few liberal Protestants could bring themselves to join the Klan. Thus, far from being a unifying force, the Klan further sharpened the cleavage between Modernists and Fundamentalists. Though not all Fundamentalists were Klansmen, virtually all Klansmen—aside from the obvious charlatans—were Fundamentalists. Fundamentalism and the Klan were perfectly mated in their anti-intellectualism, their morbid compulsion to destroy that which they did not understand, their passion for emotional release, and their frustration, as well as in their blind faith and total commitment. At the same time we should note the national leadership of American Protestantism, including almost every minister of reputation and every theologian of significance, denounced the hooded order, as did almost every national governing body of the larger denominations. Thus the Klan was not an instrument of American Protestantism in the sense, say, that the Inquisition was of the medieval church. It is crucial to understand that the Protestant denominations did not call forth the Klan; rather, the Klan sought desperately to become identified by Protestants as an ally, and it did so by tapping the historic anti-Catholic bias learned by Protestant children in cradle and conventicle and by exploiting the prideful Protestant assumption that they were the darlings of American history.

The Klan made the identification in many ways. Its symbol was a cross, and "The Old Rugged Cross" became almost the official hymn, sometimes with the alteration, "I will cherish the bright Fiery Cross. . . . " Its Kreed "reverentially" acknowledged the majesty of God. Its code of conduct was drawn from the Ten Commandments. The *Kloran* declared that "the living Christ is a Klansman's criterion of character," and Klan pamphlets bore such titles as "Christ and Other Klansmen." Every Klavern had a chaplain called a Kludd, who opened each meeting with a prayer and closed with a benediction. The fervent religiosity of the meeting reached a crescendo as the Knights gathered before the altar to sing the "Kloxology." And perhaps as they marched from the Klavern to burn a warning cross atop a nearby hill, their voices broke forth in the militant "Onward, Christian Soldiers." Perhaps, too, a few thoughtful members quieted their troubled consciences with the words from another much loved hymn, "God moves in mysterious ways, His wonders to behold."

Little wonder, then, that the Klan succeeded in attracting thousands of evangelical ministers, men already disturbed by the passing of "Old-Time Religion" and made uneasy by their own declining community status. When a Kleagle entered an area, almost invariably he made his first overtures to the local preachers, offering them membership free of the usual ten-dollar fee. Often a co-operating clergyman was thanked or a stiff-kneed one threatened by a sudden

Sunday visitation of white-robed and masked Klansmen who silently entered the sanctuary, marched down the aisles, congregated in front of the pulpit to present a purse of perhaps forty dollars. Additional hundreds of ministers were on the Klan payrolls as organizers, lecturers, and officers; and without their active labors and without the tacit endorsement of a numerically impressive element of the ministry, the Klan could not have flourished. The obscene spectacle of men of God gathered about a cross ignited by their hands is perhaps tempered only by a sense of pity for Christians possessed by such anxiety.

"My country in 1900 is something totally different from my own country of 1860. I am wholly a stranger in it." The writer continued: "The child born in 1900 would . . . be born into a new world which would not be a unity but a multiple." This lament and this prediction were made by that purest of patricians, Henry Adams, grandson and great-grandson of presidents; but the words might have been uttered by the most banal of Klansmen, for the opening years of the twentieth century saw the older Americans overwhelmed by a sense of estrangement as "their" land was flooded by a sea of new immigrants. Historians of immigration make much of the shock of alienation experienced by the "uprooted" as they migrated from the psychological security of their familiar European villages to the unknown New World. These insights are altogether valid, for the immigrant's ordeal was seldom physically easy and never emotionally painless. The obverse side of the coin, however, has been examined by fewer students. How does a man accustomed to power and prestige respond when strangers enter the land to dethrone him—and if perchance the dethronement is only in the man's imagination, it does not lessen the fear.

Between the year William McKinley enlisted as a private in the 23rd Ohio Volunteer Infantry in the Civil War and his assassination at the hands of a twenty-eight-year-old

Polish-American with the "sinister" name of Czolgosz, fourteen million people came to the United States, "new" immigrants from southern and eastern Europe accounting for over 50 per cent of the total by the 1890's. In the opening fifteen years of the new century the torrent accelerated rather than slackened, an average of 1,000,000 entering annually, and now the "new" immigrants accounted for 72 per cent. The impulse was temporarily stemmed by the war, but with the coming of peace, it renewed. From June, 1920, to June, 1921, more than 800,000 individuals entered, and consuls in Europe reported that additional millions were planning to leave. Then, in one of the most momentous enactments in American history, Congress virtually closed the gates, and the Statue of Liberty lost all relevance save for returning tourists—and a handful of immigrants. (Probably the whole twenty-five-year period after 1925 saw fewer immigrants to the United States than the single year 1907.)

There was more than a casual relationship between this surge of immigration and the resurgence of the Ku Klux Klan. These "new" immigrants, these "beaten men of beaten races," these mongrel worshipers of Bacchus or Baal or Marx, seemed no less threatening to the cherished America of yesteryear than insolent blacks and arrogant Romans. Inquired Colonel Simmons in explaining the growth of the Klan: "What were the dangers which the white men saw threatening to crush and overwhelm Anglo-Saxon civilization? The dangers were in the tremendous influx of foreign immigration, tutored in alien dogmas and alien creeds, flowing in from all climes and slowly pushing the native-born white American population into the center of the country, there to be ultimately overwhelmed and smothered." The Colonel's successor, Evans, elaborated: "When the Klan first appeared the nation was in the confusion of sudden awakening from the lovely dream of the melting pot, disorganized and helpless before the invasion of aliens and alien ideas. After ten years of the Klan it arms for defense." Nordic Americans, he continued, finally

> decided that even the crossing of salt water did not dim a single spot on a leopard; that an alien usually remains an alien no matter what is done to him, what veneer of education he gets, what oath he takes, nor what public attitudes he adopts. They decided that the melting pot was a ghastly failure, and remembered that the very name was coined by a member of one of the races—the Jews—which most determinedly refuses to melt. They decided that in every way, as well as in politics, the alien in the vast majority of cases is unalterably fixed in his instincts, character, thought and interests by centuries of racial selection and development, that he thinks first for his own people, works only with and for them, and never an American. They decided that in character, instincts, thought, and purposes—in his whole soul—an alien remains fixedly alien to America and all it means.

It is again necessary to insist on a hard point. As the Klan tapped rather than created Negrophobia and anti-Catholicism, so it did not so much inspire as reflect a pervasive Anglo-Saxon racism. The Klan can be understood only in the context of the tribalism of the times: the lynching of Leo Frank and the judicial execution of Sacco and Vanzetti; the subtle anti-Semitic discrimination instituted by eastern clubs, resorts, and universities and the crude slanders leveled at Jews by Henry Ford; the superman notions of Jack London and the elitist concepts of Irving Babbitt; the "Yellow Peril" warnings of Homer Lea and the anti-Oriental practices of native Californians; the findings prideful to Anglo-Saxons and diminishing to other "races" of the Army intelligence tests administered during the war and the conclusions implicit in "objective" sociological studies; and the consensus seemingly reached by genet-

icists such as Henry Fairfield Osborn, geographers such
as Ellsworth Huntington, psychologists such as William
McDougall, and a host of pseudo scholars such as Madison
Grant, that the American grain was being choked by alien
chaff.

It is disconcerting to note the similarities between this
xenophobia and European fascism. Both stressed racial
purity, a return to a primitive community of one blood, and
the purging of alien minority groups. And if the Klan
preached 100 per cent Americanism, was this not the
national goal during World War I? If the Klan sought to
save the country from mongrelization, was this not the
intent of the Congressional restriction laws of 1921 and
1924, laws as ardently supported by many patricians, popu-
lists, and progressives as by hooded Knights?

John Higham has given a very serviceable definition of
nativism: an intense opposition to an internal minority on
the ground of its foreign (i.e., "un-American") connec-
tions; and he has discerned three major themes each with
a separate history reaching back before the Civil War:
anti-Catholicism, Anglo-Saxon racism, and antiforeign radicalism. We have seen how the Ku Klux Klan reflected and
exploited two of these manifestations. Almost equally central to the Klan's purposes was the stamping out of radicalism in all its variants. Throughout American history,
patriots have feared their nation endangered by imported
radical ideologies. The Birchites and McCarthyites of the
mid-twentieth century experience an apprehension as old as
that which impelled the Alien and Sedition acts during the
anti-Jacobin hysteria of the 1790's. And when in the 1960's
Klansmen proclaim "FIGHT COMMUNISM," the injunction is no more imperative than that given by their fathers
to "FIGHT BOLSHEVISM." Today the enemy within is
deemed less the alien immigrant than the native-born "fellow traveler" seduced by alien ideas. Following World War

I, however, the stereotype of the immigrant radical knew its most tarnished hour.

During the war all Americans, irrespective of race or religion or ethnic background, had rallied 'round the flag, save only for some Socialists, Industrial Workers of the World, and other elements of the left wing. Thus radicalism was equated with wartime treason, the dissenter identified with the Hun. Scarcely had the United States been saved, despite the radicals' activities, than there loomed the menace of Bolshevism. And in America the advance agents of the Comintern were quite obviously aliens who somehow owed a double allegiance to Germany and Russia. Surely alien agitators were responsible for the massive labor unrest, the Seattle general strike, the Boston police strike, the "Great Steel Strike," and the thousands of additional strikes involving millions of workers in 1919 and 1920. Surely no true American laborer, unless deranged by Bolshevik propaganda, would march in May Day parades or shout, "To hell with the United States!" or join the new Communist and Communist-Labor parties. And certainly only foreigners were capable of the bombings and attempted assassinations of public officials that seemed proof positive of a vast revolutionary conspiracy.

Such was the peril, it was not enough to bar future immigration or patiently instruct foreigners in the meaning of Americanism. Heroic surgery was immediately required to cut out the cancerous growth. The "Great Red Scare" was a time of unparalleled intimidation, suppression, imprisonment, deportation at the local, state, and federal level—because at no time in American history, either before or since, had the American people been seized by such a collective failure of nerve. It is, therefore, altogether fitting that the most feared nativist movement in American history, the revived Ku Klux Klan, should date its take-off point from the "Great Red Scare." The Klan never articulated an economic program, and capitalism was not mentioned in its constitution; but it is evident that the Klan saw Americanism and radicalism in irreconcilable tension and that at least some elements in the business community supported the order as an ally in the war against all forms of radicalism, including, as it happened, labor unions.

Hopefully, the anatomy of the revived Ku Klux Klan is becoming discernible. Far from being a uniquely reprehensible episode in an otherwise sunny American pageant, it was the archetype of nativist movements, the receptacle for nativist themes flowing from the distant American past. Far from being an isolated, ugly phenomenon in an age of wonderful nonsense, it reflected the tensions of an age of revolution and embodied the anxieties of a people convulsed by change. Far from being a membership entirely of society's failures, it embraced many citizens who historically had enjoyed power and prestige, the prerogatives of the nation's senior partners. To repeat a point made earlier, the Klan may best be understood as a counterrevolutionary movement called into being by sober individuals to resist a world they neither made nor admired—nor understood. The Klan adopted as one of its mottos the command attributed to George Washington: "Put none but Americans on guard tonight!" Alas, Klansmen would not acknowledge—indeed, could not bear to acknowledge—that Negroes, Catholics, immigrants, or "radicals" had any rightful claim to the coveted title "American."

In 1927 in the southern Alabama farm country of Crenshaw, a group of Klansmen led by a Baptist minister, L. A. Nalls, flogged a divorcee, the mother of two children, who had married a divorced man. After the whipping the Reverend Nalls offered the consoling sermon: "Sister, you were not punished in anger this evening; you were punished in a spirit of kindness and correction, to set your feet aright and to show your childen how a good mother should go."

A collection for the woman was taken up among her assail-
ants and the resulting three dollars and fifty cents were
given her along with a jar of Vaseline for her wounds. This
incident and these words reveal still another color of the
chameleon-like Klan: its moral authoritarianism, its vigilantism, and its sadism.

Recent scholarship has demonstrated what must have
been self-evident to the victims of the Klan's wrath at the
time: the hooded Knights, who took as their motto, "Not
for self, but for others," regarded themselves as perfect
knights, *sans peur et sans reproche*, and therefore the
proper guardians of public virtue and private morality. And
in the postwar years, public corruption and private de-
pravity seemed endemic. Is it necessary to explicate this
point? Is it mandatory to refer once again to Hemingway's
heroes and Fitzgerald's heroines and all the beautiful and
the damned of the Lost Generation of the Roaring Twenties? The quips about rising skirts and falling morals and
the times being out of joint when the word "neck" abruptly
became a verb are not merely surface manifestations of a
society that remained at its core stable. Bootleggers, speak-
easies, rumrunners, syphilitic gangsters, organized gambling, open prostitution, lurid movies, salacious literature,
Sabbath sports, easy divorce, family disintegration, sexy
dances, purchased politicians, bought policemen—these
things, of course, were not unique to the twenties. Yet a
social and moral revolution, already apparent before the
war, was in fact dislocating the old nineteenth-century Victorian structure. The acids of modernity were in truth dis-
solving the old verities of piety, patriotism, and moral
purity, reverence for church, country, and home. To older
Americans this revolution was as menacing as the rising
tide of Negroes, Catholics, aliens, and radicals. Indeed, the
strangers in the land (together with the proverbially sexu-
ally depraved blacks) had introduced these evils into a for-

merly chaste society, and now, obviously, even the sons and daughters of the American Revolution were being infected.

Read a Klan handbill: "Every criminal, every gambler, every thug, every libertine, every girl runner, every home wrecker, every wife beater, every dope peddler, every moonshiner, every crooked politician, every pagan Papist priest, every shyster lawyer, every K. of C., every white slaver, every black spider—is fighting the Klan. Think it over. Which side are you on?" In torchlight parades white-robed men (and it probably is not happenstance that white, the emblem of purity, was chosen for the robes) carried signs: LAW AND ORDER MUST PREVAIL. COHABITATION BETWEEN WHITES AND BLACKS MUST STOP. BOOTLEGGERS, PIMPS, HANGERS-ON, GET RIGHT OR GET OUT. WIFE-BEATERS, FAMILY-DESERTERS, HOMEWRECKERS, WE HAVE NO ROOM FOR YOU. LAW VIOLATORS, WE ARE WATCHING YOU. BEWARE. GO JOY RIDING WITH YOUR OWN WIFE. THE SHERIFFS OF BOWIE AND MILLER COUNTIES HAVE MORE DEPUTIES THAN CARRY COMMISSIONS. PURE WOMENHOOD. CRAP SHOOTERS BEWARE. LOVE THY NEIGHBOR AS THYSELF, BUT LEAVE HIS WIFE ALONE. Although the evidence is fragmentary, it is quite possible that the majority of individuals flogged, tarred and feathered, branded, emasculated, and otherwise tortured and intimidated by the Klan were those who had in some way transgressed morally.

When the Klan proclaimed its opposition to "Jew, Jug, and Jesuit," its intimate relationship to Prohibition was merely underscored. There were millions of prohibitionists, of course, who never became Klansmen, but almost all Klansmen *claimed* to be as dry as a powder flask. The harsh, repressive spirit of Prohibition represented a souring of the original humanitarian passion of the early temperance reformers. Just so, the moral passion of the Kluxers was a perversion rather than a denial of progressivism's vision of a redeemed society.

And so it came to pass that thousands of good, decent citizens, genuinely alarmed by civic corruption and moral decay, failed initially to discern the Klan's own corrupt nature and welcomed it as an agency of reform. And seemingly many a community *was* rid of gamblers, bootleggers, and prostitutes because of the Klan's presence. Exulted the editor of a Texas newspaper: "It cost Goose Creek just $1200 to clean up. It cost the boys down there $1200 in fines assessed for flogging to transform a rough and tumble oil camp into a progressive and God-fearing community of industrious toilers. . . . The Ku Klux Klan has made a new and different town of Goose Creek." After one visit from Klan regulators, it was said, a tough town became "almost a Sunday School class." Vigilantism is, after all, as much a sign of a desire for law and order as it is a manifestation of lawlessness. In America vigilantism was an old and not always dishonorable tradition. In fact, in 1920 and 1921 masked farmers roamed the countryside with lighted torch in order to check the sale of cotton, and their acts of intimidation, however justified, provided an example for the Klan to follow.

The dangers of men taking the law into their own hands, the arrogance of men appointing themselves as civic censors, the voycurism and prurience implicit in Comstockery, the sadism in the act of stripping and whipping "fallen" women, the temptation to exact personal vengeance in the name of "morality"—these things are no less true because obvious. As Sartre observed, "It is *fun* to be an anti-Semite." Undoubtedly, the Klan attracted cranky professional moralists, village vigilantes, local busybodies, prudish Pecksniffs, old ladies of both sexes haunted (as Mencken sneered) by the fear that someone, somewhere, might be happy. But even Klansmen of the purest conscious motives and

highest community status failed to heed the words of George
Santayana: "Neither prosperity nor empire nor heaven can
be worth the winning at the price of a virulent temper,
bloody hands, an anguished spirit, and a vain hatred of the
rest of the world." In our effort to understand the Klan
we might heed the words of John Higham: "Perhaps, in
the pageant of American history, the white-robed Klansmen
should stand in the place of Santayana's genteel New
Englander as the Last Puritan."

When a Klansman addressed a Catholic priest, "You,
who wears his collar backwards like a mule," his audience
caught the allusion, for they were steeped in agrarian life
and lore, and when they dreamed of the past it was of a
pastoral community, a virgin land, inhibited by sturdy
yeomen, unspotted by the urban world. But urbanization
had come to the United States. In fact, the revived Klan
emerged at the precise moment when the tides of population, power, and prestige were running heavily to the city,
and at the end of the twenties only 40 per cent of the population still lived in rural areas. There is more than a casual
correlation between this demographic change and the Klan's
rise. Yet it is not a simple relationship.

Most students interpret the Klan as a rural, village, and
small-town phenomenon. This is true less in a statistical
than in a psychological sense. The Klan was reborn in
Atlanta. It enjoyed great strength in the booming cities of
the Southwest: Shreveport, Dallas, Tulsa, Little Rock (but
not cosmopolitan New Orleans). The Milwaukee unit was
the first and largest in the state of Wisconsin, and Detroit
was the center of the Klan's power in Michigan. It was
strong in Indianapolis, Chicago, Dayton, and Pittsburgh in
the heartland of America, and on the eastern shore in Nor-
folk and on the West Coast in Portland. Cities as diverse as
Denver, Tampa, and Philadelphia were spawning beds. It
is therefore misleading to presume that city dwellers were

protected by some invisible *cordon sanitaire* from the virus of the Invisible Empire. Yet it remains essentially correct to identify the Klan with the older agrarian angle of vision.

For one thing, the Klan *was* in fact a force in the villages and small towns dotting the land. For another, there had migrated to the cities farmers and villagers who, regardless of how they might be located for census purposes, retained their rural mentality. They were America's own uprooted, as lost and dislocated as the European immigrant. Stripped of their identity by the externalization, impersonalization, and depersonalization of urban industrial life, they sought desperately to define themselves by clinging to the values of their fathers and perhaps of their own childhood. The Klan had held the hope that men might preserve their ancient, agrarian values even as they now lived in an urban environment. Indeed, it was imperative that these values be imposed on the cities. Thus when Klansmen spoke of redeeming the country, in reality they meant saving the great cities of the nation, for rural and village America had not yet been lost. It was in the cities, dominated by alien hordes and ruled by politicians subservient to their wishes, that there flourished gangsterism, alcoholism, skepticism, radicalism, sexualism—in brief, the paganism that threatened to break forth from the metropolitan centers and engulf the entire land. The very enormity of the challenge heightened the Klansman's anxiety and dictated the extremism of his response.

Just as Klansmen were in the twentieth century but dreamed they were not of it, so they hoped their country somehow could be in the world but not of it. The Klan clearly drew from the wellsprings of nineteenth-century American exceptionalism and isolationism. Equally discernible is its marriage with the mood of disenchantment and bitterness that followed the Great Crusade. It is unnecessary to explicate this point at length. The Klan opposed

American membership in the World Court and, at least after 1920, in the League of Nations. It did not favor the reduction of war debts or disarmament, and it loathed pacifism. (However, the Klan did not agitate for intervention in Mexico, a foreign adventure associated with the Catholic hierarchy.) It was the old story of American innocence and European wickedness. Klansmen would have concurred in Ben Hecht's sentiment, if not in his imagery, in comparing Wilson at Versailles among the crafty Old World diplomats to "a long-faced virgin trapped in a bawdy house and calling in violent tones for a glass of lemonade." Once again it must be remarked that the spirit of the Klan fused intimately with the general temper of the 1920's. In its ethnocentrism, provincialism, and inability to accept the facts of twentieth-century life, the Klan mirrored perfectly the notion of Fortress America, a nation whose strength was the strength of ten because its heart was pure. And America's purity could be preserved only in isolation. Alas, the Klan's Manichaean view of the international scene was as murky as its vision of an America divided between the children of light and the children of darkness.

Men who sees things in this fashion, who make simplistic judgments and draw sharp distinctions between right and wrong, good and evil, who think in terms of stereotypes and moralisms, tend to be prejudiced. They also tend to be anti-intellectual. Ambiguity, irony, paradox, relativism, contingency, skepticism, suspended judgment, speculation, open-mindedness—these are the attributes of the intellectual's glory (and perhaps the source of his misery). The average Klansman was neither blessed nor cursed by them; the intellectual as Klansman was atypical. Indeed, we are of the conviction that while the Klan appealed to an entire host of Americans, poor and prosperous, disinherited and establishment-secure, southerner and Yankee, farmer, villager, and urbanite, scarcely a single intellectual claimed citizenship in the Invisible Empire. Thus the Klan both perpetuated the pervasive anti-intellectualism in American history and illuminated the growing estrangement in the 1920's between artists and scholars and the commonalty. Hiram Wesley Evans put it pointedly and poignantly:

> We are a movement of the plain people, very weak in the matter of culture, intellectual support, and trained leadership. We are demanding, and we expect to win, a return of power into the hands of the everday, not highly cultured, not overly intellectualized, but unspoiled and not de-Americanized, average citizen of the old stock. Our members and leaders are all of this class—the opposition of the intellectuals and liberals who hold the leadership and from whom we expect to wrest control, is almost automatic.
>
> This is undoubtedly a weakness. It lays us open to the charge of being "hicks" and "rubes" and "drivers of second-hand Fords." We admit it. Far worse, it makes it hard for us to state our case and advocate our crusade in the most effective way, for most of us lack skill in language. . . .
>
> Every popular movement has suffered from just this handicap. . . .
>
> The Klan does not believe that the fact that it is emotional and instinctive, rather than coldly intellectual, is a weakness. All action comes from emotion, rather than from ratiocination. Our emotions and the instincts on which they are based have been bred into us for thousands of years; far longer than reason has had a place in the human brain. . . . They are the foundations of our American civilization, even more than our great historic documents; they can be trusted where the fine-haired reasoning of the denatured intellectuals cannot.

Thus spoke the spirit of fundamentalism with its repression through anti-evolution laws and heresy trials and textbook censorship of all in modern science and scholarship threatening to a faith made truly blind by ignorance.

Thus spoke the spirit of fascism with its appeal to primitive instincts and tribal symbols. Thus spoke mediocre men maddened by the epithet's "yahoo," "boob," and "Babbitt" flung at them by all the sneering Menckens of the "Smart Set." Thus spoke Klansmen in an age when not only were ancient truths questioned, the very existence of Truth itself was coming to be doubted.

If the Klan's anti-intellectualism is apparent, its predilection for violence is not. Contemporary observers tended to exaggerate the extent of Klan violence, but perhaps recent scholarship has swung too far in its minimization of it.

In much of the North and East, physical coercion was rarely practiced, and never in some communities. The historian of the Klan in Wisconsin, for example, believes it false and dishonest to picture the Klan as threatening. Often the Klan adjusted itself to community life and lived peaceably alongside other institutions within the social order. When the Klavern assembled, the proceedings were as prosaic as the lodge meetings of George F. Babbitt. In the South and Southwest, the lash and acid were more frequently employed, but even in these areas there was a definite lessening of violence by the middle of the decade. Evans, after his assumption of technical control in 1922, disavowed coercion. Moreover, undoubtedly some crimes were committed in the name of the Klan for which the order bore no direct responsibility, and some chapters offered sizable rewards for the arrest of persons practicing violence under the guise of the Klan.

But to absolve the Invisible Empire of all acts of terror and torture simply will not wash. For one thing, perhaps the number of intimidated victims who did not report attacks exceeded the number of instances when the Klan was falsely held responsible for an outrage. For another, inevitably a secret hooded order would be attractive to the "tough guy," the psychopath driven by sadomasochistic

tendencies to deeds of cruelty; and in the total membership
of perhaps five million, there must have numbered thousands of embryonic storm troopers. Third, even when a
chapter did not authorize a special "whipping squad" garbed
in appropriate black robes and hoods (as some chapters
did), it was impossible for the leaders to control the night-
riding activities of all members. After all, it made small
difference to the victim whether his back was laid open
by Klansmen under orders or acting independently. Fourth,
there is much documentary evidence proving the Klan's employment of violence. Finally and above all, the American
people have had a long and intimate acquaintance with
brutality. Perhaps we have been compelled to spin the
myth of our gentle dispositions precisely because we find
unbearable the reality of our violence. This dark legacy
from earlier generations of Americans was exacerbated by
World War I. The war not only sanctified the killing of
Germans, it gave sanction to the practice of vigilantism
against "hyphenates," "slackers," pacifists, and all those
who were less than totally committed to the Great Crusade.
President Wilson accurately predicted, "Once lead this
people into war and they'll forget there ever was such a
thing as tolerance." Primitive passions were deliberately
whipped to a feverish pitch. And then, too soon, came peace.
As Charles W. Ferguson in *The Confusion of Tongues*
wrote: "We had indulged in wild and lascivious dreams.
We had imagined ourselves in the act of intercourse with
the Whore of the World. Then suddenly the war was over
and the Whore vanished for a time and we were in a
condition of coitus interruptus." The frustration was intolerable. It was urgent to seek release by identifying
new enemies. Klansmen found many surrogates for the
Hun. The spirit of violence appropriate to the war against
Germany was proper to the new crusade against internal
subversion.

The Klan embodied another characteristic that if not uniquely American is surely identified with the Yankee style: huckstering. In our more cynical moments the revived Klan's ancestors appear to be less convent-burning Know-Nothings, night-riding ex-Confederates, or bigoted soldiers in the army of the American Protective Association than the Connecticut peddlers of wooden nutmegs, the slippery Simon Suggs who took as his motto, "It pays to be shifty in a new country," the outrageous P. T. Barnum, and the fatuous Colonel Beriah Sellers. And in these moments of disenchantment, the Klan seems appropriate to the mood of the 1920's less because it was a time of trouble than because it was the decade of Barton and Babbitt, Gantry and Coué. On reflection, these four men were themselves anxious and pitched their appeals to insecure people whether selling advertising or real estate, salvation or mental health, thus suggesting the many faces of anxiety. In any case, at least some Klan leaders in opening a promotional meeting might well have borrowed the salutation of the night club empresario Texas Guinan, "Hello, suckers!" At least some might have taken to their hearts the admonition of W. C. Fields, "Never give a sucker an even break." And at least some might have substituted for the motto, "Not for self, but for others," the warning, "Caveat emptor."

Enormous sums of money poured into the Klan coffers and the leaders' pockets, perhaps as much as $75,000,000. The initiation fee demanded of every new member was known as the "Klecktoken." Usually the split was as follows: the Kleagle who signed the candidate and collected the fee retained for himself $4, remitting $6 to the King Kleagle who in turn extracted $1 before sending the remaining $5 to the Grand Goblin of the Domain. He retained $.50 and passed on $4.50 to the Imperial Kleagle, who in

turn kept $2.50 and paid the rest into the treasury of the
Imperial Wizard.

The Klecktoken was not the only tax levied on the citizens
of the Invisible Empire. The Gate City Manufacturing
Company of Atlanta, controlled by high officials of the order,
was given exclusive contract to furnish robes, hoods, and
other regalia. The outfit sold for $6.50, perhaps double the
manufacturing cost. "Initiation water," straight from the
"sacred" Chattahoochee River near Atlanta, was bottled
and peddled at bootleg prices, $10.00 a quart. "Horse robes,"
the carrying cases for the costumes, and trinkets such as
pocket knives were happily made available. A Klansman
paid an Imperial tax of $1.80 per year, plus a small addi-
tional duty, usually $.10 per month, levied by the state office.
The local Klan had its own per capita tax, which customarily
varied from $6 to $10 annually. A Klansman was further
expected to contribute to the rental of halls, the purchase
of Bibles and flags, the traveling expenses of local officials,
accountants' and lawyers' fees, and publishing costs.

Professing to do good, the Klan leaders did well. David C.
Stephenson, Grand Dragon of the Realm of Indiana and
points east and west, the most malevolent figure in the
entire movement, amassed from his office an estimated
fortune of $3,000,000. Imperial Kleagle Edward Young
Clarke, a born huckster, for his exalted labors received as
much as $40,000 a month. The good gray Colonel Simmons
was sufficiently effectual to demand $146,000 before re-
leasing the reins of power to Evans, as earlier he had been
sufficiently gallant not to spurn as Imperial Wizard such
tokens of appreciation from the faithful as limousines and
a mansion in Atlanta known as "Klan Krest." This passion
for the dollar was the greatest source of Klan disunity. If
we are rightly angered by the Klan's violence and bigotry,
its commercialism offends our sensibilities. That is, until we

are sobered by the thought that huckstering was very much
the fashion in the 1920's. In truth, when in all American
history was the pursuit on the dollar deemed gauche? As
in so many other ways, the Klan's commercialism was the
spirit of America writ large.

When Colonel Simmons before a Congressional investigating committee (a hearing, incidentally, that boomed the
Klan) described his new order as a purely fraternal and
patriotic organization, this was not pure dissimulation. As
one student of the movement, Norman F. Weaver, concludes: "What saved the Klan movement in Wisconsin was
its discovery that fraternalism, if wrapped attractively,
sold well. Fraternalism, good fellowship conviviality, and
boon companionship offered the Klan a fertile field to exploit. . ." The Klan appealed to grown men who had not
put away their adolescent fantasies. Indeed, like little boys
in a neighborhood club or school fraternity, Klansmen delighted in the chumminess of their secret, "select" lodge.
It was a delicious feeling to be "in on things." Frank
Tannenbaum further observed: "The danger of the Ku
Klux Klan is that it dramatizes and perpetuates a state
of excitation. It seizes upon the monotony of a small town
and gives it a daily drama. It takes him who lived an un-
eventful life, one who is nobody in particular, and makes
something of him. It gives him a purpose; makes him a
soldier in a cause." A reporter, Leonard Cline, captured this
spirit when he wrote:

> It must have provided a real thrill to go scooting through the
> shadowy roads in somebody else's flivver, to meet in lonely dingles
> in the pine woods and flog other men, to bounce down the fifteen-
> foot declivity where the ridge ends and swoop at twenty-five miles
> an hour through the flatlands around Mer Rouge, through phan-
> tasmal Lafourche swamp with its banshee live oaks waving their
> snaky tresses in the moonlight. It was perpetual Halloween. And
> even if one didn't care much for church, and took one's shot of

white lightning when one could get it, and would pay a dollar
any day for five minutes in a trollop's arms, it was reassuring to
know that religion approved and sanctified one's pranks. It made
one bolder.

Such is the fraternalism of the Americans, observed Will
Rogers, that two citizens could not meet each other on the
street without one of them pounding a gavel and calling
the other to order; and it was said that when two or three
churchmen gathered together in the name of the Lord
they formed a committee. Our very freedom, our verti-
cal and horizontal mobility, the absence of a hereditary
monarchy, established church, feudal class structure, and
national university, have made us a nation of joiners. In
a loosely constructed, traditionless, individualistic, atom-
istic society there is an even greater need for social (non-
governmental) control. "The looser the package the tighter
the string must be." Commented Tocqueville, "I know of
no country in which there is so little independence of mind
and real freedom of discussion as in America." Because we
have not been rooted to village or caste or clan, we have
been a lonely people; hence our frantic efforts to escape
this intolerable loneliness by joining clubs and lodges. In
the 1920's there were an estimated eight hundred such
fraternal societies with a combined membership of over
thirty million persons. It is possible, therefore, to view
the Klan as an effort to resolve the identification crisis of
the generation of the 1920's. We are almost tempted to
say that the typical Klansman typified Riesman's "other-
directed man."

When Thoreau observed that Americans lead lives of
quiet desperation, he might have added that they lead lives
of desperate boredom. Novelists have long discerned what
historians are coming to recognize: the ennui, intellectual
sterility, cultural vacuity, and sexual repression of village
and small-town life have exacted from their inhabitants a

fearful psychic toll. The Klan was the circus coming to
town. It was a revival conducted by Billy Sunday or Gipsy
Smith. It was a scandal involving the preacher and the
married organist. It was news that war had been declared.
It was a lynching. It was Halloween and the Fourth of July
and the County Fair. A Klan newspaper appealed to prospective members with the banner: "JUST TO PEP UP
THE GAME. THIS SLOW LIFE IS KILLING ME." To
countless men, citizenship in the Invisible Empire gave
assurance that they were still alive.

And what a grand and mysterious Empire it was! (To a
prosaic few, of course, attendance at a Klan rally elicited
only the groan, "Oh, my God, my feet hurt!") We now
know that the Invisible Empire was a very fragmented
thing, but on paper it appeared tightly structured. There
were eight "Domains" varying in size from a single thickly
populated state to a cluster of sparsely populated ones.
Each one of the forty-eight states, known as a "Realm,"
was further broken down into "Provinces," comprised of
perhaps a score of counties. Within each Province lay the
local chapters. The Invisible Empire was under the rule of
the "Imperial Wizard," the Domain under the command
of the "Grand Goblin," the Realm under the jurisdiction of
the "Grand Dragon," the Province under the control of the
"Great Titan," and the local Klan under the leadership of
the "Exalted Cyclops." The members of the Wizard's cabinet were known collectively as the "Genii." Coadjutor to
the Wizard was the "Emperor," an office created in 1922
in order to kick Simmons upstairs on his way out. The
Imperial legislature was called the "Klonvokation"; the
"Kloncilium" was primarily a judicial body. Assisting each
Grand Dragon was a council of nine known collectively
as the "Hydras." Attached to each Great Titan were seven
advisors, the "Furies." Members of the local Klan were,
in addition to the Exalted Cyclops, eleven "Terrors," the
"Klaliff" (vice-president), the "Klokard" (lecturer), the

"Kludd" (chaplain), the "Kligrapp" (secretary), the "Klabee" (treasurer), the "Kladd" (conductor of members into the meeting), the "Klarogo" (inner guard of the meeting), the "Klexter" (outer guard of the meeting), and the three "Klokann" (a board of investigators, auditors, and advisors, each member of which bore the title "Klokan"). The meeting place of the local Klan was called the "Klavern"; the monthly meeting the "Klonklave." Each meeting was conducted according to the rules set forth in the "Kloran."

The Klan had its own "Klalendar," dating from the birth of the Reconstruction order. The seven days of the week were, in order: "dark, deadly, dismal, doleful, desolate, dreadful, and desperate." The five weeks of the month were "woeful, weeping, wailing, wonderful, and weird." The twelve months of the year were "bloody, gloomy, hideous, fearful, furious, alarming, terrible, horrible, mourning, sorrowful, rightful, and appalling." Thus July 4, 1923, for example, became "The Dismal Day of the Weeping Week of the Hideous Month of the year of the Klan LVII."

The Klansmen sang "klodes," muttered passwords ("Kotop," to which the reply was "Potok," both meaning nothing), and carried on "klonversations." The latter were an exchange of code words formed from the first letters of sentences.

Ayak:	Are you a Klansman?
Akia:	A Klansman I am.
Capowe:	Countersign and password or written evidence.
Cygnar:	Can you give number and realm?
No. 1 Atga:	Number one Klan of Atlanta, Georgia.
Kigy:	Klansman, I greet you.
Itsub:	In the sacred, unfailing bond.

They would then "Klasp" left hands and, if an "alien"
(non-member) was near, whisper the warning, "Sanbog."
(Strangers are near. Be on your guard!)

The mumbo jumbo, the flimflam, was seemingly inex-
haustible: robes, hoods, parades (with visors up in friendly
communities), fiery crosses, picnics, barbecues, sky diving,
fire works, funerals, weddings (a Knight and his lady of
the women's auxiliary were often married before assembled
thousands). In areas where floggings were considered
unfashionable, Klansmen busied themselves delivering
Christmas baskets, Thanksgiving turkeys, and purses to
the needy; and hospitals, orphanages, and schools were
succored. The Klan organized a Women's Order, a Junior
Order for boys from 12 to 18, and a Tri-K Klub for young
girls; and a Krusaders unit for foreign-born Protestants,
who would have been eligible for Klan membership had
they been born in the United States. Apparently Negroes,
Catholics, Jews, and prostitutes were never wooed. All
in all, lonely men found it warming to chant with other
lonely men:

> United we stick
> Divided we're stuck
> The better we stick
> The better we Klux!

These benign activities must not be permitted to mask
the Klan's authentic diabolism. Was it in a spirit of philanthropy that in Mer Rouge the Klan trussed two young
men in wire and flung their still living bodies under the
cleated wheels of a tractor? Was it an act of patriotism
to beat to a pulp the genitals of a Tulsa Jew? Did the
Dallas Negro disfigured by the branding of the initials
KKK across his forehead deem himself the beneficiary of
the Klan's charity? Did the abducted Miss Madge Ober-

holtzer experience the Klan's love when Grand Dragon
Stephenson sadistically attacked her naked body with his
teeth, lacerating her so severely that she might have died
from the wounds had she not, in her humiliation, first
taken a fatal poison? Was it merely whimsical that the
Klan should touch off civil war in Oklahoma, coerce Oregon
into outlawing parochial schools, drench Williamson County,
Illinois, in blood, and ignite riots in Pennsylvania and New
Jersey and elsewhere? Was it true fraternalism to boycott
business establishments owned by Catholics, Jews, and
immigrants, and patronize only those displaying such signs
as "Klansman's Kafe," "Krippled Kars Kured," "Kleans
Klothes Klean" and "TWK" (Trade With Klansmen)? What
happens to the fiber of a community shadowed by the presence of a vast and mysterious Invisible Empire that "sees
all and hears all?" The mayor of Enid, Oklahoma, answered
this question: "You elbow your best friends and you do not
know whether or not you are rubbing up against a Klansman or not. Our watchword is 'Keep your mouth shut
tight and keep out of the hands of the Klansman.'" The
Oklahoma Leader caught the essence of the Klan's ugly
nature: "The Klan is the 'beatinest' thing that ever came
down the pike. It's a fraternal order for the promotion of
strife; an empire for the promotion of democracy, a criminal conspiracy for upholding the law; a peace crusade by
violence, and a new sort of Christianity that would flog
Christ for being a Jew and a foreigner."

Inevitably the Klan entered politics, and invariably it
became a divisive and sinister force. At no time did it
sponsor or support a third-party movement, but this fact
heightened rather than diminished its malevolent influence.
A Klan leader justified this political concern: "Everybody
knows that politicians nowadays cater to all kinds of
'elements' mostly selfish, some corrupt, and some definitely
anti-American. They cater to the German vote, the Catholic

vote, the Jewish vote, the Italian vote, the boot-leg vote, the vice vote, and sometimes even to the violently criminal vote. What the Klan intends to do is to make them pay some attention to the American vote, the Protestant Christian vote, and the decent, God-fearing, law-abiding vote." Candidates were expected to certify their adherence to the Klan's definition of "Americanism" and their sympathy for the Invisible Order—or suffer the consequences. Neither unadvisedly nor lightly could politicians afford (as one of them lamented) to "withstand an incalculable impact, of indefinite forces, from an invisible source, and at an unexpected time."

The Klan became a terrible element in state and local politics from North Carolina to California and from Indiana to Texas. It elected governors in Georgia and Oregon; a United States senator in Texas; congressmen in several states. In Arkansas it was so politically powerful that it held its own primaries. In Oklahoma it impeached the hostile governor after a struggle reflecting little credit on either side. In Indiana under Stephenson the Klan was the state. In communities throughout the South, Southwest, Midwest, and Pacific Coast whole municipal establishments, literally from mayor to dogcatcher, were Klansmen or subservient to the order. And the Klan's role in the presidential nominations and elections of 1924 and 1928 suggest that the Invisible Empire came perilously close to achieving the status coveted for it by Imperial Wizard Evans, that of a "great militant political organization."

The cast of Klan leaders seems incredible; that is, until we remember that the scenario was shot in the 1920's. The star of the production, albeit a dim and flickering one, was Colonel William Joseph Simmons, whose fevered imagination called the Klan "from its slumber of half a century to take up a new task." Big and hollow, pious and prissy yet profane, genteely attired in rump-sprung britches and diamond stick pin, laden with lodge badges and heavy gold watch chain, breathing a hopefully deceptive mixture of cloves and bourbon, fond of poker and the ladies (his wife was an invalid), this amiable fraud, this "engaging old reprobate," was as "full of sentiment as a plum is full of juice." What made "Doc" Simmons run? He pursued the same light as Jay Gatsby and Sammy Glick (though he would not have approved of the company) as preacher, drummer of ladies' garters, and professional lodge man (he claimed membership in twelve or fifteen fraternal orders). With his Klan, "The World's Greatest Secret, Social, Patriotic, Fraternal, Beneficiary Order," with its membership, raiment, and life-insurance fees, he whiffed at last the sweet smell of success. Oleaginous, mellifluous, lazy yet lovable, vacuous yet sly, he disarmed the American people as he did investigating congressmen with platitude, piety, and pomposity. "Are we the only people that use a mask?," he asked of his inquisitors. "If so, what about Mardi Gras celebrations in this country, and what about Hallowe'en celebrations? . . . Our mask and robe, I say before God, are as innocent as the breath of an angel." Not even Warren G. Harding could have improved on that. And is it unsporting to inquire what sort of man the sovereign citizens of the United States elected to their highest office in 1920, the precise year of Simmons' ascending star?

Simmons' star ascended in 1920 (until that year his Invisible Empire after a struggling half-decade remained almost literally invisible) because he had the wit to tap the wits of two professional promoters, Edward Young Clarke and Mrs. Elizabeth Tyler. Eyeing the main chance, these inelegant hucksters transformed Simmons' easygoing southern fraternity of patriotic whites into a violently aggressive national organization of chauvinistic native-born white Protestants. It is a compliment to their promotional abilities to say Klan membership skyrocketed under their shrewd guidance. It is a commentary on the Klan to say that in 1919 the dubious duo had been arrested, while drunk and undraped, and fined for disorderly conduct; that Clarke deserted his wife before being deserted by the divorced Mrs. Tyler; that in 1923 Clarke was arrested for transporting whisky, and in 1924 he pleaded guilty to violating the White Slave Act. Perhaps in their way Ed Clarke and Mrs. Tyler were as at home in the Jazz Age as the organization they promoted.

In November, 1922, Simmons (and soon Clarke) was pressured out of power in a palace revolution led by a Dallas dentist, Hiram Wesley Evans. Plumpish, moon-faced, spectacled, benign, platitudinous, Evans called himself the "most average man in America." Evans testifies to the banality of evil, to the sinister consequences of a blind sincerity, to the unhappy fact that sobriety and chastity are not incompatible with bigotry and fanaticism. Like another American in the 1920's, Calvin Coolidge, Evans was a "Puritan in Babylon." The country would not have missed the leadership of either "average" man. As for the gross, tough, amoral David C. Stephenson, it is sufficient to observe that had he exchanged roles with Al Capone, neither Chicago nor Indiana would have been the loser— or the winner.

By late 1924 the KKK claimed a membership of four million, perhaps even five million, though most certainly not eight million as one authority estimates. "They just throwed the doors open," complained a once dedicated Knight, "and every man that had the money, they took him in just to get his vote. . . . " It was really not a very exclusive fraternity. One needed only to be white, Protestant, and native-born—and willing to part with $10.

The Klan attracted good men, sincerely anxious about the future of "their" country, seemingly imperiled by

Negroes, Catholics, aliens, and radicals. It was a godsend
to the frustrated and insecure, unconsciously seeking scape-
goats for their sense of failure. Weak men joined because
their wills were unequal to the community pressures to
conform. The Klan carried enormous appeal to lonely men
who would join any fraternal order to erase the monotony
of daily existence. Political opportunists saw the Klan as
the highroad to power. To hucksters, the society spelled
"Ku Klux Kash."

> For it's order and trumpet and anger and drum
> And power and glory command you to come;
> The graves shall fly open and let you all in,
> And the earth shall be emptied of mortal sin.
>
> (W. H. Auden, "Danse Macabre")

Yet the membership melted away like chilled aspic on
a warm summer afternoon. Immigration no longer seemed
a threat after the restriction act of 1924. The task was
now one of Americanization through education rather than
the immediate intimidation and repression of a once cease-
less flow of new aliens. A Negro rebellion had not material-
ized, and by the late 1920's the black man was again his
docile self. Although the U.S.S.R. failed to wither away,
the feeble and feckless condition of both labor unions and
socialist parties by the middle of the decade suggested that
the fires of radicalism in the United States had now been
banked. The general prosperity and the coolness (not to
say placidity) of the Coolidge era drained reform ardor.
Many Klansmen, like many prohibitionists and, for that
matter, progressives, said farewell to reform. Ardor gave
way to apathy. Or, perhaps, to a feeling of resignation.

Decent citizens drew back in horror as the evidence of
the order's indecency mounted. How could the good people
of Indiana, for instance, continue to believe in the moral

authority of the Klan after Grand Dragon Stephenson's imprisonment? In fact, everywhere Klan leadership proved either weak or obscene. Internal wrangling was endemic. Unlike fascist movements in Europe, the KKK threw up no charismatic Mussolini or Hitler.

Official American Protestantism with increasing firmness rejected the Klan's representation of itself as a great, militant supradenominational agency. The world of journalism was almost uniformly hostile. Anti-Klan riots, anti-mask bills, and counterboycotts intimidated the timid membership. And prudent politicians increasingly learned that the Klan's blessing was a kiss of death. (After all, native-born white Protestants were themselves in many communities a minority group, as the politician recognized when he arranged to have a cross burned in front of *his* home.) Moreover, when the Klan proved unable to dominate either major party, its failure to found a third party became fatal. But, then, how could the order survive politically when it championed not a single *concrete* economic or social reform. Its appeal was essentially negative, and if it played a part (minor, we think) in the defeat of Smith in 1928, more crucial is its failure to prevent his easy nomination in the first instance. The fact of religious pluralism in America, confirmed in the life of John F. Kennedy, was foreshadowed in the career of Al Smith.

To be sure, most Klansmen remained loyal to their exclusive and prideful definition of Americanism, and they continued to cherish their dreams of an older and purer America. But they lost hope in the Klan as the agency of redemption. They were largely unmoved by rational persuasion or moralistic preaching that they had been wrong, and their drift from the Klan represented a rejection of the order itself, but not necessarily of its ideals.

Ultimately, however, the Knights unmasked and dismounted because an even larger number of Americans

recalled and honored Abraham Lincoln's indictment of the
Know-Nothing party:

> How could I be [a member]? How can any one who abhors the
> oppression of Negroes, be in favor of degrading classes of white
> people? Our progress in degeneracy appears to me to be pretty
> rapid. As a nation we began by declaring that '*all men are created
> equal*.' We now practically read it 'all men are created equal,
> *except Negroes*.' When the Know Nothings get control, it will
> read, 'all men are created equal except Negroes, *and foreigners,
> and Catholics*.' When it comes to this I should prefer emigrating
> to some country where they make no pretence of loving liberty—
> to Russia, for instance. . . .

BIBLIOGRAPHICAL NOTE

It is apparent that this essay rests very heavily on the researches
of other scholars, save only in the areas of the relationship between
the Klan and Protestantism and of civil liberties, where I have labored
in the sources. Even so, it is difficult fully to acknowledge my debts,
for in thinking about the Klan I found myself reviewing all that I had
read over many years in American social, intellectual, cultural, and
political history; and, indeed, in ancillary fields. A full and fair listing
of those authors who have illuminated for me the nature of modern
society and modern man, therefore, would be impossibly long and
unconscionably pretentious. This bibliographical note will be confined
to works dealing specifically with the Klan and is intended to be
suggestive rather than definitive.

David M. Chalmers' recent *Hooded Americanism: The First Century of the Ku Klux Klan, 1865–1965* (Garden City, N. Y., 1965), is
prodigiously researched and factually informative, but too rarely
illuminating, perhaps because of its mechanical organization. Nevertheless, it is now the best single book we have on the Klan and is
immeasurably superior to William Peirce Randel's *The Ku Klux
Klan: A Century of Infamy* (Philadelphia and New York, 1965), a
volume that need not be consulted by students of the 1920's. Also
published in 1965 is Charles C. Alexander's *The Ku Klux Klan in the
Southwest* (Lexington, Ky., 1965), a scholarly and thoughtful work,
although the theme of moral authoritarianism is overstressed. See also
his earlier *Crusade for Conformity: The Ku Klux Klan in Texas,
1920–1930* (Houston, 1962). Arnold S. Rice's *The Ku Klux Klan in
American Politics* (Washington, D. C., 1962) is good on its subject

(save in the northern states), but its subject does not explicate the full Klan story. *KKK* (Evanston, Ill., 1963), by Ben Haas, is a little book, journalistic in style and without formal documentation, yet rather interesting. A very fine examination of the Klan in one state, especially the chapters on the churches, is Emerson H. Loucks' *The Ku Klux Klan in Pennsylvania* (Harrisburg, 1936). Norman F. Weaver's "The Knights of the Ku Klux Klan in Wisconsin, Indiana, Ohio, and Michigan" (Ph.D. dissertation, University of Wisconsin, 1954) is now open to inspection and merits publication. If most writers emphasize the Klan's violent nature, Weaver demonstrates its banality, and one is almost lulled into concluding that the Klan was harmless. In another meritorious unpublished study, "The Southern White Resistance Movement to Integration" (Ph.D. dissertation, University of North Carolina, 1958), James Vander Zanden elaborates the theme implicit in the title. Benjamin H. Arvin's "The Ku Klux Klan, 1915–1925: A Study in Religious Intolerance" (Ph.D. dissertation, Georgetown University, 1952), a manuscript I failed to consult, is frequently cited by students of the Klan. Protestant bigotry is also related to the Klan's appeal by Michael Williams in *The Shadow of the Pope* (New York, 1932). I have discounted the importance of the Klan in the election of 1928 in "A Footnote to the Role of the Protestant Churches in the Election of 1928," *Church History*, Vol. XXV (June, 1956). Although Professor John Higham has termed John Moffatt Mecklin's *The Ku Klux Klan: A Study of the American Mind* (New York, 1924), a "vapid sociological interpretation," I found this pioneering work still rewarding. Higham's own discussion of the Klan in *Strangers in the Land: Patterns of American Nativism, 1860–1925* (Atheneum Edition, New York, 1963) is penetrating. Another brief, brilliant essay is by Frank Tannenbaum in *Darker Phases of the South* (New York, 1924). The crudity of the Klan in Indiana and of its leader, David C. Stephenson, is revealed by Robert Coughlan, "Konklave in Kokomo," *The Aspirin Age*, Isabel Leighton, ed. (New York, 1949). A gentler yet devastating portrait of Colonel William Joseph Simmons is drawn by Ralph McGill, *The South and the Southerner* (Boston and Toronto, 1959). The violence engendered by the Klan is documented in Paul M. Angle's account of *Bloody Williamson: A Chapter in American Lawlessness* (New York, 1952). Two contemporary books remain of interest precisely because of when they were written: Henry P. Fry, *The Modern Ku Klux Klan* (Boston, 1922), and Stanley Frost, *The Challenge of the Klan* (Indianapolis, 1923, 1924). Edgar I. Fuller, *The Visible of the Invisible Empire* (Denver, 1925), and C. Winfield Jones, *Knights of the Ku Klux Klan* (New York, 1941), may be regarded essentially as documents rather than histories. Popular and scholarly journals in the 1920's carried many articles on the Klan, but see especially those by Robert L. Duffus, entitled "Salesman of Hate: The Ku Klux Klan," "How the Ku Klux Klan Sells Hate," "Counter-mining the Ku Klux Klan," "The Ku Klux Klan in the Middle West," and "Ancestry and End of the Ku Klux Klan," *World's Work*, Vol. XLVI (1923), and Frank Bohn, "The Ku Klux Klan Interpreted," *American Journal of Sociology*, Vol. XXX (Jan., 1925) and Guy B. Johnson, "A Sociological Interpretation of the New Ku Klux Movement," *Social Forces*, I

(May, 1923). The famous New York *World* exposé appeared in a series in September-October, 1921; for the feckless Congressional investigation see *The Ku Klux Klan. Hearings before the Committee on Rules, House of Representatives,* 67th Cong., 1st Sess. (Washington, 1921). My own views on the relationship between the Klan and American Protestantism may be found in "A Note on the Relationship between the Protestant Churches and the Revived Ku Klux Klan," *Journal of Southern History,* Vol. XXII (Aug., 1956) and *American Protestantism and Social Issues, 1919–1939* (Chapel Hill, 1958). My friend and colleague George B. Tindall shared generously with me his massive knowledge of the modern South and of the revived Klan in the South, but I may not therefore presume that he shares my interpretations of the Klan.

Kenneth T. Jackson's fine study, *The Ku Klux Klan in the City, 1915–1930,* appeared too late to be used in this essay. It should be noted, however, that he estimated the total membership of the Klan to be only slightly over two million, a figure considerably lower than the estimates of most scholars.

Prohibition: The Impact of
Political Utopianism

JOSEPH R. GUSFIELD

WHEN Herbert Hoover labeled Prohibition "the experiment noble in purpose," he was only continuing to use a language of scientific procedure that made "success or failure" the dominant scholarly question to be asked about the attempt to create a dry America. Experiments are acts that resolve scientific issues, and the experience of the nation with Prohibition is trotted out and brought into the light of controversy whenever issues of law and public opinion are under the scrutiny of popular discussion. Often the 1920's and dry legislation are pointed to as evidence for William Graham Sumner's casual but powerful aphorism that "stateways cannot make folkways." In the heat of current debates about Negro civil rights we recognize that the matter is much more complex than such aphorisms would allow. As Gunnar Myrdal suggested in 1944, law may not regulate sentiment but it has much bearing on behavior and on the framework within which education and re-education go on.[1]

There is a greater significance to the experience of Prohibition than the issue of success or failure. Human experi-

[1] Gunnar Myrdal, *An American Dilemma*, (New York, 1944), Appendix I.

ments are by no means analagous to those performed in laboratories, nor was "the noble experiment" carried out in a hermetically sealed nation. Hopes and aspirations were aroused, fulfilled, and quashed; loyalties were developed and repelled; organizations were affected with particular and unique character. The United States was not the same after repeal as it had been before the Eighteenth Amendment was passed. Prohibition had some impact in producing that change. The analogy of the experiment that succeeds or fails is at best a limited one for gauging the implications of dry legislation and dry activity on American life. We must be attuned to what *happened* as well as to what *lasted*. In any analysis of the Prohibition period in American history the acceptance or rejection of the Eighteenth Amendment is an essential part of the story. But it is not the whole story nor necessarily the most vital one. A concern for contemporary American life should make us sensitive to what the quest for the dry utopia has meant for later events and issues in American society.

The issue of national prohibition was a major focus of American politics for twenty years, from the beginnings of the Anti-Saloon League campaign for federal laws in 1913 to the repeal of the Eighteenth Amendment in 1933. Most candidates for national, state, or local office could not ignore being dry or wet, or using their political art to walk delicately between. By 1928, in Al Smith's campaign for the presidency, it was a dominating issue. Even in 1932, when repeal was in the air, it was still so vital a question that both presidential candidates thought it necessary to give it their attention. The impact of Prohibition upon behavior during the 1920's is evident. What we want to do in this paper is also to assess the influence of Prohibition upon the drinking habits of Americans after repeal. Was it only an experiment that lasted for fourteen years without any effects upon the climate of morality in the United States?

What did it mean for the politics that came during and after Prohibition? Were the enemies of temperance and the advocates of repeal assuming a political identification that lasted even after beer and whiskey were again sold in the open? What did the demise of Prohibition mean to those for whom it had represented a triumph of reason and morality over the nefarious forces of sensuality and corruption? An assessment of the Prohibition Era and its place in American history cannot confine itself narrowly to the question of whether or not it succeeded in developing, for a short time, a world of sobriety and abstinence.

The debate over the Eighteenth Amendment was not, as some have suggested, a sudden intrusion into American politics. It did not spring full-blown on the American scene as a conspiracy by which a small group of determined men foisted sobriety on a wet nation.

American experience with various efforts to curtail drinking and intoxication in the United States has a long and mercurial history. Licensing acts during colonial times regulated taverns and their use. From the 1820's on, a persistent temperance movement sought many and diverse ways to limit, if not abolish, the use of spirits, beer, and wine.[2] Under the leadership of New England Federalists the early temperance movement of the 1820's was less a

---

[2] Though there is no single major history of temperance and prohibition in the United States, there are several works from which one gains an unbiased and scholarly account. John Krout, *The Origins of Prohibition* (New York, 1925) carries the history from colonial beginning to the Civil War. There is no adequate history of the movement during the last half of the nineteenth century. The period 1900–1933 has been well treated in James Timberlake, *Prohibition and the Progressive Movement* (Cambridge, 1963) and Andrew Sinclair, *Prohibition: The Era of Excess* (Boston, 1962). For an interpretation of the movement over the entire course of its history see Joseph Gusfield, *Symbolic Crusade: Status Politics and the American Temperance Movement* (Urbana, Ill., 1963). For a history of temperance in one state see Norman Clark, *The Dry Years: Prohibition and Social Change in Washington* (Seattle, 1965).

movement for abstinence than a movement for moderate and temperate usage. Hence the name "temperance" for a movement that later came to be associated almost exclusively with abstention. During the 1830's, however, as the movement became infused with the spirit of evangelical religion and the problems of Midwestern and frontier people, it aimed more often at abstinence than at moderation.[3] The goal of abolishing the liquor traffic, rather than, and in addition to, the reform of the individual drinker, emerged during the 1840's and, in the famous Maine law of 1851, resulted in the first statewide legislation prohibiting the sale of "Demon Rum." [4]

The use of law as a means to achieve reform in drinking was by no means unknown before the twentieth century. Not only had statewide prohibition been tried in many places, but a great many parts of the United States had achieved prohibition through local option at the county, city, and township levels. American local and state politics was thus well filled with the issues of the legal regulation of liquor, beer, and wine. There were many vibrant controversies over the relative merits of legislation and exhortation; over moderation versus total abstinence; over political pressure-group actions versus the development of party legislation.[5]

Though the temperance movement had advocated statewide prohibition at various times and had given such legis-

[3] The term "teetotalers" arose from the practice of placing a "T" beside one's name on temperance lists to designate a commitment to total abstinence.

[4] Colonial legislation existed in many areas licensing and regulating taverns. Krout, *The Origins of Prohibition*, chap i.

[5] The argument over tactics was continuous in temperance history, and the rationale of various positions can be seen in the argument for a third party, the Prohibition party, and for a pressure group, the Anti-Saloon League. See D. Leigh Colvin, *Prohibition in the United States* (New York, 1926) and Peter Odegaard, *Pressure Politics* (New York, 1928), chap. iii.

lation a prominent part in its activities from time to time, agitation for national legislation prohibiting sales did not occur until well into the twentieth century. That it came about at all is therefore a matter of some question for analysis. A full discussion of how Prohibition came about is beyond the scope of this paper, but it is necessary to point to some of the ways in which it became possible at the federal level if we are to understand the Prohibition Era that came later.

Success in obtaining national prohibition owes much to the work and action of the Anti-Saloon League. The formation of the Anti-Saloon League, in 1896 in Ohio, brought with it two important elements to the temperance movement. First, it centered the attention of the movement on the eradication of the saloon. Second, it initiated an era of pressure politics that was divorced from the third-party tactics of the Prohibition party. The League utilized effective means for the mobilization of public opinion and political power in the American party structure.[6] Between 1906 and 1912 seven states passed prohibition laws. By 1919, before the passage of Eighteenth Amendment, an additional nineteen states had passed restrictive legislation, and more than 50 per cent of the American population lived in dry areas. In 1913 the Anti-Saloon League reached its greatest success until then by managing the successful passage of the Webb-Kenyon Act, forbidding the transportation of intoxicating beverages into dry states. This was the first major national legislative victory of the temperance movement. When the Eighteenth Amendment was passed (January, 1919), a good deal of American society had already found such legislation appealing.

What brought about this new wave of dry sentiment and assured its political victories? In this paper I shall main-

[6] Odegaard, *Pressure Politics, passim.*

tain that a common vision of a dry America underlay the two major strands of American reform in the late nineteenth and early twentieth centuries—the progressive impulse and the Populist movement. That vision expressed the world of nineteenth-century Protestant, nativist, and agrarian-commercial American society. The roots of national prohibition, we shall argue, lay in the urban middle-class reaction to a changing and industrialized city and in the rural antipathy to the growing dominance of the city. The issue between the drys and the wets was primarily one of cultural divergence in which the power and legitimacy of ways of life were symbolized by the acceptance or rejection of abstinence and sobriety as public ideals. A major thesis of this paper is that these two strands to American reform, and to drinking reform, separated and became opposed to each other during the 1920's in part over the issue of Prohibition itself.

It is important to recognize the coexistence of both strands, and their differences, in the surge of public sentiment producing the prohibitionist victories of the early twentieth century. Recently, several scholars have suggested a revision to the thesis that Prohibition ranged rural America against the cities. Timberlake and others [7] have rightfully corrected an overstatement in pointing to the progressive and urban roots of dry belief. It is crucial, however, to recognize that the political power of rural populations was essential in securing dry supremacy at state and national levels. That power was the major source of dry political strength before, during, and after the Eighteenth Amendment wrote "Dry America" across the Statue of Liberty.

[7] Timberlake, *Prohibition and the Progressive Movement;* Norton Mezvinsky, "The Temperance Movement: 1870–1920" (Paper presented to annual meeting of the Mississippi Valley Historical Society, Kansas City, Missouri, April, 1964).

By the time the campaign for Prohibition began to gain force, the issues of drinking reform had developed their own sets of opposing supporters. Although Catholic sentiment for temperance existed in the late nineteenth and twentieth centuries, the support given to prohibition as a technique for reform was minimal, both from organized Catholic groups and from the large segments of Catholic populations in American cities.[8] The symbol of the saloon as a force of evil in American society made sense in an urban population that saw political corruption and vice at home in the saloons of urban America. Those aspects of the progressive movement that reacted to the threats of a big-business civilization and an immigrant population, saw the saloon as one source of evil, and the reform of drinking habits as a necessity for an America of Protestant virtues.[9] For the social worker, the drinking habits of the poor and the immigrant were both a slap at Protestant morality and a source of the deep-seated poverty of industrial America. The professional and small-business urban middle class had grown up and had found its dominant ideologies in a sober and disciplined framework of churchgoing people. The drinking habits of the new immigrant population were both a threat to their values and an object for deep moral concern.[10]

These considerations appear in the myriad arguments one can find in the vast mass of prohibitionist literature. In politics the argument for the sober electorate was a telling one. In the eye of the muckraker the dependence of the political machine on the saloon seemed self-evident. Just as Beecher had argued in 1820 that a whiskey-swilling elec-

---

[8] Sister Joan Bland, *Hibernian Crusade* (Washington, D.C., 1951).

[9] Timberlake, *Prohibition and the Progressive Movement,* chap. v; Odegaard, *Pressure Politics,* pp. 17–35.

[10] John Higham, *Strangers in the Land* (New Brunswick, N.J., 1955).

torate was a threat to the old aristocracy,[11] so too the progressives could argue that the demise of the saloon would help the cause of free and clean government.[12]

Prohibition appeared as a panacea for the economic ills of the society. Though liquor and beer brought in considerable revenue, it could be maintained that the worker would find his material salvation more rapidly through a change in consuming habits than in unionism or governmental welfare. Science and medicine also contributed to the growing debate over the medical values of alcohol. The belief of the early nineteenth century that alcohol was essential to health received severe blows from "scientific temperance education" and the text material that the Women's Christian Temperance Union introduced into the American educational system during the early twentieth century. For employers in an industrial society, the need for safety and the prevention of accidents had in turn added to the force of temperance arguments. A number of companies, such as United Steel and the railroads, strongly supported efforts at temperance.[13]

We should be wary, however, of deriving the support of the movement from its arguments. The same arguments had been used many times in the past and had not always proved so effective. To be sure, the growth in drinking during the early twentieth century had been considerable, and in the period 1911–14 reached the peak since Americans began keeping records on these matters following the Civil War. The saloon itself had become not only the working man's club but certainly in many cases the hiring hall for crime, prostitution, and political corruption. The brewers and distillers had been late in recognizing the strength of the tem-

[11] Lyman Beecher, *Six Sermons on Intemperance* (New York, 1843), pp. 57–58.
[12] Bartlett C. Jones, "The Debate Over Prohibition: 1920–1933" (Ph.D. dissertation, Emory University, 1961); Timberlake, chap. iv.
[13] Jones, "The Debate over Prohibition," chap. vi.

perance movement and in taking any measures that might bring about a reform of the saloon. Nevertheless, we must be careful not to overestimate the degree to which Prohibition was an urban phenomenon or the degree to which the economic logic of an industrial society pushed for temperance legislation.

The United States is one of only three countries that have experimented with prohibition on a wide scale. Finland and India are the other two. We would be hard put to relate prohibition in these three countries to economic or geographical similarities. Though some American industrialists did support Prohibition, others did not. It is worthy of note that the American man of wealth who gave the greatest degree of effort to the support of the Prohibition movement both before and after the passage of the Eighteenth American was S. S. Kresge, whose wealth was made not in manufacturing but in merchandising. There is little to indicate that manufacturing establishments, most clearly allied to an industrial society, saw in Prohibition so important a measure that they necessarily gave to it their united support.

Any analysis of the actual distribution of votes through which prohibition measures gained ascent must recognize the importance of both the rural states and the rural legislators in bringing about the passage of the Eighteenth Amendment. The South represented the greatest single source of legislative support for prohibitory measures.[14] Almost everywhere, the strength of the Anti-Saloon League represented the mobilization of church support more heavily in the rural than in the urban sectors.[15] The states that went prohibitionist earliest were not those with the highest

[14] See my discussion of the political base of prohibitionist sentiment in *Symbolic Crusade*, pp. 117–126.

[15] Odegaard, *Pressure Politics*, pp. 29–35, 121–24.

but with the smallest percentages of urban population.[16] The areas of national prohibition sentiment were strongest where the populations were Protestant, rural, and nativist. They were more likely to be found in the South and in the Midwest than in the East. Although states with high percentages of foreign-born were likely to oppose prohibition, this was less likely where the foreign population was Protestant and rural, as in Minnesota. In Mississippi, for example, it was in the rural areas with small Negro populations that one found the highest support for prohibition legislation both before and after the Eighteenth Amendment was passed and repeal had been initiated. In many of the states the ratification of the Eighteenth Amendment was brought about by votes in the state legislatures, controlled largely by rural legislators. Though the progressive movement played a role and responded well to the demands of the Anti-Saloon League, it was by no means able to wield the political power through which prohibition itself was implemented.

Both the urban middle class and agrarian America were substantially Protestant and nativist in their outlook. While they saw the cities engulfed by new groups of power, they responded both to demands of sentiment and concern for an urban and industrial poor and to the hostile threats of the cultural waves that distinguished eastern and Mediterranean Europe from Anglo-Saxon cultures. Although it was never dominant, the drys found room in their arguments for the sophisticated racism in the doctrines of eugenics and ethnic differentiation that resulted in the theories of Madison Grant and Lothrop Stoddard.[17]

[16] Gusfield, *Symbolic Crusade*, p. 109.

[17] Bartlett Jones, "Prohibition and Eugenics, 1920–33," *Journal of the History of Medicine*, XVIII (1963), 158–72.

In 1917 the Hobson resolution for submission of the prohibition amendment received the necessary two-thirds vote
in Congress. The amendment was ratified on January 16,
1919, and went into effect one year later to date. The text
of the amendment was as follows:

Section 1.

After one year from the ratification of this article the manufacture, sale, or transportation of intoxicating liquors within, the
importation thereof into, or the exportation thereof from the
United States and all territory subject to the jurisdiction thereof
for beverage purposes is hereby prohibited.

Section 2.

The Congress and the several states shall have concurrent
power to enforce this article by appropriate legislation.

A third section made the article inoperative until it had
been ratified as an amendment to the Constitution by the
legislatures of the several states.

The Eighteenth Amendment was aimed at the eradication
of the saloon and the distributor of liquor, wine, and beer.
It was not an effort to govern the buyer but to get at intoxication by obstructing the seller. It was aimed at the saloon
and at the liquor business.

Despite use of the Prohibition experience as a basis for
offhand judgments about law and morality, the entire experience has seldom been analyzed to determine whether
accounts of its impact are myth or reality. Dry adherents
have persisted in the views that the friends of "Demon
Rum" killed Prohibition by telling untruths about its impact. Those for whom it was unwelcome inhibition have,
perhaps, had a greater influence in convincing most Ameri-

can historians that the enforcement of the Volstead Act ran aground on the sharp rocks of intense public resistance.

Even with difficulties in data, we are still able to give an accurate and qualified picture of what did happen to American drinking habits during the 1920's. That picture is a complicated one, suggesting different kinds of effects to different parts of the population. It does not support either the myth of increased drinking or the death of alcoholic indulgence.

Any effort to gauge the effectiveness of prohibition legislation must meet another problem in the analysis of the relation between law and human behavior. How much enforcement is *effective* enforcement? Laws may seek long-range and long-run changes in a society rather than short-range and short-run compliance. Laws may exist and function less as direct shapers of human behavior and more as means for symbolizing what is publicly legitimate and moral. Certainly prostitution, abortion, gambling, and drug addiction exist in the United States and have existed for many decades. The laws that forbid such behavior serve many functions. Perhaps they limit the degree to which such behavior would be discoverable without them. I have suggested, in *Symbolic Crusade*, that laws frequently serve highly symbolic functions, pointing to those groups in the society that achieve public recognition of their norms and values as the legitimate ones. This is certainly the case in relation to temperance legislation. If it was flouted by those who drank, it was clear whose law and whose culture was given dominant recognition as the legitimate and sanctioned modes of behavior. No politician could openly admit use of, or be seen using, alcohol. If public leaders gave only lip service to Prohibition, that itself was an indication of what was the public and official law of the land.

In short, the evasion of laws is by no means a telling argument against their effectiveness. As Robin Williams pointed out,[18] a patterned evasion of norms exists in many cases in American society and frequently preserves both law and illegality, side by side. Though the laws of abortion exist in American life, there is a structure that makes abortion possible for those who seek it. This patterned evasion is found in more or less frequency for a great many acts of government.

What we need to know is the answer to a comparative question. Was there more or less excessive drinking than had existed before Prohibition? Were the effects such as to suggest a lessened degree of disapproval than had existed before Prohibition? In this way, the issue of the consequences of prohibitory legislation is rendered a little more capable of answer. On the other hand, it requires a greater degree of specific data often conspicuous by its absence.

The casual impressions of social workers, journalists, industrial executives, and temperance advocates is no substitute for the kind of careful measurement on which comparative analysis is based. We turn then to what we can say with a high degree of validity concerning the enforcement of Prohibition.

Having used considerable political power to effect the Eighteenth Amendment and its ratification, the dry forces had now to provide for its enforcement. Despite the considerable degree of support from public opinion and the rural-dominated state legislatures, the dry forces walked lightly. In this policy the federal and state legislatures were most co-operative. Having acceded to the intense pressure of the Anti-Saloon League and its supporters, Congress was in no mood to tweak the tail of the wets any more than it had to. The attitude toward enforcement was thus one that Charles Merz has effectively characterized as "nullification

[18] Robin Williams, *American Society* (New York, 1960), chap. x.

by non-enforcement." [19] The organization of the Prohibition
Bureau, the appropriations granted to it and to various
state agencies, and the limited disposition of courts to support Prohibition were all involved in a system of enforcement that appeared to seek compliance through patience
rather than through authoritative action.[20]

The chief measure guiding enforcement was the National
Prohibition Act, popularly known as the Volstead Act, after
Congressman Volstead who had introduced it. Under this
act the Commissioner of Internal Revenue of the Treasury
Department, rather than the Department of Justice, was
given the power to detect and suppress violations of Prohibition. The Prohibition Bureau itself was not brought under
Civil Service—a fact that gave the dry forces effective
power over the recruitment and maintenance of personnel.
Under this situation the Prohibition Bureau and the salaries
of Prohibition agents compared most unfavorably with
other personnel. They were greatly dependent upon federal
and state appropriations that were seldom large enough to
make possible an effective legal and police organization. "It
was not the business of the Prohibition Bureau to quarrel
with its peers." [21]

The result, of course, was an ineffective organization
whose morale was even further weakened by a succession of
appointed heads. The first Prohibition commissioner, John
F. Kramer, served for a year and a half until he was replaced by Roy A. Haines. Under Coolidge a new head, Gen-

[19] Charles Merz, *The Dry Decade* (Garden City, N.Y., 1937),
p. 129.
[20] Similar accounts, using different data, are found in Merz, *The
Dry Decade*; Sinclair, *Prohibition*, chap. x, pp. 13–14; Clark, *The Dry
Years*, chaps. x–xii.
[21] Merz, *The Dry Decade*, p. 129.

eral Lincoln C. Andrews, was appointed. He resigned in March of 1927 and was replaced by several different people, including the assistant secretary of the treasury and the chief chemist of the Prohibition Bureau. Not until Herbert Hoover became President was the Bureau set upon a more regular basis, recruits required to pass the Civil Service examination, and the entire activity brought under the Department of Justice.

American impressions of drinking during the 1920's owe much to the description of a "lost generation" that novelists and journalists have done much to maintain. It is a picture of flaming youth in short skirts and bobbed hair dancing wickedly in speak-easies run by tough-looking gangsters. It is a picture of orgiastic drunkenness complete with wood alcohol, bathtub gin, and illicit sex. Like many myths, it mixes truth with falsity. The general shift in American morals during the 1920's is beyond our topic. Nevertheless, the generally accepted view suggests an increase in extensive drinking, especially among the young. A more sober analysis will recognize this as behavior that was decidedly not typical. Nevertheless, whether typical or not, its dramatic impact had a great deal to do with the setting of styles both during the Prohibition Era and afterward. It had a great deal to do with the ways in which people thought about drinking and Prohibition.

Any analysis of drinking during Prohibition should begin with what we know about American drinking habits before 1920. Table No. 1 presents data on the total amount of absolute alcohol consumed in the United States and the percentage of that alcohol contributed by various diverse components.[22]

[22] Reprinted from Raymond McCarthy, ed. *Drinking and Intoxication* (Glencoe, Ill., 1959), p. 180.

TABLE 1

APPARENT CONSUMPTION OF ALCOHOLIC BEVERAGES,
PER CAPITA OF DRINKING AGE POPULATION (PERSONS AGED OVER
FOURTEEN YEARS), U.S.A., 1850–1957, IN U.S. GALLONS*

YEAR	SPIRITS		WINE		BEER		TOTAL
	Beverage	Absolute Alcohol	Beverage	Absolute Alcohol	Beverage	Absolute Alcohol	Absolute Alcohol
1850	4.17	1.89	0.46	0.08	2.70	0.14	2.11
1860	4.79	2.16	0.57	0.10	5.39	0.27	2.53
1870	3.40	1.53	0.53	0.10	8.73	0.44	2.07
1871–80	2.27	1.02	0.77	0.14	11.26	0.56	1.72
1881–90	2.12	0.95	0.76	0.14	17.94	0.90	1.99
1891–95	2.12	0.95	0.60	0.11	23.42	1.17	2.23
1896–1900	1.72	0.77	0.55	0.10	23.72	1.19	2.06
1901–05	2.11	0.95	0.71	0.13	26.20	1.31	2.39
1906–10	2.14	0.96	0.92	0.17	29.27	1.47	2.60
1911–15	2.09	0.94	0.79	0.14	29.53	1.48	2.56
1916–19	1.68	0.76	0.69	0.12	21.63	1.08	1.96
....	....	....	....	....	.....	....	....
1934	0.64	0.29	0.36	0.07	13.58	0.61	0.97
1935	0.96	0.43	0.50	0.09	15.13	0.68	1.20
1936	1.30	0.59	0.64	0.12	17.53	0.79	1.50
1937	1.43	0.64	0.71	0.13	18.21	0.82	1.59
1938	1.32	0.59	0.70	0.13	16.58	0.75	1.47
1939	1.38	0.62	0.79	0.14	16.77	0.75	1.51
1940	1.48	0.67	0.91	0.16	16.29	0.73	1.56
1941	1.58	0.71	1.02	0.18	17.97	0.81	1.70
1942	1.89	0.85	1.11	0.20	20.00	0.90	1.95
1943	1.46	0.66	0.94	0.17	22.26	1.00	1.83
1944	1.69	0.76	0.92	0.17	25.22	1.13	2.06
1945	1.95	0.88	1.13	0.20	25.97	1.17	2.25
1946	2.20	0.99	1.34	0.24	23.75	1.07	2.30
1947	1.69	0.76	0.90	0.16	24.56	1.11	2.03
1948	1.56	0.70	1.11	0.20	23.77	1.07	1.97
1949	1.55	0.70	1.21	0.22	23.48	1.06	1.98

* From Mark Keller and Vera Efron, *Selected Statitsics on Alcoholic Beverages (1850–1957) and on Alcoholism (1910–1956)*, New Haven, Journal of Studies on Alcohol, 1958.

TABLE 1 — *Continued*

| YEAR | SPIRITS | | WINE | | BEER | | TOTAL |
	Beverage	Absolute Alcohol	Beverage	Absolute Alcohol	Beverage	Absolute Alcohol	Absolute Alcohol
1950	1.72	0.77	1.27	0.23	23.21	1.04	2.04
1951	1.73	0.78	1.13	0.20	22.92	1.03	2.01
1952	1.61	0.72	1.21	0.21	22.97	1.03	1.96
1953	1.68	0.76	1.18	0.20	22.81	1.03	1.99
1954	1.61	0.72	1.18	0.20	21.73	0.98	1.90
1955	1.66	0.75	1.18	0.20	21.74	0.98	1.94
1956	1.76	0.79	1.23	0.21	21.53	0.97	1.97
1957	1.70	0.77	1.21	0.21	20.62	0.93	1.91

It should be noted that this data is based on United States tax returns and gives the gallons-per-capita population of drinking age, fourteen and over. For this reason it conflicts with the data presented in Warburton and other analyses of drinking during Prohibition.

Two things are significant in this analysis of American drinking before Prohibition. First, the first decade and a half of the twentieth century saw a considerably increased consumption of alcohol. The high point of alcohol consumption in the United States came in the years 1911–15. It is important, however, to recognize the second fact: there had been a great shift in the direction of beer-drinking and a great decrease in the use of distilled spirits. This indicates that there had been a movement away from a population consisting of a large stream of heavy drinkers (characterized by high rates of spirits-drinking) and many abstainers toward a population that indicated many less abstainers but relatively fewer heavy drinkers.[23]

[23] E. M. Jellinek, "Recent Trends in Alcoholism and Alcohol Consumption," *Quarterly Journal of Studies on Alcohol*, VIII (July, 1947), 1–43.

In analyzing the extent of drinking, we need to ask what kind of alcoholic beverages became prevalent during the dry era.[24] The most careful and impartial analysis of drinking during Prohibition is that contained in Clark Warburton's *The Economic Results of Prohibition*. Even though it was conducted at the request of the Association Against the Prohibition Amendment, Warburton found a sharp decline in the total amount of alcohol consumed.[25] His analysis, furthermore, squares very well with that by Herman Feldman [26] and the later analysis by Jellinek in 1948.[27] Warburton estimated the amount of alcohol consumed by three methods—the analysis of components used for production, deaths from cirrhosis of liver, and police arrests for drunkenness. All of these show the same general tendencies toward a sharp decline in the amount of alcohol consumed between 1920 and 1923 with an increase over the next seven years. Nevertheless, as Table 2 (below) indicates, the per capita usage at all times was considerably below that of the pre-Prohibition period of 1911–14. It remains evident, then, that Prohibition did succeed in curtailing, even if

[24] It should also be noted that beer-drinking is associated less with drunkenness than is liquor, both because of its lower alcohol content and because it is more likely to be consumed in conjunction with eating.

[25] Clark Warburton, *The Economic Results of Prohibition* (New York, 1932). Warburton utilized reports of the production of the components of alcoholic beverages, arrests from drunkenness, and estimates from death rates and from cirrhosis of the liver. All of these require major assumptions concerning other usages of the same components, the uniform validity of crime rates, and the relationship between cirrhosis of the liver and alcoholism and can best be considered as systematic estimates.

For another analysis of the effectiveness of Prohibition, see John Burnham, "The Prohibition Experiment of the 1920's" (Paper presented at the meeting of the Mississippi Valley Historical Society, Kansas City, Mo., April, 1964).

[26] Herman Feldman, *Prohibition: Its Economic and Industrial Aspects* (New York, 1930).

[27] Jellinek, "Recent Trends in Alcoholism and Alcohol Consumption".

not stopping, the heavy drinking that had characterized the early twentieth century in the United States. Warburton's figures, based as they are on the general population rather than the population of age fourteen and over, probably overestimate the amount of alcohol usage during the 1920's as compared to the earlier period. Jellinek's later analysis

TABLE 2

ESTIMATES OF THE CONSUMPTION OF PURE ALCOHOL
IN THE UNITED STATES, 1920–30 (GALLONS PER CAPITA)

YEAR	ESTIMATE FROM SOURCES OF PRODUCTION	ESTIMATE FROM DEATH RATES	ESTIMATE FROM ARRESTS FOR DRUNKENNESS	FINAL ESTIMATE	INDEX OF CONSUMPTION OF ALCOHOL 1911–14 = 100
1920	....	.64	.16	....	....
1921	.26	.82	.43	.54	32.0
1922	.90	.92	.81	.91	53.8
1923	1.17	.97	1.05	1.07	63.3
1924	1.08	1.02	1.05	1.05	62.1
1925	1.13	1.07	1.06	1.10	65.1
1926	1.24	1.11	1.11	1.18	69.8
1927	1.08	1.15	1.15	1.12	66.3
1928	1.23	1.13	1.25	1.18	69.8
1929	1.31	1.09	1.18	1.20	71.0
1930	1.03	1.09	....	1.06	62.7

Sources of data: Estimate from sources of production: Table 30, Warburton, *The Economic Results of Prohibition*, p. 72. Estimate from death rates: Table 37, *ibid.*, p. 89. Estimate from arrests for drunkenness: Table 44, *ibid.*, p. 102. Final estimate: Average of the estimate from sources of production and the estimate from death rates.

of alcohol consumption in the United States (those in age groups of fourteen and over) suggests that the rate of alcohol consumption per capita during Prohibition for those of drinking age at about one-half of that for the average of the four years preceding Prohibition.[28] Jellinek has used later alcoholism rates to shed light on 1920's drinking. These rates for alcoholism from 1920 to 1945 show a decided drop as compared with 1910 and 1915 rates. Since chronic alcoholism is a reflection of past drinking habits (beginning approximately ten to fifteen years earlier), it is indicated by deaths of cirrhosis of the liver and is good evidence for changes brought about during state and national prohibition in the early twentieth century.

We can conclude then that Prohibition was effective in sharply reducing the rate of alcohol consumption in the United States. We may set the outer limit of this at about 50 per cent and the inner limit at about one-third less alcohol consumed by the total population than had been the case before Prohibition and at the point of peak usage in the United States.

When we come to survey the different forms of alcohol usage, however, the picture becomes a little more complicated and a little closer to the lurid and impressionistic one of the novelist and the popular historian. It is highly significant, however, that the abolition of the liquor traffic had different effects at middle-class than at lower-class levels of the urban population.

We have already pointed out that the increase in total alcohol consumption during the first decade of the twentieth century was accompanied by a continuing drop in the percentage resulting from the consumption of distilled spirits. Prohibition succeeded in reversing that relationship. To a very large extent, according to Warburton, the decrease

[28] The American population of the 1920's contained a higher percentage of older people than it did in the previous decade. Consumption rates based on total population, as Warburton's are, actually ignore the fact that the population of the 1920's had a higher percentage of potential drinkers than did the earlier decade. Using only the population above fourteen would result in lowered rates for the 1920's.

in total alcoholic consumption was the result of a great drop in the use of beer. As Table 3 shows, the diminished use of beer was as great as a total drop of 85 per cent during 1921–22 and a drop of more than two-thirds during 1927–30. According to Warburton's calculations, there was actually an increase in the gallons-per-capita usage of spirits. This seems reasonable given two facts about illicit sale of alcoholic beverages during the dry era. The first is that the price of alcohol increased enormously. The second is that, per unit, there was more money to be made in the sale of hard liquor than in the sale of beer. Both were difficult to manufacture at home, but liquor was just as easy

TABLE 3

CONSUMPTION OF ALCOHOL BEVERAGES IN THE UNITED STATES
BEFORE AND AFTER THE ADOPTION OF PROHIBITION
(GALLONS PER CAPITA)

PERIOD	SPIRITS	BEER	WINE	PURE ALCOHOL
1911–14	1.47	20.53	.59	1.69
1921–22	.92	1.49	.51	.73
1927–30	1.62	6.27	.98	1.14

Sources of data: 1911–14, Table 2, Warburton, *The Economic Results of Prohibition*, p. 26; 1921–22 and 1927–30, Tables 45 and 46, *ibid.*, pp. 104, 106. Figures for spirits, wine, and beer taken from the estimates from sources of production.

as beer if not easier. As now, so too then, hard liquor was more often the choice of those in the higher-income levels than among lower-income groups.

Warburton concludes "that under Prohibition the working classes consumed not more than half as much alcohol per capita as formerly; and that the expenditure of this class upon alcoholic beverages is probably a billion dollars less than it would be without national Prohibition.

"That the per capita consumption of alcohol by the business, professional and salaried classes has been affected but little by Prohibition; and that due to higher prices this class is spending at least a billion dollars a year more for alcoholic beverages than it would be spending without national Prohibition." [29] The differential between the classes has been noted as well in the impressions of social workers [30] and a testimony of executives observing workers.[31]

It would be fair to say then that Prohibition did affect drinking behavior. The impressionistic notion that rural areas were more clearly affected than urban is substantiated by the pattern of bootlegging. The total consumption of alcohol did drop. Even after the upsurge following the initial effects of the act, it still remained well below the rates of consumption in the pre-Prohibition years. It is also the case, however, that hard drinking was apparently substituted to some degree for beer, especially in those urban groups that represented high-income levels. Its greatest impact in eradicating drink was thus on the working classes, and, paradoxically, coinciding as it did with the shift of morals in the general prosperity of the 1920's, it may well have increased the hard and excessive drinking among precisely those groups that had in the past been pace-setters and style-setters. As may often happen, Prohibition was least effective in curtailing the drinking among precisely those groups that were most clearly visible to the mass media of communication.

[29] Warburton, *The Economic Results of Prohibition*, p. 262.

[30] Martha Bruère, *Does Prohibition Work?* (New York and London, 1927).

[31] Whiting Williams, testimony before the Wickersham Commission. Quoted in Burnham, "The Prohibition Experiment of the 1920's," p. 11.

If one attempts to adduce the economic results of Prohibition, he is in an even more difficult morass, one in which it is extraordinarily difficult to separate the general effects of historical conditions from those which are specifically the results of legislation. The general increase in automobile usage in the United States was so great in 1920 as to mask any efforts to determine Prohibition's impact upon automobile accidents. What is true, however, and this became of considerable importance later, is that the national and state governments lost visible revenue as alcoholic beverages disappeared from the lists of taxable items. It was also coupled with the fact that the existence of Prohibition did lead to curtailment of certain specific jobs in the brewery and the distilling industries. To suggest that these were balanced by the ultimate economic gains is to pose an intangible and indirect effect against an immediate and visible one. For brewery and distillery workers such long-run considerations were cold comfort in the face of present unemployment.

During the 1920's the existence of the bootlegger and of syndicated crime made many headlines. The gangs and gang warfare of Chicago and the dramatic quality of Al Capone impressed themselves upon American mentality. American crime had begun to change considerably with the growth of large cities and the development of big business in crime—gambling, prostitution, and other economic services performed for clients rather than victims. That bootlegging was an industry of considerable magnitude is certainly unquestionable. Without Prohibition, of course, a bootlegging industry would have been nonexistent. It should be pointed out, however, that large gangs of a business nature had already been in existence before the advent of bootlegging. Capone himself came to Chicago from New York to function in the organization run at that time by Big Jim Colosimo, whose basic source of revenue came from the houses of prostitution in Chicago, well before Prohibition presented new opportunities.

The history of the underworld matches the history of American big business in many respects. It is one of increasing consolidation and centralization as small enterprises give way to large organizations.[32] In the complex and often ruthless competition by which the underworld became organized, there was increasing evidence that a high degree of central control would lead to a disappearance of the rougher tactics made necessary by an unregulated market economy. The last echoes of this can be found in the famous St. Valentine's Day Massacre, when the Capone gang reputedly brought the severest of all sanctions to bear against "unfair competition." The firm of "Bugs" Moran and Company was found operating outside the zone that had been agreed upon as their sales and merchandising territory, and seven executives died in defense of free enterprise.

To summarize this mass of evidence is not easy. Perhaps we may do best to quote Herman Feldman, who wrote in 1927:

> People who discuss the economic effects of Prohibition or, for that matter, any of the other effects of Prohibition, too often go to one of two extremes. The largest group attributes everything that had happened since about 1919 to 1920 to Prohibition, some finding the conditions insufferable while others are full of praise. The second group consists of skeptics who are so much impressed by the fact that other things could explain present day circumstances that they seem unwilling to admit that Prohibition has had any effects at all. . . . Its effects may well be exaggerated, but they should certainly not be waved aside as negligible.[33]

[32] Daniel Bell, "Crime as an American Way of Life," in D. Bell, *The End of Ideology* (New York, 1960), chap. vii.

[33] Feldman, *Prohibition*, p. 1.

The full story of any law, moreover, is not to be found solely in what happened while it was on the books. If drinking behavior changed during the 1920's as this paper argues, we should expect that it did not readily return to what had existed before the 1920's. In short, we need to search for some more permanent and lasting effects of the Prohibition Era in the later experience of Americans with alcohol in the periods after repeal. Here again we should find that the United States by no means has gone to a drunkard's dubious reward with the advent of repeal, nor did the Prohibition Era succeed in drying up the well-springs of drinking habits. Nevertheless, it does appear evident that the experience of a dry society, even though less than perfect, did not contribute to a wave of excessive alcoholism. What we find, instead, is that those cultural sources that had produced abstinence continued to play their role and those that had enforced moderate drinking continued to grow. In this respect the experience with Prohibition appears to have had little permanent effect on American drinking behavior per se.

In order to understand American drinking behavior, we must recognize the sharp differences in the various ways in which the different ethnic and religious groups of the United States utilize alcohol. Extensive use of beer was introduced into the United States largely by the Germans and Swedes. The use of beer, as we have pointed out above, reflects a strong relationship between eating and drinking as does the use of wine among the French and the Italians. A highly Protestantized country, such as the United States, has been given to more extreme patterns of use and non-use of alcohol, ranging from total abstinence to drunkenness. Studies of Italians and of Jews in the United States have shown that it is quite possible for cultures to sanction the use of alcohol and yet be surrounded with controls that limit

the impact of alcoholism.[34] The Irish have represented still
another motif of high rates of non-abstinence and high
rates of chronic alcoholism.[35] These studies indicate that
as immigration increased in the United States, it brought
into American society patterns in the uses of alcohol different from those encompassed by Protestant virtues. As
our society became increasingly an urban one, the styles
of life of the middle class in turn reflected newer modes of
entertainment and leisure in which liquor and beer came
to play distinctly different roles.

Harold Pfautz has shown some of this in his study of
the depictions of alcohol in popular fiction at the turn of
the twentieth century and later at mid-century. Pfautz
found that the earlier fiction was less likely to impute
useful properties to drinking than were later works. Both
periods in his mode-of-content analysis were equal in the
frequency with which they perceived alcohol as harmful
to the individual and as a focus for social interaction. What
was true, however, was that the later fiction tended to
place far more value on the social functions of alcohol than
did the earlier literature.[36] Pfautz's work provides additional support to our general understanding of the use or
place that alcohol has come to play in American entertainment and in the moderate drinking habits of the urban
middle class. In a culture that has come to prize fellowship
and ease of human relations, the relaxing effects of alcohol
permit quicker dissolution of reserve among people and
facilitate group formation.

It is this general tendency toward a more moderate
drinking pattern that characterizes the drinking behavior

[34] Charles Snyder, *Alcohol and The Jews* (Glencoe, Ill., 1958);
Giorgio Lolli, *et. al.*, *Alcohol in Italian Culture* (Glencoe, Ill., 1958).

[35] Robert F. Bales, "Attitudes Toward Drinking in the Irish
Culture," in D. Pittman and C. Snyder (eds.), *Society, Culture and
Drinking Patterns* (New York, 1962), pp. 157–87.

[36] Harold Pfautz, "The Image of Alcohol in Popular Fiction:
1900–1904 & 1946–1950," *Quarterly Journal of Studies in Alcohol*,
VIII (September, 1947), pp. 265–73.

of Americans today. The general alcohol consumption in the United States by no means has risen greatly in the post-Prohibition period, and the long-run trend toward moderation appears to have continued. Studies in 1945 and 1946 both demonstrated that about one-third of the American population considered themselves abstainers from all alcoholic beverages.[37] The Gallup Poll has remained, with one debatable exception, remarkably constant in its findings of abstinence. A recent national survey finds 29 per cent of its respondents indicating their commitment to total abstinence.[38] Even a 1962 study of San Francisco adults found 24 per cent were abstainers.[39] As Table 4 below

TABLE 4

PERCENTAGE CONTRIBUTION OF DISTILLED SPIRITS, WINE, AND BEER
TO THE APPARENT CONSUMPTION OF TOTAL ABSOLUTE ALCOHOL
IN THE UNITED STATES, 1850–1957,
BASED ON TABLE 1 ABOVE

| YEAR | TOTAL ABSOLUTE ALCOHOL* | PERCENTAGE OF TOTAL | | |
		Distilled Spirits	Wine	Beer
1850	2.07	89.6	3.7	6.7
1911–15†	2.56	36.7	5.9	57.4
1940	1.56	42.9	10.3	46.8
1957	1.91	40.3	11.0	48.7

* Gallons per capita population of drinking age, fourteen and over.
† Average figures.

[37] Raymond McCarthy, ed., *op. cit.*, p. 179.

[38] Harold Mulford, "Drinking and Deviant Drinking," *Quarterly Journal of Studies of Alcohol*, XXV (December, 1964), 634–50. Mulford's 1963 study shows 71 per cent of population drank. Riley and Marden (1946) found 65 per cent. Compared with Riley and Marden, Mulford found greatest increase among the small-town residents and among those over thirty-five.

[39] Genevieve Knupfer and Robin Room, "Drinking in a Metropolitan Community," *Social Problems*, XII (Fall, 1964), 224–40.

shows, the total absolute alcohol consumed in the United States, although increased somewhat in recent years, has not fallen back to the 1911–15 levels. So, too, if one examines the components in American drinking, the substitution of beer for whiskey that occurred in the early twentieth century has continued. It is remarkable that a large amount of the increase in alcohol consumption since 1940 has been a function of the increased use of wines in American life All this supports the general tendency toward a more moderate set of drinking habits in which both abstinence and indulgence are less normal.

Of course, it is impossible to know to what degree this is a function of the Prohibition Era. What is important to recognize, however, is that neither the passage of the Eighteenth Amendment nor the repeal of it appeared to have had decisive effects upon American drinking habits or upon sentiment. If it did, we could only surmise that it tended to accentuate the moderate use of liquor and to some degree to diminish the high point in American alcohol use of the early nineteenth century, thus supporting the long-run trend toward moderate use of alcohol. Certainly the analysis of local-option elections since repeal, like the public opinion polls, does not indicate any remarkable shifts in basic sentiment. In 1939, 18.3 per cent of the American population lived in locally dry areas. In 1959 this percentage had only declined to 14.7 per cent.[40] During the period 1947–59 there were 12,114 local elections held in the United States on issues of liquor control, and most of these left the existing situation intact.[41] The conception of alcoholism as a moral imperfection rather than a disease still continues to persist in many areas. Thus Mulford and Miller found in an Iowa survey that 45 per cent of their respon-

[40] Based on annual reports of the Distilled Spirits Institute, 1939, 1959, p. 51.
[41] Gusfield, *Symbolic Crusade*, p. 161.

dents viewed the alcoholic as morally weak, although surveys in Connecticut have shown a much higher percentage who viewed alcoholism as a disease.[42] As compared with European countries, liquor in America is still limited in availability. The bars found in the theaters and museums of Europe are rarely encountered in America.

The Prohibition period, with the experience of hard drinking in the middle class, and the absence of beer and liquor among the working classes may, however, have contributed to a different kind of shift in American drinking habits. It is certainly the case that two things appear to have occurred: the middle-class components are more likely to be non-abstainers today than might have been true at an earlier period before Prohibition, and lower classes appear to be more abstaining. Certainly all the surveys have indicated that middle and upper classes represent higher levels of drinking than working and lower classes.[43] Abstinence has declined among the college-educated groups, and with it the less evangelical and highly prestigious denominations such as the Presbyterians, the Congregationalists, and the Methodists, who had been so firm in their support of Prohibition, have waivered and become much less enamored of abstinence.

Although drinkers are perhaps no more frequent than was true in the pre-Prohibition Era, their character and status has considerably changed. As one informant put it: "There has been a breakdown in the middle classes. The

[42] Harold Mulford and Donald Miller, "Public Definitions of the Alcoholic," *Quarterly Journal of Studies of Alcohol*, XXII (June, 1961), 312-20.

[43] John W. Riley, Jr., and Charles F. Marden, "The Social Pattern of Alcoholic Drinking," *Quarterly Journal of Studies on Alcohol*, VIII (September, 1947), 265-73; Knupfer and Room, "Drinking in a Metropolitan Community"; Mulford, "Drinking and Deviant Drinking." Mulford's story shows a slight *decrease* in percentage of drinkers among lower-educated persons when compared with Marden's 1946 study.

upper classes have always used liquor; the lower classes have always used liquor. Now the middle class has taken it over. The thing is slopping over from both sides."

The Prohibition period did not serve to set in motion a vast antipathy to abstinence. It did not check the continued long-run trend away from the excessive use of distilled spirits in the United States. The 1920's experience of upper-middle-class urban drinking was consonant with the later shifts in the class usages of alcohol in the United States, resulting in moderate use by a formerly abstinent middle class. It was effective in diminishing the total of alcoholic consumption in the United States while it was in operation. Its lasting effects, then, in terms of American drinking and behavior appear to have been relatively few, although it may have to some degree acted to support other cultural shifts that were changing class patterns in the use of alcohol in the United States. In order to appreciate the impact of the Prohibition Era on American life we need also to look at its role as a political issue, a role that suggests other kinds of cultural meanings than those we have already examined in terms of direct effect upon drinking.

In many ways the movement for national prohibition was an inexpedient one. By 1913 an equitable arrangement seems to have developed in which temperance sentiment was recognized by both law and behavior in those areas where it was strongest. Where dry sentiments were weak, the populace continued to act in accord with what they thought to be culturally legitimate. Enforcement in urban areas, where cultural support was small, had been tried and had been shown to be a doubtful possibility. It should have seemed impossible to the reformer to enforce legislation against so deep a resistance. Instead of seeking a possible compromise on a national level, however, the Anti-Saloon League and its supporters pushed their power as far as it could go into a law that made no distinctions between beer and liquor and gave no solace to those for whom drinking was part of the way of living.

The issue of enforcement, however, hides some crucial functions of Prohibition as a symbolic issue in American life. If the norm against alcohol was often evaded, there was no question after 1919 about whose law it was. The Eighteenth Amendment made very plain the legal and public commitment of the American society to the utopia of the dry. Perhaps Billy Sunday was carried away by his own moral fervor when he described a world in which "the reign of tears is over. The slums will soon be only a memory. We will turn our prisons into factories and our jails into storehouses and corn cribs. Men will walk upright now. Women will smile, and the children will laugh. Hell will be forever for rent." [44] The flamboyant orator's rhetoric expresses the fundamental moral conception of Prohibition that lies so deeply within the American and Protestant ethos. It is impossible to understand the politics of the 1920's adequately, and its consequences, without understanding the interrelationship between moral stands, cultural commitments, and political conflict.

In describing the myriad of forces that supported Prohibition, the one common denominator that united the sometimes disparate body of reformers was Protestant theology and its antipathy to the kinds of leisure that alcohol represented. If some overzealous supporters described the battle for Prohibition as a veritable Armeggedon, they were not without truth. They saw the drinkers and the opponents of Prohibition as people who stood for cultural values that

[44] Quoted in Harry Elmer Barnes, *Prohibition Versus Civilization* (New York, 1932), p. 68.

were anathema to the dry. As one observer put it, "Criminals, bandits, ex-convicts and thugs; street-walkers, harlots, prostitutes and degenerates are against Prohibition. But the good church people, the humanitarians, those who try to uplift and help others are for Prohibition." [45]

In this disjuncture between the drinkers and the abstainers, we find the same kind of cultural dichotomy that Horace Greeley had recognized at the base of political loyalties and animosities in the 1844 elections in New York State when he wrote, "Upon those working men who stick to their business, hope to improve their circumstances by honest industry and go on Sundays to church rather than the grog shop, the appeals of Loco-Focoism fell comparatively harmless; while the opposite class were rallied with unprecedented unanimity against us." [46] As we have seen, this distinction had a certain validity. It was in the cities that one found the saloon at its height and the problem of alcohol consumption at its greatest. It was the immigrants and the Catholics who provided the greatest contrast in values to the sober middle-class Protestant. These conflicts were focused around the issue of Prohibition. They were given sustenance by the nativism and racial theories that were then so current. [47]

In this context consumption and abstinence take on meanings as signs and symbols of group loyalty and differentiation. The styles of life to which people are committed in their status groups are signs to us of who they are. As important elements in the make-up of one's standards of living, they become symbols of membership and loyalty. Thorstein Veblen has shown this very clearly in his discussion of the theory of the leisure class. The fur-

[45] *Ibid.*, p. 31.
[46] Quoted in Lee Benson, *The Concept of Jacksonian Democracy* (Princeton, N.J., 1961).
[47] Jones, "Prohibition and Eugenics."

nishings we use, the clothes we wear, and the foods we eat are those that are part of our specific culture. They are also enjoined upon us as ways of demonstrating that we are what we claim to be. In American society, drinking, like sex, is also an aspect tinged with a high degree of moral judgment. Whether one is a "drunken bum" or a "dried-up blue nose" is a matter of considerable moral moment. Hence, drinking in American society is affected with an intensive set of cultural designations.

Politically, this implies that the designation of the public morality is also a determination of cultural dominance.[48] The quest for a given piece of legislation has meaning that is symbolic of, or in substitution for, instrumental goals. For cultural dominance to be symbolized by a piece of legislation, its mere existence is sufficient; enforcement is not essential. To have gained the legislative victory itself is to have gained the mark of cultural dominance; to be able to say, "Give deference to my way of living and degradation to yours".

As a code of living, temperance performed two functions vis-à-vis its opponents. First, it existed as a style of life that was set forth in opposition to less stern orientations to family, to neighbors, and to a hierarchial authority in which leisure involved a separation between work and play and not a preparation for it. In this sense the effort to make others temperate (abstinent) was an act of coercion, dominated by a defense against a threatened overwhelming new cultural impulse. Second, temperance was an invitation to those, especially the newly arrived in the United States, to adopt the habits that spelled success and prestige in American life. It was in this respect an invitation toward

---

[48] Clark, *The Dry Years*, pp. 113–22, shows the split between middle class and lower class as deeply related to dry and wet antagonisms in the twentieth century in the state of Washington. The symbolic nature of the issue is discussed throughout my *Symbolic Crusade*.

assimilation in which urban social problems were to be
solved by the lower classes adopting the values by which
middle-class citizens would permit them to enter their gates.
The passage of Prohibition made clear that the cultural
dominance of the old middle-class was proclaimed; Anna
Gordon, president of the WCTU put it in an address in
1915: "Total abstinence is no longer a ridiculed fanaticism.
It sits in regal state on the throne of empires and of
kingdoms and sways, in ever increasing measure, the
voting citizenship." [49]

If this cultural confrontation existed before Prohibition,
it did so in a somewhat muted fashion. It was a major
consequence of Prohibition and of the Prohibition Era that
it served to make both sides more homogeneous and consequently to polarize the cultural diversities within American
society. In understanding the ways in which Prohibition
functioned as a symbol of cultural conflict, we must now
turn to the sources of growing commitment and antipathy
during the 1920's.

The polarizing effects of the campaign for national prohibition were made manifest in an editorial of the Anti-
Saloon League's journal, the *American Issue*.[50] "The liquor
issue is no longer one of Wet and Dry arguments. Hence-
forth, it is to be a question of Wet men and Dry men."
The campaign for Prohibition had the effect of widening
the gulf between the cultures involved in the defense of
drinking and of abstinence. Because it sought political decisions, rather than moral suasion, the Anti-Saloon League
and the dry forces tended to organize both sides around
concrete issues. Because they sought a total victory, they

[49] *Annual Report,* National Woman's Christian Temperance Union,
1915, p. 93.
[50] *American Issue,* XX (January, 1912), 4.

made it extremely difficult for more moderate dry allies
to stay in the same camp.

One aspect of this was the almost total demise of Catholic
organizational support for prohibitionist legislation. Although the Catholic Abstinence Union and many of the
Paulist fathers had been a source of aid in efforts to curtail
drinking, they could not go along with the extreme position
represented by Prohibition. When the Catholic Clergy Prohibition League of America was founded in 1919, it had
relatively small backing in contrast to the earlier more
moderate efforts. "Most Roman Catholics, however, opposed
Prohibition and became especially hostile after the reform
began to reach the larger cities where Catholic strength
was concentrated." [51] Two major non-evangelical Protestant
churches, the Episcopalian and both Lutheran synods, did
not climb on board the dry wagon. The Jews, who also
represented an immigrant population, were similarly hostile
to prohibitory legislation. The effect, then, of the campaign
for Prohibition was to stamp it even more clearly as a
middle-class, Protestant, and nativist activity.

Despite the fact that the progressive movement was a
major source for urban middle-class support for Prohibition,
as Timberlake has shown, it yet remains the case that the
drive for Prohibition tended to increase the gap along class
lines between components within the progressive movement.
Thus the labor movement, especially with the development
of the American Federation of Labor, was by no means
any longer a major ally of temperance. Although Terence
Powderly, the founder and head of the Knights of Labor,
had been actively allied with the temperance organizations
of the late nineteenth century, his concern was by no means
mirrored in the labor movement of the twentieth century.

[51] Timberlake, *Prohibition and the Progressive Movement*, p. 32.

Gompers was concerned with moderating the use of liquor, but both he and most of the labor movement were by then, in culture and temperament, opposed to both abstinence and the tactics of legislative prohibition.[52]

The progressive movement, though it was dominated very much by the urban middle class, nevertheless gained very important strength from its general concern with the welfare of labor and the industrial worker. In this sympathy progressivism was anti-industrial and an opponent of the new business classes. Prohibition, so thoroughly identified in the urban areas with the Protestant middle class, split the progressive movement on the issue of drinking. To the worker it smacked of paternalism and class exploitation. Samuel Gompers, with considerable foresight, remarked to a Congressional committee that Prohibition would be discriminatory against the worker. "The cry is against this discrimination, which is almost inevitable, except so far as a business man or a man of means may be himself a total abstainer. Where a wage earner can not get a glass of beer, still a very large proportion of the men of means can have and do have a stock of intoxicating drinks to last men their lives." [53] The visible exemption of the urban rich from the restrictions of Prohibition made the gap evident to the urban poor.

Despite the activity of urban progressives, a major consequence of the Prohibition campaign was to intensify the conflict between the city and the country. As we have shown above, it was in the rural areas that the Prohibition forces found their greatest support. When the Webb-Kenyon Act was passed in Congress in 1913, the sources of support came far more from areas where old-stock middle classes

[52] Despite Timberlake's assertion that Prohibition was a phase of progressive reform, he admits that "other Progressives, especially those identified with urban-labor-immigrant elements, disliked the reform and fought it" (*ibid.*, p. 2). Also see his discussion of labor and Prohibition, pp. 88–95.

[53] *Ibid.*, p. 94.

were strong than from those of the industrial and immigrant population.[54] An analysis of percentage of state populations under prohibition by state or local laws in 1913 shows that dry laws were far less likely to occur in urbanized than in rural states.[55]

The same thing is true if one compares the Populist vote in the late nineteenth century to the prohibitionist status of states in 1919. In counties where Populist vote had been high, there the prohibitionist support was strongest. The earliest of the states to be drawn into the wave of prohibitory legislation after 1906 were in the South, and it was in the South that one found the strongest support for national prohibition and prohibitory legislation. Those who were likely to see this as largely a reaction to the Negro are mistaken. County-by-county analysis in Mississippi and Alabama revealed that the strongest sources of support were in the rural counties that had been Populist in the late nineteenth century and that had a low percentage of Negroes. In the urban counties the support was much less, and in rural counties with high percentages of Negroes, largely disenfranchised, Prohibition found considerable opposition. What differentiated the Prohibitionist from the pro-wet forces in these southern areas was largely the existence of evangelical Protestant religion.

We are not implying here that Prohibition can be explained as a Populist reform. What we do suggest is that great opposition to Prohibition came from the eastern, urban states where large percentages of Catholics and immigrants were to be found. Major urban and industrial areas like Illinois, New York, and Pennsylvania were the last to ratify the Eighteenth Amendment. The strongest areas of national prohibition sentiment were not the industrialized states nor the industrialized sectors of rural states. They

[54] *Ibid.*, p. 163; Sinclair, *Prohibition*, p. 154.
[55] Gusfield, *Symbolic Crusade*, pp. 102–3.

were largely areas that were Protestant, rural, and nativist;
in the South and in the Midwest rather than in the East.
This is not to deny that the progressives did play an important role in Prohibition campaigns. This they certainly
did, as Timberlake has shown. In California they played
perhaps the greatest role, but in Los Angeles County,
where the Populist candidate for President in 1892 had
pulled 14 per cent of the votes and the Prohibitionist 4 per
cent, one found intense support for the Anti-Saloon League
and the Progressive campaigns of 1909–13.[56]

The saloon and the drinker increasingly appeared to the
Protestant middle class, both urban and rural, as a symbol
of a culture alien to the ascetic character of American
values. What was important was not so much that people
drank but that they upheld the validity and the rightness
of liquor and beer within an accepted way of life. There
were many strands in the Prohibitionist campaign, derived
from many ideological sources of a nineteenth century commercial and agrarian society. The reform movements that
swept the United States in the late nineteenth and early
twentieth centuries, especially in the form of progressivism
and Populism, were important roots for the Prohibition
movement. But in the process of pursuing Prohibition, both
the gaps between the older social system and the newer one
and the elements involved in these movements themselves
came into conflict. At the root of these conflicts were cultural
differences that were symbolized by the very effort to make
the American Protestant version of the good life embedded
in law.

The result was that what for one group was a part of
its daily existence and a legitimate and welcome source of
leisure was, to the dry forces, a vice whose eradication was

[56] *Ibid.*, p. 104; Gilman Ostrander, *The Prohibition Movement in
California, 1848–1933* (Berkeley, Calif., 1957), p. 105.

essential. Consider the cultural overtones of superiority in the argument of a Prohibition advocate: "The hope of perpetuating our liberties is to help the foreigners correct any demoralizing custom, and through self-restraint as-similate American ideals." [57] The result of the Prohibition campaign was to increase the cultural conflict that had long been involved in temperance activity. "The Anglo-Saxon stock," declared the journal of the Anti-Saloon League, "is hardiest and fittest. . . . If we are to preserve this nation in the Anglo-Saxon type, we must abolish [saloons]".[58] For those who were the objects of such abolition, the attempt seemed only one of hostile aggressiveness.

As the nation entered the Prohibition Era on the night of January 16, 1920, the issues had already been drawn and the conflicts and symbols already stated. The only new argument to emerge for the drys was that abstinence was now the law of the land, and the devotees of law and order must obey. The wet rejoinder, after the first few years, was that Prohibition had been tried and was found to be unenforceable. Though the arguments from science, reli-gion, economics, and other areas of knowledge were con-tinuously stated and restated by friend and foe, the basic for and against positions of rural-urban, of middle-working class, and Protestant-Catholic were apparent and more evident day by day. What was new and what made the Prohibition Era so consequential for later American politics was the tendency toward an increasing and vigilant moral-ism among the drys and a fusion of these qualities with particular political parties and leaders. In the course of this, the moderates and the progressives were increasingly pushed to one or another side. When repeal came, it came

[57] Barker, *The Saloon Problem*, pp. 49–50. Quoted in Timberlake, *Prohibition and the Progressive Movement*, p. 118.
[58] *American Issue*, XX (April, 1912), 1.

to a country that was tired of the moralisms of the drys and the wets and preoccupied with a totally different kind of problem.

The progressive impulse had played a significant part in the Prohibition campaign. But even before Prohibition was achieved, there was a widening split. Although the urban, middle-class, and progressive supporters of Prohibition were highly visible, their role in the major Prohibitionist organizations was by no means this apparent. The WCTU, which had in the late 1890's been deeply committed to Frances Willard's Do-Everything policy, had been active in such diverse movements as female suffrage, the rights of labor, penal reform, and even cremation, as well as influenced by the general tenets of Christian socialism. After the Anti-Saloon League began its Prohibition campaigns in 1906, however, this ladies' wing of the temperance movement began to retreat from its wider concerns into a far more specific and concerted attack on the liquor traffic.[59] The Anti-Saloon League itself was based upon a very explicit policy of isolation from all other issues. The title of its major periodical, the *American Issue,* was its basic point of difference from the Prohibition party and from many earlier temperance organizations. Even the famed Methodist Board of Temperance, Morals, and Social Legislation was far less concerned with the latter two items than with the first. When Prohibition arrived, those organizations that had been so successful in mobilizing political strength had become isolated from other major progressive movements of the early twentieth century.

The urban middle classes, so much wedded to the progressive ideology of clean government and paternalism toward industrial workers, were far less hostile to the urban society than was the case among the rural components of Prohibition. As groups, they were less likely to be drawn

[59] Gusfield, *Symbolic Crusade,* chap. iv.

into some of the highly bombastic and hostile attitudes that came to govern Prohibition rhetoric and action during the 1920's. As residents in urban America, they were quick to feel the consequences of Prohibition for middle-class drinking and for organized crime. The easier enforcement of Prohibition in the towns and country areas made rural people far less susceptible to the belief that Prohibition was unenforceable and productive of excessive crime. As the era continued, the defection of the moderate progressive left the field still further open to the neo-Populists. When the Federal Council of Churches of Christ, the leading organ of expression of the social gospel and high-status churches in the United States, announced its opposition to continued Prohibition, it sounded the beginnings of a shift that proved highly destructive to the drys.[60]

By the 1920's the progressive movement had run its course. Teddy Roosevelt and Woodrow Wilson had both departed, and the effort of La Follette was a last weak shot at revival. The alliance between temperance and nativism began to produce excessive and unsophisticated ideologies that pushed the urbanites further from identification with rural colleagues. It should be noted that in point of fact the northeastern urban progressives in the Progressive party of 1916, when the prohibition issue was raised, did not support it. The party convention opposed prohibition in its meetings in 1912.[61]

In this respect I am in agreement with Sinclair and in disagreement with Timberlake. Timberlake sees Prohibition as largely an extension of the progressive reform, whereas Sinclair and I are likely to see it as one element but much overshadowed by the rural political base and sentiments

[60] Sinclair, *Prohibition*, pp. 290–91. It might also be suggested that this polarization among Protestants accentuated the shift in drinking standards, distaste for the dry's single-minded political zeal undermining the standard he so zealously pursued.

[61] *Ibid.*, pp. 95–96.

of antiurbanism and nativism. During the Prohibition Era
the forces of nativism, antiurbanism, and religious fundamentalism gained strength. Both defensiveness over the
enforceability of Prohibition and the very success in
achieving it added to an expansiveness that took the form
of a strong effort to expand the rural virtues embodied in
Prohibition into other areas. Perhaps, too, as Virginius
Dabney has suggested, the dry leaders felt themselves
threatened by the obviously increasing strength and numbers of the Catholic, immigrant, and working-class people
of the big cities.

In his rhetoric and in his career William Jennings Bryan
embodied much of what Prohibitionists stood for. His action
in the 1920's reflected a good deal of what was happening.
Although he had carefully refrained from taking a stand
on liquor questions during his presidential campaigns, despite his obvious personal pro-dry feelings, during the 1920's
he came to feel that the Prohibition issue was now a dominant one. He spoke out most strongly in the effort to make
the Democratic party a stauncher vehicle for Prohibition
sentiment and to prevent its domination by urban and eastern forces. The 1924 convention was a bitter one. It linked
Bryan and the drys to the support of the Ku Klux Klan.
In this respect, as in so much of the rhetoric of the drys,
the nativism and anti-Catholicism of the Prohibitionists
were made to seem the central tenets of a wider movement.
Those urban supporters who had found in Prohibition a
significance given by concern for social welfare and for industrial efficiency were more likely to be rebuffed by legislation that had now been given a decidedly different kind of
symbolic significance. In 1924 the Prohibition party even
passed planks to support the placement of Bibles in the
schools and for legislation to enforce the Americanization
of aliens.[62]

[62] *Ibid.*, p. 87.

The dry victory, and the later fight against repeal, made the conflicts between cultures more intense and polarized even more the forces of the urban and the rural, the Catholic and the Protestant, the immigrant and the native. Prohibition was thus not an isolated issue but one that pitted cultures against each other. Given the constitutionality of Prohibition and the experience with the denunciation of the German brewers during World War I, the loyal drys added patriotism to the other arrows in their quiver. It was a patriotism directed less against external enemies than toward the urban and immigrant cultures in American cities. Ella Boole, then the president of the WCTU, said in 1928 to its national convention that "this is the United States of America, my country and I love it. . . . As my forefathers worked and struggled to build it, so will I work and struggle to maintain it unsoiled by foreign influences, uncontaminated by vicious mind poison." [63]

Bryan's own qualities, so effective on the prairies, were not calculated to gain loyal followers on the cement sidewalks. He embodied the prejudices and the virtues of rural America. At the Scopes trial, he was not simply a pathetic old man; his effort to shore up fundamentalist religion against the attacks of sophisticated science in turn continued that resistance to the modern that is in part at the root of the antiurbanism in Prohibition. In a mania for purity in literature, attack on the cigarette, and the demand for the eradication of jazz, the drys moved increasingly to an alliance with a general movement of fundamentalist conservatism in American manners, morals, and politics. It is in this sense that we speak of the radicalization of Prohibition reform. Both sides moved toward a more rigid statement of diverse orientations toward life.

To some degree the increasing polarization was a function of the fact that the issues were posed as political choices.

[63] *Union Signal* (Dec. 15, 1928), p. 12.

The split that Bryan had dramatized in the Democratic party began the set of events that tended increasingly to turn the Prohibition issue into one of party identifications. What the Anti-Saloon League had sought to avoid came into being—the identification of the Republicans with Prohibition and of the Democrats with Repeal. In large measure the national legislative victories had been a function of a coalition between southern Democrats and middlewestern and western Republicans. The Hobson resolution submitting the Eighteenth Amendment to the states was originally defeated in 1914. In 1917 its passage was secured by the increased votes that came from Republican gains in the House from midwestern states.[64] Nevertheless, neither the presidential campaigns of 1916, 1920, or 1924 had pivoted around the dry issue. Although Wilson and Harding had vetoed various pro-dry measures, such as Wilson's veto of the Volstead Act, they had all steered clear of any identification on either side of the issue.

The campaign of Alfred E. Smith for the presidency was a vital link in the processes by which repeal was achieved and by which the American political parties gained a great deal of their present stylistic differences. The conflict of cultures that Smith's candidacy mirrored had already been more than foreshadowed in the 1924 convention. The very fact that an urban Catholic, an avowed wet, was the candidate of a major political party was in itself an affront to the sober, Protestant middle classes that had put through Prohibition and that had for so long dominated American political life.

Theda Tray has written that while Hoover and Smith were talking about issues, "the rest of the population was talking about Al—where he went to church, what kind of a lid he wore, what liquids he took with his meals, how he was born and brought up in Tammany Hall and the way he

[64] Sinclair, *Prohibition*, p. 163.

pronounced 'foist.' " [65] In Smith the wets had found a perfect symbol of a way of life—a man who had championed social welfare, whose sentiments and speech showed clearly the sidewalks of New York on which he had been reared. He was the best of the machine politicians and a deep defender of the urban underdog who "worked in factories, spoke broken English, and wanted a good time on Sundays." [66] Herbert Hoover was, of course, the very opposite in manner and in speech. In so many ways he was the rural epitome of the American success story: the efficient engineer who had worked his way up from humble farm beginnings and who had made his mark in the effective organization of charity. At last the struggle was out in the open, and it led the Prohibitionist forces into a zealous fight against the devil. In a typical statement the Anti-Saloon League yearbook said in 1931, "When the great cities of America actually come to dominate the states and dictate the policies of the nation, the process of decay in our boasted American civilization will have begun." [67] Bishop Cannon, the Anti-Saloon League, the Methodist and other evangelical Protestant churches, the WCTU—all threw themselves behind Herbert Hoover, departing from their long policy of avoiding specific recommendations in presidential elections. Even the Prohibition party, for the first time since its beginning, in 1872, supported another party's presidential candidate and failed to nominate one of their own. Such a split made it extraordinarily difficult for the Progressive and social welfare-oriented urban Prohibitionists. The bigotry of the

[65] Quoted in *ibid.*, p. 304. For a general description of the 1928 campaign see Moore, *A Catholic Runs for President* (New York, 1956).

[66] Gusfield, *Symbolic Crusade*, p. 125. For an account of Smith's voting power in urban areas see Samuel Lubell, *The Future of American Politics* (New York, 1952).

[67] *Anti-Saloon League Yearbook. 1931* (Westerville, Ohio, 1931), p. 9.

open anti-Catholicism in which Cannon and other Prohibition leaders engaged further turned the knife in the wounds that a vindictive policy of nativism had developed during the 1920's.

Hoover's victory, in a clear endorsement of Prohibition, should of course not hide what is evident today in Smith's defeat—the rise of Democratic majorities in the American big cities. These cities had already been the bastion of wet votes.[68] Samuel Lubell has recounted the importance of the Smith campaign in presaging the development of the Democratic party as the champion of the urban underdog ethnic minorities. Not only was it the case that the Catholic and Jewish populations were increasing more rapidly than were middle-class Protestants, but the cultural conflicts represented in part by prohibitionist issues tended to drive some of the immigrant groups that had been Republican closer to the Democratic party.[69]

What Smith had accomplished, in relation to the Prohibition issue, was to swing the wet centers of the population behind the Democrats. Sinclair's analysis of the vote in 1930 in the House of Representatives on the Jones Law shows this clearly. The drys, though winning a great victory in numbers (284–90), captured very little of the northern vote. Although the North had provided over half of the wet vote in 1917, now it provided just under two-thirds. The Republican party had become even more dry, whereas the Democrats were more split than ever.[70] In short, Prohibition had become identified with the Republican party. The basis for a compromise had increasingly diminished. When repeal came, it was as a vindiction of all that urban

[68] With the exception of Los Angeles and several southern cities, no major American city was pro-dry.

[69] Lubell, *The Future of American Politics.*

[70] Sinclair, *Prohibition,* p. 353.

and industrial America had come to stand for in the dialogue of American politics.

If Smith's defeat and the shifting nature of political polarization in the United States foreshadowed the possibility of repeal, the events of the 1920's had already begun to sharpen the opposition. The growth and development of the Association Against the Prohibition Amendment and the development of a Women's Auxiliary in the late 1920's had produced something that had not clearly existed before 1920—an independent organization of wets. As long as the liquor and beer industries were behind all efforts to publicize a wet position, their hearing in public was limited. However, growing dissatisfaction with the law had brought into being groups of people of high social position who could not easily be dismissed. The early defection of the DuPonts from the ranks of temperance supporters and their enthusiastic backing of the Association Against the Prohibition Amendment represented a serious blow to dry forces. The championing of Repeal by Mrs. Charles Sabin, a woman of social prominence, was another blow to the dry cause.

The shifts in public opinion might have been borne and the amendment saved, at least in relationship to distilled spirits, had it not been for the major event of the depression. It was the Great Depression that killed the Eighteenth Amendment more than any other single act or process. In 1929 Prohibition was still part of the Constitution. It had survived the attack of the 1928 election. The Prohibition Bureau, under Hoover, for the first time was placed on a sound footing under Civil Service in the Department of Justice. A strong effort to enforce the law seemed in existence. The Wickersham Report, though critical of enforcement, laid the groundwork for an adequate discussion under which some compromise between wet and dry might have

been achievable. That the dry forces were still quite strong
has already been indicated in our analysis of the vote on
the Jones Law. The depression, however, made the issue of
Prohibition a minor one, less calculated to instil enthusiastic
loyalties in either direction.

The argument of economic consideration now took precedence. In 1926 only a few unions had actively opposed the
law in Congressional hearings. In 1930 and 1932 union
representatives constituted a great source of the advocacy
of Repeal, on the grounds that it would put men back to
work in such jobs as lithography (making bottle labels),
glass blowing, and among hotel and steward groups.[71] Further, the argument that new sources of tax revenues were
necessary and needed appeared to play an extremly important role among businessmen who had championed Prohibition as the route to a sober and reliable work force.
Even those great stalwarts of the dry reform John D.
Rockefeller and S. S. Kresge had left the movement in 1932.
For the first time in many, many years the Anti-Saloon
League was suffering from a deficiency of funds.[72] More
importantly, tangible economic issues became paramount,
and the cultural differences between the lower-class urban
workers and the rural farmers became minimal when they
were both so desperately in financial difficulty.

The depression, however, had another important effect
upon the consequences of Prohibition for American life.
Having so thoroughly identified the Republicans with dry
sentiment and with Herbert Hoover, they quite clearly
underlined the antipathy of the urban and immigrant masses
for the party that appeared to be the spokesman of the white
Anglo-Saxon Protestant. Not only did the Republican party
come to be viewed as the party of big business, but it was

[71] See my discussion of these Congressional hearings in Gusfield,
Symbolic Crusade, pp. 127–28.
[72] Clark, *The Dry Years*, pp. 227–29.

also deeply associated with the party that had turned its back on the urban poor, the Catholic and the Jew and the working man whose leisure had little room for the dry utopia.

It is in its implications for the setting of styles in American politics that Prohibition has had a considerable importance in American life.

In becoming associated with the cause of the dry, the Republican party hardened its cultural overtones as the party whose heyday was the period of the 1920's—the high point of old middle-class political supremacy and a prosperity that celebrated the effectiveness and virtue of a business civilization. The Great Depression dissolved the magic power of the old symbols and set in its place a conception of government closer to the welfare orientations of the urban, immigrant, and industrial poor. In Al Smith and in the New Deal, the Democrats moved more clearly out of the 1920's and the world of William Jennings Bryan. These images of political parties have continued to play significant functions in voter perceptions of Republicans and Democrats—the Republicans as the party of "big business" and the Democrats as the party of the "underdog." Public opinion polls have been consistent in reporting such designations among American voters.[73]

We have already suggested that the era of Prohibition tended to polarize the cultural diversities in American life. In splitting off the welfare-oriented and progressive strands in Prohibition from the nativist and Populist strands, the 1920's more completely effected the bond between political party choices and cultural loyalties. The differential availability of beer and liquor for working and for middle classes underlined the symbolism of the Republicans as the party

[73] Bernard Berelson *et al.*, *Voting* (Chicago, 1954), p. 79; Angus Campbell *et al.*, *The American Voter* (New York, 1960), pp. 149–67; Lubell, *The Future of American Politics.*

of the old middle class, the Protestant establishment, and the agrarian past.[74] The Democrats emerged more clearly as the party of the urban frontier, the champion of a good life of leisure and comradeship. Against the utopia of an efficient and moral civilization, soberly dedicated to production and perfectability, there was clearly posed the utopia of the happy consumers, sharing in the fruits of the economy and practicing a "live and let live" attitude to the differences of a pluralistic society.

The linkages between party and cultural styles involves as well distinctly diverse views of government and its obligations and limits. Richard Hofstadter has described this in remarking on the contrast between the progressive's conception of government and that of the big city machine and its followers.[75] For the urban middle class that supported progressivism, government was a vehicle for achieving moral purposes and the public good. Clean government and the rational electorate were his virtues, and the corruption and organization of the machine were deeply vicious. The saloon, in its alliance with the political boss, was anathema. The good citizen, in the progressive utopia, saw government as a vehicle in which he was the driver, not the passenger. The urban immigrant, on the other hand, saw society as a hierarchical structure in which authority did favors for those on the bottom in return for favors toward those at the top. The impersonal, moralistic vision of politics that the drys upheld was the common property of the old middle class, both urban and rural. A

[74] We should be careful not to confuse the farmer and the small town. Farmers show much less fealty to the Republican party than often supposed. Much of the solid Republican strength lies in the rural non-farm communities and does not display the erratic quality of the farm vote, which is more closely related to immediate farm prices. See Lubell, *The Future of American Politics*, chap. viii; Seymour Lipset, *Agrarian Socialism* (Berkeley and Los Angeles, 1950), chap. i.

[75] Richard Hofstadter, *The Age of Reform* (New York, 1956), pp. 180–84.

more personal practice that mixed human concern with ethnic loyalty was the stuff on which the urban politician based his power. Lincoln Steffens quoted the Boston "boss" Martin Lomasny as saying that what people wanted was mercy, not law and justice.[76]

In their efforts to enshrine a Protestant Sunday as the ideal of American consumership, the drys set their face against the tolerant and indulgent cultures that had come to make up much of the new industrial populations. Their own logic and their intense need for the establishment of moral supremacy in public forms made compromises with the wets increasingly difficult. A politics of compromise was itself difficult for such moralists to accept. As the issues became sharper, became more clearly cultural in content, and became linked to political parties, political loyalties and ethnic identities were more clearly linked to stylistic differences.

Perhaps here we touch upon deeper shifts in American life that were beginning to emerge in the 1920's and in turn appear to have been in process of changing American orientations toward consumption, toward leisure, and toward the use of alcohol. We have already pointed out that America, over the past eighty years, has shifted from a nation of excessive drinkers and abstainers to one of far more moderate consumption of alcohol. The intensive use of alcohol as a means of escape (and consequently the defensive reaction against it) appears to have given way to the use of alcohol in facilitating social camaraderie. In this respect Americans, in their quest to extend and maintain good fellowship, are more inclined to accept playfulness and leisure and less inclined to show continuous concern with production and work. The general shifts in American character that David Riesman has made so vivid are presaged in the 1920's. Kinsey, in his famous study of the

[76] Lincoln Steffens, *Autobiography* (New York, 1931), p. 618.

sexual behavior of the human female, dates a sharp shift in American sexual morality from the appearance of the generation born after 1910.[77] Certainly the 1920's saw a tremendous increase in what may be called the cultural mobility of the American population, especially in urban centers. It was the era in which communication and transportation were greatly increased by the appearance of the automobile, the movies, and the radio. It was an era of affluence, in the main, and one in which the moralities of a sterner Protestantism were under attack both by the winds of change and by the appearance of whole new populations that were less committed to the utopia of the sober Sunday. After the 1920's the conflicts between the alien and the native, between urban and rural, Protestant and Catholic, became less vivid than those between adherents to styles of fundamentalism and modernism, conflicts that cut across the different religious and residence groups.[78]

The sentiments that American Prohibition expressed are by no means dead, although they have lost a great deal of their prestige and political dominance. Abstinence is still the commitment of a large segment of the American population. What is true, however, is that the domination in cultural and political terms that it represented, the domination of the nineteenth-century Anglo-Saxon Protestant, has ended in American life. It is this that was the meaning of the struggle over Prohibition and that has made its loss so bitter for those who have identified with it. "For when all the old Prohibs are dead—as soon they will be—one may look in vain for the old America." [79]

[77] Alfred Kinsey *et al.*, *Sexual Behavior in the Human Female* (Philadelphia, 1953).

[78] This has also been discussed recently in sociological literature as conflict between "cosmopolitans" and "locals." See the discussion of these cultural styles in Gusfield, *Symbolic Crusade*, Chapter VI.

[79] Clark, *The Dry Years*, p. 127.

Fiction of the Jazz Age

FREDERICK J. HOFFMAN

THE title of this essay suggests not only that the time from 1918 to 1930 involved us in a very special, a unique, world, but also demands that the fiction published during these years be distinctive. I have no absolutely reliable measure either of the 1920's or of its fiction. Like the use of statistics in argument, evidence *can* be cited to support the idea of an unusual American society enjoying for a few years an unusual life, and of a fiction that held a mirror to this life.

It becomes a matter of scaled values. To take the term "Jazz Age" by itself, one might say that it argues a quite free, say, even an irresponsible, "Age." This is a cliché about the decade, and it conjures up images of Gilda Gray, Grover Whalen, Jimmy Walker, and others, and Warren Gamaliel Harding playing poker with his buddies in the White House. It is true that there was an easing of tensions after World War I; since we were on the winning side and had suffered not much more than slight inconveniences, and since we were temporarily enjoying the illusion that there would be no more wars, the tone of the decade was special. This is true even though the country's economy was only superficially prosperous, the distance between haves and have-nots quite noticeable, and at Versailles the seeds of World War II had been sown.

In other words, although the "Jazz Age" phrase describes only a partial view of the 1920's, it refers to a sizable segment of our society—and that one of the most articulate. The attitude itself has been overemphasized in subsequent histories of the decade and of its literature; in no case does it adequately comprehend the genuine spirit of the 1920's; it points to surface glitter—the sort of world indicated by the epithet in the society of F. Scott Fitzgerald's short stories, of his flappers, of wealth, of a world in which (he said later) rewards were quick and success came early.[1] "Even when you were broke you didn't worry about money, because it was in such profusion around you. . . . Charm, notoriety, mere good manners, weighed more than money as a social asset. . . . " (*Crack-Up*, pp. 21–22)

But in these words, and in others, there is more than surface gaiety; for Fitzgerald was not only the master reporter of the Jazz Age, he was, or he ultimately became, its most sensitive judge. He managed the reporting easily enough; in fact, it was all too easy and too much a temptation for him to report on the behavior of the decade's golden lads and lasses. In one of his Notebook entries, under "Girls," he wrote: " . . . She was lovely and expensive, and about nineteen." (*Crack-Up*, p. 133) These three characteristics summed up quite effectively the superficial qualities of his people; and they *were* real enough qualities, for Fitzgerald's great popular attractiveness was due in part to his being able to define a part of an age, the part that has led to the decade's being called the Jazz Age.

[1] See "Echoes of the Jazz Age," in *The Crack-Up*, ed. Edmund Wilson (New York, 1945), pp. 13–22. This essay was first published in *Scribner's Magazine*, November, 1931.

Nevertheless, one does not remain nineteen; the pressure of time upon his people is ever-present.[2] In a crucial scene, Nick Carraway, the narrator of *The Great Gatsby* (1925) suddenly becomes aware of his thirtieth birthday (Fitzgerald was himself twenty-nine when *The Great Gatsby* was published) ; there is much said, in the person of Jay Gatsby, about "repeating the past." The following exchange with Carraway has an especial poignancy (they are discussing Daisy Buchanan's ability to recover her love for Gatsby after five years) :

> He broke off and began to walk up and down a desolate path of food and rinds and discarded favors and crushed flowers.
> "I wouldn't ask too much of her," I ventured. "You can't repeat the past."
> "Can't repeat the past?" he cried incredulously. "Why of course you can!"
> He looked around him wildly, as if the past were lurking in the shadow of his house, just out of reach of his hand.[3]

Of course, Carraway is right; you may have the illusion of retrieving the past, but what you actually have is an altogether different time, and you are beyond the range of the past when you most think you have it. The idea of time's hovering near, of the basic risk of overevaluating youth, is an important part of most of the decade's best novels and stories. The unreality of the 1920's—in some quarters, at least, the time and the circumstances *did* seem unreal—made these years appear at times to be a moral hiatus between two "substantial" and morally serious times,

[2] See Richard Lehan's *F. Scott Fitzgerald and the Craft of Fiction* (Carbondale, Ill., 1966) for a thorough study of the peculiar effect of time upon Fitzgerald's work.

[3] *The Great Gatsby* (New York, 1925), p. 133.

the prewar Victorian and the post-crash Marxian. Much
of Fitzgerald's moral judgment of the decade came in retrospective glances at it. Charlie Wales, hero of one of his
finest short stories, "Babylon Revisited," looks back at the
years recently past and thinks of them as a time without
"character":

> . . . He believed in character; he wanted to jump back a whole
> generation and trust in character again as the eternally valuable
> element. Everything wore out.[4]

Fitzgerald is the decade's most skilful judge and analyst,
and he is at his best here. At his worst, he is merely friv-
olous, and his work seems merely to glance obliquely off
the shining surface. His first novel (his "early success," as
he later described it), *This Side of Paradise* (1920), is
really about the "generation" that was three or four years
younger than he, whom he observed from the maturity of
his twenty-four years. It is a "classical" form of the *bil-
dungsroman,* but it is so many other things that only Fitzgerald's youthful and unanalytic enthusiasm could have
given it an élan that makes it readable today. But it is not
without its contemporaries: Stephen Vincent Benét's *The
Beginning of Wisdom* (1921), Ben Hecht's *Erik Dorn*
(1921), Floyd Dell's *The Moon-Calf* (1920) and *The Briary-
Bush* (1921), John Dos Passos' *Streets of Night* (1923),
and Carl Van Vechten's *Firecrackers* (1925) and *Parties*
(1930) are additional examples. Although there is much
variety within these books, much the same type of material
is drawn upon in each: exuberant, romantic youth, whose
early introduction to experience either was responsible for
slyly amusing scenes or was exploited as somehow "pro-
foundly moving."

[4] "Babylon Revisited," in *Taps at Reveille* (New York, 1935),
p. 387. The story was first written in 1931.

This is an exemplary kind of Jazz Age fiction, but it is only one kind. Other types need to be reviewed: the expatriate novel (Hemingway's *The Sun Also Rises*, 1926, is the "representative anecdote," [5] but there are others); the novel of war experiences (once again, a novel of Hemingway's is the best example: *A Farewell to Arms*, 1929); the nostalgic or retrospective novel, which is written on the assumption that the postwar period was vastly inferior to the past (Willa Cather's *The Professor's House*, 1925, is the best example, but such of her contemporaries as Edith Wharton and Ellen Glasgow also dramatized the view); finally the parodic novel, directed usually at the American middle class and supporting a bias most strongly presented in H. L. Mencken's magazine, the *American Mercury* (of course, Sinclair Lewis' *Babbitt* is the supreme example here). I shall discuss each of these in turn.

No one who has recently read Hemingway's *A Moveable Feast* (1964) can have failed to have at least a small sense of the "bliss" that it was to be alive in the 1920's, if not in Dubuque, at least in Paris. That book is a primary example of the practice of making literature out of the weaknesses of others (perhaps the nastiest and the most effective of all literary exploitations of the *roman à clef* misdemeanor). It shows Hemingway in the years before he was internationally known, living in Paris, on *la rive gauche*, getting along on very little, loving when there wasn't money enough for any other pleasures, sitting alone in a cafe through an afternoon and writing a story, "Up in Michigan." This was Hemingway, the ur-expatriate, to whom living in Europe was a thing you thought naturally good, because "Soldier's Home" (that is, the normality to

[5] For a discussion of this term, see my *The Twenties* (New York, 1955), pp. x–xii.

which the soldier found he had to return) just wasn't interesting after the war.

Like other major conditions of the postwar world, expatriation had its superficial, as it had its complex, moments. There were many American novels that described expatriation superficially, or exploited it for its nuisance value. As the grand gesture of renunciation, the act of leaving the United States for Paris had its dramatic values, and in the fiction of the time the gesture had a value equivalent to that attached to the act of leaving Split Lip, Kansas, for Greenwich Village. The eastward movement, as a gesture reversing Horace Greeley's directions, was toward New York and eventually toward Europe. The great American expatriates were T. S. Eliot, Gertrude Stein, and Ezra Pound; none of these wrote a novel to dramatize his experience, though all of them applied themselves to its varieties of emotional experience. Early poems of Pound (*Hugh Selwyn Mauberley,* for example) and Eliot are often effectively critical of both the United States and Europe. Glenway Wescott's stories, in *Goodbye, Wisconsin* (1928), also dramatize the need to move away from home to the East and to Europe. In any event, by the mid-1920's the offices of Paris' little magazines (Ford Madox Ford's *Transatlantic Review*, Pound's *Exile*, Jolas' *Transition*, and the recently arrived *Little Review* of Margaret Anderson and Jane Heap were among the best) were trying, in their art, to come to terms with Pierre, Des Moines, Eau Claire, or East Saint Louis.

Much of the best American fiction of the decade was written in Europe: the most American of them all, *The Great Gatsby* and Glenway Wescott's *The Grandmothers,* (1927), were written in southern France; Louis Bromfield spent many of his productive years in France; and of course, one of the greatest dowagers of them all, Edith Wharton, wrote steadily at her villa, Pavillon Colombe, not far from Paris. These facts do not necessarily suggest that they wrote expatriate fiction, though expatriation was certainly one of the general governing influences in what they did write.

The *real* expatriate fiction, which explores the meaning of cultural dislocation, of cultural difference, in the manner of Henry James's Lambert Strether (*The Ambassadors*, 1903) setting Woollett, Massachusetts, against Paris, was a comparatively rare thing. There are many spoofs of the American tourist, by Sinclair Lewis, Donald Ogden Stewart, and others. But *tourisme* is not expatriation; and the full emotional and psychological values belonging to a person who has chosen to live outside his country are explored only in so complex a book as *The Sun Also Rises*.

Here the full impact of postwar deprivation is seen. The characters are nervously aware of their expatriation, as well as of the reasons why they should be separated from their own countries. On a few occasions they try to enunciate forms of moral order, but none of these seems to be quite appropriate or suitable. Robert Cohn, who is most anxious to define himself in terms of a culture, is considered hopelessly romantic by Jake Barnes and a nuisance by others. There is something to be said for Cohn as a gadfly, a character whose unpleasant task it is to point out the weaknesses of others. But mostly, the worlds of Paris and Pamplona that the novel describes demand moral improvisation, "grace under pressure," and a day-to-day adjustment to circumstance.

There are many aches and pains in the novel, but the major ache comes from an absence suffered by everyone, even by Cohn: the absence of standards that can be trusted, securities that won't be momentarily upset, assurances that are worthy of more than a second's span of attention. Because of these failures, the major emphasis in *The Sun Also Rises* is upon a quiet-acceptance world, best repre-

sented by the fishing trip in the mountains at Burguete. But
there is still a more important *modus vivendi*, the bullfight,
which (even though it is largely a spectatorial sport, as the
Mass is a spectatorial art-form) imposes a discipline upon
an artificial set of circumstances that are nevertheless
dangerous and will end in death.

Hemingway is careful not to make a moral expedient of
the bullfight. It is true that nothing is accomplished or
decided in *The Sun Also Rises*; the characters do not emerge
from their experience reformed, or even much advanced
over their earlier conditions. The early view of a novel as
developmental gives way here to the idea of it as static, at
best describing a series of scenes in which groups of persons are involved and in which they behave as they can.
Hemingway's novel is not so much a series of actions as it
is a non-literary ballet. The fact of its curiously quiet and
static world makes *The Sun Also Rises* a quite admirable
dramatization of its title; for it is true that "One generation
passeth away, and another generation cometh: but the
earth abideth forever. . . ." [6] Principally, the novel seems
to advise patience and resignation to a situation that, while
not intolerable, is nevertheless vexing and abnormal.

Nowhere else has the full significance of expatriation
been explored. And, of course, by implication and by direct
reference, the fact of World War I stands as one of the
primary causes. The fiction of the Jazz Age is in many
ways a postwar fiction. Some of it, of course, is about the
war experience, an engagement of great importance and
the most significant of American military involvements
since the Civil War. Much has been said, and more will be
said, about the two principal war fictions. It is true that

[6] Quotation from Ecclesiastes 1:4, used as part of the epigraph
of *The Sun Also Rises*.

many of the novelists who wrote about World War II were conscious of the great master, Hemingway, and tried to emulate his successes. But the fact is that the experience of World War I was far more innocent than that of the second war. This is true because an ideology intervened between the two wars, and a great racial scandal engaged the full moral attention of the new writers. That is, in the 1930's writers were (or most of them were) taught the validity and the "saving qualities" of Marxism. It was a powerful incentive and a great comfort. As for the "racial scandal," few American writers lacked a sense of both dedication and horror in their description of the Nazi enemy; the antagonist was both more powerful and more loathsome than he was in World War I. The literature of World War II is scarcely innocent, though some of it (Harry Brown's novel *A Walk in the Sun*, 1946, for example) is neatly reductive and seems to be about nothing but the scene of the fighting.

In the views of Hemingway, Dos Passos (*One Man's Initiation*, 1920, and *Three Soldiers*, 1921), Laurence Stallings (*Plumes*, 1924), E. E. Cummings (*The Enormous Room*, 1922), and Thomas Boyd (*Through the Wheat*, 1923), the experience of World War I is represented by the innocent soldier's meeting head-on with violence, finding no appropriate terms in which to describe it, and reacting finally to it by means of a "separate peace," an actual or an implied desertion of its allies.

This sense of an enforced separation from the "side of the angels" (Edith Wharton's great bastion of Western civilization) is in a real way associated with the figure of exile; the war is, genuinely, a source of exile, since it forces its hero into a state of isolation from which he finds it difficult to recover. In all of the novels I have mentioned above, the essential result is a withdrawal into one or another kind of personal relationship from the large, confused dis-

CHANGE AND CONTINUITY: THE 1920's

organization that war forces upon a man. The love of Lieutenant Frederic Henry for Catherine Barkley is notoriously an example of this disengagement. Of course, Hemingway makes it clear that love is a false alternative to war, whether through Rinaldi's fear of venereal disease or because of the death of Catherine in childbirth. Henry does momentarily feel that "We could feel alone when we were together, alone against the others." [7] But this is only a temporary sense of security. In the end he tries to find himself once again in the figure of the dead Catherine, but

> it wasn't any good. It was like saying good-by to a statue. After a wihle I went out and left the hospital and walked back to the hotel in the rain (p. 355).

The gesture of resignation, which is also assumed in the behavior of Jake Barnes in *The Sun Also Rises*, marks the end of innocence, or sentimentality, or romantic self-reliance, call it what you will. It is a considerable advance over Huckleberry Finn's gesture of defiance (when he says, of the question of returning Jim to his owners, all right, then, I *will* go to hell) ; that is, it is an advance in the recognition of the futility of human decisions. The grand, heroic act of making *our own* moral decisions and abiding by them, which is a strong part of our cultural inheritance, is here (and in many war novels of the decade) set aside by a circumstance that is beyond the human will to contain. Therein lies the strength of *A Farewell to Arms*: its having suggested a limit to the grand Emersonian gesture; not that the earlier naturalists had not already sounded such a note, but that they had done it crudely for the most part, whereas Hemingway put the stamp of the master stylist upon it, the man of strong and controlled feeling.

[7] *A Farewell to Arms* (New York, 1929), p. 266.

If the 1920's are to be seen clearly, they must also be understood as a time that was heartily despised by some of those living in it. Henry James never got beyond the second year of the war, but he had been sensitively aware of the several cracks in the wall, which he described in *The Princess Casamassima* (1886). It was up to several of his most devoted imitators—Willa Cather and Ellen Glasgow, among them—who survived the war to go on and speak with amazed incredulity of the postwar world. "The world broke in two in 1922 or thereabouts." [8] Miss Cather said in 1936, when she was sixty years old; and she did little to try to repair the damage.

It is not because Miss Cather was a "traditionalist" that I select her work as an illustration of this aspect of the 1920's. There were better, or more confirmed, traditionalists than she: John Crowe Ransom, Allen Tate, and Humanists like Paul Elmer More and Irving Babbitt, who hated the principal lines of modernism and made a literature from alternative proposals. But, except for Tate's *The Fathers* (1938), no fiction was written by them.

The Professor's House is designed to describe the two worlds that emerged from the "break" in 1922 "or thereabouts." Typically, Professor St. Peter is a student of history, of the past; he prefers staying in the old house, where his study is in the attic, to going to the vulgar new one, paid for by the exploitation of an invention inherited from Tom Outland (the symbolism of the names is almost too obvious), one of his favorite students who had died in the war. Miss Cather had also written a war novel, *One of Ours* (1922), but she did not go the way of Edith Wharton, who, in *A Son at the Front* (1923) and elsewhere, came out quite frankly in favor of civilization and "proper art." Nevertheless, *The Professor's House* is an object lesson in the

---

[8] Prefatory Note in *Not Under Forty* (New York, 1936).

matching of past against present. It is here that the professor is rescued from what appears very close to a willed
death, though it is not a suicide, and that he does eventually come to the new house. But his final acts are simply
and undramatically empty gestures.

The Professor's House is a representative organization of
a number of attitudes and dispositions found in the writers
of the 1920's. The effort to comprehend what Mrs. Wharton
once called "this after-war welter" [9] became increasingly
difficult to those whose art had been fashioned before the
world broke in two. The world of the 1920's—the first real
decade of the twentieth century—required a new form; and
it was provided by Hemingway in fiction, and in poetry by
Pound, Eliot, and Hart Crane. Miss Cather's novel dramatized the nostalgia for the past, for the non-violence and
the comprehensibility of the pre–World War I past. She
also had the sense to admit that such nostalgia was not
altogether useful, though it might be understandable and
even, in some cases, pardonable.

No review of 1920's fiction is complete without attention
to Sinclair Lewis—not because he was a great novelist but
because his works belong to a great American tradition of
journalistic debunking. Lewis' fiction corresponds to the
world of H. L. Mencken's essays on the middle-middle class
and of his collections of absurdities in the monthly Americana section of the *Mercury*. The style of both of them is
a matter of rearranging fragments and shards of what is
actually historical truth into such a pattern that they add up
to absurdity. This is the art of parody, of literary caricature,

[9] In *A Backward Glance* (New York, 1934), p. 362, she says of
the postwar scene: "The war was over, and we thought we were
returning to the world we had so abruptly passed out of four years
earlier. Perhaps it was as well that, at first, we were sustained by
that illusion."

in which a small excess becomes a large excess through overemphasis.

The style of *Babbitt* (1922), *Elmer Gantry* (1927), and *The Man Who Knew Coolidge* (1928) features exaggeration. Almost anyone can recognize a portion of actuality in any given incident; as, indeed, anyone can recognize that Mencken's quotations in "Americana" are really quotations and not fakes. There is, in spite of evidence to the contrary, a tenderness in his treatment of Babbitt (though Elmer Gantry is handled viciously enough) that makes one always suspect sympathy rather than scorn. And this is what we have had for a comic tradition in the United States—journalistic parody, caricature, the "soft-hearted absurd," the clown who is a victim—of Babbitt, Robert Benchley, W. C. Fields, *et al.*, in typically absurd situations. It is a comedy of the small person: Babbitt, when he endures the outraged sneers of his contemporaries, is no larger than Charlie Chaplin in a typical clown-victim scene.

Of course, Lewis cannot maintain the pressure. Eventually, his novels give way to sentimentality; and the hero of *Dodsworth* (1929) becomes a "good man" in the Jimmy Stewart—or, perhaps better, the Cary Grant—tradition. Eventually, the typical American comedy became that of the violent snafu, of Joseph Heller's *Catch-22* (1961). But in the 1920's it was a comedy in which the artist was linked to his victim by bonds of sympathy; essentially, it is the patter and scene of the vaudeville situation, invested with as much self-mockery as its victim can sustain and still survive.

The fiction of the 1920's is sufficiently varied to resist any easy definitions. Surely the phrase "The Jazz Age" applies to only a small part of it; nothing could be further from the tone that phrase suggests than the work of Willa

Cather, Edith Wharton, Ellen Glasgow, and Ernest Hemingway. In many ways these novelists penetrated beneath the surface reality that any catch-phrase suggests; and— at least in the first three cases—their origins were in the past.

Nevertheless, it is time that a certain American fiction is justified as peculiarly the result of conditions set up by the postwar situation and encouraged by a social ease and an apparent prosperity. That this time should once more be the subject of a number of analyses testifies, not necessarily to the strength of the literature itself, but to the hardiness and energy of our continuing interest in it. The 1920's are the true sign of beginnings in our own century.

However naïve some of the attitudes and poses may now seem to us in subsequent phases and currents of experience to have been, they have become the models of twentieth-century behavior. This may be either a hateful or an admirable fact; I have no interest in deciding which. The truth is that the Victorian sentiment had gone as far as it could by 1914, and the events since then have demanded basic changes, which our literary artists have been the first to describe and define for us. It is indispensable to a culture that its arts formalize the moral and social positions that we ultimately hope to assume ourselves. The complexity and depth of Jazz Age fiction are valuable because, from them, we have reached the position, the attitudes toward modern reality, that it is now possible for us to take. That is, we are perhaps two decades behind the aesthetic "law-givers"; that rebellion often (surely not always) becomes our established world. This is to assume that they rebel intelligently against something that is not intelligent. Much of the nostalgia about the 1920's comes from the fact that some writers in the decade were both free and sensible, though they may not have seemed to be either in their time.

The Revolution in Morals

GILMAN M. OSTRANDER

ALTHOUGH the United States had emerged by the opening of the twentieth century as the industrial colossus of the world, American society was still predominantly a rural and small-town society. Two-thirds of the American people were still living on the farm or in communities of less than 2,500, deeply rooted in the American past and deeply suspicious of the social changes resulting from the industrial revolution and the rise of the city. Inevitably they were affected by the coming of the railroad and the rise of industry, and inevitably they grasped at the resulting opportunities to improve their economic conditions in revolutionary ways. Religion and the moral order, however, were based upon changeless principles and were not to be affected by changes in the economy.

Righteous villagers and farmers were convinced that theirs was the society that most closely conformed to the laws of God and that theirs was no less than the mission to save America from the challenges of the modern world. How this American majority wished to train future generations to carry out their moral mission is to be found in the McGuffey School Readers, one hundred million of

which were sold during the course of the second half of
the nineteenth century. In these readers, as Lewis Atherton
has pointed out, there was no notice given of the coming of
the railroad or of the rise of the city, although these books
were used in city schools as well as by farmers' children.
They concerned themselves with village life and farming and
with the religious and moral precepts to be derived from
that environment. A firm assumption upon which they
were written was that America was a Protestant common-
wealth, and that it was the foremost duty of American
schools to inculcate true religious principles in the minds
of their pupils:[1]

> A little child who loves to pray.
> And read his Bible too,
> Shall rise above the sky one day,
> And sing as angels do;
> Shall live in Heaven, that world above,
> Where all is joy, and peace, and love.

The pupil was taught that his admission to heaven required,
in addition to Bible-reading, abstention from alcohol and
tobacco as well as from those practices specifically proscribed by scriptures. The sages and patriots of America's
past had followed these precepts, he was told, and their
good conduct had made possible the establishment of the
great American republic; continuing good conduct was a
necessary condition for its perpetuation.

Social activity in small-town America of 1900 was church-
centered, probably to as great a degree as had been the
case a half-century earlier, and church members continued
to be zealous brothers' keepers. Churches earnestly pursued

[1] Lewis Atherton, *Main Street on the Middle Border* (Bloomington,
Ind., 1954), p. 69. This discussion of rural social and religious life is
based largely on Atherton, *Main Street*, Chapter III.

the task of disciplining erring members with punishments ranging from public rebuke to excommunication. It was the unquestioned conviction of every sincere member of an evangelical church that everything that happened in the universe occurred according to the purposes of God. This belief in the providential significance of everyday happenings was akin to the seventeenth-century Puritan belief in the religious significance of portents. God's ways were inscrutable, as when he took away little babies or virtuous persons who were engaged in useful work; the only human recourse in the face of these mysteries was faith and prayer. Church congregations prayed for rain as the Indians had before them and then accepted whatever followed as being in accordance with the specific intentions of a personal God.

To the extent that American society was farm-centered, it was also family-centered. The family was a self-contained economic unit in a way that was not possible in the city. Where children in the city might become economic liabilities, they remained economic assets on the farm, and relatively large families continued to be the rule. There was ample biblical authority to establish the father as the undisputed patriarch of the family, and his authority was no more to be questioned by his wife than it was to be questioned by his children while they remained in his house.

Courtship in rural and small-town America took place at church socials, picnics, and dances, often without being very much chaperoned, and generally—from the perhaps dubious evidence of many reminiscences—in an atmosphere of bucolic innocence. Girls were taught as early as possible that marriage was their destiny and that only nice girls were in a position to marry advantageously. The rule was not so rigid so far as boys were concerned, but they were taught to distinguish between the nice girls and the others and to conduct themselves accordingly.

They were, however, two sides to the track in small-town America. Saloons were beginning to be voted out of these communities by 1900, but not much had as yet been done along this line. They were still frequented during the day by respected men in the community and at night, especially Saturday night, by a rowdier element. Farm laborers, who did not stay long in any one community, got drunk regularly on Saturday night and brawled in the streets, along with disreputable native sons. Local sons who went to the dogs generally saw their advantage in leaving town for good, but if they remained, some sort of place would still be found for them in the disapproving community, for they were permanently entitled to some sort of status by right of birth.

For that matter, so long as a man did not make a public spectacle of himself, he could get away with a good deal of "fooling around" and still retain a decent place in society. The small towns had their own red-light districts, just as the big cities did. Muncie, Indiana, the city that was the basis for Robert and Helen Lynd's *Middletown,* supported in 1890, with a permanent population of about 6,000, between twenty and twenty-five houses of prostitution, each of which employed from four to eight girls.[2] There was always gossip about what went on between, say, the superintendent of schools and the new teacher, and much of this gossip was fairly readily verifiable. This sort of thing was expected and looked for. Men would always be what they always had been. Young women were taught that sex in marriage was a necessary evil and that prostitution was a necessary evil. The distinction between sexual intercourse within marriage and prostitution was therefore not absolute. Under these circumstances, the important thing for

[2] *Middletown* (New York, 1929), p. 113.

men who could not control themselves was that they observe the outward forms of respectability.[3]

Even disregarding these inevitable moral failures that occurred in every community, there did not exist the moral consensus in small-town America that the upright would have liked to have seen. For one thing, these communities had not altogether escaped the social impact of nineteenth-century immigration, even though the immigrants had concentrated themselves in the larger cities. These smaller communities had their Irish and Italians and Greeks and Poles and even Chinese, and they were likely to have their Germans in considerable numbers. Among these, the Germans were looked upon as the most respectable—good farmers and hard workers who had arrived in the community with a sufficient competence to acquire land or buy a store and establish themselves on a solid economic basis. The trouble with the Germans was that they persisted in customs alien to the community. They organized their *Turnvereins* and sang loudly and drank beer flagrantly. Other national groups indulged in other peculiar customs.[4]

There remained at least one further element disturbing to Main Street orthodoxy. Economic ruling groups developed —the prosperous lawyers, bankers, merchants, and large-scale farmers—who tended to remove themselves from the community in some ways and to live according to a somewhat different set of moral precepts. It was quite in character for the scion of a good family to leave the Methodist

[3] Oscar Handlin, *Race and Nationality in American Life* (Boston, 1957). Chapter VI discusses late nineteenth-century medical ideas relating to sex.

[4] John Higham, *Strangers in the Land* (New Brunswick, N.J., 1955). Merle Curti, in *The Making of an American Community* (Stanford, 1959), concludes that alien ethnic groups were fairly well absorbed into the community, on the basis of an extremely intensive study of Trempealeau County, Wisconsin.

or Baptist church for the Episcopalian, where the doctrine
of original sin was not rightly understood and where a
latitudianarian view was taken of moral conduct. These
people took trips to Chicago and to New York and perhaps
even to London and Paris, and they tended to conform to
the standards of the big city as against the traditional
values of America. Their conduct was somewhat disturbing
to Main Street orthodoxy in 1900, as was the *Gemütlichkeit*
and Catholicism of the otherwise proper, prosperous
German-American burghers, not to speak of what went on
across the railroad tracks. Still, these towns and surrounding farms were fundamentally wholesome, God-fearing
communities, and still able to view themselves as comprising the backbone of the nation and the best hope for
its salvation.

Many men and women in the cities also feared God and
lived upright lives, but for them it took much more money
to do it conveniently than was the case with their country
cousins. In 1900 there were three American cities with
populations in excess of one million—New York leading, of
course, with 3.4 million people—and 36 cities with 100,000
inhabitants or more. Virtually all of these possessed their
roaring red-light districts and their crowded ghettos. The
growth of even the smaller cities resulted in overcrowded
conditions in tenement areas and worked to depress wages
and living conditions generally. Religion was virtually out
of the reach of many in America's slums, whereas the bar-
room and the brothel were right next door. According to
Jacob Riis's count, there were, below New York's Fourteenth
Street, 4,065 saloons to 111 places of worship of all kinds.
Organized neighborhood gangs, in common with the saloons
did much to establish the social order in slum areas. "The
gang," Riis wrote, "is the ripe fruit of tenement house
growth. . . . Its gangs are made up of the American born
sons of English, Irish, and German parents. . . . The

assimilation of Europe's oppressed hordes, upon which our Fourth of July orators are fond of dwelling, is perfect. The product is our own." [5]

It was not so viewed by most middle- and upper-class Americans, however. The teachings of scientific philanthropists and social gospelers notwithstanding, the slum-dwellers were still looked upon as savages beyond the pale, the degraded classes against which upright America must defend itself. The conscience of progressive America was stirred by the condition of these unfortunates, but it did not really sympathize with them. The staunch progressive, determined to make America a better nation for his children to live in, was apt not to notice the plight of the Irish or Italian upstairs maid living on a wage of a few dollars a week.[6] It was this progressive representative of the comfortable classes who set the dominant moral tone in the cities in the early twentieth century. And when the younger generation kicked over the traces, it was the children of the respectable upper-middle classes, rather than those from the slum areas, who led the nation as a whole into the new age of moral freedom.

Wealth leads to temptation, just as poverty does; but wealthy Americans at the turn of the century did not suppose, in theory at least, that great wealth exempted one from the normal standards of moral conduct. Lavish display of wealth was the hallmark of society among the plutocrats. A hundred or more servants were maintained by the very rich to service lavish mansions, and the struggle was unremitting to keep up with the Vanderbilts. Those who could afford to do so built palatial "cottages" at Newport and gave parties the costs of which ran into six figures. But this social life, though vulgar, was intended to be

[5] Jacob Riis, *How the Other Half Lives* (American Century ed., New York, 1957), pp. 158, 164.

[6] Lucy Salmon, *Domestic Service* (New York and London, 1901).

thoroughly decorous. The chaperone was omnipresent at the upper-class social gatherings of young people. Wrote one New York gentleman, "Even when I was thirty years old, if I had asked a girl to dine with me alone, I would have been kicked down her front steps. If I had offered her a cocktail, I would have been tossed out of Society for my boorish effrontery." [7]

Behind this Victorian façade, however, a lot of things were going on, if one is to lend the least credence to the gossip column of the popular New York weekly magazine *Town Topics*. Week after week the "Saunterer" in *Town Topics* reveled in tales of high society adultery, incest, illegitimacy, abortion, transvestism, and nymphomania, giving broad clues as to the participants and sometimes coming right out and naming names. It may be doubted that Saunterer's charges were all accurate, but it may not be doubted that high society enjoyed them thoroughly. It would not do to be caught reading the magazine, but the Saunterer was avidly followed by the social set. According to the son of etiquette authority Emily Post, *Town Topics* "found its way into almost every cottage in Tuxedo Park, as it did into the cottages, villas, and mansions at Newport. It was read upstairs, downstairs, and backstairs." [8] American high society was characterized both by an impossibly strict moral code and by a blatant and pervasive prurience.

Protestant middle- and upper-middle-class New Yorkers, living decent, orderly lives in substantial brownstone houses, represented a rather small minority of the population; but, more than any other element in the city, they represented traditional Bible-guided, family-centered America. They had reason to disapprove on moral grounds of high life in Tuxedo Park, just as they had reason to disapprove of the

[7] Frederick Lewis Allen, *The Big Change* (New York, 1952), p. 11.
[8] Andy Logan, "That Was New York," *New Yorker*, Aug. 14, 1965, p. 55, in an article that deals extensively with *Town Topics*.

morals of Mulberry Bend. In the worlds of business and politics they had reason to fear for an America threatened by socialism from below and plutocracy from above. Therefore, in the opening years of the twentieth century, in common with middle-class Americans throughout the nation, they joined in the progressive movement to restore the nation to moral order as well as to true republican principles.

In somewhat uneasy alliance with progressivism in most parts of the nation were the prohibitionists, working through most of the Protestant churches of the nation under the direction of the Anti-Saloon League. In contrast to the progressives, the prohibitionists were rural-oriented and literalistic in religion. Prohibitionists were persuaded that the single greatest obstacle to the regeneration of society was the drink evil and that with prohibition the way would be prepared in one stroke for that regeneration. By the time of the triumph of Prohibition, however, the forces in support of it had already ceased to represent the national consensus, and probably its ratification was made possible only by the fact that rural native America enjoyed a disproportionate representation in the state legislatures that ratified it. A revolt had already broken out in America against this provincial moralism, and Prohibition served only to feed the fires of this revolt in the twenties.

Even while evangelism and moral reform reverberated throughout the nation in the opening years of the twentieth century, silent dissent from established religious belief was taking place widely, and native American intellectuals were beginning to attack openly and rudely the most cherished of American assumptions. "The present age is a critical one and interesting to live in," wrote the philosopher George Santayana during the high noon of progressivism and prohibitionism. "The civilization characteristic of Christendom has not yet disappeared, yet another civilization has begun to take its place." [9] America was indeed at an Armageddon of sorts, and in the battle that took place the forces of nativist, moralistic Protestant orthodoxy, at the moment of apparent victory, went down to crashing defeat.

As is true of all major revolutions, the American revolution against traditional morals was led by intellectuals. Darwin's *Origin of Species,* appearing in 1859, had touched off a debate immediately in America, despite the distractions of the sectional controversy and the Civil War. The war, itself, had served as a catastrophic repudiation of optimistic American asumptions, and, at the same time, it had served as a national demonstration of the working out of the law of survival of the fittest. Amid the great debate over Darwin, evolutionary biology appears early to have become widely and easily accepted in America, at least in the northern urban areas, many jokes and allusions being bandied about concerning ape men and missing links. It soon established itself in the curriculum of all but the most fundamentalist northern colleges, and by the opening of the twentieth century it was part of the intellectual equipment of most college-educated Americans. Belief in evolution logically necessitated abandonment of biblical literalism and abandonment also of belief in man as specially created by God. Some ministers and scientists attempted systematically to reconcile evolution with the existence of an immortal soul in man, without much success. Many people were not to be talked out of their immortal souls, even while accepting evolutionary biology, but the basis for faith had been weakened. [10]

Evolutionary theory was even more shattering to traditional beliefs in its destruction of the changeless

[9] Henry May, *The End of American Innocence* (New York, 1959), prefatory quotation.
[10] Stow Persons, "Evolution and Theology in America," in Stow Persons (ed.), *Evolutionary Thought in America* (New Haven, 1950).

Newtonian universe, operating according to immutable laws, including immutable moral laws. This new concept revolutionized thinking in philosophy and in the social sciences, but it was in literature that it most vividly demonstrated its destructive power so far as the traditional moral order was concerned. A school of literary naturalists emerged in America at the close of the nineteenth century. Crane, Norris, Dreiser, and London differed greatly in content and style, but they were united by a common assumption. The universe was a mindless movement of forces, providing no objective basis for a fixed moral law. Man struggled in this universe as did other animals, and the course of his life was determined for him by forces over which he had little control. Like other animals, he was the product of his instincts and his environment.

This deterministic and relativistic view of man and the Godless universe had come to be generally accepted by American intellectuals a generation before Walter Lippmann lamented in 1929, quoting Aristophanes, that "Whirl is King, having driven out Zeus." [11] In 1922 there appeared a collection of writings by American intellectuals, edited by Harold Stearns, on *Civilization in the United States*. This collection failed to include an article on religion among the thirty topics selected. The editor felt obliged to comment on the omission in his preface. "The bald truth is," he wrote, "it has been next to impossible to get any one to write on the subject; most of the people I approached shied off. . . . "

> Almost unanimously, when I did manage to procure an opinion from them, they said that real religious feeling in America had disappeared, that the church had become a purely social and political institution, that the country is in the grip of what

[11] Walter Lippmann, *A Preface to Morals* (New York, 1929), prefatory quotation.

> Anatole France has aptly called Protestant clericalism, and that,
> finally, they weren't interested in the topic.

He noted, however, that the subject had not been altogether
neglected, being discussed in the essay on "Philosophy"
and again in the one on "Nerves." [12]

The beginnings of what Henry May has called the end
of American innocence can be at least faintly discerned
during the closing years of the nineteenth century. Thomas
Beer named the 1890's the Mauve Decade, deriving his title
from Whistler's definition of mauve as "pink trying to be
purple." "The Americans of the '90's," Beer wrote, "achieved
a frame of mind that was apparent even to small boys;
when the ladies said 'actress,' they meant something else."

> . . . The decade became a little more liberal in conversation and
> in print. . . . "whore," came from its covert once or twice,
> rendered as "w----," which deceived nobody but gave everybody
> a sense of daring. Children were told that it stood for "where"
> and didn't believe it.[13]

American intellectuals were becoming increasingly self-
conscious about American provincialism in morals as in
other areas. The decadence of Swinburne and Oscar Wilde
appealed to some of them, and the amoral and anti-Christian
philosophy of Nietzsche gained an American following. De-
cadent little magazines made their fleeting appearances: the
Chapbook in Chicago, the *Lark* in San Francisco and *M'lle*
in New York.[14] Most successful among such magazines was
the *Smart Set,* which came under the editorship of H. L.
Mencken and George Jean Nathan in 1914. By that time

[12] Harold Stearns (ed.), *Civilization in the United States* (New
York, 1922), pp. v–vi.
[13] Thomas Beer, *The Mauve Decade* (New York, 1926), pp. 125–26.
[14] May, *End of Innocence*, pp. 198–99.

American intellectual amoralists had established their capital in Greenwich Village and had found their prophet in Sigmund Freud.

Freud's American influence dates from his visit to the United States in 1909 to deliver a series of lectures at Clark University. He later commented in surprise on how warmly he had been received in "prudish America." American intellectuals flocked to Freudianism before his writings had been translated into English and therefore before most of them could have gained any real understanding of his ideas. For them Darwin had already served to demolish the world of orthodox American Protestantism. For many of them Freud introduced a system that provided the basis for an entirely new morality, or perhaps a sanctioned immorality. Outside Greenwich Village, Freud was taken seriously also, and sex ceased to be taboo as a subject for discussion in educated mixed groups.

By the 1920's Freudian terminology had entered the American vocabulary: id, ego, superego, repression, complex, psychoanalysis, Freudian slip. Sexual restraint, which had been accepted as basic to social stability, was now blamed for virtually all the ills that society suffered. Freudian psychology was a much more titillating subject than Darwinian evolution, and borrowings from it were soon evident in motion pictures and popular literature, as well as in the works of the critically acclaimed writers. It soon was influencing millions of Americans who had hardly heard of Sigmund Freud. In the academic world opposition to Freud was mounting, but this affected his popular influence little.[15]

By the outset of the twenties the revolution in morals was already virtually complete so far as many American

[15] Oscar Cargill, *Intellectual America* (New York, 1959), Section VI, is the most thorough discussion of the impact of Freud on American ideas.

intellectuals were concerned. Stearns's *Civilization in the
United States* shed remarkably little light on the thirty subjects discussed by its authors. Its significance lay in what it
revealed about the authors themselves. Their articles were
almost uniformly cynical, shallow, and negative, almost
blindly opposed to American society and all its moral shibboleths. Intellectuals had done little toward drawing plans
for a new moral order, but destructively they had already
completed their part of the task.

Though it was the "lost generation" of intellectuals who
made articulate the repudiation of the old moral order, it
was their despised Philistine America that gave body to
the new concepts in the age of the flapper. The younger
generation had already started on its way to freedom
before the war, although it was by no means as far along
in revolt as were the intellectuals. The most evident symptom was the much-discussed "dance craze," for ragtime
was in vogue in the northern cities even before the wartime
closing of the New Orleans brothels sent jazz musicians
on their way to Chicago and New York. In 1911 Irving
Berlin had written "Alexander's Ragtime Band," the waltz
had suddenly faded in popularity, and the dance craze was
on. There were the Fox Trot, the Horse Trot, the Grizzly
Bear, and many others. One girl, according to a popular
song of 1912, declared that "mother said I shouldn't dare/
To try and do the grizzly bear," but girls nevertheless did
try to do it. Of these new dances, the Bunny Hug was
singled out by critics for special censure.[16]

Young women were already divesting themselves of some
of the clothing their parents had worn. Skirts rose from
the ground to the ankle, and some undergarments were
shucked off altogether. The president of the New York

[16] Mark Sullivan, *Our Times* (6 vols.; New York, 1926–35), IV,
242–56.

Cotton Exchange announced in 1912 that these changes in dress had "reduced consumption of cotton fabrics by at least twelve yards of finished goods for each adult female inhabitant." [17] By 1915 the evolution of the new American woman had advanced sufficiently for H. L. Mencken to herald her arrival and bestow upon her the name of flapper.

> Observe, then, this nameless one, this American Flapper. Her skirts have just reached her very trim and pretty ankles; her hair, newly coiled upon her skull, has just exposed the ravishing whiteness of her neck. . . .
>
> Life, indeed, is almost empty of surprises, mysteries, horrors to this Flapper of 1915. . . . She knows exactly what the Wassermann reaction is, and has made up her mind that she will never marry a man who can't show an unmistakable negative . . . is inclined to think that there must be something in this new doctrine of free motherhood. She is opposed to the double standard of morality, and favors a law prohibiting it. . . .[18]

Then the war came for America, with its excitement, confusion, social disorientation, and call for service. Several million American men and a good many women went overseas to England and France. Mademoiselle from Armentièrs may not have made a lasting impression on most of them, but the whole violent disruption of their lives had an enduring effect. On the home front, bands played, lovers said good-bye, women went into war work, and everybody knew that everything was different and that life must be led according to new rules. Then, just as all was started, it all stopped. Armistice was declared, the boys came home, and a great deal of adrenalin, which was to have been used up on the enemy, was expended during the next few years domestically.

[17] *Ibid.*, IV, 273.
[18] May, *End of Innocence*, p. 339.

There followed a postwar period of disillusionment that remained a matter for puzzled comment by foreign observers, especially as it was reflected in American literature of the 1920's. Compared to Europe, America had been lightly touched by the war; yet the cynicism arising out of the war and its conclusion seemed to be more deeply felt in America than in the European nations that the war had ravaged. Americans loudly and rudely repudiated the moralistic idealism of the Wilsonian war aims along with the moralistic idealism of Wilsonian progressivism. The fighting war had directly touched relatively few Americans, but the mood that received its classic expression in Hemingway's *A Farewell to Arms* and *The Sun Also Rises* was widely shared. After the war the flapper almost at once made herself the flaming symbol of this cynical spirit.

Within the space of a half-dozen years, women's skirts rose from the ankle to the knee. The number of inches between the hemline and the ankle was rightly taken as the index of the revolutionary change in morals and manners that accompanied and followed the war, and responsible elements in the nation moved to check the revolution by putting women back into their old clothes. Fashion writers warned that the American woman had "lifted her skirts beyond any modest limitation," and they decreed that she should drop them the next year. The YWCA issued a national "Modesty Appeal" and reported that it was getting good results. Bills were introduced in the Utah legislature fixing skirts at three inches above the ankle and in the Virginia legislature fixing necklines to within three inches of the upper part of the throat, but the girls went right ahead with what they were wearing.[19]

[19] Frederick Lewis Allen, *Only Yesterday* (New York, 1931), Chapter V, remains the best account of the American flapper and is the main basis for this discussion.

Some of them took to smoking publicly and conspicuously, and proprietors of public places, who would have ejected them five years earlier, retreated. Then they were overrunning the speak-easies. The pre-Prohibition saloons had been male sanctuaries where primarily beer had been dispensed. In the speak-easies mixed drinking of mixed drinks was the rule, the women bellying up to the bar with the men, skirts short, stockings rolled below the knees, and corsets sometimes checked at the cloak room. Many young women who did not frequent the speak-easies nevertheless felt obliged to school themselves in social drinking in their own homes and in those of their friends. Drinking, formerly proscribed for middle- and upper-middle-class women, became, under the pressure of Prohibition, socially mandatory in many of those circles.

The girls were petting also, and the "petting question" was anxiously discussed on and on in the ladies' magazines and elsewhere. The rule earlier had been that a nice girl did not allow a man to kiss her unless they were engaged to be married. By the early 1920's the polling of coeds showed that fairly indiscriminate petting was the rule. When it came to the question of extramarital sexual intercourse, fewer of these coeds were inclined to give their unqualified approval, but that question also was much mooted and in a spirit of open-mindedness that was frightening to fathers and mothers.

In sex as in other matters the girls were determined to demolish the double standard. They did not approve of a society in which men were free to wander back and forth across the tracks while women had to choose their side and stay there. In this wish they had been abetted by progressive reformers and later, during the war, by the Navy and War departments, which had fought against the red-light districts. The wartime antivice campaign had been highly successful, and thereafter the era of the roaring red-light district was substantially at an end except in some larger cities and some industrial and mining towns.[20]

The war opened up unprecendented career opportunities to American women, and these opportunities were eagerly taken advantage of. In 1900 about one out of five American women was gainfully employed, but most of these were miserably victimized in sweatshops. Among the better people at that time it had been a matter for sorrow and concern that a girl one knew was reduced in circumstances to the point where she was obliged to take employment as a schoolmistress. The war turned the working girl into a patriot and opened up many opportunities to her, the single most important field being secretarial work. At the war's end women fought with some success to retain these positions and to enter new lines of activity formerly closed to them.

The American housewife was freed for outside activities as never before. The tendency in the twenties was to move to smaller houses or to apartments, and at the time when immigration restriction laws reduced the supply of servants, the much more manageable electrical household appliances took their place. Throughout American history the number-one killer of women had been childbearing. Advocates of birth control, led by Margaret Sanger, had long fought their cause against bitter official and unofficial opposition. Opposition continued throughout the 1920's, but the average size of families declined rapidly during the same period.

That the emancipated women in the 1920's did not know quite where to go with their new freedom was indicated

[20] Prostitution in America's major cities is surveyed in great detail in a series of books by Herbert Asbury: *The Gangs of New York* (New York and London, 1928), *The Barbary Coast* (New York, 1933), *The French Quarter* (New York and London, 1936), and *Gem of the Prairie* (New York and London, 1940).

in the styles, which combined short skirts and make-up with bobbed hair and boyish figures. Nevertheless, the flapper was the symbol of the Jazz Age. So far as men were concerned, alterations in morals and manners were in large measure forced upon them by the new relationship they found themselves in with respect to the new American woman.

The flapper as a type was on the way out even before the coming of the depression, giving way to the siren. Mothers had followed the fashions set by their daughters early in the decade. Then in the late 1920's both mother and daughter let their hair grow a little longer and dropped the hemline of their skirts five or six inches below the knee. They did not do this under social pressure, however; by the end of the decade the issues aroused by petting and short skirts had ceased to burn brightly, which is to say that the women had won that battle.

By 1930 the United States had become statistically an urban nation. More than half of its population was living in communities of 2,500 or more, and the automobile had made the city readily accessible to the farming regions. In almost all of the major cities first- and second-generation immigrants still made up a majority of the population. In most cities native American Protestants continued to control business and to set the social tone, but this differed from city to city. On the one hand, Boston retained, rather desperately, a properly Bostonian air amid the welter of newer immigrants. On the other hand, San Francisco's ruling class had been made up largely of non-Anglo-Saxons since the days of the gold rush, and the personality of the city was as cosmopolitan as that of Boston was provincial. Like San Francisco, St. Louis and New Orleans had been non-Anglo-Saxon in origin and had retained something of their old Gallic flavor, and Cincinnati and Milwaukee continued to be influenced by their sizeable German populations. Los Angeles, by extreme contrast, was the most Protestant of any sizeable American city, and it was very mindful of its heritage of American Puritanism. A booster for the city had written that "it is a city of churches and schools and civic bodies, deeply interested in the best. The type is that of the highest moral and ethical citizenship." [21] Willard Huntington Wright, one-time editor of the *Smart Set*, agreed. The city had been formed, he wrote, by the "rural pietist obsessed with the spirit of village fellowship, of suburban respectability. . . . Hypocrisy, like a vast fungus, has spread over the city's surface. . . . Los Angeles is overrun with militant moralists, connoisseurs of sin, experts on biological purity." [22]

In most cities where the non-Protestants outnumbered the Protestants, the newer immigrants had been effectively segregated into ghettos and kept down by bad wages, and their social influence had thereby been minimized. In the 1920's, however, Congress passed two enactments that, in their consequences, did much to reconcile many among the older Protestant population to the more recent immigrants: the Volstead Act, passed to enforce prohibition, and the National Origins Act, passed to limit severely further immigration from southern and eastern Europe.

The National Origins Act of 1924 was illiberal and racist in intent, but in its consequences it proved enormously beneficial to the recent immigrant groups against whose former countrymen it was directed. These recent immigrants had formerly been despised and feared by older generations of Americans as the vanguard of an endless

[21] Dana W. Bartlett, *The Better City* (Los Angeles, 1907).
[22] Carey McWilliams, *Southern California Country* (New York, 1946), pp. 157–58.

army of foreign rabble that threatened to subvert American society. Following immigration restriction, however, these recent immigrants became part of an exclusive American community. They came to see themselves in this light, and they came increasingly to be so viewed by the older Americans. When that happened, there developed a greater appreciation for their contributions to American culture, and American culture became more cosmopolitan than it had formerly been.

More than anything else it was Prohibition that brought many older Americans to the conclusion that these newer arrivals were not such bad fellows after all. Drinkers and drys alike had supposed that Prohibition, once written into the Constitution, would be generally obeyed by a law-abiding nation, but such proved to be not remotely the case. Only during the first year of the experiment was Prohibition even moderately successful. Then it absolutely collapsed. Systems were perfected for smuggling, moonshining, and bootlegging; and soon almost anybody who wanted his tipple could obtain it easily, even out in the countryside.[23] The bootleggers and the proprietors of speak-easies were drawn mainly from the newer immigrant population, and these became minor heroes to the people they served. The blustering and ineffectual Anti-Saloon League became an object of fun for many Americans, including many who had soberly advocated Prohibition in the first place. There emerged a distinctly anticlerical sentiment among urban middle-class Americans, such as had already been voiced by American intellectuals. Thus protected by immigration restriction and harassed by Prohibition, middle-class, urban Protestant Americans began to blur the distinctions that formerly had set them apart in their own minds from the newer arrivals. (Some among the newer arrivals who

[23] Charles Merz, *The Dry Decade* (Garden City, N.Y., 1931).

involved themselves in the bootlegging industry, meanwhile, took advantage of Prohibition to organize nation-wide crime syndicates that have remained a part of the American moral structure ever since.)

Probably most Americans in the twenties were convinced that the chief contribution of the United States to civilization lay in the fields of business enterprise and technology, and they were not by any means alone in this opinion. Teams of experts came from the corners of the earth to see how this miracle had been achieved. The Germans coined a word for it, *Fordismus*. In Russia, it was said, Henry Ford was honored above all other foreigners. From the coming of the Puritans through the rise of democracy, America has always had a message for the world. Of all America's messages, this materialistic one was the message that has been most eagerly received.[24]

American intellectuals confused creative achievement in the realm of material things with materialism of the spirit. They lumped them together and damned them without qualification and without a second thought. Other Americans took an exalted and idealistic view of their nation's achievement. What it had accomplished had been no less than the democratization of the way of life that in other nations was restricted to the privileged few. It had created an affluent society and a democratic leisure class.

In the 1920's millions of Americans became part of the carriage trade. The carriage had always been a hallmark of gentility (for the American businessman had not invented materialism), and in the early years of the century this had been true of the automobile, which had been custom-made and very expensive. It had been the view of Woodrow Wilson that nothing had done more to advance socialism in America than the automobile. Henry Ford had had a

---

[24] See George Soule, *Prosperity Decade* (New York, 1947), for a discussion of economic conditions in the twenties.

different idea, however, and in the 1920's millions of Americans owned their own mass-produced Model T's, which at one point could be purchased for less than $300. One of the most startling sights in America, in the view of foreign observers, was the factory parking lot filled with workmen's cars.

The American majority was also given the leisure time to enjoy its new opportunities. In the nineteenth century the working day had commonly been from dawn to dusk, six days a week, the seventh day presumably being reserved for rest and prayer. The ten-hour day had been the best that the worker could hope for. In 1890 the average work week was estimated at 60 hours. In 1926 it was estimated at 49.8, and Americans at last had time on their hands. Real wages had risen substantially in the meantime, so Americans had more money in their pockets than ever before.

What would this do to their morals? Employers had long followed the pious practice of keeping wages down for the reason that the added money would simply go down the rum hole. Employers had also always defended long working hours as the only means of keeping the lower classes out of trouble. The 1920's was, among other things, the first experiment in the history of modern civilization, except during periods of depression, in mass leisure.

Perhaps surprisingly, the increased time and money, instead of debauching the working classes, proved an elevating influence, at least by the rum-hole standard. Where the old saloon had been known as the poor man's club, the speakeasy's clientele was drawn to a greater extent from the middle and upper-middle classes; and intoxication, so far as it manifested itself in public, was afflicting "a better class than formerly and a much younger class," according to the chief supervisor of dance halls in San Francsico.[25]

[25] Martha Bruère, *Does Prohibition Work?* (New York and London, 1927), p. 55.

What appears to have been the case is that blue-collar workers, untrained in the art of leisure, spent most of their free time working around the house and yard and listening to the radio with their families. Beyond that, sports provided them with their chief recreation. Fishing and hunting were the two sports in which they themselves participated to any great extent. Otherwise they remained spectators of baseball, football, boxing, and horse racing. They memorized baseball statistics and followed the exploits of Red Grange and Babe Ruth. This gave them plenty to talk about when they got together in their idle hours, as is still the case.

Public-spirited persons of cultured taste hoped that the people would take advantage of their increased leisure by doing more reading, and they did. Newspaper circulation increased greatly, and in 1919 Bernard McFadden launched *True Story Magazine,* which achieved a circulation of almost two million by 1926.[26] Asserting that "its foundation is the solid rock of truth," it featured such articles as "The Primitive Lover," "Her Life Secret," "How to Keep the Thrill in Marriage," and "What I Told My Daughter the Night before Her Marriage." Women have always made up the main reading public in the United States, and the two most popular themes for them have always been those of religion and seduction. The social developments of the twenties did not greatly alter this. To the extent that change is to be seen in that era, the change was in the direction of a greater interest in literary works.

The "lost generation" of writers enjoyed thinking of themselves as alien to the Philistine American majority. Sinclair Lewis, upon receiving the Nobel Prize for Literature in 1930, delivered an acceptance speech entitled "The American Fear of Literature," in which he criticized his

[26] Allen, *Only Yesterday,* p. 71.

fellow Americans for failing to support their creative artists. This was the same Lewis whose *Main Street* had sold more than 400,000 copies in 1920 to rival *The Sheik* as the best-selling book of the year and whose subsequent novels had all sold just about as briskly in his native land. Lewis had enjoyed greater success than most other serious-minded writers. It is, neverthless, true that America in the 1920's supported its best writers as it had never done previously.

Happily, the new technology created new forms of popular entertainment at the same time that it created the new leisure class. Chief among these were the radio, the phonograph, motion pictures, and the automobile. In 1890 theatergoers in Muncie were limited to the Opera House, where performances were irregular. The theater would be dark for as much as a month at a time. In 1924 Muncie supported nine motion-picture houses, operating daily the year around. The western was the staple at five of the theaters, but movies with sex appeal drew the largest crowds. Patrons were attracted in large numbers to *"Alimony*—Brilliant men, beautiful jazz babies, champagne baths, midnight revels, petting parties in the purple dawn, all ending in one terrific smashing climax that makes you gasp." Others such as *Sinners in Silk, Women Who Give,* and *Rouged Lips* similarly tried for gasps. Opinions varied widely as to the influence these movies exerted on their audiences, composed mainly of children and women; but to the extent that they were influential, the direction is evident.[27]

The impact of the automobile upon morals in America was undoubtedly greater than that of the movies and is easier to determine. By the end of 1923 there were two cars for every three families in Muncie, a good many of the car-owners being without bathtubs in their homes. The automobile had replaced the house as the chief status symbol in

[27] Lynd and Lynd, *Middletown,* p. 266.

the community, and car-owners declared themselves willing to go without food or decent clothing rather than give up their automobiles.[28]

One of the revolutionary results of the automobile was the institution of instalment buying, which established itself in the twenties. The traditional American virtue of thrift was undermined systematically and with great success by the advertising companies, and a finance-company officer in Muncie estimated that between 75 and 90 per cent of automobiles purchased locally were bought on the instalment plan. Living beyond one's means, a sin to previous generations, became the thing to do.

There were those who argued that the automobile served to keep the family together by providing a diversion the whole family could share together. The opposite opinion, however, was the one more frequently expressed. Methods of courtship changed. In the days before the automobile, courtship might very likely consist of a boy and a girl attending a church social and then walking back to the girl's house to sit on the sofa and talk to her parents. What the automobile did, as Frederick Lewis Allen pointed out, was to take that sofa out of the parlor and put it on wheels and move it off into the woods. A judge in Muncie declared that of thirty girls brought before his court during a year for "sex crimes," nineteen had committed their acts in automobiles. And whether it was used for sex purposes or for more conventionally acceptable diversions, the car, and who was going to get to use it, became a major source of family conflict.

Cicero in the first century B.C. was worried that the younger generation was going to the dogs, and spokesmen for the older generation have frequently been of this opinion since then. A lot was said to that point by members of the

[28] *Ibid.*, pp. 235–59, for social impact of the automobile.

older generation in the twenties, and during that decade there was much in what they said. It is no doubt true that every generation rebels to some extent against its elders, and it is also of course true that many young people in the twenties did not. The decade of the 1920's, nevertheless, remains the watershed in the history of American morals. It was the grandmothers of the present generation who hiked up their skirts, bobbed their hair, put on lipstick, and went out in the car with the boys to the speak-easy to drink bootleg liquor and do the Black Bottom. The twenties was the decade when there occurred, to some extent in the country as well as the city, the urbanization of American morals.

The New Psychology:
From Narcissism to Social Control [1]

JOHN CHYNOWETH BURNHAM

IN 1931 Frederick Lewis Allen in his delightful book *Only Yesterday* synthesized a now familiar picture of the decade of the 1920's. [2] He characterized as a unit the period that began with the end of the Great War and closed with the spectacular signals of the onset of the Great Depression. Although Allen focused on changes in American life during the 1920's, his portrait of those years has left the indelible impression that they constituted a unit in terms of both public mood and the style of living to which readers of middle class and mass media appeared to aspire.

As historical analysis of the 1920's has proceeded, Allen's image of the decade as a unit has become increasingly untenable. In spite of the impact of the war and the depression, the decade now appears to have encompassed a period of critical change in American life. Instead of constituting a unit, it was a watershed. On one side were the progressive years and the rebellion of the intellectuals that began about

[1] Many thanks are due to colleagues in addition to the editors who generously offered suggestions for improving this essay: Paul C. Bowers, Hamilton Cravens, Roy Lubove, Gerald D. Nash, John C. Rule, and Jack Tager.

[2] Frederick Lewis Allen, *Only Yesterday: An Informal History of the Nineteen-Twenties* (New York, 1931).

1912.[3] On the other side came a period when spokesmen for their generation frankly embraced a mass, bureaucratic society and perhaps even the elements of the welfare state. Images from Allen's narrative will continue to permeate discussions of the Jazz Age, but the new periodization gives a more accurate idea of the direction in which American history was moving in the first decades of the twentieth century.

During the 1920's one of the most crucial changes occurred in precisely the area that Allen depicted most effectively: public mood and style of life. The phenomenon of the decade that gave the best intellectual representation of the change was the "new psychology." The new psychology was a popularization of conceptions of the human animal and his motives. Although its elements had been present since about 1912 or even earlier, only in the 1920's did the new psychology become one of the characteristic fads of the age and at the same time both symptom and cause of critical social change.[4]

In the early 1920's the new psychology was of great interest because of its relationship to the cult of the self in which Jazz Age Americans were caught up. In a remarkable reversal from an earlier day, social norms produced not only self-centered attitudes but self-indulgent behavior. To this narcissistic preoccupation the new psychology contributed both the idea of the hidden self, with its many

[3] Henry F. May, *The End of American Innocence: A Study of the First Years of Our Own Time, 1912–1917* (New York, 1959); Henry F. May, "The Rebellion of the Intellectuals, 1912–1917," *American Quarterly*, VIII (1956), 114–26; Arthur S. Link, "What Happened to the Progressive Movement in the 1920's?", *American Historical Review*, LXIV (1959), 833–51.

[4] Hornell Hart, "Changing Social Attitudes and Interests," in President's Research Committee on Social Trends, *Recent Social Trends in the United States* (New York, 1933), I, 395. See also, for example, *Psychological Review* and *Journal of Nervous and Mental Disease* in the 1910's.

ramifications, and a rationalization for the self-indulgent behavior.

In the later years of the decade expositors of the new psychology became involved in an interest in social control that was taking a turn different from an earlier interest in the same subject. Because the new psychology provided information about the instincts, drives, and wants of men, it suggested new ways in which they might be controlled. "The belief that we are at last on the track of psychological laws for controlling the minds of our fellow men," wrote Abram Lipsky in 1925, "has brought about a revolution in the popular attitude towards the science that teaches how to do it. . . . Out of this change has sprung the universal interest in psychoanalysis, psychotherapy, hypnotism, character-analysis, mob-psychology, salesmanship,—all connoting a technique with which one may control the minds of others." [5]

THE PHENOMENON

The book that gave its name to the movement, *The New Psychology and Its Relation to Life*, was written by an Englishman, A. G. Tansley.[6] An earlier generation of Americans had known another "new psychology"; indeed, E. W. Scripture of Yale had written a book in 1897 bearing that title.[7] The new psychology of Scripture and his contemporaries was an experimental physiological psychology. It consisted primarily of exploring the functioning of sensory processes in normal adult humans. The new psychology of the 1920's represented a revolt against this "dry, academic" psychology, and Tansley, for example, meant explicitly by the term "new psychology," psychoanalysis.

[5] Abram Lipsky, *Man the Puppet: The Art of Controlling Minds* (New York, 1925), p. 11.

[6] London, 1920.

[7] *The New Psychology* (London, 1897).

Psychoanalysis represented the first of three phases through which the new psychology went. After psychoanalysis came an emphasis on endocrine glands, and after the glands, behaviorism. Regardless of its changing face, however, there was a distinctive continuity in the new psychology. Tansley, for example, recognized that he was not speaking of psychoanalysis in any narrow sense; he wanted basically to present a " 'biological' view of the mind." [8]

Although behaviorism and the glands had, like Freudianism, come into American technical and *avant-garde* literature about 1912, psychoanalysis clearly dominated the first phase of the new psychology.[9] In an incredible number of publications the literate public had endless opportunities to learn about Freud's psychological theory: the unconscious, the psychic censor, repression, the instincts (especially the sex instinct), and the psychological mechanisms and symbols by means of which drives can gain indirect expression in thought and behavior. Likewise, abnormalities, psychoses and neuroses, significant slips of the tongue and pen, the curative powers of self-awareness, and various facets of psychoanalytic therapy gained publicity. Although the output of more or less popular books and articles on psychoanalysis was beginning to decline perceptibly by the middle 1920's, its influence persisted. Attacks, if not so many expositions, continued to appear. The impact of psychoanalytic ideas on literature, another index of influence, seemed to be cumulative during the decade.[10] The later decrease in expositions of Freud's teachings, in short, reflected their assim-

[8] Tansley, *New Psychology*, p. 5.

[9] See, for example, L. L. Thurstone, "Contributions of Freudism to Psychology," *Psychological Review*, XXXI (1924), 175. Monroe A. Meyer, in *Mental Hygiene*, IX (1925), 649–50, said that a bookseller told him that there were then in print about a hundred "psychoanalytic works of the more or less introductory type, designed for popular consumption."

[10] See, for example, Frederick J. Hoffman, *The Twenties: American Writing in the Postwar Decade* (New York, 1955), and W. David

ilation into popular thinking. Writers of the new psychology representing both glandular and behavioristic points of view, as a matter of fact, usually incorporated, and thereby perpetuated, psychoanalysis in the new psychology.[11]

Competent, professional psychoanalysis was not involved in the new psychology. There were a few full-time analysts left from before the war, such as A. A. Brill in New York, and in the 1920's a small but growing number of young physicians took up analysis. Many of them went abroad for special training.[12] Between them and the denizens of Greenwich Village and intellectual salons there was considerable intercourse, both professional and social, but neither the Bohemians nor the analysts were usually involved in the flurry of publications about the new psychology. The fact is that the specialists, when confronted with popular writers' distortions and dilutions of Freud's ideas, usually reacted with either silence or agonized protest.[13]

Relatively early in the 1920's, a few very active publicists established glandular theories of personality as a part of the new psychology.[14] The shift was quite noticeable, and one observer commented at the time on the sudden change:

Sievers, *Freud on Broadway: A History of Psychoanalysis and the American Drama* (New York, 1955). "Psychoanalytic" (and likewise "Freudianism") is, as noted below, used here in the loosest sense, as it was in the new psychology. In literature, for example, Jung's thinking probably had more influence than strictly Freudian psychoanalysis.

[11] See, for example, John B. Watson, *Behaviorism* (New York, 1925), pp. 239–40.

[12] The history of the competent, specialized practice of psychoanalysis in the United States is a subject in itself and is not taken up in the present paper; see C. P. Oberndorf, *A History of Psychoanalysis in America* (New York, 1953).

[13] No attempt is being made in the present essay to explore the image of the new psychology in contrast to technical psychoanalysis as it existed and was distorted in the 1920's, nor to explore the reasons for the distortions.

[14] For example, Louis Berman, *The Glands Regulating Personality: A Study of the Glands of Internal Secretion in Relation to the Types of Human Nature* (New York, 1921).

"How swiftly the spotlight of popular interest shifts from one part of the stage to another! The eyes of distressed humanity turn eagerly toward any quarter that appears to promise health and happiness. . . . Those who recently were reading Freud and Jung have now taken up with Berman and Harrow. Those who formerly were rushing to have complexes extracted are now anxious to have glands implanted." [15]

Following the example of a young New York internist, Louis Berman, these gland enthusiasts exploited not only the established knowledge that gland dysfunction can cause certain diseases and severe personality changes but the recent work of physiologists who had shown the connection between emotion and glandular secretions. The connection between libido and the glands was of course well known; but gland psychology suggested that one's entire personality depended upon the balance of body chemicals. Specific secretions, according to the theory, can produce indolence and agitation, depression and megalomania. The public at large knew little of the general theory but fed eagerly on sensational stories about treatment with gland extract and gland transplantation. Even well-informed intellectuals took the exaggerated claims of the endocrine enthusiasts surprisingly seriously.[16]

Relatively late in the decade, the new psychology came more and more to emphasize behaviorism. Behaviorism was a mechanistic stimulus-response psychology. Behavioral investigators, using human and animal subjects alike, avoided traditional psychological concepts such as consciousness, cognition, and will. Instead, they carried out severely scientific experiments on how organisms in a

[15] Edwin E. Slosson, "From Complexes to Glands," *Scientific Monthly*, XV (1922), 189.

[16] See, for example, Lewellys F. Barker (ed.), *Endocrinology and Metabolism, Presented in Their Scientific and Practical Clinical Aspects* (New York, 1922), and the mental hygiene and education publications of the middle 1920's.

carefully controlled environment react to specific stimuli. For some years behaviorism had included as a fundamental unit of explanation the Pavlovian conditioned reflex. Behaviorism had been a serious reform movement within professional psychology since 1913. In the 1920's, especially after 1925, its founder and chief exponent, John B. Watson, who was himself a distinguished experimentalist, had taken to publicizing behaviorism flamboyantly. Behaviorism, like psychoanalysis, had a number of implications, many of them iconoclastic, and generated an intense opposition.[17]

The new psychology in all of its phases was a distinctly popular phenomenon and was therefore subject to both extreme oversimplification and sensationalism. The competence of its expositors varied, but in popularization even the most capable seldom maintained high levels of scientific precision. Many were flatly incompetent to present more than a grossly distorted version of the ideas about which, allegedly, they were writing. Psychoanalysis, particularly, suffered from emasculation and misrepresentation. With all of their intellectual imprecision, however, the general ideas in the new psychology are discernible and can be discussed on that level.

[17] See David Bakan, "Behaviorism and American Urbanization," *Journal of the History of the Behaviorial Sciences*, II (1966), 5–28. See, in general, Lucille Birnbaum, "Behaviorism in the 1920's," *American Quarterly*, VII (1955), 15–30, and Lucille Terese Birnbaum, "Behaviorism: John Brodus Watson and American Social Thought" (unpublished doctoral dissertation, University of California, Berkeley, 1964), especially p. 291. See also discussion below, p. 376. There were attempts to add other components to the new psychology. The most notable was made late in the twenties by advocates of Gestalt psychology, which aroused much interest among professional psychologists. Aside from a few explanatory publications and even a few attacks, however, this attempt failed. Gestalt, significantly, lacked the potential for practical application possessed by the other elements of the new psychology and in other ways failed to mesh with American society of the 1920's. See, for example, Louis Berman, *The Religion Called Behaviorism* (New York, 1927), which was more an advocacy of Gestalt than an attack on Watsonianism (Berman was he of gland fame, incredibly enough); Edward S. Robinson, "A Little German Band: The Solemnities of Gestalt Psychology," *New Republic*, LXI (1929), 10–14.

Because it was a popular phenomenon in the period when, as Allen pointed out, ballyhoo reigned, the new psychology was bound to contain at least an element of faddism. Yet the waxing and waning of psychoanalysis, gland psychology, and behaviorism was not entirely a matter of public whim. The proof lies in the great exception, Couéism, which, in contrast to the rest of the new psychology, was ephemeral because it lacked scientific support sufficient to sustain it.

In November, 1921, the Swiss physician who founded the movement that bore his name, Emile Coué, made a triumphal tour of England. Americans immediately imported Couéism from England, and in January, 1923, Coué himself came to the United States. He received a ballyhoo welcome from midwestern as well as New York journalists that gave his message a currency along with mah-jongg. Coué was viewed essentially as a secular faith healer. His technique was vulgarized into a person's repeating to himself, "Day by day, in every way [emphasize the every], I'm getting better and better." Supposedly, this "autosuggestion" cured both physical and psychological difficulties and improved the character. A rhymster for *Life* suggested the enthusiasm and exaggeration of the publicity:

> Would you be freed from every kind
>   Of woe and make your forces double?
> Bamboozle dark Subsconscious Mind,
>   That ever-present source of trouble.
>
> .   .   .   .
>
> No matter what your goal or aim,
>   You must not doubt yourself a minute,
> But say, "Of course I'll win the game!"—
>   Subconscious Mind will make you win it.[18]

[18] See, for example, C. Harry Brooks, *The Practice of Auto-suggestion by the Method of Emile Coué* (New York, 1922); this volume inspired the quoted "Rhymed Review" by Arthur Guiterman, in *Life*, LXXX (1922), 31, used by permission of H. T. Rockwell.

Coué based his work on the standard psychology of suggestion, which in turn had been inferred largely from the phenomenon of hypnosis (at the time thought to be suggestion in an extreme form). In addition to the conscious mind, so the theory goes, there is a subconscious mind that helps determine behavior. A repeated suggestion aimed at the subconscious will eventually influence it. This had been a well-known theory for many years before the 1920's, and a type of psychotherapy consisting of suggestions made by the physician was frequently employed. The idea of do-it-yourself suggestion, however, was relatively new on the popular level. This novelty made autosuggestion susceptible to ballyhoo, and the scientific aura of the panacea gave it a respectability lacking in other faith cures.[19] For years afterward expositors of the new psychology often mentioned Couéism, along with suggestion, in eclectic treatises; but for the most part, it, like any other fad, disappeared without a trace.[20]

THE BACKGROUND

Contributing to both the acceptance and the image of the new psychology throughout the twenties were the mental testing and mental hygiene movements. Each had its own existence but interacted with the new psychology in important ways. Mental testing was largely intelligence testing.

[19] See, for example, Joseph Collins, "Couéism," *North American Review*, CCXVI (1922), 190–99; Harry N. Kerns, review of Satow, *Hypnotism and Suggestion*, in *Mental Hygiene*, VIII (1924), 414: " . . . One wonders why the public is asked to read another book on this question."

[20] Even the gland fad left behind a solid contribution on a technical physiological level. The lack of professional backing for Couéism sets it apart. A. Kardiner, for example, in a review of Northridge, *Modern Theories of the Unconscious*, in *Mental Hygiene*, IX (1925), observed caustically that "Coué's views are given such space and dignity as to cast serious doubt upon the author's ability to criticize his material" (p. 419).

The public, alerted before the war to the dangers of feeble-mindedness, was entertained in the postwar period by the concept of one's mental—as opposed to chronological—age (IQ). Statistical standardization of the tests and their use by the Army in the war gave them added social significance. Intelligence and other mental tests appeared to offer a way in which scientific study of man could be really useful. Up until then psychology had been for the most part a science remarkable because of its lack of potential for practical application. The tests were of great importance because they suggested that psychology had practical value. This cult of practicability carried over to all of the components that went into the new psychology and eventually guided it in a direction that could not then have been foreseen.[21]

Mental hygiene was a more complex movement. It grew out of both the psychotherapy movement of the prewar period and the discovery of shell shock by physicians and the public, a discovery that had any number of consequences. The psychotherapy movement began about 1906 and infiltrated both medicine and popular thinking. Fields as disparate as literature, politics, and religion felt the impact of the movement. Psychotherapists of the time assumed that environment—and especially social environment—is very important in determining both normal and abnormal human behavior. The success of the physicians using psychological or "moral" means to treat mental illnesses suggested that a more general reform of society and the individuals in it was possible.[22] Like many other aspects of progressive thought, the psychotherapy movement did not survive the experience of World War I in a recognizable form. It simply vanished, either absorbed or replaced by the mental hygiene movement. Indeed, many of the leaders

[21] See discussion, pp. 389–90.

[22] John C. Burnham, "Psychiatry, Psychology and the Progressive Movement," *American Quarterly*, XII (1960), 457–65.

of the psychotherapy movement were also leaders of the mental hygiene movement.

Because psychoanalysis had been introduced as, and continued to be, an important part of the psychotherapy movement, it is paradoxical that while psychotherapy as a movement withered, psychoanalysis flourished after the war. The Freudian phase of the new psychology is the more surprising because World War I had had a devastating effect upon the growth of psychoanalysis within American medicine. Freudianism, an Austrian import, was suspect because of its supposed Teutonic origins. In the backwash of anti-German feeling, the American Psychoanalytic Association almost disbanded itself in 1919.[23] The phenomenon of shell shock and its consequences heighten the paradox of the fad of psychoanalysis.

Physicians had seen "shell shock" as early as the Russo-Japanese War of 1904-5, but the trench warfare of World War I caused the malady to appear with sometimes epidemic frequency. Soldiers—and good soldiers—often developed severe symptoms of mental illness, such as hysterical (i.e., psychosomatic) blindness, paralysis, tremors, terrors, and even hallucinations, that rendered them unfit for fighting. As the name implies, the disease was at first ascribed to shock caused by the concussion of exploding shells. The shock presumably disrupted the normal functioning of the nervous system. When careful inquiry revealed that shell shock was more common among troops who had not been exposed to shelling (or, indeed, any action at all) than among those at the front, physicians concluded that shell shock was a common neurosis, a mental illness without any apparent physical cause. The term persisted, however, partly to mask the fact that these ill war heroes had "weak nerves"; that is, were either constitutionally

[23] Oberndorf, *A History of Psychoanalysis in America*, pp. 135–36.

inferior or mildly mentally ill without any reference to war experiences.

The shell shock diseases called attention to environmental causes—as well as to environmental types of treatment— and therefore tended to vindicate the belief of the psycho- therapists that these illnesses were, at least functionally, psychological in nature. (Many prominent practitioners, of course, insisted in the name of theoretical materialism that there were real physical changes that just were not dis- cernible by methods then available.) As knowledge about shell shock spread, the public became increasingly aware that one's mind could play tricks on one and produce neurotic symptoms and uncontrollable behavior. Even those of the public for whom shell shock represented physical injury to the nerves necessarily became aware of how com- mon and agonizing nervous diseases could be. By turning the neurosis into a war wound, the experience of World War I mitigated public attitudes toward mental illnesses more effectively than years of humanitarian propaganda.[24]

The war also created a profession to treat these ill- nesses outside of the mental hospitals. The specialists in nervous and mental diseases had divided themselves by function into two distinct groups: the neurologists and the hospital physicians. The neurologists concentrated on organic diseases of the nervous system, but many of them participated in the psychotherapy movement and did some outpatient psychotherapy. The mental hospital physicians

[24] The literature on shell shock is immense; one convenient sum- mary is Mabel Webster Brown and Frankwood E. Williams, *Neuro- psychiatry and the War: A Bibliography with Abstracts* (New York, 1918). For examples of popular literature, see Frederick W. Parsons, "War Neuroses," *Atlantic Monthly*, CXXIII (1919), 335–38, and, indicative of how late in the decade the idea was still filtering down, "Second Wind," *Saturday Evening Post*, CXCVIII (May 8, 1926), 8 ff.

tended to keep to their asylums where they did more managing of the patients than curing them. Both neurologists and hospital physicians appeared before the public as alienists, or expert witnesses in legal proceedings. After World War I the new specialist, the neuropsychiatrist or psychiatrist, appeared. No longer exclusively a hospital physician or legal expert, the psychiatrist became in the twenties a healer, in either a hospital or an outpatient setting. It is significant, for example, that in keeping with this changing image the *American Journal of Insanity* changed its name in 1921 to *American Journal of Psychiatry*.

This popular conception of the psychiatrist resulted largely from the work of the mental hygiene movement.[25] The mental hygiene movement had been launched in 1908 by Clifford Beers, a former mental patient who enlisted the support of the country's leading specialists in nervous and mental diseases in a diffuse movement to improve the treatment of mental patients and in general foster mental health. As it became clear that the United States would probably become involved in World War I, the newly formed National Committee for Mental Hygiene approached the surgeon general and requested to be included in the war effort. A special committee of leading psychiatrists urged the Army Medical Department to create a special staff and service for nervous and mental diseases. The committee cited not only the statistics of increases in mental illnesses among European soldiers but the fact that "mental diseases were approximately three times as prevalent among the troops on the Mexican border last summer as among the

[25] The standard histories of this movement are not very revealing; see, for example, Albert Deutsch, "The History of Mental Hygiene," in J. K. Hall, *et al.* (eds.), *One Hundred Years of American Psychiatry* (New York, 1944), pp. 325–65.

adult civil population." The Army eventually accepted the program of the committee.[26]

By the end of the war several hundred specialists had been enlisted and several hundred more trained to operate a special neuropsychiatric service within the Army Medical Department.[27] Because of the low caliber of many hospital physicians, other doctors had often regarded the entire speciality with some contempt. In the war, however, psychiatrists found themselves fully recognized and appreciated for the first time. The recognition, acquired so abruptly, led these ambitious men to expect, and rightly so, that they could do even better in the 1920's.[28]

The relationship of the psychiatrists, their patients, and their admirers to the new psychology is reflected in the movement that had so successfully infiltrated psychiatry into the army. During the 1920's and even the early 1930's mental hygiene flourished and grew.[29] It had something for everybody: neurologist, psychotherapist, psychologist, social worker. The key to its scientific and medical success—as well as its political expediency—was the team approach.

The team approach grew out of the work of William Healy, the neurologist who founded the child guidance movement. In the 1900's he had been approached by a number of reformers in Chicago, led by Jane Addams, who were concerned about juvenile delinquents. The reformers believed that science ought to be applied in order to discover why the children had gone wrong. In 1909, therefore, they

[26] Norman Fenton, *Shell Shock and Its Aftermath* (St. Louis, 1926), chap. i; M. W. Ireland (ed.), *The Medical Department of the United States Army in the World War* (Washington, 1929), X, chap. i, and pp. 489–91.

[27] Ireland, *The Medical Department*, X, *passim*.

[28] For example, Pearce Bailey, "Applicability of the Findings of the Neuropsychiatric Examinations in the Army to Civil Problems," *Mental Hygiene*, IV (1920), 301–11.

[29] The mental hygiene movement is best followed in appropriate volumes of *Mental Hygiene*. General treatments also appear in the standard bibliographical indexes of the day.

commissioned Healy to carry out comprehensive studies—
psychiatric, physical, psychological—of individual offenders
brought before the Chicago juvenile court. Healy did the
medical and psychiatric studies himself but also employed
a psychologist (primarily to administer mental tests). The
two of them, of course, discussed the cases informally and
often conferred with social workers from other agencies.
After 1917, when Healy moved his operations to Boston,
he added social workers to his own staff and instituted
the formal case conference to bring together the opinions
of experts with different competences, each of whom had
studied the same individual case. Healy used as a model the
medical case conference of specialists, in which each one
presented his particular view of the case and then the group
together tried to reach a diagnosis.[30]

The team absorbed and tended to obliterate the special
approaches of the neurologist, the psychiatrist, the psychologist or clinical psychologist, and the social worker. A
psychiatrist at Buffalo State Hospital thus observed in 1924
that within a few years a remarkable change had taken
place in that psychotherapy could no longer be distinguished
from psychiatry.[31] Whenever a new emphasis or technique
appeared, the mental hygienists could incorporate it and
call it their own; such was the fate in the 1920's of Couéism,
of gland therapy, of the mental testing movement, of both
theoretical and applied behaviorism. Each was absorbed by
adding it to the team.[32]

[30] Lawson G. Lowrey and Victoria Sloane (eds.), *Orthopsychiatry,
1923–1948* (New York, 1948). Oral history interviews of William
Healy and Augusta Bronner, conducted by John C. Burnham, 1960–61
(copies deposited in the Harvard University Library and at the
Judge Baker Guidance Center, Boston).

[31] H. L. Levin, review of Yellowlees, *Manual of Psychotherapy*,
in *Mental Hygiene*, VIII (1924), 1077.

[32] The function of eclecticism in the science and therapy of mental
illnesses—of which mental hygiene was a sophisticated and extremely
clever example—is a large subject. Some account of it appears in
J. C. Burnham, *Psychoanalysis and American Medicine, 1894–1918:
Medicine, Science, and Culture* (New York, 1967).

With democratic egalitarianism (or perhaps it was lack of discrimination), the movement welcomed not only medicine, psychopathology, and neuropathology but "psychology, sociology, education, and other fields having to do with human behavior and the conduct of life." [33] If the members of the mental hygiene team were united on any point besides the value of co-operation, it was this: they all studied the adaptation, both physical and mental, or, more accurately, "biological," of the individual. In this emphasis they came close to the view of the dominant school in American psychiatry, eclectic dynamic psychiatry. Dynamic psychiatrists, in addition to emphasizing individual life patterns and their adaptive function, included important elements from psychoanalytic psychology.[34]

One further aspect of the mental hygiene movement deserves special notice: its emphasis on child mental hygiene and child rearing generally. Within psychiatry—and typically, dynamic psychiatry—the idea of the importance of early life was traceable directly to the influence of Freud, although popular attitudes that created the "age of the child" had other, equally important determinants.[35] Observers at the time remarked on the unbelievable growth of both medical and popular literature about childhood and child rearing during the 1920's, a proliferation that lasted well into the 1930's.[36]

[33] Frankwood E. Williams, "A Selected List of Books on Mental Hygiene and Allied Subjects," *Mental Hygiene*, VIII (1924), 327.

[34] See Alfred Lief (ed.), *The Commonsense Psychiatry of Dr. Adolf Meyer: Fifty-two Selected Papers* (New York, 1948); Burnham, *Psychoanalysis and American Medicine.*

[35] See discussion, pp. 381–82.

[36] See, for example, William B. Terhune, "Modern Trends in Juvenile Mental Hygiene," *Education*, XLIV (1923), 65. Bernard Glueck, "Constructive Possibilities of a Mental Hygiene of Childhood," *Mental Hygiene*, VIII (1924), 651, connected child mental hygiene to an "unprecedented interest in child health, and child welfare generally. . . . " The incidence of articles indexed in the *Readers Guide* provides concrete confirmation of these impressions.

The dominance of the mental hygiene movement in the Jazz Age raises again the paradox of the psychoanalytic phase of the new psychology. Not only did mental hygiene almost completely supersede psychotherapy but the mental hygienists were not necessarily friendly to psychoanalysis. Even shell shock was used commonly to demonstrate the unsoundness of Freud's beliefs—or what were imagined to be Freud's beliefs. A good example is Sidney I. Schwab, a St. Louis neurologist who in 1906 had been the first person to introduce the term "psychoanalysis" into the United States. In 1920 he asserted that the war neuroses, which clearly had no sexual determinants, had shown Freud to have been basically mistaken.[37] The secret of the success of popularized psychoanalysis lay in the cult of the self and its sequel. That is, a significant part of the literate American public discovered in Freud's teachings (and their distortions) ideas that fitted in with, first, their preoccupation with self and, second, their interest in the controllability of man. That these narcissism and control themes occurred also in the gland and behavioristic phases of the new psychology is a remarkable demonstration of the new psychology phenomenon.

The Cult of the Self

It is ironic that people who viewed their own times as an "Age of Crowds" should see the rise of a strong sense of the urgency of finding one's self. Or perhaps the irony reflects the reality that in the mass society of the twenties depersonalization called forth compensatory attitudes from a large proportion of the atoms of the faceless—and presumably lonely—multitude.

[37] Sidney I. Schwab, "Influence of War Concepts of Mental Diseases and Neuroses," *Modern Medicine*, II (1920), 192–99.

One of the striking developments of the 1920's was the culmination on a mass scale of public interest in personal, introspective accounts of private experiences. A mass market for popularized personal documents grew primarily out of two sources: the lovelorn column of the newspaper and the cult of physical, that is, bodily, development.[38] As a matter of fact, it was the editors of *Physical Culture,* the McFadden Company's health and exercise magazine, who initiated the phenomenon. Their offices had been flooded by unsolicited letters of an essentially confessional nature that contained the details of intimate secrets. The editors got the idea of publishing them, and *True Story Magazine* was born. Its success was immediate and unbelievable, and a host of imitators sprang up.[39]

These cheap magazines appealed, as the editors of *True Confessions* observed in 1924, to readers whose reaction was that "that experience is very like my own." [40] Another aspect of this appeal of the confession magazines was the fact that the material in them tended to be guilt-laden or aberrant in some way so that variations from mass society conformity appeared more common—and easier for the reader to deal with in himself—than might otherwise have been the case. It is very much to the point, therefore, that candid and confessional autobiographical fragments were central in popular expositions of psychoanalysis. Psychopathologists often observed that the neurotic's memories in effect caused his illness, and the case reports in the new psychology literature had all the appeal—and more—of true confessions. The relatively frequent, often didactic, use of psychoanalysis in fiction and drama as a device not

[38] Nothing could underline as subtly and surely as this latter source the presence of narcissim in the phenomenon under discussion.

[39] Ernst Theodore Kreuger, "Autobiographical Documents and Personality" (unpublished doctoral dissertation, University of Chicago, 1925), pp. 16–17.

[40] *Ibid.,* p. 31.

only for characterizing but for suggesting dramatic problems (mother-son relationships, for example) is testimony to the interest generated by personal revelation.[41]

In other ways, however, psychoanalysis as set forth by the writers of the new psychology tended to diminish the personal and to reinforce the loss of identity and the sense of unreality fostered (presumably) by mass society. In the new psychology the apparent was not the real, and the real was never apparent. One leading exposition was entitled *Unmasking Our Minds;* the author's purpose was explicitly to help the reader discover his real self, under the assumption that it was not obvious.[42] How the new psychology led to confusion of appearances and realities was caught by the writer of a satiric "Nutshell Novel" of 1924 of the variety, "A Psycho-Analytical Idyll":

> Zachariah Hardshell and his beautiful daughter, Clammie, lived on a small farm where they struggled with Poverty and Bull Weevils. Trillion Plunks, the village banker, had warts on his nose, a mortgage on the farm, and designs on Clammie. But Clammie hated him. So Trillion dumped them into the county road. He was very cruel. He often kicked dogs, especially in the motion picture version of the novel.
>
> Byron Keats came along, playing his violin, and found them in the road. He was kind to them. He picked some wild flowers for Clammie. She loved him.
>
> But she couldn't marry him. At first she didn't know why. Then it Dawned Upon her. She didn't love him. She hated him for being a Softie. She loved Trillion because he was a Brute.
>
> She married Trillion and he beat her. That made her happy. But Trillion hated her for letting him get away with it. That made him miserable. Thus was poor old Zachariah avenged. He spent his old age Gloating.

[41] *Ibid.*, pp. 31, 39. Freud had early noticed and condemned those who read case histories as if they were novellas; Sigmund Freud, *Collected Papers* (New York, 1959), III, 15.

[42] David Seabury, *Unmasking Our Minds* (New York, 1924).

Byron Keats picked some more flowers. He didn't amount to
much anyway. He had a complex on destruction. 'Way down
inside of him he was bloodthirsty. That was what made him
such a Softie.[43]

The themes of deceptive appearance and concern with
self came together in the idea of the hidden self. Popular
expositions of psychoanalysis confirmed and extended the
widely held belief that each person has a real self deep
inside, the discovery of which, for some reason, may be
desirable. "Dark hidden things," wrote Sherwood Anderson,
describing the effects of psychoanalysis, " . . . came out
and found expression for themselves, and the miracle was
that, expressed, they became often very beautiful." One
of the better-known documents of the new psychology, for
example, was called *Your Inner Self*. "Self-exploration,"
wrote David Seabury in 1924, in *Unmasking Our Minds*,
"may suggest some answer to such questions as: 'What am
I like? What are my strong and weak points? What unconscious conditions suppress and injure me? How can I understand my family, my children, my friends? What effect
does my own nature have on health, happiness, marriage,

[43] Chester T. Crowell, "Nutshell Novels," *New Republic*, XL
(1924), 44. The idea of the illusory nature of appearances was not only
important but one of the fundamentals in the credo of the age. It
represented an aspect of general disillusionment (see Christopher
Lasch, *The New Radicalism in America (1889–1963): The Intellectual
as a Social Type* [New York, 1965], pp. 254–55) as well as of the
currents discussed in the present essay. The denunciations of in-
sincerity and hypocrisy and the cult of frankness, both of which
were conspicuous in the postwar world, were other aspects of the
feeling that the obvious is not the real. Rationalization, one of the
major conceptual contributions of the new psychology, was exciting
because it showed specifically how people fooled themselves and why
the traditional, rational explanations for human behavior were both
convincing and erroneous. See, for example, James Harvey Robinson,
*The Mind in the Making: The Relation of Intelligence to Social
Reform* (New York, 1921), pp. 40–48.

career? How can I solve these problems?' " [44] As Seabury suggested, literate Americans of the Jazz Age typically considered knowledge about the interior self—and cognate understanding of others—to be of the greatest importance.

In literature, obsession with the unobvious and unconscious aspects of personality was destructive of artistic effectiveness. In attempting to portray the flow of free associations, for example, writers often lost the inner consistency that gives characterization its convincing—and interesting—quality. Novelists, for instance, tended to write about their inner feelings and emphasize impulses that they imagined had origins deep in the unconscious. Authors described, sometimes directly, sometimes symbolically, polymorphous perverse and other primitive elements in behavior or motivation as if they conveyed to the reader more meaning than was really the case.[45] In addition to deliberate obscurantism, from the concept of the hidden self writers developed the literary device of a character's being saved by the revelation of his inner self. That is, either some shock or circumstance brought about significant self-understanding, or else the dramatic action was resolved by the "deus ex clinica." [46] Literature of the decade was strewn with the wreckage of stories and plays in which the psychiatrist offered a clumsy means (often an overnight psychoanalysis) of resolving the dramatic conflicts. If the new psychology provided inspiration and tech-

[44] Sherwood Anderson, quoted in Hoffman, *The Twenties*, p. 206; Louis E. Bisch, *Your Inner Self* (Garden City, N. Y., 1922); Seabury, *Unmasking Our Minds*, p. x.

[45] See, for example, Hoffman, *The Twenties*, pp. 204–5.

[46] See, for example, Elsa Barker, *Fielding Sargent: A Novel* (New York, 1922), and Sievers, *Freud on Broadway*, pp. 80, 95–96. Sievers, *ibid.*, p. 138, quotes the critic Alexander Woollcott, suggesting that the action in a supposedly psychoanalytic play in 1927 is a good example of putting very conventional drama in a faddish Freudian form: "If what ails the girl can be said to be hidden, then so is the Woolworth Building."

nical details for the literary exponents of searching-for-the-self, they, in turn, contributed to popular knowledge of the new psychology, usually within the context of a sentimental narcissism.

One impetus to the fervent search for the hidden self was the idea that one's *real* self had potential that the everyday one did not. James Oppenheim, a former poet and lay analyst who wrote for a Los Angeles newspaper, used Jungian psychology[47] in his book on *Your Hidden Powers*: " . . . Every human being has hidden powers which must be brought to light and used. . . . Not only is a knowledge of human nature a great power, because we can more successfully deal with others, but it is all essential in learning how to deal with ourselves, how to solve our problems and develop ourselves for the sake of our happiness, our health and our well being." [48]

The chief purveyors of the new psychology, such as Oppenheim, asserted that man's potential—and particularly their own—was seldom fulfilled. If they were not great artists, the fault lay in external circumstances rather than in personal shortcomings. Influenced by Marx, for example, many intellectuals had spoken of the tyrannies of society that held creativity and intellectuality in chains. When the intellectuals realized that early twentieth-century society was not oppressing them, they found—in part through the new psychology—that it was their interior psyche, the

[47] Jungian psychology was a variant of psychoanalysis, emphasizing the immediate causes of a neurotic illness (as opposed to life history) and such mystical concepts as a Lamarckian racial unconscious. In conformity to the usual American eclecticism, writers customarily did not distinguish Jung's work from Freud's but utilized them alternately without regard for consistency.

[48] James Oppenheim, *Your Hidden Powers* (New York, 1923), pp. 5–6. This conception of the unrealized powers of the hidden self was usually not Freudian or even broadly psychoanalytic, but had its origin in the psychopathology of Janet, of which Coué represented a distortion.

internalization of conventional upbringing, that constrained their actions and withered originality.[49] In this context a person could realize the hidden powers of his self—discoverable through psychoanalysis—not so much by simple revelation of the hidden powers as by unmasking and breaking the interior chains.[50]

In the behavioristic phase of the new psychology, the idea of internalization of external inhibitions persisted, but often in a simplistic form. The behaviorists viewed the personality as the congeries of habit systems built up by conditioned reflexes. Where the behavioristic view was not just a translation of psychoanalytic concepts, the Watsonians suggested that the traditional association psychology served to explain how habit systems of adults originated.[51] Except in so far as the behaviorists emphasized a few primitive fear and sex reactions, their extreme environmentalism tended to change the emphasis of the new psychology from searching for the inner self to finding out how a person got to be the way he was.[52]

The new psychology expositions of the early 1920's had shifted remarkably in emphasis from comparable writings of the prewar period. For years there had been any number of books and articles addressed to the "nervous." The tone of these progressive period tracts was embodied in two motifs: self-improvement (the authors were generous with exhortation) and, either directly or indirectly, social improvement and service. Expositors of psychoanalysis before

[49] Lasch, *The New Radicalism*, pp. 142–43.

[50] See discussion, pp. 387–89.

[51] For example, John B. Watson, *The Ways of Behaviorism* (New York, 1928), especially p. 120.

[52] The argument might be made here, and will be made below, that like so much of the late 1920's, the behavioristic phase of the new psychology in its emphasis on external social control belongs with the 1930's, not the early 1920's. See Birnbaum, "Behaviorism: John Broadus Watson," p. 345 and *passim*.

the war, for example, often stressed the idea of sublimating one's primitive desires into useful social activity.[53] In the twenties the authors of the rapidly proliferating literature of the new psychology changed the emphasis from self-improvement to self-justification; they moved from the progressive idea of service to the postwar idea of discovering one's wants, needs, and desires (usually in the hidden self or primitive chemical and reflex systems) and gratifying them.[54]

The method of justifying one's present condition was simple: no matter what you do, according to the new psychologists, your motives are impure. Therefore, why improve? Behind every action the new writers found a base motive. "Don't you even know, mother," said Claire, the flapper daughter in John Howard Lawson's *Loudspeaker*, "that everybody's thoughts are obscenely vile? That's psychology." [55] André Tridon, a lay analyst in New York and prolific publicizer, in one chapter showed that people who talk about the weather are inhibited, "poor, weak, underdeveloped human beings . . . not daring to love and admire violently anything or anybody . . . "; that pompous persons have a tendency to schizophrenia and "compensate for their intellectual inferiority by unbearably good manners and an annoying form of accuracy"; that snobs are "neurotics afraid of life and of competition . . . ," regressed in their exclusiveness "to the prenatal level in which the child is protected against all of life's problems but death"; that

[53] Burnham, "Psychiatry, Psychology and the Progressive Movement." See, for example, James J. Putnam, *Human Motives* (Boston, 1915).

[54] See, for example, the contemporaneous observations of Stanley P. Davies, "What Grown-Ups Cry For: Has an Eager Public Been Oversold on Mental Hygiene?", *Survey*, LXVII (1931), 253–54, 280–81. Similarly, a quipster in *Life*, LXXXI (1923), 8, caught some of the underlying appeal of Couéism: "One thing about auto-suggestion: It is practically the only suggestion the average man will take."

[55] John Howard Lawson, quoted in Sievers, *Freud on Broadway*, p. 143.

those who begrudge praising others are trying "unconsciously to kill those who [unlike themselves] do create by never mentioning them . . . "; that superstitious people, besides having inadequate nerve and gland stimulation, "are obsessed by a sense of guilt, which, unfortunately, has a solid foundation of fact [in the unconscious], and they fear retribution"; that those who go to watch the spectacle of a destructive fire are envious sadists—"everyone is at heart a jealous brute who enjoys whatever damage is inflicted upon someone else's person or property." Tridon went on to analyze, similarly, animal lovers, busybodies, conservatives, and cardplayers, among others.[56]

The popular pseudo-Freudians reserved their sharpest scorn for the reformer, a contrast to the prewar psychoanalytic writers' tendency to urge social reform. It was explained that moral superiority originated in a most unrighteous secret self that was in danger of breaking loose. The "puritan" who was sensitive to sexual subjects suffered from "suppressed Pornophilia" and probably was hypersexual in nature. "We are told of certain professional reformers," wrote new psychologist William J. Fielding, "who have large collections of obscene pictures. . . . "[57]

When the gland psychology came in to supplement and supplant psychoanalysis, the wicked unconscious in each of us acquired palpable reality. Writers of the gland epoch attributed virtually every characteristic action to impulses generated by the chemicals secreted by the ductless glands. [58] Even the mental testing and IQ craze was utilized

[56] In the bargain Tridon passed on tips on the serving of food; André Tridon, *Psychoanalysis and Man's Unconscious Motives* (New York, 1924), chap. v.

[57] William J. Fielding, *The Caveman Within Us, His Peculiarities and Powers: How We Can Enlist His Aid for Health and Efficiency* (New York, 1922), pp. 264–69.

[58] In combination with psychoanalytic explanations, the environment was believed to affect glandular functioning and so to account in organic terms for what had appeared to be an essentially psychological relationship of cause and effect. See, for example, the inde-

as a justification for not changing one's self. Because intelligence tests had suggested that feeble-mindedness was a
major—and often unobvious—factor in criminal and other
abnormal behavior, the IQ was often incorporated into the
concept of the hidden self (and the public, it turned out,
tended to confuse mental subnormality with abnormality).
Unsuspected brilliance could also be discovered in the real
self. As a Yale psychologist, Howard W. Haggard, wrote
'Tisn't What You Know But Are You Intelligent? "Intelligence," he said, "is the capability to do productive thinking." It is not necessary to know "what Leonardo da Vinci's
two most famous paintings are." Or who wrote *Carmen.*
Or, apparently, to do any disciplined thinking at all.[59] One
could, in short, justify his lack of self-improvement simply
by pointing out his potential—a remarkable reversal of
prewar devotion to acquiring character and culture.

When behaviorism came to supplement and replace
psychoanalysis and the glands in the make-up of the new
psychology, one's present behavior was ascribed to the accident of environmental conditioning as well as one's gut
reactions. In this way the idea of self-justification continued
to be a basic theme in the new psychology. It was easy to
trace one's character to the circumstances and automatic
emotional reactions that conditioned and gave rise to his
"habit systems." As Ross L. Finney of the University of
Minnesota pointed out in a book attacking behaviorism,
behavioristic mechanism implied that one experience—and
the conditioning that results—is as good as another. There
was therefore, again, no serious motivation to change
oneself.[60]

---

fatigable André Tridon, *Psychoanalysis and Gland Personalities* (New
York, 1923).

[59] Howard W. Haggard, *'Tisn't What You Know But Are You
Intelligent?* (New York, 1927), especially pp. 5–7.

[60] Ross L. Finney, "Behaviorism's Silence as to Human Values,"
in William P. King (ed.), *Behaviorism: A Battle Line* (Nashville,

Watson himself offered the most convincing evidence of the conservative nature of behaviorism. Although he was famous for his dictum that by manipulating environment he could make any infant develop into any specified kind of person, from beggarman to lawyer or chief, Watson always in fact qualified the assertion. By 1928 he confessed that although theoretically even adults should be able to change their personalities by reconditioning, modern man lacked the necessary means of thoroughgoing control to effect a significant reconditioning. People were too spineless, too lazy and careless, said Watson, to be able to change themselves. As he grew older, he said, he became convinced that "the zebra can as easily change his stripes as the adult his personality." [61]

Regardless of specific content, the behaviorists in their popularizations echoed the same iconoclastic tone as the vulgarizers of psychoanalysis. Where the psychoanalytic writers ruthlessly showed the real self to be found in the mind, the behaviorists were talking about the real self of the gut, that is, reflex actions. [62]

The expositors of the new psychology in centering on the self almost invariably spoke in terms of motives. This preoccupation with motives was one of the marks of the

---

1930), p. 177. A. A. Roback, "Intelligence and Behavior," *Psychological Review*, XXIX (1922), 54–55, noted that intelligence testing made assumptions similar to those of behaviorism in that from both points of view intelligence is passive, i.e., mechanical—the machinery, rather than active or a part of the drive itself. Both the IQ movement and behaviorism pictured intelligence as a passive, automatic reaction to a stimulus.

[61] Watson, *The Ways of Behaviorism*, p. 138; Birnbaum, "Behaviorism in the 1920's," pp. 21–22, discusses on one level the inconsistency in behaviorism. Compare in general Birnbaum, "Behaviorism: John Broadus Watson."

[62] Birnbaum, "Behaviorism: John Broadus Watson," especially pp. 291 ff., contains the interesting characterization of behaviorism as an "outsider's" psychology. See the observations of Paul Hanly Furfey, "After Psychoanalysis—What?", *Catholic World*, CXXVII (1928), 681–85.

age.[63] Psychoanalysis and its successors revealed that the cause of even the most innocent, everyday behavior could be shown to be impulses that were clearly improper and immoral, or at least uncivilized, in nature. H. M. Kallen, who knew both Academia and Bohemia in New York, asserted about his own times that "men have ceased to be clear in their hearts about their own motives and actions, and have become suspicious of those of their fellows." [64] The hidden, even unconscious, motive was known long before, in the writings of eighteenth-century political philosophers, for example, and the *avant-garde* had for some time used Marxian insights to discredit the motives of apparently altruistic contemporaries. The new psychology emphasized a far more primitive type of motive and the ways in which a man rationalized and hid such motives from himself.

Even in Marxist analysis, the motives of men had some rational goal in terms of the function of the individual within the social system of production. The new psychology tended to emphasize the irrational, to deny at all the efficacy of reason on the level of motive.[65] A long period of intellectual preparation, including currents such as naturalism, decadence, and primitivism, the writings of Zola, Nietzsche, and Marx, had effectively introduced ideas of the irrationality and animality of man.[66] In a time of general disillusionment after World War I, the new psycholo-

[63] See, for example, Horace Bidwell English, "Dynamic Psychology and the Problem of Motivation," *Psychological Review*, XXVIII (1921), 239–48; K. S. Lashley, "The Behavioristic Interpretation of Consciousness," *Psychological Review*, XXX (1923), 348.

[64] "Is Minding Behaving?", *New Republic*, XXIX (1922), 285–86.

[65] Of course, this motivation was presented in a context of belief that "facing the truth," with subsequent rational action, would have beneficial effects on both the individual and society.

[66] Every student of the period will have his own list of movements, of social background factors, and of influential thinkers. See, for example, Oscar Cargill, *Intellectual America: Ideas on the March* (New York, 1941).

gists, too, expressed disenchantment with the nature of man. Two immediate factors also helped account for the success of the disillusionist aspect of the new psychology: the war experience, when cherished beliefs turned out to be propaganda, and the popular impact of science, especially evolutionary thinking. One acute contemporary observer listed three propositions that were in vogue in the 1920's: "That men are moved by the same instincts as the lower species; that instinctive conduct is mechanically determined; and that the reasons conventionally given for conduct are mostly sophisticated 'rationalizations'. . . . "[67]

It was during the 1920's that the famous instinct controversy in sociology and psychology occurred, and its contents and resolution were often included in expositions of the new psychology. One of the chief aspects of the development of the psychology of motivation was the appearance of dynamic psychologies, in which the concept of instinct was used to account for the actions of man.[68] Among the lists of human instincts that various writers suggested, those of Freud and William McDougall predominated. It was in the eventual defeat of McDougall's viewpoint that the new psychology reflected most interestingly the spirit of its times.

McDougall, writing originally in 1908, had explained human behavior in terms of a number of instincts—such as the acquisitive and the gregarious—that he found expressed in well-refined adult human ways and, specifically, in civilized institutions.[69] The new psychology tended either to analyze all behavior back into instincts that are

[67] George A. Coe, *The Motives of Men* (New York, 1928), p. 45. *Ibid.*, Chapters I-VII, gives a good summary of the relationship of science, World War I, and industrial society to the cult of irrationality of the new psychology.

[68] The standard treatment is L. L. Bernard, *Instinct: A Study in Social Psychology* (New York, 1924).

[69] William McDougall, *An Introduction to Social Psychology* (Boston, 1916).

strictly animal, in a traditional sense, such as sex and
hunger; or, as in behaviorism, instinct was largely discarded and man's behavior construed to be the result of
accidental associations of primitive visceral and behavioral reactions. It was no accident that behaviorism grew
out of non-verbal, biological animal psychology. Where
specifically human drives did show up in the new psychology, they tended to have amoral connotations, such as the
will to power or narcissistic self-love. The glands, as Theodore Dreiser illustrated very well, suggested a somatic
concomitant for both blind, reflex action and primitive
instincts as determinants of supposedly adult, civilized
actions. What he had once referred to as "chemisms" took
by 1925 the form in the hero of "the Efrit of his own darker
self." [70]

That man has bestial passions was of course an ancient
idea. In addition, Nietzsche and other writers had made
common the idea that the supposedly compensatory noble
instincts of man—as posited by many nineteenth-century
thinkers—were in truth only myths. But this early
twentieth-century conception of man's passions, emphasizing his irrationality, differed from Hobbes's conception of
man in modifying the familiar idea of hedonism and introducing an element of wilful impulsiveness uncommon for
some time in Western thinking on man's nature. "The
gorilla in us," wrote Tridon in 1924, "is starved for fresh
air, exercise, wild motions, explosive manifestations of
mirth. And the gorilla in us now and then avenges himself
by compelling us, in neurotic attacks, to act like a gorilla.
... " [71] This emphasis on the animality of man, however,

[70] Robert E. Spiller, et al. (eds.), Literary History of the United
States (2d rev. ed.; New York, 1953), pp. 1201–2; Theodore Dreiser,
An American Tragedy (New York, 1925), II, 56.
[71] Psychoanalysis and Man's Unconscious Motives, p. 106.

did not give the new psychology its distinctive tone. The bestial passions tended, in actual exposition, to be rather boringly conventional passions; and the will to power, for instance, was surprisingly well articulated and adult. The new psychology had its impact in emphasizing not the bestial so much as the infantile and the abnormal.

Like other elements of the new psychology, the emphasis on the persistence of childish elements in adult behavior had developed in the period before World War I. As reflected in education and in other areas, America had "discovered the child," although in a culture long known for its indulgence of children, the child-centered school could hardly be described as a surprising development. Biological thinking of the day suggested that the process of growing and maturing—and adapting to the environment —both foreshadowed and determined adult patterns of life. Freud's assertions that early life patterns would persist into adulthood found a receptive audience. The behaviorists gloried in bringing infants into the laboratory, using infantile behavior patterns to fill out their general psychology. Where in the progressive period the perspective had tended to be backward, tracing back the ways in which violations of the supposedly natural course of childhood had produced effects in adults, in the 1920's the perspective was forward looking: the environment and experiences that were provided for the child were of overwhelming importance because of their influence on later life.[72]

The cult of child rearing and child mental hygiene that was so typical of the twenties signified the concern of the

[72] See Richard Hofstadter, *Anti-Intellectualism in American Life* (New York, 1963), pp. 364–65, 368–69; Lasch, *The New Radicalism*, pp. 86–87; Birnbaum, "Behaviorism in the 1920's," pp. 26–30. *Life*, LXXXIII (1924), 24, pictured a nurse in a modern nursery saying, "A penny for your complexes, Master John."

age with the childish—and more specifically, the infantile—
elements in the hidden self.[73] The educators especially
seized upon the idea of self-expressionism in order to foster
creativity in children and, presumably, adults. "The creative impulse is within the child himself," wrote the authors
of a major pedagogical document of the period.[74] This idea
of course sounded very much like some traditional
romantic ideas, but it appeared—not always with logical
consistency—in the "scientific" context of psychoanalysis
and behaviorism.[75]

Since both the animality and infantilism of man were
emphatically "natural," the deliciously rebellious flavor of
the new psychology showed up best in the harping of its
expositors upon the pervasive existence of abnormality in
supposedly innocent human actions. "Civilization is a study
in pathology and perversion," asserted one new psychologist.[76] (Nor, it should be added, is there any more effective
argument justifying one's shortcomings than pointing out
the prevalence of the same or worse in the population in
general.) For some, the very exposure of the forbidden
subject of abnormality was, perhaps understandably,
unpleasant. "It is certainly somewhat trying," remarked
the Jesuit psychologist E. Boyd Barrett, "to be reminded
in every new book on psychology of the abnormal characteristics of pyromaniacs and homosexuals." The appeal of

[73] Very frequently when the hidden self expressed itself in neurotic
ways, they were understood to represent inappropriate adaptations
essentially infantile in nature. Indeed, "infantile" was used commonly
as a synonym for "neurotic" when describing thought or behavior.
There was, in other words, a distinction between the childish content
or impulse in the hidden self and the choice between adult or infantile
modes of expressing the content.

[74] Harold Rugg and Ann Shumaker, quoted in Lawrence A.
Cremin, *The Transformation of the School: Progressivism in American Education, 1876–1957* (New York, 1961), p. 207, which should
be seen in general.

[75] See discussion, pp. 387–89.

[76] Samuel D. Schmalhausen, *Why We Misbehave* (Garden City,
N. Y., 1928), p. 104.

the new psychology, he asserted, did not need to rest on a morbid curiosity about side-show freaks.[77]

Yet the writers of the new psychology in all its phases did exploit—in however sugar-coated a form—expositions of abnormality. Tridon in writing thirty-one chapters on *Psychoanalysis and Love* spent two chapters on fetishism, two on neurotic lovers, two on non-monogamous love, two on jealousy, two on homosexuality, three on sadism-masochism, and one each (emphasizing abnormality) on virginity, modesty, and prostitution. Additional chapters likewise contain subheadings such as "Having Her Fixation-Fling." [78] The more urbane of the rebellious writers could find in every traditional human institution an amazing amount of abnormality. One such author, Samuel D. Schmalhausen, must have come close to establishing a record in a chapter he entitled "Family Life: A Study in Pathology." He not only contended that the "family is the cradle of incest" but pictured it as holding its members in "neurotic bondage." Parents continuously, he asserted, "are predisposing their children to neurotic and psychotic break-down, to social maladjustment and misery, by preventing them from achieving ego-adequacy." And he concluded pessimistically about marriage: "When two human beings, . . . loaded with defect and derangement [as are all modern couples], attempt to bring to one another sexual joy and ego-tranquillity and human fellowship, one need not be an expert either in statistical reasoning or in psychopathology to realize with a start how very few the chances of harmony and beauty and fulfillment." [79]

The simultaneous interest in self and interest in the abnormal reflected the common concern of the time about

[77] "Psychology or Science," *New Republic*, LII (1927), 343.

[78] André Tridon, *Psychoanalysis and Love* (New York, 1922).

[79] Samuel D. Schmalhausen, "Family Life: A Study in Pathology," in V. F. Calverton and Samuel D. Schmalhausen (eds.), *The New Generation: The Intimate Problems of Modern Parents and Children* (New York, 1930), pp. 275–99.

"normality." The public in general had become vividly
aware of the idea of normality when intelligence tests
became standardized and widely publicized. The idea of
deviation in the form of feeble-mindedness was refined to
include personality traits. Not surprisingly, therefore, in
the 1920's a number of personality tests appeared, designed
to detect personality deviations. So great was the concern
about normality that a discipline known as industrial
psychiatry grew up to try to eliminate misfits from industry
just as they had been screened out of the Army. The mental
hygiene movement similarly popularized this concern about
abnormalities of every kind: eccentricities could in a rather
romantic way take on the quality of portending sinister
events in the hidden self. The possibility that abnormality
might include most people—which fascinated the self-
centered—grew not only out of the discovery of abnormality
in garden-variety aspects of life but out of the publicity
about shell shock, which underlined the well-established
idea in popularized psychiatry that it is difficult to draw
a line between normal and abnormal.[80]

As the new psychologists introduced both primitive passions and abnormal behavior into their expositions, they
inevitably and characteristically gave much attention to
sex. The new psychology popularized two ideas: first, the
importance of sexual desires and drives, and, second, the
presence of sexual factors in a wide variety of supposedly
non-sexual phenomena. One psychiatrist in the mental
hygiene movement, Arthur G. Lane, admitted candidly that
"The new psychology . . . has created unwarranted antagonism in many minds, and morbid curiosity in many others,
because of the prominence given to the sexual instinct as
the main driving force that motivates all human conduct."[81]

[80] The concept of normality and concern about it is of course a
very large subject of which only the above hint can be given here.
[81] Arthur G. Lane, review of Green, *Mind in Action*, in *Mental
Hygiene*, VIII (1924), 422.

The new psychology, with its high sexual content, paralleled the sex education movement and the change in moral standards traditionally associated with the new freedom of women and World War I.[82] What was notable about the sex content of the new psychology was its adolescent character—adolescent in consciously sexualizing not only the hidden self but all human phenomena, and adolescent in using the sexual content for purposes of expressing a more general rebelliousness.

To a surprising extent the very freedom to talk about sexual matters generated a great deal of energy devoted to testing that freedom, and expositions of the new psychology provided a vehicle for discussing in a scientific or reasonable guise matters that otherwise would have been considered offensive, forbidden, or just plain puerile. Pornography was hidden in the case history; any word could appear in print as long as "neurosis" or "complex" appeared with it.

As disillusionment became an end in itself for the intellectual rebels and their followers, the iconoclasts found that imputing sexual qualities and motives to people's actions was an effective way to discredit them. The Marxists had, of course, for a long time used the conception of marriage as legalized prostitution to attack capitalism. In the 1920's such general attacks on institutions because of their effects on the relations between the sexes—and now with a tithe of abnormalities thrown in flourished. Writer Floyd Dell, in his well-informed and sensitive essay on *Love in the Machine Age*, for example, condemned any number of social and economic institutions because of their undesirable effects on lovemaking.[83] The religious establishment was

[82] See, for example, Ben B. Lindsey and Wainwright Evans, *The Revolt of Modern Youth* (New York, 1925), especially pp. 66–67; May, *End of American Innocence*, especially pp. 340–47; John C. Burnham, "Psychoanalysis and American Civilization before 1918" (unpublished doctoral dissertation, Stanford University, 1958), chap. ix.

[83] Floyd Dell, *Love in the Machine Age: A Psychological Study of the Transition from Patriarchal Society* (New York, 1930).

especially vulnerable to sexual analysis. The pious naturally reacted with anguished objections. Barrett, the Jesuit, for example, denounced the idea that religion was simply a disguised expression of sexual instincts. "This blasphemous theory has, unfortunately, made its way into current literature," he admitted. "Hints and innuendos inspired by it are dropped here and there. Religious ritual is likened to pagan orgies. Devout and pious believers are described as neurotic, and in a veiled way it is suggested that they are homosexual. Heaven is spoken of as a disguised sex-dream. Religious symbols are spoken of as *phallic*. . . . " [84]

The connection between sexual emancipation and the new psychology was clear to everyone. Ben Hecht, testing the limits of emancipation, provided a good example by dedicating his work to

> the reformers—the psychopathic ones who publicly and shamelessly belabor their own unfortunate impulses; to the reformers (once again)—the psychopathic ones trying forever to drown their own obscene desires in ear-splitting prayers for their fellowman's welfare; to the reformers—the Freudian dervishes who masturbate with Purity Leagues, who achieve involved orgasms denouncing the depravities of others; to the reformers . . . the psychopathic ones who seek to vindicate their own sexual impotencies by padlocking the national vagina, who find relief for constipation in forbidding their neighbors the water closet. . . . [85]

Nor was sexual rebelliousness the exclusive domain of psychoanalysis and its close relatives. The fact that popularizers of the influence of the glands devoted a large part of their expositions to the gonads testified not only to their business sense but to the beliefs of both the writers and

[84] E. Boyd Barrett, *The New Psychology: How It Aids and Interests* (New York, 1925), p. 310.

[85] *Fantazius Mallare: A Mysterious Oath* (Chicago, 1922), p. 13.

their readers. Similarly, behaviorism, in the laboratory more purely "scientific" than was tolerable to many psychologists, in the hands of Watson and other popularizers sounded essentially the same as vulgarized psychoanalysis in stressing the importance of proper sexual education and the extreme importance of sex in all life matters.

It was psychoanalysis, nevertheless, that bore most of the burden of the common popular association between the new psychology and sex. The usual belief was that Freud had shown that (1) repressions—presumably sexual in nature—were at the root of many nervous illnesses; and (2) the less repressed a person was, therefore, the healthier he was. This popular conception coincided in time with a widespread belief that sexual mores were changing and led to the conclusion that psychoanalysis and the whole new psychology were partly responsible for the change in moral standards.

Liberated spokesmen for the Jazz Age as well as their critics shared this belief. "We studied Freud, argued Jung, checked out dreams by Havelock Ellis, and toyed lightly with Adler," asserted a precocious teen-age writer. "And all these authorities warned us of the danger in repressing our normal instincts and desires. . . . " Playwright Rachel Crothers, in her heavy-handed satire *Expressing Willie*,[86] recognized the common belief with the song lyrics, "Express Yo'se'f My Chile," in which one is warned not to suppress himself but to let all his emotions "rise to the top." Playwright Crothers explicitly contrasted the injunction of 1924 to "*Ex*press yo'se'f" with the type of child training and advice to young ladies known in a former time and embodied in exhortations to suppress one's feelings and impulses. Expositors of the new psychology such as Tridon implied

[86] Elizabeth Benson, quoted in Hoffman, *The Twenties*, pp. 89–90. Rachel Crothers, *Expressing Willie, Nice People, 39 East: Three Plays* (New York, 1924), pp. 42–43.

continuously that expressing one's true self—more than was customary—would be the royal road to health and happiness.[87]

The extent of the change wrought by the new psychologists' tender concern about repression is reflected best in the sex education movement. During the 1920's the sex educators played down their customary emphasis on abstinence for the sake of preventing disease from fear of causing too much repression. One critic of the new psychology, for example, who charged that Schmalhausen's book *Why We Misbehave* deserved to be called *Why We Should Misbehave*, still showed himself remarkably timid about asserting that a little repression, at least, is harmless.[88]

Unreconstructed critics of the new psychology alone remained relatively unconcerned about repression, possibly because they understood the fundamental issues. One of the most vitriolic, Harvey Wickham, recognized the similarity between popularized psychoanalysis and behaviorism. Both are materialistic, he wrote, and both are mechanistic. "The two philosophies," he continued, "have but one effect—to

[87] For example, André Tridon, *Psychoanalysis: Its Theory and Practice* (New York, 1919), chap. xxi. Although often invoking the idea of sublimation and socially useful expressions of forbidden impulses, such writings as Tridon's lacked the moralistic flavor of prewar expositions of psychoanalysis. The question has often been raised whether sexual behavior did change in the Fitzgerald period or not, and if so, whether fear of repressions—learned from the new psychology—was a cause or just a symptom or rationalization for the change. It was true that adventure-seeking young ladies went to Greenwich Village and cast off their repressions. But had Freud been unknown (or known more accurately), the adventure-seekers could have been asserting their emancipation rather than gratifying their impulses, and, indeed, had done just that in an earlier period. (This example was suggested by Waldo Frank, who knew Greenwich Village well, in an interview). Without attempting to answer probably unanswerable questions, it is still possible to observe that the new psychology was very frequently associated with expressions of new attitudes (regardless of behavior) toward sexual matters.

[88] S. C. Kohs, "We've Gone Psychiatric," *Survey*, LXIV (1930), 189-90. See in general *Journal of Social Hygiene* for these years.

sanction *laissez-faire* in matters of sex. A verbalized but otherwise unconditioned 'gut-reaction' is but a conscious 'libido' freed from the suppression which might create a 'complex.' Dr. Watson's superiority lies in his insistence upon education where sex is not involved. Freud's superiority is literary." [89]

Even the sexual emphases of the new psychology, in the context of emphasizing man's wants rather than his duties, were often understood to be self-indulgent, or at the least self-centered.[90] This theme of egocentricity flourished especially in the psychoanalytic period of the new psychology. The behaviorists also incorporated it by emphasizing, for example, the uniqueness of each organism. With the behavioristic phase, however, came the second characteristic of the new psychology, one that set popularized psychology of the later 1920's off from the immediate postwar period and, in one way, connected it to the 1930's. This was the theme of control—social control.

SOCIAL CONTROL

When the psychologists used the mental test in World War I to bring attention to the usefulness of psychology, they gave impetus to the development of an important aspect of modern bureaucratic society.[91] In the 1920's the mental tests were used primarily in the schools, but as part of the new psychology were also applied to industry. During the war the military had adopted three devices from the psychologists: the intelligence tests to weed out those whom

[89] *The Misbehaviorists: Pseudo-Science and the Modern Temper* (New York, 1928), p. 130.

[90] One of the amusing and perhaps remarkable evidences of the hegemony of narcissistic attitudes in the twenties was the rehabilitation of masturbation in the sex education literature of the times.

[91] See discussion, pp. 397–98.

it was not worthwhile to train; systems of rating subordinates so as to introduce a semblance of objectivity; and aptitude tests. After the war, segments of industry, with much encouragement from psychologists, ostentatiously adopted or at least experimented with the three devices.[92]

The industrial use of psychological tests reflected a major shift in attempts at scientific management. Scientific management had, in the progressive period, typically focused on the job, as exemplified in the Taylorization, or rationalization, of industry and time-motion study. Gradually the conception grew that centering attention on the worker rather than the job might turn up ways to increase output. From the one-best-way approach to a task, the new thinking turned to a recognition of individual differences in the workers. Thus personnel work, with its own literature, scientific management, and paternalism in industry, with its dual goals of increasing production and killing unionism with kindness, all called attention to the importance of the worker. After stable employment conditions replaced the high labor turnover period of the immediate postwar years, and after the evident failure of much of the testing to achieve practical results—around 1925—interest in mental tests declined. But the basic quest of industry for a practical industrial psychology remained.[93]

The new psychology, as a psychology of motivation, had great potential for any applied psychology. As one professional psychologist noted at the time, "A rather insistent demand for an adequate psychology of motivation has always been made by those who are interested in the control of human nature. It has come from economists, soci-

[92] Loren Baritz, *The Servants of Power: A History of the Use of Social Science in American Industry* (Middletown, Conn., 1960), chaps. i-iv.

[93] *Ibid.*; for example, see Douglas Fryer, review of Strong and Uhrbrock, *Job Analysis and the Curriculum*, in *Mental Hygiene*, VIII (1924), 848–49.

ologists, educators, advertisers, scout masters, and investigators of crime. . . . " [94] The businessmen, especially, because of their interest in controlling human nature, wanted to know how to predict it. As Loren Baritz has pointed out, with the growth of large bureaucratic organizations, managers needed to avoid the unpredictable, even the unpredictable human element. "The goal was to create an organization so perfect that . . . it would be run by law, not men." [95]

In the first stage of the attempts to apply the new psychology as such to industry, writers suggested that industrialists take into account the instinctual drives of their employees. Ordway Tead, for example, produced a book on *Instinct in Industry* in which, for the sake of completeness, he even took up "the sex instinct" as applied to the factory. Since Tead (who used primarily McDougall's conception of instincts) spoke chiefly in terms of the direct expression of instincts, the chapter dealt mostly with seduction and stands as a parody on itself and the not uncommon idea of applying general concepts of instincts directly to the problem of control of labor.[96]

Meanwhile, the psychology of advertising and selling had developed early in the century as one of the first areas in which psychology could be applied.[97] For some time the standard motivations of man appeared in the literature of both psychology and business as elements to which advertisers and salesmen could appeal. Then in the period of the new psychology, while the basic idea of appealing to

[94] F. A. C. Perrin, "The Psychology of Motivation," *Psychological Review*, XXX (1923), 176.

[95] Baritz, *Servants of Power*, p. 6.

[96] Ordway Tead, *Instincts in Industry: A Study of Working-Class Psychology* (Boston, 1918), especially chap. iii. See Baritz, *Servants of Power*, chaps. i-iv.

[97] See, for the general setting, Otis Pease, *The Responsibilities of American Advertising: Private Control and Public Influence, 1920–1940* (New Haven, 1958), especially chap. vii.

men's wants remained the same, advertising psychologists largely abandoned the concept of human instincts as such and turned instead to the specific, determinable wants of men. As Henry C. Link, an advertising psychologist, explained, the new psychology of selling led to "studying people's wants and buying habits as the best clue to what they *will* buy, in contrast with the older emphasis on overcoming their sales resistance to articles which we think they *should* buy." To Link the market survey was fundamentally behavioristic, and certainly this departure represented the applied psychology version of the movement—again, largely behavioristic—to avoid speaking in terms of theoretical human instincts.[98]

A similar development, a second stage, within industrial psychology was even more revealing. The personnel specialists began to talk about the specific wants of the individual workers rather than generalizing about them. Control of the workers and preclusion of "labor problems" was now thought of in terms of dealing with the concrete and immediate set of desires of each worker. The wants could either be satisfied or they could be tempered, diverted, or otherwise controlled. Although writers on industrial psychology tended to assert that they had the workers' good at heart, control obviously could lead to exploitation.[99]

When Benjamin Stolberg, a well-known Marxist writer, denounced psychology for its sellout to capitalism, he could present a strong case. Not only had a group of leading scientific psychologists formed their own corporation—The Psychological Corporation—to spread the use of psychology by businessmen (at considerable profit to the psychologists,

[98] Henry C. Link, *The New Psychology of Selling and Advertising* (New York, 1932), p. xiii and especially chap. iv. See Birnbaum, "Behaviorism: John Broadus Watson," p. 114.

[99] See, for example, Sadie Myers Shellow, review of Watts, *An Introduction to the Psychological Problems of Industry*, in *Mental Hygiene*, VIII (1924), 610.

as it turned out), but industrial psychological consultants were making effective use of the idea of dealing with immediate wants of workers so as to prevent either a major problem or any questioning of the situation. The worker was supposed to be at fault, not the system, and he was supposed to adjust to it. "The key-word of psychology today," asserted Mary Parker Follett, one of the best-known writers on industrial psychology, "is desire." She developed a system of solving labor problems by open and candid analysis of the wants and desires of the parties involved, during which process the reduction of the conflict to simple, specific elements took much of the fight out of both sides. A smart manager, she said, would study habits and reaction patterns and anticipate them, thereby bringing them under control.[100]

Perhaps it was appropriate that in the "business civilization" of the 1920's the concept of social control should have had experimental application in industry and that important techniques in the bureaucratic manipulation of people should have been pioneered by business. The idea of social control was an old one. Originally the concept had centered on the informal controls that society exercises over the individual, the mores or folkways. Out of the possibility of manipulating these informal controls rather than, say, laws or orders, came the idea of social management.[101]

After the war, many intellectuals sensed that old social patterns had disintegrated or were in the process of doing so. Many of these thinkers therefore eliminated the concept

[100] Benjamin Stolberg, "The Degradation of American Psychology," *Nation*, CXXXI (1930), 395–98. See, for example, E. E. Southard, "The Modern Specialist in Unrest: A Place for the Psychiatrist in Industry," *Mental Hygiene*, IV (1920), 550–63. M. P. Follett, "The Psychological Foundations: Constructive Conflict," in Henry C. Metcalf (ed.), *Scientific Foundations of Business Administration* (Baltimore, 1926), pp. 114–31.

[101] See, for example, Stow Persons, *American Minds: A History of Ideas* (New York, 1958), pp. 431–32.

of determining social patterns from among the major underpinnings of their world views; such thinkers instead began utilizing the new psychology of the inner self.[102] It was inevitable, then, that the new psychology, while replacing the older assumptions on which previous ideas of social control had been based, would contribute new approaches to the subject. The behaviorists, especially, explicitly emphasized the idea of predicting behavior in order to control it. Advocates of the new objective psychology were acutely aware of what one *avant-garde* writer discovered only in 1924: its "crying and significant social meanings." [103]

In the new psychology, writers did find aspects of the individual that might be used for purposes of social control. ". . . The disillusioned—not disheartened—liberalism of to-day," observed William Ernest Hocking, a Harvard University philosopher, in explaining contemporary interest in the problem of human nature, "turns itself heart and soul to psychological enquiry. It perceives that there is a human nature which invites the use of the same principle that Bacon applied to physical nature,—something having laws of its own which must be obediently examined before we can hope to control it." [104] It was in searching for means of control that the postwar thinkers found the irrational. In 1925, in his book describing *Means of Social Control,* sociologist F. E. Lumley expressed this fact in his conclusion that "control by the methods discussed has been accompanied by and charged with a very large amount of primitive or childish *feeling.*" And Lipsky, in his *Man the Puppet: The Art of Controlling Minds,* remarked on "the growing real-

[102] See, for example, Caroline F. Ware, *Greenwich Village, 1920–1930: A Comment on American Civilization in the Post-War Years* (Boston, 1935), p. 248.

[103] V. F. Calverton, "The Rise of Objective Psychology," *Psychological Review,* XXXI (1924), 425.

[104] *Human Nature and Its Remaking* (2d ed.; New Haven, 1923), p. 13.

ization" that knowing "the nature of the psychological dispositions . . . make[s] control possible." [105]

Just as the businessman found that direct appeals to basic human nature would not lead to control, so thoughtful Americans learned from the use of propaganda during the war the way in which the irrational in man can be manipulated. Walter Lippmann, in *Public Opinion*,[106] one of the most influential books of the decade, stated the common conclusion that predictability does not follow from knowing the basic drives and interests; what was needed for social control was the knowledge of how each individual will perceive a situation, how his conceptualization of reality as he knows it will in turn activate his drives and instincts, not in their primitive form but in their practical, habitual, and adult form. In business the market survey provided one model; in public life, public opinion polls. The test of validity was not hypothetical drives but actual behavior.

The new psychology contributed, therefore, in many ways to the preoccupation of the people of the 1920's with controlling other people. An outstanding example was H. A. Overstreet's famous book *Influencing Human Behavior*.[107] Here was a chapter, "The Appeal to Wants." Here was the idea of changing people by changing their habit systems. Here were explanations of behavior such as "rationalization." All of them were synthesized in a context of common sense to the end of enlarging the individual's feeling of power and control, on the one hand, and on the other hand, self-valuation and self-importance.

It is easy to show how the new psychology reflected and exemplified main currents in American society and culture in the 1920's: how self-centered, self-indulgent attitudes and an emphasis on men's desires laid the foundation for

[105] Frederick Elmore Lumley, *Means of Social Control* (New York, 1925), pp. 395–96; Lipsky, *Man the Puppet*, p. 262.

[106] New York, 1922.

[107] New York, 1925.

social control, how the search for the interior self led to attempts at external control of people.[108] At first used by business in the twenties, the new psychology emphasis on social control portended much for the 1930's.

The new psychology was involved in the expression of many phenomena and attitudes distinctive to the twenties. It was part and parcel of the change in manners and morals that F. Scott Fitzgerald and Frederick Lewis Allen portrayed so vividly. And the new psychology was also involved in trends of the decade that may eventually appear more significant than changing moral standards (such as, for example, the remarkable intellectual assault on the institution of motherhood) but which scholars have thus far hardly explored.[109] In most of these examples the role of the new psychology was no greater than that of other cultural forces, such as the popular discovery of primitive cultures through the work of such anthropologists as Margaret Mead. The new psychology was so involved in cultural changes of the 1920's as ultimately to raise the question whether its importance can be determined with any precision or even suggested meaningfully.

But important as it was as the mirror and index to an era, the new psychology provided, if not the tool for cultural change, at least the avenue of its expression. The new psychology suggested a meaningful way to work out in practice the relatively vague concepts of social control that had developed in the progressive period.

The new social control movement adopted from the health crusades of an earlier period the concept of improving the

[108] Lasch, *The New Radicalism*, p. 146, has come to a similar conclusion in a different context: "The study of the inner man could degenerate into a technique of manipulating him in accordance with your own designs"; and Lasch goes on to add, "it could degenerate indeed into a technique of totalitarian control."

[109] See, for example, Sievers, *Freud on Broadway*, pp. 76–79; Harvey O'Higgins and Edward H. Reede, *The American Mind in Action* (New York, 1924), pp. 20–25.

world not by social action but by a patient program of individual treatment of large numbers of people. As tuberculosis and syphilis were fought not primarily by general laws but by curing everyone who was sick, so the mental hygienists and other new psychologists wanted to change the social mass—one atom at a time. The change can be epitomized in the shift from general prohibition laws to the individual treatment of the alcoholic by a psychiatrist—or Alcoholics Anonymous.

More clearly than even the businessmen, the social workers showed the impact of the new psychology in their emphasis upon individual therapy and adjustment and its use as a melioristic device. Social workers had been a powerful and important element in the prewar progressive movement and in harmony with that movement had emphasized the role of environment in the lives of their clients. As a consequence, the social workers gave much attention to general social reform measures as well as to the dependent people with whom they worked directly. By the late twenties casework, under the influence of psychiatry, tended to abstract the client from his "environmental and cultural milieu" and to emphasize his internal attitudes and even his emotional life. The inner man, not the outer environment, was to be adjusted.[110] By offering the technique of conditioning, the behaviorists, too, furnished a concrete method whereby their aspirations for social control could be worked out in practice, case by case, person by person, without any troublesome recourse to general social reform.

The new psychology of the twenties, whether in the form of mental hygiene, psychiatric social work, or business personnel and welfare practices, provided the technique for

110 Roy Lubove, *The Professional Altruist: The Emergence of Social Work as a Career, 1880–1930* (Cambridge, Mass., 1965), chaps. ii, iii, iv. The professionalization process within social work was itself introspective in character, focusing on professional norms and the practitioner's adjustment to them.

modern bureaucratic society: [111] in addition to control through mass movements, advertising, the propaganda and voluntary actions typical of, say, World War I, now there was control through the bureaucratic society in which the inner need, the individual desire, was carefully manipulated and indulged, person by person, so as to prevent the childish, brutal, perverse, or savage in any man's hidden self from disrupting the predictability of civilization.[112]

The agencies of control in bureaucratic society were still the experts, as in the progressive period, but now their expertise was directed toward individuals rather than general problems. Floyd Dell, who typified the intellectuals of the early twentieth century, reflected the sentiment generated by the new psychology in suggesting that social salvation lay in the *deus ex clinica*, the psychiatric treatment of everyone.[113] More typical of the extravagant bureaucratic society to come was the team approach, the committee of experts, looking not for desirable social changes, but trying to help the individual in a world taken as given.

[111] Daniel R. Miller and Guy E. Swanson, *The Changing American Parent: A Study in the Detroit Area* (New York, 1958), especially Chapters II and VIII, provide the conception of the bureaucratic welfare society.

[112] *Ibid.*

[113] *Love in the Machine Age*, pp. 405–7. Schmalhausen, in *Why We Misbehave*, pp. 74–75, epitomized the impact of the new psychology when he observed that "psychologic corrective of economic doctrine is a first-rate contribution to our enlightenment."

Metropolis and Suburb:
The Changing American City

CHARLES N. GLAAB

THE facts of demography, presented in their customary statistical form, are not the kind of information likely to arouse public attention and controversy. Yet at each decennial census from the mid-nineteenth century on, commentators on the American social scene had noted with alarm the steady and seemingly inexorable urbanization of the country's population. To a nation whose traditions emphasized the value of the sturdy, independent farmer on his freehold, the urban-rural ratio in the 1920 census had particular symbolic importance: for the first time, the census reported, a majority of the people in the United States could be classified as urban, with 51.2 per cent of the population living in incorporated municipalities of 2,500 or more.

In a sense this finding only confirmed a long-standing reality. Nineteenth-century changes in technology, transportation, and communication had assured that the city would shape the character of American society. By 1920 the customs and the standards of the city had to a large extent already been imposed on the countryside. But this did not mean diminishment in the intensity of the anti-urban sentiments that had pervaded American culture. On

the contrary, they became even more vigorous, for the
"agrarian myth" was part of an ideology that had evolved
in defense of groups losing their economic power and social
status in society. And ideologies may be most effective
when they least reflect current reality.

During the decade of the 1920's the old city-country
polarity frequently influenced events—in the effort to re-
strict immigration, in the struggle over prohibition, in the
crusade for religious fundamentalism, and in the election
of 1928. Sometimes, the polarity now became that of small
town and large city, but this did not alter the argument.
People could still accept at face value the famous photo-
graph of Calvin Coolidge seated on a hay wagon with rake
in hand, his clothes spotless, while in the rear his assistants
stand by an automobile waiting to whisk him back to the
city. Writers of articles and stories in popular magazines
still employed the imagery of the soulless city. To find "real
values," to regain honesty, courage, and independence, one
had to flee the city. "I have had to do things, terrible
things, things no decent man should have done," says a
hero of a *Cosmopolitan* short story who finds peace in the
wilderness. "Thank God that's all behind me now. Out here
I can be a real person again." [1] On a higher level, twelve
southerners in their notable manifesto *I'll Take My Stand*,
published at the end of the decade, defended an idyllic
rural life that probably never existed. "Back to the land,"
a position popularized by Ralph Borsodi, who established
a subsistence homestead outside New York City in 1920
and preached the joys of the Thoreauvian way of life, became an organized movement that influenced federal re-
settlement policy with the coming of the depression. Its
advocates offered a classical Jeffersonian defense of the
farm against the city. "The farms have always produced

[1] R. B. Gray, "Tiger, Tiger," quoted in an unpublished paper by
Lionel Johnson, "Images of Urbanity: City People in the Popular
Literature of the Twenties."

our great leaders in finance, industry and statesmanship," Robert A. Green testified before a House committee. "The vast population must depart from the congested industrial centers and cities and once again become self-sustaining on our vast and fertile farms, pasture, and prairie lands. Herein lies the real hope for the bright destiny of America." [2]

The traditional view of country and city, which persisted during the 1920's, was that they represented distinct and opposed environments. In the nineteenth century, and earlier of course, there was a measure of truth in the view, particularly in a physical sense. Despite the presence of suburbs, which might date back to early in the century, cities were reasonably compact; their limits were certain; a few miles journey from the center of any downtown brought one to the rural countryside. But in the period falling roughly between World War I and the early 1930's, this situation was drastically altered. Cities began to spread out; suburbs multiplied; small towns were joined to larger cities by bands of residential development; the metropolis extended its influence over vast adjacent areas that might vary in population density or in land use but that often were not really distinguishable as either country or city.

The emergence of the sprawling super-city, with its new patterns of urbanization, added new dimensions to the traditional urban problems. Although everyday debate might still center on a conflict between city and country, many thinkers and reformers in the 1920's began to develop new conceptions of the social environment that emphasized the community, the neighborhood, and the region. What was needed, they suggested, was not to solve just a single urban problem but rather to reorder a whole environment that

---

[2] *I'll Take My Stand: The South and the Agrarian Tradition* (Harper Torchbooks Edition, New York, 1962). See particularly Andrew Nelson Lytle, "The Hind Tit," pp. 201–45; Ralph Borsodi, *Flight from the City* (New York, 1933); Green is quoted in Paul K. Conkin, *Tomorrow A New World: The New Deal Community Program* (Ithaca, N.Y., 1959), p. 33.

often transcended city and country. In the 1880's the rapidly growing cities had seemed a major threat to American civilization. In the 1920's many saw the huge metropolis that had begun to obliterate all the old distinctions between city and country as the same kind of danger. In that group of trenchant essays on American life, *Civilization in the United States: An Inquiry by Thirty Americans,* Lewis Mumford, who became one of the better-known students of the city during the decade, sounded a theme that informed much of the analysis of urban society during the period. "Our metropolitan civilization is not a success," he wrote. "It is a different kind of wilderness from that which we have been deflowered—but the feral rather than the humane quality is dominant; it is still a wilderness. The cities of America must learn to remould our mechanical and financial regime; for if metropolitanism continues they are probably destined to fall by its weight." [3]

A wealth of statistical material documents the dramatic growth of the metropolitan super-city, which many observers found to be a key force shaping American civilization in the 1920's.[4] The large American cities substantially increased in population during the decade—New York by 23.3 per cent from 5,620,048 to 6,930,446; Chicago by 25 per cent from 2,701,705 to 3,376,438; Detroit by 57.4 per cent from 996,321 to 1,568,662; Los Angeles by 114.7 per cent

[3] Lewis Mumford, "The City," in Harold E. Stearns (ed.), *Civilization in the United States: An Inquiry by Thirty Americans* (New York, 1922), pp. 19–20.

[4] For statistical material and demographic analysis of this development, see *15th Census of the U.S.—Metropolitan Districts* (Washington, D.C., 1932); W. S. Thompson, *The Growth of Metropolitan Districts in the United States: 1900–1940* (Washington, D.C., 1947); Amos H. Hawley, *The Changing Shape of Metropolitan America: Deconcentration Since 1920* (Glencoe, Ill., 1956); Donald J. Bogue, *Population Growth in Standard Metropolitan Areas, 1900–1950* (Washington, D.C., 1953); Donald J. Bogue, *The Population of the United States* (Glencoe, Ill., 1959). A basic work on the 1920's is R. D. McKenzie, *The Metropolitan Community* (New York, 1933).

from 576,673 to 1,238,048. Even more significant was the population growth in areas near large cities. As early as 1880 the federal census had noted the metropolitan region that had begun to form around New York City. In 1910 the census bureau, noting the inadequacy of the simple definition of "urban" based on the classification of people in municipalities of a certain size, applied the concept generally and presented data on central cities and their contiguous related areas for twenty-five metropolitan districts. Whether one employs this older device or the more refined device of the standard metropolitan area, which was introduced in 1950 and applied to past censuses, the conclusions that emerge from an examination of population change are comparable. First, there was a great increase in the size of the larger metropolitan areas. Nearly 71 per cent of the total population growth in the period from 1920 to 1930 occurred in the metropolitan districts, and much of this occurred in the larger ones. The New York–Northeastern New Jersey metropolitan district, for example, had a population growth greater than the gain in 28 states and the Chicago district more than the gain in 21 states.

TABLE 1

GROWTH OF METROPOLITAN DISTRICTS, 1900–1940

YEAR	NUMBER OF DISTRICTS	TOTAL U.S. POPULATION IN MILLIONS	TOTAL POPULATION OF DISTRICTS IN MILLIONS	PERCENTAGE OF U.S. POPULATION IN DISTRICTS	PERCENTAGE OF U.S. POPULATION INCREASE IN DISTRICTS
1900	44	76	19	25.5	....
1910	44	92	26	28.3	41.9
1920	58	106	36	34.0	55.5
1930	97	123	55	44.6	70.8
1940	140	132	63	47.8	53.0

Second, after 1920 the outlying areas of metropolitan regions (as demonstrated in the statistics on "metropolitan rings" outside the central cities) grew much faster than the central cities themselves.

TABLE 2

GROWTH OF STANDARD METROPOLITAN AREAS, 1900–1940

YEAR	NUMBER	POPULATION IN DISTRICTS IN MILLIONS	RATE OF GROWTH DURING PRECEDING DECADE		
			SMA Total	Central Cities	Rings
1900	52	24.1	....	....	....
1910	71	34.5	32.6	35.3	27.6
1920	94	46.1	25.2	26.7	22.4
1930	115	61.0	27.0	23.3	34.2
1940	125	67.1	8.3	5.1	13.8

The decade from 1920 to 1930 saw the complete emergence of the modern residential suburb, and this was reflected in spectacular growth rates for some of the better-known suburbs: Beverly Hills, 2485.0 per cent, Glendale, 363.5, Inglewood, 492.8, Huntington Park, 444.9 (suburbs of Los Angeles) ; Cleveland Heights, 234.4, Shaker Heights, 1000.4; Garfield Heights, 511.3 (suburbs of Cleveland); Grosse Pointe Park, 724.6, Ferndale, 689.9 (suburbs of Detroit); Webster Groves, 74.0, Maplewood, 70.3, Richmond Heights, 328.3 (suburbs of St. Louis) ; Elmwood Park, 716.7, Oak Park, 60.5, Park Ridge, 207.9 (suburbs of Chicago). Numerous new towns and villages appeared around large cities, as demonstrated in the incorporation statistics for the decade. Of the 38 new incorporations in Illinois, 26 were located within the metropolitan regions of Chicago or St. Louis; of the 33 in Michigan, 22 were suburbs of Detroit; and of

Ohio's 55 incorporations, 29 were near Cleveland. Cities in the 2,500–10,000 bracket showed a rapid growth rate for the period, chiefly because so many of them were located on the fringes of metropolitan areas.[5]

Many of the specialized functions that had been centered within the city were also suburbanized in the decade of the 1920's. In 1919, for example, 11 central cities in the 40 largest manufacturing counties had accounted for 85 per cent of the nation's manufacturing workers; by 1937 this share had fallen to just under 60 per cent. The number of wage earners in the eleven central cities decreased during the period from 2,045,789 to 1,808,692, while in the outlying areas the number increased from 365,403 to 1,218,465. The bulk of the increase occurred during the period from 1919 to 1929, when most new factory construction took place outside of large cities. The growth of industrial suburbs was an important aspect of suburbanization during the 1920's. Similarly, many of the commercial functions of the nineteenth-century city showed a marked tendency to deconcentration during the period.[6]

A number of influences contributed to the decentralization of cities. Cheap electric power, which could now be transmitted over considerable distances, freed manufacturing from centralized steam power. Improvements in communication, particularly the telephone, permitted information to be transmitted nearly instantly over great distances. Rapid fixed transportation systems contributed to the greater mobility of labor. But the most important development stimulating rapid suburbanization in the 1920's was, of course, the mass use of the automobile. At the turn of the century the automobile was still only a toy of the rich,

[5] McKenzie, *The Metropolitan Community*, pp. 183, 71.
[6] Harold McLean Lewis, *Planning the Modern City* (New York, 1949), p. 91; Harlan Paul Douglass, *The Suburban Trend* (New York, 1925), pp. 87–89.

with only 8,000 motor vehicles registered in 1900. By 1910 the number had grown to 468,500; in 1915, to 2,490,932. Then came the tremendous postwar expansion of the industry: motor vehicle registration jumped from 9,239,161 in 1920 to 19,940,724 in 1925 to 26,531,999 in 1930.[7] Enough automobiles were in use to put the entire population of the United States on the road at one time.

In the first two decades of the century, cities had spread out along the lines of interurban railroads, and the suburbanized sections of the metropolis resembled thin tentacles extending from the central city in radial fashion. Highways, particularly in older and larger cities like Chicago and New York, first tended to follow the established railroad lines. The new residential and industrial suburbs made possible by the automobile became part of the older pattern of growth. Gradually, however, as road-building greatly expanded during the decade, the interstices of the metropolitan areas began to be filled in. New cities like Los Angeles, whose metropolitan district had grown to 2,318,526 by 1930, lacked railway systems and spread out along streets and highways that opened new routes of travel. As a consequence, cities that were a product of the motor age did not develop the highly specialized, clearly defined central business districts characteristic of older cities. The transportation systems of older cities, on the other hand, still tended, even after the automobile came into general use, to funnel traffic into the center, greatly intensifying the problem of congestion.[8]

[7] *Historical Statistics of the United States 1789–1945* (Washington, D.C., 1949), p. 223.

[8] For discussion of the influence of transportation on metropolitan patterns, see Homer Hoyt, "The Influence of Highways and Transportation on the Structure and Growth of Cities and Urban Land Values," in Jean Labatut and Wheaton J. Lane (eds.), *Highways in Our National Life: A Symposium* (Princeton, N.J., 1950), pp. 201–6; Leo F. Schnore, "Metropolitan Growth and Decentralization," *American Journal of Sociology*, LXII (1957), 171–80.

During the latter part of the 1920's, engineers perfected, and governments adopted, the various devices that were part of a high-speed system of highway transportation— the grade separation of highway from city street, the traffic circle, and the divided dual highway. These techniques, along with new bridges such as the George Washington in New York and the Camden-Philadelphia, and an innovation such as the Holland Tunnel under the Hudson, permitted easier movement of automobile traffic throughout the huge, sprawling metropolitan region. By the end of the decade, however, the rush-hour, weekend, and holiday traffic jam had become all too familiar to many city dwellers.[9] The institution during the 1920's of comprehensive urban traffic systems involved a high degree of governmental control and planning; this, and many of the actions of municipalities, runs counter to the established conception of the laissez-faire character of public policy during the period.

The automobile, in addition to changing the spatial pattern and organization of established cities, also added a new dimension to one of the oldest economic activities associated with urbanization—the promotion of new cities and urban real-estate speculation. The celebrated Florida land boom of mid-decade was tied to the automobile. Tourists from the northeastern seaboard, by driving south for only a few days, could escape winter temporarily. During the early twenties people flocked to Florida in ever increasing numbers. Hundreds of promoters and salesmen went to work selling lots—usually on option through a "binder"— and advertising new town sites. Much of the boom went on in Miami, which grew from a population of 30,000 in

---

[9] Spencer Miller, Jr., "History of the Modern Highway in the United States," in Labatut and Lane, *Highways in Our National Life*, pp. 106–7. For contemporary accounts of traffic problems, see "Los Angeles and Its Motorjam," *Literary Digest*, LXXXI (1924), 68–71; "Detroit's Struggle with the Traffic Problem," *American City*, XXX (1924), 612–15.

1920 to 75,000 by 1925. But, as on so many past urban frontiers opened by transportation, fabulous claims were advanced for fabulous new cities—Silver Heights, Coral Gables, Picture Bay, Montezuma Manors, Sea Cove Crest, and Biscayne Bay. The number of lots platted in Florida during the boom, according to some estimates, reached 20 million, which with a little overcrowding would have been sufficient to house the entire population of the United States. Large profits were sometimes realized in series of frenzied property transactions. Before the boom a New Yorker bought a stretch of land in West Palm Beach at a low figure and sold it for $800,000 in 1923. The tract was then turned into city lots that sold for one and a half million dollars; by 1925 the tract was evaluated at four million dollars. One Carl Fisher bought a tract in Miami Beach for $8,000,000, paying $3,000,000 down. Two weeks later he had sold it for $11,000,000, collecting a down payment of $4,000,000. The boom continued through 1925; early in 1926 it began to fall off slightly as fewer people appeared in Florida for the winter. A severe hurricane struck the state on September 18, 1926, turned many of the shoddily constructed developments to ruins, ended the boom, and wiped out virtually all the ambitious speculators. Although in the long run a good share of the land involved in the boom was utilized as urban property, as late as ten years afterward the bulk of the lots were weed-grown or under water.[10]

The Florida land boom is often considered another bizarre episode of a decade of excess. Yet it was part of a pattern of overdevelopment of land for urban purposes encouraged by

[10] For a colorful account of the Florida land boom, see Frederick Lewis Allen, *Only Yesterday* (Bantam Edition, New York, 1959), pp. 191–205. A basic article is Homer Vanderblue, "The Florida Land Boom," *Journal of Land and Public Utility Economics*, III (1927), 113–31. See also Eugene Rachlis and John E. Marqusee, *The Land Lords* (New York, 1963), pp. 87–130.

the use of the automobile. Portions of Los Angeles County experienced subdivision development similar to Florida; 75 per cent of the total platted area of Burbank, California, for example, was vacant in the early 1930's. In 1929, 175,000 of Cleveland's 375,000 lots were empty; over 65 per cent of the lot area in Duluth, 50 per cent in Portland, Maine, 30 per cent in El Paso was unused in the early 1930's. Similar premature subdivisions occurred in the metropolitan area of New York. The announcement of plans for the George Washington Bridge set off a boom in Bergen County, New Jersey, characterized by many of the features of the Florida boom. A large section of farm land was platted and divided by paper streets; lots were sold at auction, through high-pressure mail campaigns, and by newspapers as part of their subscription efforts. But little of the area was actually developed. During the 1920's lots sufficient for all the inhabitants of the five boroughs of New York were platted on Long Island. By late in the decade, nearly half these lots had become county property owing to unpaid taxes. The chaotic development of subdivisions in the 1920's greatly complicated the problems of urban leaders in trying to provide municipal services over vast thinly settled areas and in attempting to establish some degree of social order on the rapidly burgeoning American metropolises.[11]

In addition to leading to vast, excessive subdivision development, the urban land boom of the 1920's radically inflated property values in the heart of cities. Particularly where automobile routes tended to follow older fixed forms of urban transportation—which had been built in a fashion to funnel people to central points in the city—considerable expansion took place in the central business districts. Ex-

[11] *Urban Planning and Land Policies: Volume II of the Supplementary Report of the Urbanism Committee to the National Resources Committee* (Washington, D.C., 1939), pp. 217–19.

pansion contributed to an optimism that caused property values to rise. In 1920 the total value of land in American cities of over 30,000 population—only about one-fifth of one per cent of all the land in the United States—was estimated at $25 billion; by 1926 this figure had doubled to $50 billion. During the same period the value of American farm land dropped from 55 to 37 billion dollars, a figure 33 per cent less than the value of land in cities above 30,000. Real estate on Manhattan Island was assessed at over five billion dollars in 1930, which was more than the value of the farm land in 23 states in 1925. The corner of State and Madison in the heart of Chicago's Loop was leased during the decade at a rate of $50,000 a front foot, a figure equivalent to $21,780,000 an acre. One small holding at 1 Wall Street in New York City sold for $100,000 a front foot, a rate of nearly $44,000,000 an acre.[12]

To some extent, all cities experienced a similar inflation of land values, but this did not occur in uniform fashion through downtown districts. In Milwaukee, for example, the land occupied by the taller buildings of the city ranging from six to twenty-four stories increased in valuation by 80 per cent between 1920 and 1930 and the buildings themselves by 95 per cent. Yet the assessed value of the rest of the land in the downtown district actually decreased by 30 per cent while the assessed value of buildings increased only slightly. In general, when the upward expansion of business districts in cities supplied the need for additional commercial space, the commercial core of the city tended to shrink away from neighboring blighted areas, contributing to additional slums and blight. This might cause some drop in speculative land values, as demonstrated in the Milwaukee example, but land values were still too high to permit the sites to be used for any new construction besides

---

[12] John D. Hicks, *Republican Ascendancy, 1921–1933* (Harper Torchbook Edition, 1963), p. 117; Hoyt, "The Influence of Highways," in Labatut and Lane, *Highways in Our National Life*, p. 204.

commercial buildings and expensive apartments. Since only a limited amount of space was needed for these purposes, many sections of the downtown remained blighted, and the process of decay continued.[13]

The deconcentration permitted by the automobile did have the desirable effect of relieving population congestion in the center of cities, a long-standing urban problem that had developed in some eastern cities early in the nineteenth century. Older parts of St. Louis along the river, for example, lost 50,000 people between 1910 and 1930, resulting in the lowering of densities throughout the city to below 80 persons per acre, but the remaining residential areas in the interior of the city had by the early 1930's turned into slums.[14] Suburbanization in the 1920's extended the opportunity for individual home ownership and permitted a number of people to live in better surroundings, but it was part of a process of changing urban development that led to deterioration and decay of the heart of cities. Many of the familiar problems of today's cities had their origin in this decade of urban growth tied to the use of the automobile.

The general inflation of city land values and the expanding prosperity of many sections of the economy during the 1920's stimulated the great era of skyscraper-building in American cities. The Woolworth Building of New York, completed in 1913, set the style. Chicago's group of towers along the Chicago River built in the early years of the decade differed little from the new "Woolworth Gothic" buildings that sprang up in New York. Cleveland, Pittsburgh, San Francisco, and Kansas City developed the jagged skylines distinctively characteristic of the twentieth-century American city. By 1929 American cities had 377 skyscrapers of more than 20 stories in height, largely built

13 *Urban Planning and Land Policies*, pp. 269–70.
14 *Ibid.*, p. 222.

without concern for the character of the surrounding urban
space and without concern for the patterns of traffic created
by the buildings. Even on the cities of the plains the skyscraper was as much demanded as on the tight land plots
of lower Manhattan Island. "A 60-story tower in New
York evokes a 70-story tower in Chicago," wrote the architect Hugh Ferriss in 1929. "What is more serious, a 60-
story tower in New York evokes a 70-story tower directly
across the street. The skyscraper is said to be America's
premier architectual contribution to date, popular fancy
pictures . . . 70-story skyscrapers side by side for miles." [15]
Many of the nation's tallest buildings were begun in 1928
and 1929 and only completed after the depression. The
most famous skyscraper of all, the Empire State Building
was finished in 1930 and for many years was a white ele-
phant in a city that during the depression had more than
enough office space. Although architects criticized the skyscraper for its lack of esthetic distinction and planners
criticized it for its contribution to grave traffic congestion,
it was through the jagged towering skylines of great cities
that many observers perceived the character of the new
urban civilization. The German director Fritz Lang was inspired to make his classic motion picture "Metropolis," with
its striking vision of the urban future, after a visit to Manhattan in the mid-1920's. The French historian Bernard
Faÿ, who visited New York late in the decade, echoed the
sentiments of many travelers to the city in finding the mass
of skyscrapers an appropriate symbol of a new order:

> The very thing which I admire most in New York is its adapta-
> tion to the continent. In this sense, its architecture is intellectually
> reasonable, logical, and beautiful. Skyscrapers are the dwellings

[15] Hugh Ferriss, *The Metropolis of Tomorrow* (New York, 1929),
p. 62. For a general account of the architecture of the period, see
John Burchard and Albert Bush-Brown, *The Architecture of America:
A Social and Cultural History* (Boston, 1961), pp. 299–386.

of the supertrusts; they are Eiffel Tower cathedrals which shelter Mr. Rockefeller, the Emperor of Petroleum, or Mr. Morgan, the Czar of Gold. . . . Some say that New York crushes them—and not without reason; the individual is overwhelmed by these great buildings. This is not an architecture for men, like the Parthenon or the châteaux of the Loire and Versailles. It is an architecture for human masses. Such buildings do not shelter or isolate men as do those of Europe. They gather and shuffle them. Often more than five thousand persons are united under one roof. . . . The New York skyscrapers are the most striking manifestation of the triumph of numbers. One cannot understand or like them without first having tasted and enjoyed the thrill of counting or adding up enormous totals and of living in a gigantic, compact, and brilliant world.[16]

During the 1920's American cities went upward and outward. Decentralization altered the pattern of urban functions within cities. Moreover, the character of urban population and its distribution throughout the areas of the city also changed. The decade of 1900–1910 was the last in which foreign immigration contributed substantially to the growth of American cities. In 1907, the high year for the decade, 1,285,349 immigrants had arrived in the United States. With the outbreak of war in Europe, the number fell to 326,700 in 1915 and reached a low point of 110,618 in 1919, with European immigration constituting less than 25,000 of the total. Immigration revived in the early 1920's reaching 805,228 in 1921, but the legislation establishing a quota system passed in that year and revised in 1924 reduced annual immigration to around 300,000 in the years from 1925 to 1929. There are no statistics indicating exactly what proportion of immigrants settled in cities, but it is clear that from at least 1870 on the foreign-born had tended to concentrate in larger cities. As a result, by 1920,

---

[16] Quoted in Bayrd Still, *Mirror for Gotham: New York As Seen by Contemporaries from Dutch Days to the Present* (New York, 1956), pp. 298–99.

31.5 per cent of the total population in cities over one million and 23.3 per cent of the population in cities between one-half and one million was foreign-born. By contrast, only 11.3 per cent of the population in cities from 2,500 to 10,000 and only 6.5 per cent of the total rural population was foreign-born.[17]

With immigration from abroad sharply restricted, cities in the 1920's achieved their large growth in population through internal migration, since city-dwellers did not reproduce at replacement levels until the period after 1940. One of the more significant aspects of this rural-urban migration was the movement of the southern Negro to the cities of the East and Midwest. From 1820 to 1910 the urbanization of the white population of the United States had always been at a more rapid rate than that of the Negro. Owing largely to the demand for labor in northern cities during World War I, this trend was reversed. During the 1910–20 decade the percentage of native white population classified as urban increased by 6 while that of Negroes increased by 6.7. The trend was intensified during the next decade, with the percentage of native white population classified as urban increasing by 4.9 while that of Negroes increased by 9.7.[18]

This changing population pattern modified the social character of larger cities. The older ethnic colonies in cities had always contained a fairly high proportion of population not of the predominant group. In addition, these colonies had been relatively impermanent. As members of an ethnic group achieved greater economic and social status, they moved throughout the city, and some more recently arrived immigrant group would begin to occupy the area. The Negro colonies in northern cities, which grew rapidly in the 1920's,

[17] *Historical Statistics of the United States, 1789–1945,* p. 33; Bogue, *The Population of the United States,* p. 139.

[18] Bogue, *The Population of the United States,* pp. 126–27.

were much more homogeneous, and, as time proved, much more permanent. Wards in New York and Chicago had percentages of Negro population that approached 95 by 1930. The Negro ghetto created a new kind of urban problem. Racial segregation drastically limited the possibility of upward mobility by individual or group. The Negro subcities, with populations of over 225,000 in Chicago and New York by 1930, were areas where few could benefit from the economic and cultural advantages of the city but where all the long-standing urban problems of crime, poverty, and disease existed in aggravated form.[19]

The segregation of the Negro reflected a general tendency to increased economic and cultural segregation in the emerging metropolitan cities. During the decade the wealthier and more powerful members of the community continued their movement to the outer zones of the city and to the new suburban regions. A study of over 2,000 substantial Detroit families, for example, demonstrated a striking deconcentration of the city's elite. In 1910 nearly 52 per cent of this group lived within a three-mile radius of the main business center of Detroit, and only 9.7 per cent outside the municipal boundaries. By 1930 these percentages were nearly reversed with only 7.5 per cent of the substantial families near the business district and 50 per cent in suburban areas. Numerous studies of economic zones within cities and of spatial zones away from the center during the 1920's demonstrated clearly the cultural advantages and the greater stability of the outer regions of metropolitan centers. Crime, the need for public welfare, and infant mortality decreased sharply in the outer areas and usually in direct proportion to the distance of the area from the center of the city.[20] Traditionally the city had been resented because its extremes of wealth and poverty seemed a denial

---

[19] McKenzie, *The Metropolitan Community*, p. 242.
[20] *Ibid.*, pp. 184–86, 248.

of American equalitarian beliefs. In the metropolis of the 1920's these inequalities appeared more obvious, more rigidly confined, and more permanent.

From the middle of the nineteenth century, American reformers had been concerned with problems that had special urban dimensions—health, poverty, and the slum. These classic urban problems did not disappear in the supercities of the twentieth century. Housing the poor of the cities, for example, continued to be one of the principal concerns of urban reformers during the decade. But the complexity of the new metropolitan communities forced those concerned with American cities to try also to find ways of reordering the whole urban environment. Proposals for new kinds of cities and for comprehensive plans that encompassed whole urban regions now became part of the discussion of the future of American cities. During the 1920's most of the conceptions that became a permanent part of plans for cities were formulated and debated. With the coming of the depression, these conceptions were to have a significant effect on public policy toward urban life.

The inspiration for many of the new plans for cities, as was frequently the case with urban innovation in the United States, came from Europe. Particularly influential was the "garden city" idea of Ebenezer Howard, a London court reporter and reformer. In 1898 Howard had proposed a new kind of community that would combine the best features of town and country. The size of the garden city would be limited to 30,000 people. A permanent greenbelt would surround it, and enough industry would be developed in carefully specified areas to ensure the community's self-sufficiency. The land on which the city was built would be owned by the community as a whole and administered by a public authority. All leases would contain specific and detailed building requirements, and areas of greenery would be preserved throughout the city. Howard argued that the rising land values occasioned by a growing city would pro-

duce rents high enough to pay for municipal services. Under
the system of public control, the profits of growth would
go to the community rather than to the speculator, since
only limited dividends could be paid to the original investors
in a garden city project. The system would also ensure
that there would be no temptation to modify land use or to
increase the planned density of the city. Howard foresaw
garden cities being founded throughout England, providing
a way of checking the continued growth of the huge, congested industrial cities. A number of nineteenth-century
American planners, led by Frederick Law Olmsted, the de-
signer of Central Park in New York, had advanced proposals for planned communities that would preserve a
natural setting in the fashion of the garden city. But
Howard's plan went much further: it provided for a whole
new city, not just a residential suburb, and introduced a
radical conception of land ownership. The successful establishment of the first garden city of Letchworth, England,
begun in 1903, led to a world-wide garden city movement;
interest was reinforced by the start of a second community
called Welwyn in 1919. Letchworth and Welwyn were the
only two cities built in accord with Howard's over-all plan,
but his ideas were adopted by a number of American planners and architects. Although they seldom embodied any
significant aspects of Howard's plan, "garden villages,"
"garden suburbs," and "garden homes" became the fashion
of the day in the 1920's. In addition, there were serious
efforts to incorporate elements of his proposal into a number of private efforts in community development. Later,
the garden city was to inspire the federal government's
greenbelt-town experiments in the 1930's.[21]

21 Howard's proposal is contained in Ebenezer Howard, *Garden
Cities of To-morrow* (London, 1945). For an excellent, brief dis-
cussion of the garden city in America, see Conkin, *Tomorrow a New
World*, pp. 59–72. For a critical view of the influence of the garden
city concept, see Jane Jacobs, *The Death and Life of Great Cities*
(Vintage Edition, New York, 1963), pp. 17–21.

The French architect Le Corbusier was responsible for an influential plan to bring the garden city to the metropolis and accommodate it to the automobile and the skyscraper. His Radiant City, first suggested in 1920, would be composed of a group of 700-foot-high towers surrounded by 250 to 300 yards of park, a plan that would permit housing 1,200 people to an acre and yet leave 95 per cent of the ground open so that the "whole city is a Park." Le Corbusier's design, tied to the concept of the huge superblock, included an elaborate system of great arterial roads for automobiles that were separated from pedestrian routes. By the close of the decade his ideas had begun to influence the writings of American architects and planners concerned with finding new approaches to the building of cities.[22]

Utopian proposals for cities that required drastic reconstruction by government and new forms of property ownership could not be expected to make rapid headway in a nation strongly committed to traditions of individual enterprise. Yet the planning and zoning movement, which flourished in the 1920's, did reflect to a limited extent the same kind of concern with the whole environment of metropolis that had motivated Howard and Le Corbusier. In part, the vogue for planning in the United States had its origins in the City Beautiful movement of the turn of the century. The effort to beautify the centers of cities through the construction of new public buildings and civic centers that had been inspired by the Chicago Columbian Exposition of 1893 produced comprehensive advisory plans for city redevelopment such as the one Daniel Burnham proposed for Chicago in 1909. The attention paid to these proposals led municipalities to establish planning commissions and

[22] Le Corbusier (Charles E. Jeanneret-Gris), *The City of Tomorrow and Its Planning* (New York, 1929), pp. 164–78; Burchard and Bush-Brown, *The Architecture of America*, pp. 356–57.

planning boards with advisory powers. Before 1914 there were seventeen such agencies. Between 1914 and 1922, 207 new agencies were established, and another 161 were added from 1923 to 1926. Toward the end of the decade the power of planning commissions tended to be increased, and their number had grown upwards of 735 by 1930.[23]

Closely related to the establishment of planning commissions was the passage of zoning regulations, for zoning was ordinarily a part of plans for city redevelopment and growth. The techniques of zoning had initially been applied in German cities beginning in 1900, but zoning in the United States was largely a development of the postwar period. Before 1916 only five American cities had zoning regulations, but New York's adoption in that year of a zoning law for the entire city popularized the approach. Between 1916 and 1920 twenty-five cities passed zoning laws, and by 1930 the number of zoned cities had risen to 981. After several years of litigation, the United States Supreme Court finally upheld this type of governmental regulation in 1926. The earliest zoning ordinances in the United States were designed mainly to keep residential areas free from business and industry and only regulated land use in various districts of the city. The laws passed after 1925 tended to be more comprehensive and regulated not only land use but the height and bulk of buildings as well. A study in 1929 indicated that of the 754 municipalities with zoning, 475 had comprehensive ordinances controlling the use, height, and area of buildings. Measures requiring setbacks on the upper portions of taller buildings contributed to the uniformity of the tower skyscrapers of

[23] McKenzie, *The Metropolitan Community*, pp. 294–99. For the relationship of the planning movement of the 1920's to earlier planning traditions, see John W. Reps, *The Making of Urban America: A History of City Planning in the United States* (Princeton, N. J., 1965), pp. 497–525.

the 1920's, and in general led to more consistent building styles in American cities.[24]

Although zoning and planning were advocated by urban reformers who were genuinely concerned with trying to make cities better places in which to live, the movement to some extent merely intensified certain problems of the metropolis. Building requirements often contributed to the segregation of groups within the city on the basis of wealth. Many residential suburbs, for example, were kept as enclaves of wealth through rigorous zoning requirements. Until they encountered court difficulties, early zoning measures in southern cities were rather frankly aimed at maintaining the segregation of Negroes. It has been argued that zoning requirements represented an effort by older inhabitants of cities to maintain control of the downtowns they were abandoning. In this way they protected their investments at the same time they kept newcomers to the city confined.[25]

Business interests often supported planning and zoning not out of an altruistic concern to improve the quality of urban life, but rather because they recognized that these programs would make cities economically more efficient and easier places in which to do business. Powerful support for the basic New York zoning law of 1916 came from Fifth Avenue merchants, who were distressed by the encroachment of garment industry plants into their shopping district. The reports that preceded the law appealed to this

[24] McKenzie, *The Metropolitan Community*, pp. 299–301; Coleman Woodbury, "Some Suggested Changes in the Control of Urban Development," *Journal of Land and Public Utility Economics*, V (1929), 249. For the German background of zoning, see Roy Lubove, *The Progressives and the Slums: Tenement House Reform in New York City, 1890–1917* (Pittsburgh, 1962), pp. 229–30.

[25] Richard C. Wade, "The City in History—Some American Perspectives," in Werner Z. Hirsch (ed.), *Urban Life and Form* (New York, 1963), p. 74; "The Social Aspects of Zoning," *Survey*, XLVIII (1922), 418; Robert A. Walker, *The Planning Function in Urban Government* (2d ed., Chicago, 1950), pp. 85–89.

kind of sentiment. "The natural result of a poor utilization of its land areas by a city is high rents for occupiers and low profits for investors," stated the New York Committee on Building Heights in 1913. "It may seem paradoxical to hold that a policy of building restriction tends to a fuller utilization of land than a policy of no restriction; but such is undoubtedly the case. The reason lies in the greater safety and security to investment secured by definite restrictions." [26]

The report on the St. Louis city plan of 1918 reflected the dual objectives that underlay the planning and zoning movement. City plans, the report argued, were tied to the goals of American democracy; they provided a way of advancing "human contentment and human growth" through scientific experiment and through applying the techniques of modern social science to the problems of the metropolis. Yet planning could also be a means to promote industrial and commercial prosperity.

> Only by forethought can the city hope to take advantage of vast commercial opportunities which the new era is to bring forth. The Plan Commission aims to take immediate and effective steps to relieve the Mississippi River, the city's greatest natural resource from bankruptcy. . . . All modern men who are convinced of the hopelessness of future individual effort, know that the time has come, if the city is to prosper, to replace individual effort by community forehandedness. The development of the terminal system and the construction of new bridges logically follow; while, unless the city is provided with adequate sewers, water-supply and scientific garbage disposal, the money for all industrial improvements will have been spent in vain.[27]

[26] Quoted in Harold M. Lewis, *Planning the Modern City* (New York, 1949), p. 260. For the background to the New York zoning law, see Lubove, *The Progressives and the Slums*, pp. 238–45.

[27] Introduction to *St. Louis After the War* reprinted in "The Supreme Question Facing Our City and Country To-day," *American City*, XX (1919), 1–2.

Other extensions of the "City Efficient" idea during the 1920's—the visiting teacher movement, mental hygiene clinics, and the expansion of parks and playgrounds—were supported as measures that would advance economic prosperity of the city. For example, business leaders endorsed the building of additional parks and playgrounds with the argument that they would increase the efficiency of factory workers. A spokesman who found that parks were "wisely industrial" and "wisely economic" as well as "wisely human" argued also that they would "enhance the desirability of nearby land, thus yielding more taxes to the municipality and boosting the sales value of the property to the owner." [28]

As a result of the general support of measures designed to make the complex urban environment more efficient, the supposedly laissez faire period of the 1920's witnessed a considerable extension of the activities of municipal governments not only in such new fields as traffic control and zoning but also in relation to the older, established urban services. A census study of municipal spending in cities of various size groups from 1915 to 1929 showed a general per capita increase in expenditures (measured in 1915 dollars) that varied from 55 per cent in cities of 50,000–99,999 to 30 per cent in cities of 300,000–499,999. Much of this increase went to support expanded municipal services in public health, education, and recreation. A survey of governmental activities in 34 representative cities during the above period demonstrated wide adoption of a variety of specialized new services ranging from the provision of public health nurses and children's clinics to community centers and vocational guidance. In accord with the efficiency ideal, numerous cities introduced such measures as

[28] William Butterworth, "Community Recreation—a Wisely Human, Wisely Industrial, Wisely Economic Thing," *American City*, XXXIX (1928), 82.

centralized purchasing, public improvement planning, and executive budgets. Expenditures for the fundamental urban functions—police, fire, and water—also increased at more rapid rate than population growth.[29]

One of the most noted extensions of government authority in the 1920's—the Port of New York Authority—represented an effort to cope with metropolitan problems by establishing agencies that cut across the traditional units of government. In 1917, in response to a struggle between New York and New Jersey interests over railroad freight rates to various parts of the Port of New York, the U.S. Interstate Commerce Commission denied New Jersey's claim for a favorable rate differential and recognized the significance of the growing metropolitan region. The Commission observed that "historically, geographically, and commercially New York and the industrial district in the northeastern part of the state of New Jersey constitute a single community." [30] This decision led eventually to the creation in 1921 of a permanent interstate agency responsible for the administration of the Port.

Regional planning commissions established in the 1920's for areas in and around Boston, New York, Chicago, Los Angeles, Toledo, and other places reflected a similar awareness of the developing metropolitan character of American society. These commissions were primarily advisory and often dealt only with one or two specialized problems. The Los Angeles commission, for example, was concerned chiefly with highways and subdivision control; the Milwaukee commission, with park planning and county zoning. Disciples of planning vigorously argued the inadequacy of this kind of limited approach. But as a result of the popu-

[29] Carroll H. Wooddy, "The Growth of Governmental Functions," *Recent Social Trends* (one volume ed.; New York, 1933), pp. 1312–15.

[30] Quoted in Austin J. Tobin, "Management Structure and Operating Policies in Public Authorities—The Port of New York Authority," *C.I.O.S.* (1963), pp. 1–2.

larity of the regional planning movement, cities and counties greatly extended their use of agencies that dealt regionally with problems of sewage, water, and parks. By the middle of the decade, the specialized metropolitan commission—a device used in Boston for providing sewerage facilities as early as 1889—had become a relatively common institution of local government. The regional planning movement of the 1920's also produced a landmark in the history of planning, the eight-volume *Regional Plan of New York and Its Environs*. This privately financed study, which cost over a million dollars to prepare and took ten years to complete, provided an enormous amount of data about the most significant of American metropolitan regions. Many of its proposals relating to railroads, waterway and harbor improvements, airports, civic centers, and parks and boulevards were eventually adopted by local governmental agencies in New York and established precedents for actions in other urbanizing regions.[31]

During the 1920's, zoning, planning, and other measures of control over the urban environment were established in large part through the efforts of business groups tied to the City Efficient movement. Similarily, many of the conceptions that were a part of garden city and other plans for new-style towns and cities were initially applied by businessmen who were not unduly concerned with creating the good community but who foresaw that their utilization might enlarge the profits to be made in real-estate development. The term "garden city" was often used to describe any planned new community that preserved a natural setting. Torrance, California—one of several planned suburban industrial communities developed in the early years

[31] Flavel Shurtleff, "Fifteen Years of City Planning in the United States," *Municipal Index, 1924*, pp. 28–30; George Gove, "Regional Planning—Theory and Progress," *Municipal Index, 1925*, pp. 53–54; Roy Lubove, *Community Planning in the 1920's: The Contribution of the Regional Planning Association* (Pittsburgh, 1963), pp. 109–22.

of the century—was labeled by its founder, the industrialist Jared Sidney Torrance, as the "greatest and best of the garden cities of the world." [32] In 1914 the limited-dividend principle, which had been a fundamental part of Howard's plan, was employed in the development of a suburban area of Boston called the "garden suburb" of Billerica. Nowhere, however, was more than a portion of Howard's plan utilized; often in the 1920's "garden city" became a description of any suburban housing development.[33]

One of the most famous suburbs of the 1920's, the spectacularly successful Shaker Heights outside of Cleveland, provided an example of how the new planning conceptions could be applied to real-estate development. The community served as a model for hundreds of less successful experiments in controlled suburban development. Shaker Heights was the creation of two business tycoon brothers, Oris P. and Mantis J. Van Sweringen, who had started out as office clerks, had briefly owned a bicycle shop, and had become interested in real estate at the turn of the century. After a successful experience with developing a tract of land beyond the Cleveland street-car line and then persuading a local street-car company to extend its tracks to their holding, the two promoters purchased 1,400 acres of country land, which had once been the site of a Shaker religious community. Their plan, carefully conceived from the beginning, was to develop a rigorously controlled residential suburb having different-priced homes in distinct areas so that the cheaper houses would not depress the prices of the more expensive ones. The Van Sweringens employed many of the features of suburban residential development that were to become standard: abandonment of the traditional gridiron and the substitution of curving and semi-

[32] Dana W. Bartlett, "Torrance," *American City*, IX (1913), 311; *Urban Planning and Land Policies*, pp. 46–47.

[33] Conkin, *Tomorrow a New World*, pp. 66–67.

elliptical roads running from main automobile boulevards;
the preservation of natural park areas throughout the
development; and rigorous architectural, building, and
decorating requirements. With the opening of a rapid-
transit system to the community in 1920, Shaker Heights
began to boom. From 1919 to 1929 nearly 300 new houses
were built each year; the community's population jumped
from 1,700 to 15,500. The price of one-hundred-foot lots
increased from $20 a foot to over $200 a foot in some sections of the development; by the end of the decade, the
evaluation of the property had climbed to $80,000,000. The
Van Sweringens used their profits from real estate to
engage in some of the more grandiose railroad speculations
of the decade, and until their pyramid of holding companies collapsed in the 1930's, occupied a high rank among
American corporate leaders.[34]

The Van Sweringens were taciturn, unlettered, self-made
men who offered no public analysis of the significance of
their innovations in suburban residential development. In
contrast, Jesse D. Nichols, whose Country Club District of
Kansas City, Missouri, attracted international attention
in the 1920's, became a forceful spokesman of the zoning
and planning movement. In his real-estate operations, he
was genuinely concerned with establishing new patterns
of business and residential location that would alleviate
some of the problems of the sprawling metropolis. Nichols
grew up on a farm near Olathe, Kansas, graduated from
the University of Kansas, and studied economics at Harvard University, where he wrote a thesis on land development. On a visit to England during his student days, he
was impressed by the parks, lawns, and gardens of the
smaller English cities and later argued that the notion for
the Country Club District was conceived at that time. After
leaving Harvard, he got his start in business building

[34] Rachlis and Marqusee, *The Land Lords*, pp. 60–86.

houses for workers in Kansas City, Kansas, and with capital accumulated from this venture, in 1905 began buying property south of Kansas City, Missouri. The residential district he established was a success from the beginning. It was eventually to cover 6,000 acres, one-tenth of the area of the city.

By the 1920's the Nichols Country Club District had already become one of the most extensive restricted residential developments in the country, and the techniques he employed were widely copied by real-estate men elsewhere. Comprehensive deed restrictions on all property sold by the Nichols company controlled land use, minimum cost of buildings, open space, set-back lines, and sales to Negroes. The Nichols company was probably the first to employ the device of self-perpetuating deed restrictions. These were automatically continued unless a majority of the owners in an individual subdivision moved to change them at least five years before the expiration of the usual 25-year term of initial subdivision deeds. Nichols also sponsored the formation of self-governing Homes Associations, which received charters from the state. These Associations, which had grown to twelve in number by 1926, levied assessments on residents and provided a variety of governmental, cultural, and recreational services such as garbage and snow removal, lawn contests and flower shows, and maintenance of parks and playgrounds initially provided by the Nichols company. Students of the city, including a number of English visitors who made comparisons with the garden city, pointed to the Homes Associations as a desirable system to promote the spirit of neighborhood in the impersonal metropolis. City planners from as far away as South America and Australia visited the Country Club District in the 1920's. The British planner Charles Read echoed their local public reactions when he commented that no man in the world had done as much as Nichols "to carry beauty and comfort into every-day life." [35]

In the 1920's Nichols also won attention for his development of the first large decentralized shopping center in the United States, the Country Club Plaza Shopping Center, begun in 1922. In the early 1920's Nichols visited the garden cities of Welwyn and Letchworth and also toured Spain to get ideas for the project. His carefully planned and controlled shopping center successfully harmonized Spanish-style architecture with the natural setting of the district. The design for the center was widely copied by suburban developers, but few other planners were able to preserve the harmony and architectural integrity that Nichols insisted upon.[36]

Owing primarily to the attention his Country Club District received, Nichols in the 1920's became a national leader in the real-estate industry. In his speeches he consistently defended zoning and planning. Zoning, he suggested, could provide a means of ensuring "air, light, sunshine, and decent surroundings" for the laboring man as well as for the owner of the large estate; it would bring "order instead of chaos into American building." Lack of planning intensified the problem of the automobile; traffic congestion was largely the result of the "stupid application of the conventional checkerboard scheme without regard to grades or traffic needs." In addition to pointing out that planning could make cities more livable, Nichols always emphasized to business audiences that planning could also be profitable. "City planning," he told the Kansas City Chamber of Commerce in 1921, "is based on love, ambition,

[35] For an account of the development of the Country Club District, see *Urban Planning and Land Policies*, pp. 83–85.

[36] Victor Gruen, *The Heart of our Cities: The Urban Crisis, Diagnosis and Cure* (New York, 1964), pp. 189.

and profit. . . . If you are ambitious for the growth of your business, your institution or your city, if you believe in its future growth, you plan for healthy expansion." [37]

Nichols, like many less practical theorists of the city, was acutely sensitive to the ugliness of the new metropolitan environment that was rapidly being created in the 1920's. In a 1926 essay on shopping centers he developed this theme:

> In American cities of any considerable size our new outlying business centers frequently are becoming the ugliest, most unsightly and disorderly parts of the entire city. New traffic throats of congestion are being created that will sooner or later call for the expenditure of gigantic sums of public funds to relieve. Buildings of every color, size, shape, and design are being huddled and mixed together in a most unpresentable manner. A mixture of glowing billboards, unsightly rubbish dumps, hideous rears, unkempt alleys, dirty loading docks, unrelated, uncongenial mixtures of shops of every type and use, with no relation to one another; shacks and shanties mixed up with good buildings; perfectly square, unadorned buildings of poor design, are bringing about disorder, unsightliness, and unattractiveness that threaten to mar the beauty and good appearance of the residential regions of American cities. . . . The abandonment of formerly beautiful residential areas, neglected and blighted former business sections, should arouse in everyone a determination to protect the appearance of his city as well as the property values themselves.[38]

Nichols was aware of the problems of the metropolis and attempted to do something about them. His innovations

[37] Mary Katherine Goldsmith has kindly furnished me with several quotations from Nichols' speeches and writings from her unpublished work on Nichols.

[38] J. C. Nichols, "The Planning and Control of Outlying Shopping Centers," *Journal of Land and Public Utility Economics*, II (1926), 17–18.

helped to provide a better way of life for many city-dwellers. But not everyone could benefit from the amenities of Nichols' Country Club District. Deed restrictions kept out Negroes, a practice not invalidated by the Supreme Court until 1948. Construction requirements assured that lower-income groups would not live there. By the early 1930's the area contained a homogeneous population of upper-white-collar and professional families.[39] The Country Club District reflected the difficulties in private efforts to develop new living patterns in cities. Well-planned industrial villages and luxurious residential suburbs did virtually nothing to provide housing for the poor. And this was one of the most significant problems of the metropolis. In the 1920's real-estate men like Nichols frequently accepted the need for government regulation of urban expansion through city plans and zoning laws. But they did not of course advocate any significant departure from the established practices of private ownership and private development of land in cities. It remained for reformers outside the real-estate business to argue the necessity for more drastic approaches to the problems of the metropolis during the 1920's.

Much of the initial agitation for new policies toward cities stemmed from experiments in housing during World War I. The shortage of housing for low-income groups that had been developing in the early part of the century became so serious during the war that it interfered with production, and as an emergency measure the federal government instituted a program of public housing. Through two agencies, the United States Shipping Board's Emergency Fleet Corporation and the Department of Labor's United States Housing Corporation, the government built, sponsored, and controlled a number of housing projects for war-workers. Developments like Yorkship Village (later the Fairview section of Camden, New Jersey) and Union Park Gardens near Wilmington, Delaware, provided reasonable, attractive, and well-designed housing. The projects also

[39] *Urban Planning and Land Policies,* p. 85.

permitted American architects and planners—many of them imbued with garden city concepts—to experiment with new kinds of urban design, including curvilinear street systems, the row house, and balanced residential neighborhoods. Despite protests, Congress when the war ended liquidated the programs as quickly as possible. But the memory remained. Throughout the 1920's housing reformers and planners pointed to various aspects of the wartime program as a model for government action in housing.[40]

The acute housing shortage that followed the armistice indicated the need for new policies. Shortages of capital and inflated construction costs checked the anticipated resumption of normal building, which had provided the justification for the quick termination of the government programs. Building increased after 1921, and was one of the factors sustaining the mixed prosperity of the decade, but expansion was accompanied by a disproportionate rise in building costs. From 1923 to the end of the decade, wholesale building material costs remained 80 to 100 per cent higher than before the war. Rents also rose much faster than wages. One survey of 178 cities, for example, showed a rise in rents of 85 per cent between July, 1914, and June, 1924.[41]

In addition, there was considerable deterioration in the older tenement areas of American cities. Studies in the 1920's generally substantiated the point that became common currency in the next decade—that one-third of the nation was ill-housed. By 1930, census reports indicated that over 6,000,000 homes in cities, over 25 per cent of the total, did not meet minimum standards.[42] The studies of the new urban sociologists, including Clifford R. Shaw's examina-

[40] *Ibid.*, pp. 56–69; Roy Lubove, "Homes and 'A Few Well Placed Fruit Trees': An Object Lesson in Federal Housing," *Social Research,* XXVII (1960), 469–86.

[41] Lubove, *Community Planning in the 1920's*, pp. 19–21.

[42] Edith Elmer Wood, *Slums and Blighted Areas in the United States* (Washington, D.C., 1935), pp. 3–4. See also Federal Emergency Administration of Public Works, Housing Division, *Urban Housing: The Story of the P. W. A. Housing Division, 1933–1936* (Washington, D.C., 1936), pp. 4–7.

tion of juvenile delinquency in Chicago and the Lynds' analysis of Middletown, demonstrated a relationship between
inadequate housing and social disorganization. Numerous
statistical investigations during the decade documented the
problems of public health that resulted from bad housing.[43]

Because of the seriousness of the problem, much of the
discussion of the future of cities during the 1920's had housing as its central emphasis. City planners and housing reformers generally agreed that private builders operating
within a free market were simply not able to provide satisfactory low-cost housing. They offered a variety of solutions
to the problem that were often based on garden city concepts and on the wartime experiments in public housing:
cheap rapid transit subsidized by government to enable
workers easily to reach garden communities built in the
country where land costs were low; efforts by municipalities
to aid private builders or to establish local co-operative
housing projects; federal housing loans to low-income workers or to limited-dividend philanthropic building companies; various kinds of federal subsidies and tax concessions
to builders; and comprehensive government slum clearance
programs.[44]

As a result of this agitation, there were efforts during
the decade to encourage the establishment of limited-dividend and co-operative housing projects. A precedent-break-

[43] For summaries of these studies, see Wood, *Slums and Blighted
Areas in the United States*, pp. 7–15; *Urban Planning and Land
Policies*, pp. 201–5; Federal Emergency Administration of Public
Works, *Urban Housing*, pp. 10–13. For a recent assessment of the
approach of the sociological studies of the 1920's, see Maurice R.
Stein, *The Eclipse of Community: An Interpretation of American
Studies* (Princeton, N.J., 1960), pp. 13–69.

[44] Arthur Gleason, "The Lack of Houses: Remedies," *Nation*, CX
(1920), 548; Edith Elmer Wood, "How To Get Better Houses,"
Journal of Home Economics, XVI (1924), 4–9, 65–70; John J.
Murphy, *The Housing Famine: How To End It* (New York, 1920),
passim, reflect some of the contemporary points of view.

ing Wisconsin law of 1919 permitted counties and cities to purchase stock in co-operative housing companies, and a Milwaukee co-operative company, with support from the city, erected 105 houses, at an alleged savings of $1,500 a house. Other private housing co-operatives, totalling forty in number at mid-decade, were organized, virtually all of them in New York City. The New York State Housing Law of 1926 provided tax exemptions to limited-dividend housing projects, permitted municipalities to exempt the projects from local taxes, and set maximum rents for authorized projects. Two co-operatives and one limited-dividend company built a total of six projects in New York City under the law. In short, private and public efforts to supply low-cost housing during the decade were so restricted that they had virtually no effect on the general problem. But the years of agitation of the housing question did produce a body of information and a number of approaches on which future public programs could be built. By the end of the decade there was increasing recognition of the fact that some type of government intervention in housing had become a necessity.[45]

A group particularly influential in establishing this point during the decade was the Regional Planning Association of America, an informal association of planners, architects, social theorists, and housing experts who began meeting in 1923. The organization included many of the leading students of city problems: Clarence Stein, an architect who was most responsible for the formation of the group; Lewis Mumford, a social theorist and planner; Frederick L. Acker-man, an architect, planner, and follower of Thorstein Veblen; Charles H. Whitaker, editor of the *Journal of the*

[45] Bayrd Still, *Milwaukee: The History of a City* (Madison, Wis., 1948), p. 528; Federal Emergency Administration of Public Works, *Urban Housing*, pp. 61–64; Lubove, *Community Planning in the 1920's*, p. 42.

American Institute of Architects; Benton MacKaye, a disciple of Thoreau and an experienced forester; and Henry Wright, an expert on housing costs and site planning. The RPAA evolved from other groups concerned with the postwar housing crisis, and good housing for the poor remained a dominant concern of the organization until it broke up around 1933. But the group went much further and attempted to formulate ways to plan whole metropolitan regions. Their program emphasized the development of a new kind of regional city that would preserve small towns and villages and renew metropolitan centers through a comprehensive, flexible ordering of the relationships between population, resources, and institutions.[46]

As part of their effort to develop more reasonable and more livable urban communities, the RPAA turned to Howard's garden city as a beginning. In 1923 Stein convinced Alexander M. Bing, a New York real-estate man, to support RPAA plans for building residential communities along garden city lines. Bing sponsored the formation of a limited-dividend housing company, the City Housing Corporation; between 1924 and 1928 the corporation built the first of its two garden city–style communities, Sunnyside Gardens, New York. Sunnyside was located on a seventy-acre tract in the borough of Queens on land purchased from the Pennsylvania Railroad. Unable to obtain modification in the existing gridiron plat for the area, Stein and Wright, who designed the community, were forced to work with the gridiron block; but despite this handicap they laid out an attractive development of row houses and apartments enclosing large central gardens. Contrary to the hopes of its founders, the project did not supply housing that accom-

---

[46] The history of the group is thoroughly examined in Lubove, *Community Planning in the 1920's.* For an account by one of the founders, see Lewis Mumford's introduction to Clarence S. Stein, *Toward New Towns for America* (New York, 1957), pp. 12–15.

modated low-income groups. Even though the dividends of the City Housing Corporation were limited to 6 per cent and certain economies in efficient site planning were realized, Sunnyside did not provide housing that was competitive with that built by large-scale, private speculative builders.[47]

The RPAA's most significant effort—and one of the most significant housing efforts of the decade—was carried out in New Jersey on a 1,258-acre site some seventeen miles from New York. Sunnyside had been a kind of trial run; Radburn, New Jersey, was to be a real garden city of 25,000 people. Before the project could be completed, the depression hit; Bing's corporation was thrown into receivership; and Radburn remained a town of about 1,500. But in the period between 1928 and 1931, Radburn was considered the closest approximation of a garden city in America, and was internationally hailed as the "town for the motor age." Radburn had no unique features of building or design, but it artfully synthesized most of the ideas that were a part of proposals for planned communities in the 1920's—the 40-acre superblock, interior parks, curvilinear streets, and perhaps, most significantly, a system of roads that separated the automobile from the pedestrian. Benton MacKaye's 1930 plan for the "townless highway," which anticipated most of the features of the modern turnpike, was suggested by the Radburn experiment. But Radburn was at most only a limited success. Because of high land costs, no greenbelt was provided, and the founders were never able to attract industry as they had hoped to. Rather ironically, in the 1930's Radburn became a suburb of white-collar commuters instead of the self-sufficient, neighborly community that the RPAA leaders had hoped to establish within the modern regional metropolis.[48]

[47] Stein, *Toward New Towns for America*, pp. 17–37; Lubove, *Community Planning in the 1920's*, pp. 58–62.
[48] *Urban Planning and Land Policies*, pp. 97–101.

Radburn was the most famous experiment in American community planning during the 1920's. The failure of its founders to realize their objectives was typical of most efforts to cope with the problems of the metropolis during the decade. During a period in which the huge sprawling supercity assumed its present form and made its influence felt over the length and breadth of the land, most public debate on the subject was still informed by the old conception of city and country as polar ways of life. The accepted efforts of control that became popular during the decade— zoning, controlled private residential development, and the decentralized shopping center—created new problems while providing only limited solutions to old ones. But these measures did firmly establish the principle that a large degree of collective control over urban growth was necessary; the 1920's saw a considerable expansion of municipal regulation and public works, particularly in relation to automobiles and highways. Moreover, most of the approaches that became a part of national plans for cities in the New Deal period were evolved during the decade. Radburn, for example, served as the prototype for the greenbelt cities, and Lewis Mumford could reasonably argue that had it not been for the ideas that the RPAA "put into circulation during the twenties, the Greenbelt Towns undertaken by the Re-settlement Administration in 1935 would have been inconceivable." [49] Similarily, the housing programs and the experiments in regional planning of the New Deal were the outgrowth of the proposals of the preceding decade. In 1932 Franklin D. Roosevelt prophetically recognized that "something new" had developed out of the earlier experiments in city planning—"not a science, but a new understanding of problems that affect not merely bricks and mortar, subway and streets; planning that affects also the

[49] Introduction to Stein, *New Towns for America*, p. 15.

economic and social life of a community, then of a county, then of a state; perhaps the day is not far distant when planning will become a part of the national policy of this country." [50] Here was implied recognition of the central view of many of the urban theorists of the 1920's—that city and country were no longer separate and distinct, that the urban problems of the past had now become the social problems of the nation.

[50] Franklin D. Roosevelt, "Growing Up by Plan," *Survey*, LXVII (1932), 483. Conkin, *Tomorrow a New World*, pp. 70–72, develops the influence of the planning movement on Roosevelt's thinking.

NOTES ON THE CONTRIBUTORS

JOHN BRAEMAN teaches history at the University of Nebraska and is the author of a forthcoming biography of Albert J. Beveridge.

DAVID BURNER teaches history at the State University of New York, Stony Brook, and is the author of *The Politics of Provincialism: The Democratic Party in Transition, 1918–1932.*

JOHN C. BURNHAM teaches the history of American science at the Ohio State University, and is author of *Lester Frank Ward in American Thought* and *Psychoanalysis and American Medicine, 1894–1918.*

ROBERT H. BREMNER, professor of history at the Ohio State University, is the author of *From the Depths: The Discovery of Poverty in the United States* and *American Philanthropy,* and the editor of *Essays on History and Literature.*

DAVID BRODY is professor of history at the University of California, Davis, and author of *Steelworkers in America: The Nonunion Era* and *The Butcher Workmen.*

PAUL A. CARTER, associate professor of history at Northern Illinois University, has written *The Decline and Revival of the Social Gospel.*

GILBERT C. FITE is research professor of history at the University of Oklahoma and the author of *Peter Norbeck: Prairie Statesman* and *George N. Peek and the Fight for Farm Parity.*

CHARLES N. GLAAB, author of *Kansas City and the Railroads* and co-author of *A History of Urban America,* is professor of history at the University of Toledo.

JOSEPH R. GUSFIELD, professor of sociology at the University of Illinois, is the author of *Symbolic Crusade*.

The late FREDERICK J. HOFFMAN was Distinguished Professor of English at the University of Wisconsin, Milwaukee. Among his many books are *Freudianism and the Literary Mind, The Twenties, The Mortal No*, and *The Imagination's New Beginning*.

ROBERT MOATS MILLER, professor of history at the University of North Carolina, is the author of *American Protestantism and Social Issues, 1919–1939*, and one of the authors of the three-volume *The History of American Methodism* and *The Negro in the South Since 1865*.

BURL NOGGLE, associate professor of history at Louisiana State University, is the author of *Teapot Dome: Oil and Politics in the 1920's*.

GILMAN OSTRANDER, professor of history at Michigan State University, is the author of *The Prohibition Movement in California* and *The Rights of Man in America, 1606–1861*.

MARK PERLMAN is professor of economics at the University of Pittsburgh and the author of *Labor Union Theories in America* and *The Machinists*.

INDEX

Change and Continuity
in Twentieth-Century America:
The 1920's

MODERN AMERICA
Number 2

Change and Continuity
in Twentieth-Century America:
The 1920's

Edited by

John Braeman
Robert H. Bremner
David Brody

Ohio State University Press